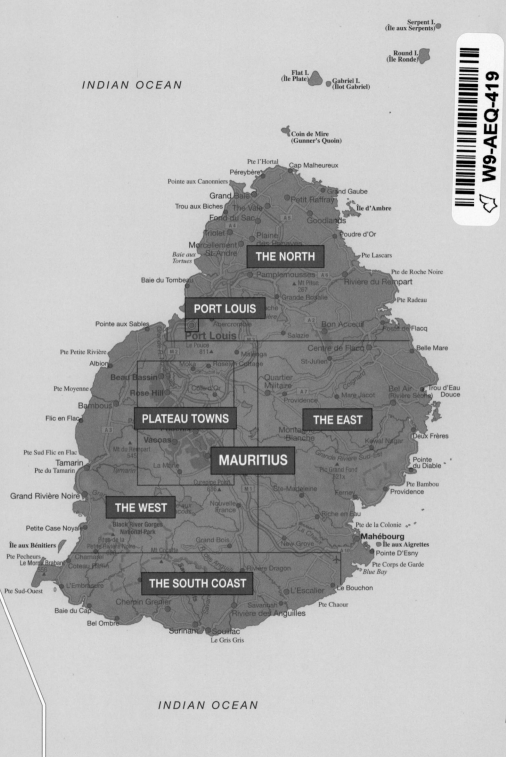

INDIAN OCEAN

Serpent I.
(Île aux Serpents)

Round I.
(Île Ronde)

Flat I.
(Île Plate)
Gabriel I.
(Îlot Gabriel)

Coin de Mire
(Gunner's Quoin)

Pte l'Hortal
Cap Malheureux
Péreybère
Pointe aux Canonniers
Grand Gaube
Grand Baie
Petit Raffray
Trou aux Biches
The Vale
Île d'Ambre
Fond du Sac
Goodlands
Triolet
Plaine
des Papayes
Poudre d'Or
Morcellement
St-André
Baie aux
Tortues

THE NORTH

Pte Lascars
Pamplemousses
A6
Baie du Tombeau
▲ Mt Piton
267
Pte de Roche Noire
Grande Rosalie
Rivière du Rempart

PORT LOUIS

Pte Radeau
Abercrombie
A2
Bon Acceuil
Pointe aux Sables
Poste de Flacq
Port Louis
Salazie
Le Pouce
811▲
Pte Petite Rivière
Malenga
Belle Mare
Albion
M2
Centre de Flacq
Moka
Roselyn Cottage
St-Julien
Pte Moyenne
Colmarel
Quartier
Military
Beau Bassin
Côte d'Or
A7
Bel Air
Trou d'Eau
Rose Hill
Mare Jacot
(Rivière Sèche)
Douce
Providence
Bambous

PLATEAU TOWNS

THE EAST

Flic en Flac
A3
Montagne
Blanche
Deux Frères
Vacoas
Mt du Rempart
545
Pte Sud Flic en Flac
La Mare
MAURITIUS
Grande Rivière Sud-Est
Tamarin
Pte du Tamarin
Pic Grand Fond
521▲
Pointe
du Diable
Tamarin
Curepipe Point
686▲
Ste-Madeleine
Pte Bambou
Grand Rivière Noire
M1
Ferney
Providence
Nouvelle
France
Riche en Eau

THE WEST

Petite Case Noyale
Black River Gorges
National Park
Pte de la Colonie
Île aux Bénitiers
Piton de la
Petite Rivière Noire
Grand Bois
Mahébourg
Île aux Aigrettes
Pte Pecheurs
Mt Cocotte
New Grove
A10
Pointe D'Esny
Le Morne Brabant
556
Chamarel
Pte Corps de Garde
Pte Sud-Ouest
Coteau Raffin
Blue Bay
L'Embrasure
Rivière Dragon

THE SOUTH COAST

L'Escalier
Le Bouchon
Chemin Grenier
Baie du Cap
Savannah
Pte Chaour
Bel Ombre
Rivière des Anguilles
Surinam
Souillac
Le Gris Gris

INDIAN OCEAN

N

Mauritius
0   5 km
0   5 miles

INSIGHT ⊙ GUIDES

MAURITIUS, RÉUNION & SEYCHELLES

⦿ Walking Eye App

YOUR FREE DESTINATION CONTENT AND EBOOK AVAILABLE THROUGH THE WALKING EYE APP

Your guide now includes a free eBook and destination content for your chosen destination, all for the same great price as before. Simply download the Walking Eye App from the App Store or Google Play to access your free eBook and destination content.

HOW THE WALKING EYE APP WORKS

Through the Walking Eye App, you can purchase a range of eBooks and destination content. However, when you buy this book, you can download the corresponding eBook and destination content for free. Just see below in the grey panels where to find your free content and then scan the QR code at the bottom of this page.

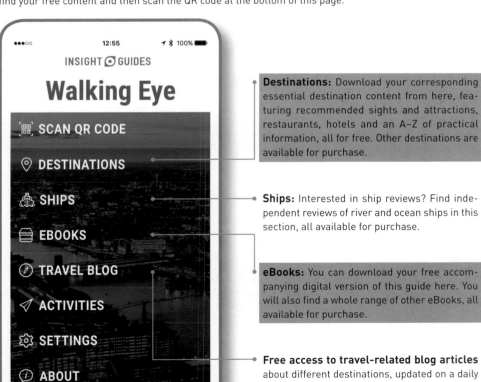

Destinations: Download your corresponding essential destination content from here, featuring recommended sights and attractions, restaurants, hotels and an A–Z of practical information, all for free. Other destinations are available for purchase.

Ships: Interested in ship reviews? Find independent reviews of river and ocean ships in this section, all available for purchase.

eBooks: You can download your free accompanying digital version of this guide here. You will also find a whole range of other eBooks, all available for purchase.

Free access to travel-related blog articles about different destinations, updated on a daily basis.

HOW THE DESTINATION CONTENT WORKS

Each destination includes a short introduction, an A–Z of practical information and recommended points of interest, split into 4 different categories:

- Highlights
- Accommodation
- Eating out
- What to do

You can view the location of every point of interest and save it by adding it to your Favourites. In the 'Around Me' section you can view all the points of interest within 5km.

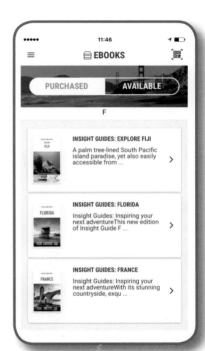

HOW THE EBOOKS WORK

The eBooks are provided in EPUB file format. Please note that you will need an eBook reader installed on your device to open the file. Many devices come with this as standard, but you may still need to install one manually from Google Play.

The eBook content is identical to the content in the printed guide.

HOW TO DOWNLOAD THE WALKING EYE APP

1. Download the Walking Eye App from the App Store or Google Play.
2. Open the app and select the scanning function from the main menu.
3. Scan the QR code on this page – you will then be asked a security question to verify ownership of the book.
4. Once this has been verified, you will see your eBook and destination content in the purchased ebook and destination sections, where you will be able to download them.

Other destination apps and eBooks are available for purchase separately or are free with the purchase of the Insight Guide book.

CONTENTS

LEGEND
𝒫 Insight on
◎ Photo Story

THE BEST OF MAURITIUS, RÉUNION & SEYCHELLES: TOP ATTRACTIONS

△ **Piton de la Fournaise, Réunion**. One of the most active volcanoes on the planet, producing blood-red fire fountains and rivers of lava. Hike through lunar landscapes to reach the summit. See page 184.

▽ **Vallée de Mai, Praslin, Seychelles**. Mistaken for the Garden of Eden by British general Charles Gordon in 1881, this is the primeval forest that time forgot, dense with coco de mer palms and their suggestive fruit. See page 313.

△ **Grand Baie, Mauritius**. A vast, horseshoe-shaped turquoise bay dubbed the Creole Côte d'Azur is the island's tourism hub, with plenty of beaches and excursions to choose from and après-sol entertainment. See page 111.

△ **The Cirques, Réunion**. Three huge caldera-like valleys, the remains of an extinct volcano, form a landscape of lush gorges, waterfalls and jagged peaks – all the more stunning when seen from a helicopter. See page 221.

△ **The Outer Islands, Seychelles**. A plethora of remote beaches, each one as stunning as the last. Most islands are uninhabited and remain largely unexplored; wildlife experiences are superb, from Aldabra giant tortoises to whale sharks. See page 337.

△ **Le Morne Brabant, Mauritius**. Former hideout of runaway slaves, the forbidding bulk of Unesco-listed Le Morne mountain rises from a hammerhead peninsula fringed with fine sands and luxury resorts. See page 145.

▽ **Adrenalin-pumping adventure, Réunion**. The dramatic terrain of Réunion was made for all manner of activities, from white-water rafting and canyoning to horse trekking, paragliding, bungee-jumping and scuba diving. See page 179.

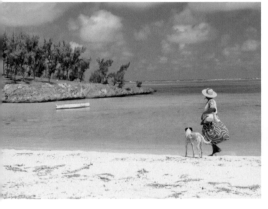

△ **A trip to Rodrigues, Mauritius**. This rustic island, just a 90-minute flight hop, is Mauritius' best-kept secret. Go for hiking, table d'hôtes, tranquillity and laid-back Creole charm. See page 153.

▽ **Black River Gorges National Park, Mauritius**. Hiking in the forested interior, criss-crossed with walking trails, is a must for nature lovers, with waterfalls and rare endemic plants and birds. See page 142.

▽ **Anse Lazio, Praslin, Seychelles**. Consistently tops the polls as the best beach in the world for its butter-soft sands and sculptural boulders. See page 312.

THE BEST OF MAURITIUS, RÉUNION & SEYCHELLES: EDITOR'S CHOICE

The pristine sands of Anse Soleil.

SPORTING ACTIVITIES

Diving. The coral reefs of the Indian Ocean, notably around Rodrigues and Seychelles, support hundreds of species of fish, which snorkelling and glass-bottom boats will also allow you to glimpse. See pages 87 and 263.

Big game fishing. Spending a day on the ocean wave doing battle with a marlin is big business in Mauritius: sit back in the fighting chair, strap on your harness, and wait for

the bite. See page 268.

Casela World of Adventures, Mauritius. The island's premier eco-adventure park and bird sanctuary offers a vast range of activities, from ziplining and quad-biking to walks with lions and cheetahs, and more. See page 140.

Kitesurfing, Le Morne Peninsula, Mauritius. 'One Eye' at Le Morne is one of the world's best spots for kitesurfing, with beginner's lessons nearby. See page 145.

Hiking, Réunion. More than 1,000km (620 miles) of numbered trails, known as the Grandes Randonnées, criss-cross Réunion, a walker's paradise. See page 182.

A sweetlips swimming over coral, Seychelles.

BEST BEACHES

Île aux Cerfs, Mauritius. Limpid waters, lovely beaches and water-sports galore make this east-coast island a favourite with day-trippers. See page 121.

Northern Islands, Mauritius. The pristine sandy beaches and coral gardens of tiny Îlot Gabriel (Gabriel Island) and larger Île Plate (Flat Island) are far from the madding crowd. See page 114.

Trou d'Argent, Rodrigues. This pirate haunt, accessible only by foot, is among the best preserved beaches on the planet. See page 159.

L'Hermitage, Réunion. This long, white-sand beach is lined with casuarina trees and protected by a coral reef. See page 209.

Beau Vallon, Mahé, Seychelles. Busiest beach in the Seychelles and lined with hotels but still pristine and excellent for bathing. Clear water and good reefs make it a popular diving and snorkelling spot. See page 292.

Anse Soleil, Mahé, Seychelles. Small and perfectly formed, this picturesque cove on Mahé's west coast is overlooked by the Anse Soleil Beachcomber hotel. See page 289.

Anse Source d'Argent, La Digue, Seychelles. Dazzling white sand and swaying palms; the calm sea – thanks to a protective reef – makes this an ideal beach for snorkellers. Neck and neck in the polls with Anse Lazio. See page 328.

CULTURE AND HERITAGE

Vieux Grand Port and Mahébourg, Mauritius. The Dutch landed at Vieux Grand Port in 1598, where the remains of Fort Frederick Henry and 18th-century cannons can still be seen. At Mahébourg's National History Museum, eclectic exhibits tell the tale of the colonial periods under the Dutch, French and British. See page 122.

L'Aventure du Sucre, Mauritius. Sugar cultivation and its history,

stylishly presented. See page 114.

Grand Bassin, Mauritius. Dominated by sculptures of the Hindu gods Shiva and Maa Durga, this volcanic crater, known as the Lake of the Ganges, is a sacred place of pilgrimage. See page 145.

Plantation houses and cases créoles. Before the concrete tide takes over these lovely wooden homes, with their airy verandas and delicate 'lacework', visit St Aubin

and Eureka (Mauritius) or Villa Carrère and Villa Folio (Réunion). See pages 132, 149, 194 and 224.

Musée de Villèle, Réunion. Once home to notorious coffee and sugar producer Madame Desbassyns, this colonial mansion houses memorabilia and fine French East India furniture. See page 210.

Dauban Mausoleum, Silhouette, Seychelles. Modelled on the Madeleine church in Paris,

the imposing six-columned mausoleum set amid coconut palms pays homage to the Dauban family, owners of the island for more than 100 years. See page 304.

Arts and craft scene, Seychelles. Small art studios and galleries are dotted around Seychelles' main islands, selling paintings, batiks, craft and ornaments, and there's often a chance to meet the artist while you're there. See page 255.

WILDLIFE WATCHING

Île aux Aigrettes, Mauritius. Look out for the bands of pink pigeons, immortalised by naturalist Gerald Durrell in his book *Golden Bats and Pink Pigeons*. See page 125.

François Leguat Giant Tortoise and Cave Reserve, Rodrigues. A top attraction, with limestone caves, native plants and a colony of Aldabra tortoises. See page 157.

Whale-watching, Réunion. Snorkel with humpback whales between June and September, or admire them from a boat as they breach. See page 181.

Kelonia turtle sanctuary, Réunion. This conservation project, which has captive-breeding and release programmes, will interest children and adults with its exhibits and large tanks. See page 209.

Ste Anne Marine National Park, Seychelles. Established in the 1970s, the park protects six islands and prolific marine life including dolphins and turtles. Day trips by glass-bottom boat or subsea viewer depart from Victoria. See page 295.

Aride Island Nature Reserve, Seychelles. Home to more breeding sea birds and more sea bird species than Seychelles' other granitic islands put together, there are also jaw-dropping views at the pinnacle of the nature trail. See page 321.

Bird Island, Seychelles. The sooty tern colony is the most famous attraction here, but guests are encouraged to help with the island's hawksbill turtle conservation project too. See page 333.

PARKS AND GARDENS

Pamplemousses Botanical Gardens, Mauritius. A maze of shady palm-lined avenues lead to beautiful sights such as the Lily Pond, concealed under the floating leaves of the giant Amazon water lily. See page 116.

La Vallée de Ferney, Mauritius. Nature trails run through forests with more than 100 native plants and daily appearances from the endangered Mauritian kestrel. See page 125.

Jardin de l'État, Réunion. A botanical collection born from the European trees brought to the island by botanist Nicolas

Bréon in 1817. The centrepiece of the gardens is a natural history museum. See page 194.

Conservatoire Botanique de Mascarin, Réunion. A magnificent botanical garden landscaped into themed areas, with a restored 19th-century villa, stables, hunting lodge and old family kitchen. See page 209.

Jardin du Roi, Mahé, Seychelles. Originally laid out in 1771 for the cultivation of spice plants, the present garden is reminiscent of 18th- and 19th-century farms. See page 287.

Whales and dolphins, Réunion.

Looking down over Bird Island in the Seychelles.

The Trou de Fer waterfall in Belouve forest on Réunion.

Children play by fishing boats at sunset on Mahé.

Idyllic waters at Praslin, Seychelles.

INDIAN OCEAN ISLANDS

The main draw may be white beaches and crystal waters, but beyond these are exotic cultures and breathtaking landscapes to explore.

A small boat off Mauritius.

Visitors who have already been to both Mauritius and Seychelles always have a firm favourite: 'The beaches are better on the Seychelles'; 'But the people are so wonderful in Mauritius... and I've never seen such hotels...'; 'But what about the diving?'.

And what about Réunion? Until recently this corner of France in the Indian Ocean, with its breathtaking volcanic landscapes and opportunities for outdoor adventure, was France's best-kept secret. But in the last few years the island has promoted its attractions further afield and it is now appearing in an increasing number of brochures, mainly as a twin-centre holiday with Mauritius.

Réunion, with Mauritius, forms part of the Mascarenes, along with Rodrigues, Mauritius' isolated, serene sister island, with its unspoilt beaches, chilled Creole culture and ecotourism.

All these Western Indian Ocean islands share the same history to a certain point: all were colonised and cultivated with sugar, tea or vanilla plantations, and their populations are the descendants of explorers and colonists, slaves and indentured labourers. Kreol in one form or another is spoken in all of them, and some of their songs and dances share similar roots, as do their cuisines. But there is also great diversity, both culturally and in the tourist experience.

The cultural diversity of these islands, whose roots spread across three continents, is more visible in the Mascarenes than in Seychelles. The culture of Mauritius, from its politics to its cuisine, is heavily influenced by Asian customs and

Restaurant in Sennevile, Mauritius.

beliefs, while Rodrigues aligns itself more to the people and character of Africa. In Réunion, where culture is rooted in Gallic tradition, *boulangeries* sell baguettes and croissants alongside Creole specialities.

Seychelles, an archipelago of 115 mainly uninhabited islands, boasts chart-topping beaches, world-class diving and birdlife to make ornithologists weep. With the first settlers arriving little more than 200 years ago – a mix of French colonists, African slaves and Indian workers – Seychelles has a relatively new culture. Thankfully the government's commitment to conservation has resulted in more than half the landmass being given over to nature reserves and national parks.

This guide aims to bring out the truth behind the clichés so often attached to these tropical islands, and also to introduce the lesser-known islands and features of the region.

Children playing on tree swing of aerial roots in Pamplemousses Botanical Gardens.

PEOPLE OF THE INDIAN OCEAN

Indian Ocean islanders are all descendants of immigrants –
pioneers or pirates, settlers or slaves – and at least three
continents are represented among them.

The only thing that distinguishes a Mauritian or Seychellois away from home is the French lilt of their English. Otherwise you could be forgiven for believing that you are meeting a person of European, Asian or East African origin. And, leaping across a few generations, you would be right. The diversity, intermingling and surviving distinctions of the ethnic groups, who have arrived over the past 400 years, create the intriguing hotchpotch of cultures and physiognomies that characterise the Western Indian Ocean peoples today.

ETHNIC DIVERSITY

Travellers to the islands of the southwest Indian Ocean often remarked on the ethnic diversity of the inhabitants. Charles Darwin, visiting Mauritius in 1836 on the *Beagle*, noted that 'the various races of men walking in the streets afford the most interesting spectacle'. He would have seen Arab and Persian traders dressed in long, flowing robes, Malagasy with elaborate hairstyles, turban- and langouti-clad Indians, and Chinese shopkeepers with long plaits.

The piecemeal settlement of the islands helps to explain the diversity of the inhabitants. In the 17th and 18th centuries, small groups of French prisoners and pioneers, along with a few Malagasy, Indians and Malays, set up bases, initially in the Mascarenes, and later in Seychelles and Rodrigues. With the importation of women from these same regions, the foundations of 'white' and 'coloured' communities were laid. Free immigrants were offered grants of land and encouraged to produce cash crops such as cotton, coffee or spices for export to Europe, or to cultivate foodstuffs and raise livestock which could be used to provision the ships calling at the islands on their way to or from the Indies.

A warm welcome at Mahe International Airport.

Merchants, adventurers, pirates and refugees from many nations were soon attracted to these new centres of trade and maritime construction, and the demand for skilled labour spiralled. Asians were cheaper to employ than Europeans, and agreements signed with Indian artisans led to the establishment of a wealthy free 'Malbar' class in the islands by the late 18th century. The crews of sailing ships were also frequently sourced from Asia, and were known as 'Lascars'. Many were Muslims. To this day the term 'Malbar' is local slang for people of Indian origin in both Mauritius and Réunion, but visitors should avoid using it, as it can also be considered an insult.

Slaves and convicts from countries as diverse as Guinea, the Canary Islands, Bengal, Java and

Timor were also off-loaded from passing ships to the labour-hungry colonists. From the mid-18th century, however, organised slaving voyages brought large numbers of Mozambicans and Malagasy to the islands, so they became the dominant ethnic groups, swallowing up the diverse pre-19th-century minorities into a Creole population that increasingly reflected this East African cultural heritage.

> *Some French Mauritian families are genuine descendants of aristocrats who fled the French Revolution, while more outlandish claims of noble descent from Arab princesses and heroic corsairs can be heard in rum shops across the islands.*

ASIAN IMMIGRATION

The conversion of Mauritius and Réunion into plantation societies in the late 18th and early 19th centuries led to the large-scale introduction of estate workers, chiefly from India. Mauritius recruited

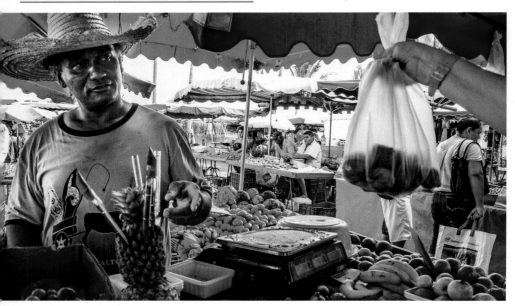
Buying fresh fruits in Réunion.

⊘ ARTISTS' IMPRESSIONS

In the days before photography, artists travelled from place to place, capturing and publishing famous moments – such as the conquest of an island (for example, R. Temple's drawings of the British conquest of Mauritius in 1810), or sketching and labelling 'types' of exotic peoples for a curious European audience. L.A. Roussin and A. D'Hastrel published *Albums of Réunion* in 1863 and 1847 respectively, while Alfred Richard illustrated individuals as diverse as the 'Persian Groom', the 'Indian Labourer' and the 'Muslim Barber' for his *Types de l'Île Maurice* which was published in 1850.

indentured labour from several states: Biharis and Tamils were the most numerous; Marathis and Telegus arrived in smaller numbers. Réunion recruited mostly Tamils. Principally Hindus, some Muslim and Christian Indians were also indentured. Smaller numbers of African and Chinese labourers arrived over the same period. In the 1860s and 1870s several thousand 'Liberated Africans' were brought to Seychelles and Mauritius. They are thought to have mostly come from Malawi.

Merchants and other service migrants followed these population flows: Gujarati merchants and Chinese traders (chiefly Hakka and Cantonese speaking) established themselves in wholesale and retail, first on Mauritius and then across the region. Chinese women did not immigrate in large numbers until the turn of the 20th century, and the earlier relationships established by Chinese men produced a substantial Creole-Chinese population on the islands.

Seychelles and Rodrigues, less well suited by size and terrain to sugar cane cultivation, received fewer Asian immigrants and have remained principally Creole societies.

OLD INEQUALITIES, NEW ATTITUDES

The Mascarene and Seychelles island groups are all ex-slave societies in which the three

been relaxed recently, leading to a rediscovery of separate Hindu and Creole identities.

The ethnic compartmentalisation of present-day Mauritian society is more apparent. Here, a white settler class has survived and maintains its ethnic exclusiveness by marrying within its ranks and with acceptable outsiders – typically white Europeans and, increasingly, white South Africans, who have a shared experience of enclave status in a multicultural environment. The old three-tier society has been replaced by one of five

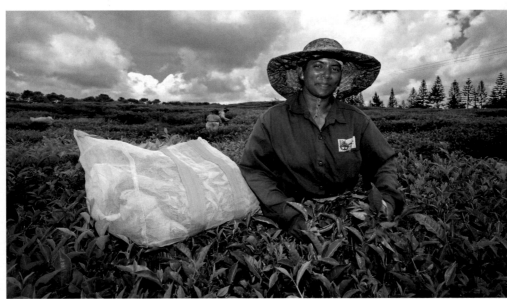

Woman harvesting tea at Bois Chéri Tea Factory, Mauritius.

tiers of the population – whites, 'coloureds' and slaves – were clearly demarcated and discouraged from intermarrying. Distinctions, grounded in membership of these 'colour-coded' groups remain, in varying degrees, on all the islands.

Vestiges of this old hierarchical society seem to have little relevance in modern Réunion and Seychelles, where intermarriage is now the norm, with equality of opportunity an official policy. A light-skinned elite nevertheless remains influential in Seychelles politics and society, while in Réunion, a new class of z'oreilles (white metropolitan French) is complained of as having favoured status. Integrationist French policy in Réunion, which ensured that generations of Tamils have taken Christian first names, has

☉ CREOLE OR KREOL

In its historical sense, the term 'Creole' meant someone born on an island and was applied to all island inhabitants, regardless of their ethnicity. Thus Napoleon's consort, Josephine de Beauharnais, was a French Creole of Martinique. This is still very much the case on Réunion today. In more racially segmented Mauritius however, the term 'Creole' applies only to islanders of African origin.

A colonial language often became the basis of a new lingua franca, also called 'Creole'. To avoid confusion, the language is often spelt 'Kreol', as it is throughout this book.

or more subgroups which each claim specific caste, religious and regional distinctions, maintained through intermarriage. Most Mauritian communities view marriage with a foreigner as a preferable option to an alliance with a Mauritian of another ethnic group. Intermarriage is not unusual, but it is not yet the norm. Politically, ethnic divisions are reinforced by a constitution that provides electoral safeguards for minorities and by a tradition dating from Independence of selecting candidates and even ministers according to their

Celebrating Dipvali on Réunion.

⊘ BRAIN-TEASERS

Kreol *sirandanes* or riddles are a legacy of the African storytelling traditions that are now disappearing in the Indian Ocean islands. When someone had a few riddles to tell they would shout 'Sirandane!', their audience would reply 'Sampek!' and the brain-teasing session would begin. Here are some typical examples:

Dileau dibout? Canne. Standing water? A sugar cane.

Dileau pendant? Coco. Hanging water? A coconut.

Menace dimoun, napas koze? Ledoigt. I threaten but I do not speak? A finger.

Ki lalangue ki zames ti menti? Lalangue zanimaux. Whose tongue never lies? An animal's.

community. Every prime minister apart from Paul Bérenger has come from the Vaish sub-caste of the North Indian Hindu community, numerically the most powerful ethnic group in Mauritius.

DISTINCTIVE TRADITIONS

Despite a shared history, and collective musical, linguistic and other traditions, each of the Indian Ocean islands has evolved a unique brand of Kreol and a distinctive set of social customs and religious practices. The African cultural heritage is strongest in Seychelles and Rodrigues, where the proportion of Afro-Creoles is highest. Réunion is greatly influenced by France and the Francophone world – the zouk rhythms of Martinique are as popular as Paris fashions. In Mauritius, the preponderance of people of Indian origin means that cinemas here are as likely to show Hindi as French films, the sari and the *shalwar kamiz* (trousers and tunic) are common forms of dress, and bhojpuri bands compete with sega and European music for the hearts and minds of the island's youth. The ubiquitous red flags or *jhandi* which can be seen in front of houses throughout the island signify that the occupants are Sanatanist or orthodox Hindus – an eloquent symbol of the cultural dominance of this community in modern Mauritius.

While there are latent tensions between ethnic groups, the Indian Ocean islands are characterised more by syncretism, and participation in each other's celebrations, than by communal conflict. Many non-Tamils make vows to participate in the Cavadee fire-walking ceremonies (see page 74) and people of all religions light candles at the Catholic shrines.

Superstition and sorcery cut across ethnic divides: individuals perceived to possess the requisite skills – from traditional practitioners of alternative medicine to specialists in the art of black magic – attract followers from every community, and may be called in to administer remedies, settle quarrels and banish evil spirits.

The food of the islands is perhaps the best expression of a shared ethnic heritage: Creole cuisine incorporates European, Asian and African influences and offers dishes to suit every palate, from creamy gratins to Indian-style curries and Chinese-style fried noodles.

LINGUA FRANCA

The peoples of the Seychelles and Mascarene Islands are united by variations of a shared spoken language, which exist as a symbol of their shared identity today.

As a legacy of their shared history of settlement during periods of French rule, the mother tongue of the inhabitants of the Seychelles and Mascarene Islands is Kreol. The various forms of Kreol spoken have evolved from adaptations of French to which a sprinkling of words and speech patterns from the other languages of immigrants has been added.

The formative period of Indian Ocean Kreol in the late 17th and 18th centuries has left its mark on the language. The Breton origins of many early French settlers means that traces of their regional language survive in modern Kreol, while the influence of Malagasy immigrants is reflected in local words such as *fangourin* or cane sugar juice, which derives from the Malagasy term *fangorinana*. South Indians who arrived on the islands in the 18th century as slaves and artisans have left their mark in culinary terms. The herb known as *kaloupile* in Réunion, *karipoule* in Mauritius and *karipile* in Seychelles is derived from the Tamil word *kariveppilai* or curry leaf.

Kreol is often thought of as one language, when in fact Réunion (Réyoné) Kreol, Mauritian (Morisyen) Kreol and Seychelles (Sesel) Kreol are three separate languages not necessarily mutually intelligible. A native speaker of Réunion Kreol will not understand all Mauritian Kreol, and will understand very little Seychelles Kreol.

Over time, the islands have developed particular speech patterns. Seychelles Kreol is said to be more sing-song in style, while Réunion Kreol has been greatly influenced by the Francophone world, particularly the French Caribbean. Mauritian Kreol uses many words deriving from its large population of North Indian origin. Other expressions derive from the Bhojpuri dialect spoken widely in rural Indian villages on the island.

The emphasis given to Kreol in the various islands is strongly linked to political factors. Because Réunion is a *département* of France, the French language is given priority, and is used in all official communications and in the written media. In Mauritius and Seychelles, where French rule was succeeded by British government, English is the official language. In Seychelles, however, Kreol also has this status and is treated equally in the media and government institutions. In Mauritius, as in Réunion, Kreol is spoken but rarely written. However, the language has gained greater respect in recent years, with the publication of a French-Kreol dictionary.

For all the islands, these varying political solutions to the language question pose further problems. Middle-class Seychellois complain that the prominence given to Kreol restricts the opportunities for their children to become proficient in French. Réunion suffers from being a Francophone island in an Indian Ocean that is largely Anglophone. Mauritius, with its multiplicity of competing

Shopping in Port Louis.

Asian ancestral languages and chiefly French media, is continually struggling with internal dissent and controversy. The island is becoming increasingly Francophone, while the education system is slanted towards the use of both English and Oriental languages, although Kreol is an optional language in schools.

As a rule, English is widely understood in Seychelles and Mauritius, but not in Réunion. French is the preferred language of communication in Mauritius and Réunion, but will not be appreciated by all Seychellois. Switching from English to French and back will not daunt a Mauritian. A few words of basic Kreol acquired in any of the islands should help you communicate in all of them. A pronunciation guide and glossary of basic terms and phrases appear on page 360.

Dinarobin Beachcomber Golf Resort & Spa is one of several luxurious resorts in the region.

THE IMPACT OF TOURISM

Seychelles and Mauritius continue to lure celebrities, Réunion is no longer such a well-kept secret, and Rodrigues is yet to be 'discovered'.

The development of tourism is relatively recent in the Western Indian Ocean and its growth and quality have been carefully monitored. Planners, all too aware that the islands' natural assets are what attract visitors, have kept conservation very much at the forefront of their development schemes. There are no sprawling miles of concrete coastal resorts here, and the isolated location of the islands, together with high standards of service and beautiful natural beaches, mean that the tropical island paradise experience as presented in the brochures and glossy magazines actually lives up to expectations.

TOURISM DEVELOPMENT

Trendiness has been a key factor in determining the way tourism has evolved both in Mauritius and Seychelles, which are at different stages of development. Seychelles was the first island group to be popular with European visitors, and by 1979 tourism was the chief earner. Sporadic political conflict, however, as in Madagascar and the Comoros, slowed economic growth in Seychelles while Mauritius remained stable. Despite the coup d'état and succeeding radical governments, Seychelles still attracts a steady stream of holiday-makers. The beaches are as stunning as ever and are often rated among the world's best in travellers' surveys (see page 31). Nevertheless, this has not been enough to stop Seychelles from being overtaken by Mauritius, which has been riding the crest of a popularity wave for some years now. The 'Vanilla Islands' alliance has been set up to encourage tourism between Seychelles, Mauritius, Réunion, Madagascar and the Comoros, promoting twin-centre holidays that combine the beaches of Mauritius, for example, with adventure in Réunion or Madagascar.

Infinity pool at Maradiva Villas Resort & Spa.

The Mauritian tourist industry has concentrated all its energies on developing the luxury end of the market, building splendid hotels and gaining a reputation for excellent service. Since 1993, the island has outstripped Seychelles in tourist numbers and currently welcomes over 1.3 million tourists a year (visitors to Seychelles numbered around 350,000 in 2017). Indications are that this figure will reach 1.8 million by 2028, exceeding Mauritius' own population.

STATE VS THE PRIVATE SECTOR

Politics has also affected the development of tourism in the region. The state has a deeper level of involvement in tourism on 'socialist' Seychelles than on 'capitalist' Mauritius. While it was the government that initiated tourist development in Seychelles, the role of the private sector in the building of exclusive resorts in Mauritius was significant. Seychelles' population of 95,000

> *It used to be said that Mauritius is a three-star destination with five-star hotels while Seychelles is a five-star destination with three-star hotels, but Seychelles facilities are rapidly catching up.*

Shangri-La's Le Touessrok Resort & Spa.

is low compared to Mauritius, which has almost 1.3 million inhabitants, so labour and production costs are less advantageous. In addition to this, the wages of workers in the Seychelles hotel sector are regulated, as are the number of privately owned guesthouses and the prices they can charge. All of these factors contribute to a higher cost of living than on Mauritius.

Seychelles recognised the fact that to maintain its appeal and the high quality that people have come to expect, it needed to reinvest. The result is some of the best private island resorts in the world, such as luxury eco retreat North Island and celebrity favourite Frégate Island Private. High-end hotel chains have also set their sights on the prime stretches of sand, so

in recent years Constance Lemuria Seychelles and Raffles Resort have sprung up on Praslin, the Four Seasons, Banyan Tree and Maia opened on Mahé and the latest five-star causing a stir is luxurious Six Senses Zil Payson on Félicité.

CELEBRITY SPOTTING

Whatever the economic and political ups and downs, both Mauritius and Seychelles are still hot favourites among the rich and famous. Celebrities and royalty in search of an exclusive destination the paparazzi can't get to opt for Seychelles, where whole islands can be hired out – Frégate, Cousine and D'Arros, all privately owned, are perfect hideaways for those who can afford to pay for the privilege of having a tropical island to themselves. The Seychelles' most famous guests were the Duke and Duchess of Cambridge, Prince William and Catherine, who honeymooned on North Island in 2011, as did George Clooney and Amal Alamuddin in 2014. The Miss World competition has been staged here on more than one occasion; its co-ordinators exploited the paradise cliché to the full, billing the event as a unique opportunity to see 'the most beautiful girls on earth in the most beautiful place on earth'.

With its larger tourist industry, Mauritius has more five-star hotels than Seychelles. Seychelles had no five-star facilities until the late 1990s, but this has since changed dramatically and new hotels have capitalised on the twin advantages of more private islands and better beaches than Mauritius. Both countries have hotels in the 'leading hotels in the world' category. They cater to every whim of their celebrity guests, providing security, a high standard of service and world-class chefs. Supermodels, footballers, pop stars and film stars regularly appear in glossy magazines, captured languishing in their designer swimwear by the poolside cafés and seaside bars of Mauritius' most fashionable hotels. Old favourites Shangri-La's Le Touessrok Resort & Spa (photogenic and popular as a Bollywood location), One&Only Le Saint Géran and the Royal Palm Beachcomber Luxury, popular with visiting heads of state, compete with newer glitzy resorts such as Constance Prince Maurice, The St. Regis Resort Mauritius and LUX* Grande Gaube. Lesser mortals cannot expect automatic access to these hotels. If you want to have lunch or dinner it's best to make a reservation first.

AFFORDABLE LUXURY

In principle, these islands are luxury destinations. A two-week holiday at a good hotel on Seychelles or Mauritius can cost several thousand pounds per person. That said, you don't have to be a celebrity or tycoon to enjoy the best that the region has to offer. There are so many small islands in the Seychelles group that anyone can find their own 'private' cove complete with swaying palms, fine white sand and turquoise lagoon. Cruising the granitics sounds like an expensive luxury but there are a range of options available for those with a more limited budget. Honeymooners and others looking to splash out on an exceptional holiday can spend their fortnight on islands such as La Digue, where cars are rarely seen, or enjoy the utter isolation of Denis or Frégate, where your very own island wedding can be arranged. Cousine is also an exclusive hideaway, with five villas that can be reached by helicopter.

The tourist industry on Mauritius targets the well-heeled lover of luxury and exclusivity – charter flights are limited here. This is

Canonnier Beachcomber Golf Resort & Spa.

⊘ COASTAL FORTS AND QUARANTINE SITES

The Indian Ocean islanders feared two things above all else – enemy attack, which their small populations could not easily fend off, and the introduction of contagious disease, which drastically reduced their numbers. The dangers came from visiting ships, and elaborate measures were taken to protect their coastlines. Defence and quarantine buildings were erected on shores and islets – precisely those areas that are most in vogue today as tourist sites. Flat Island off the north coast of Mauritius was a quarantine station, while Seychelles' Île Curieuse was once a leper colony. Some hotels have incorporated these ruins into their grounds. Canonnier Beachcomber Golf Resort & Spa in Mauritius is built on the site of an important fortress and a quarantine station. The old defence walls are now an integral part of the hotel and the mounted cannon still point out to sea. Maritim Resort & Spa, further along the coast, offers guests and non-residents the opportunity to walk around 18th-century ruins of a French arsenal and Oberoi Mauritius provides private dining in the old Gunpowder Room. Mauritius also has some of the best preserved Martello towers in the world (see page 140). On your travels, you may come across the ruins of old lime kilns. The French spent a great deal of time and manpower in the manufacture of lime, which they used for the building of roads and in construction work.

the destination of choice for those who want to exploit the service and amenities of a five-star hotel and the tropical beach on its doorstep to the full. However, such luxury can be surprisingly affordable, with competitive packages, including all-inclusive deals, offered by some 120 luxury hotels and an increasing number of accommodation options, from 'glamping' to self-catering. The key to a successful holiday on Mauritius lies in choosing the right accommodation to suit you, both in terms of style and location. The latest trend is to stay in more than one

The palm-fringed pool at Constance Prince Maurice.

hotel or resort for contrasting experiences, and self-catering options are increasing, with the addition of luxurious properties in recent years.

NATURAL ASSETS

While both Mauritius and Seychelles have been effectively marketed as idyllic beach holiday destinations, their other natural assets have been widely exploited to draw in people looking for more than just a 'sun, sea and sand' experience. The Seychelles government is anxious to attract the 'discerning and environmentally aware' tourist and promotes the archipelago as the Galapagos of the Indian Ocean. Top of its list of highlights are two Unesco World Heritage sites – the Vallée de Mai on Praslin (home to the rare and indigenous coco de mer nut) and far flung Aldabra Atoll. Other designated bird sanctuaries and tropical forests attract twitchers and trekkers, while live-aboard cruises around the Outer Islands are becoming increasingly popular. In 2018 the government agreed to create two new marine parks the size of the UK in exchange for a portion of its national debt being written off, which will further ensure its natural assets are protected.

In Mauritius although water sports, including kitesurfing, diving and big game fishing – the annual World Marlin Fishing competition is a major event on the fishing calendar – remain big business for those who can afford it, ecotourism ventures inland are being promoted as an alternative activity, with some success.

The flora and fauna of Seychelles and the Mascarenes is in many respects unique and, like all

⊘ THE WORLD'S BEST HOTELS

The hotels of Seychelles and Mauritius are the Indian Ocean's best assets, and continue to win awards on the world stage.

Mauritius boasts three members of The Leading Hotels of the World (Constance Prince Maurice, Maradiva Villas Resort & Spa and Royal Palm Beachcomber Luxury), and Seychelles has two (Maia Luxury Resort & Spa and Constance Lemuria). Mauritius is also the beautiful and proud setting of two Small Luxury Hotels of the World, Heritage Le Telfair Golf & Wellness Resort and Paradise Cove Boutique Hotel, as well as one Relais & Châteaux hotel, 20 Degrés Sud.

In 2017, Mauritius and the Seychelles were named among *Condé Nast Traveller*'s Readers Awards 'Best islands in the world'. At the World Travel Awards 2018 – the Oscars of the travel industry – Mauritius was crowned the 'Indian Ocean's leading honeymoon destination', Oberoi Mauritius was voted the 'Indian Oceans Leading Hotel', One&Only Le Saint Géran in Mauritius was voted the 'Indian Ocean's leading resort', and Hilton Seychelles Northolme Resort & Spa was voted the 'Indian Ocean's leading luxury villa resort'. Seychelles' Four Seasons Resort at Desroches Island appeared on the *Condé Nast Traveller*'s Hot List in 2018.

small island ecologies, endangered. Coral reefs are notoriously fragile and prone to destruction by overzealous exploitation. Seychelles has a long tradition of ecotourism, with several islands declared nature reserves and access to them limited to the daytime. Mauritius is belatedly recognising the advantages of exploiting the few remaining areas on which unique species have survived. Thankfully, it's now following the example set by the Seychelles government in requiring permits for visits to some of its islets and in opening them up to responsible, supervised nature tours. Île aux Aigrettes, off the southeast coast, is home to the only remaining example of coastal savannah, which the dodo and other local birds found a natural habitat, and tours have been set up by the Mauritius Wildlife Foundation (see page 125).

HOLIDAYING ON A BUDGET

Backpackers are not encouraged, but there are ways of staying more cheaply on the islands. The resorts of Grand Baie/Pereybère and Flic-en-Flac in Mauritius offer numerous flats and guesthouses where a studio can be rented for around £25 (US$37) a day. Once you have paid for your flight, this is the one island in the region where you can live more cheaply than at home, and some seasonal workers from European coastal resorts choose to spend the winter here, staying for the three to six months that is allowed them on a tourist visa. Prices of imported goods are higher than in Europe, but essential foodstuffs are subsidised, and if you bring your own luxury items, you can live very cheaply.

Seychelles also has a number of small guesthouses; though not particularly cheap compared to other countries, they are less expensive than hotels, the service is much more personal and standards are generally high. Self-catering establishments are also good quality, such as Anse Soleil Beachcomber chalets, and shopping for yourself brings down costs: shop prices for drinks are half those charged by hotels, while local produce, including fish, is inexpensive.

ADVENTURE PLAYGROUND

Réunion is the most expensive of the Indian Ocean islands because its economy is artificially boosted with regular injections of French capital. Prices are somewhat higher here than in mainland France. It has long been popular with French visitors – as an overseas *département* there are no customs or immigration checks for arrivals from the métropole (mainland France) – but its lack of coral-fringed beaches and its monolingualism have lessened the island's appeal to non-French tourists. The Réunionnais themselves often take their annual holidays on Mauritius where, beyond the big hotels, the cost of living is much lower.

As its coastline doesn't fit the tropical island profile, Réunion has escaped invasion from

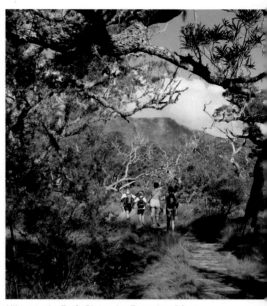

Hiking in the Forêt Plaine des Tamarins, Réunion.

international tourists. Most of us still need persuading that hiking – even to an active volcano – is more fun than lounging by a palm-fringed lagoon, and until recently the island's breathtaking landscape remained a well-kept secret from all but the French and the ardent adventure traveller. However, Réunion is now being featured by more UK tour operators as part of a 'beach and adventure' twin-centre holiday with Mauritius.

The tourist authorities were quick to recognise and exploit its potential as a paradise for backpackers and thrill seekers, and over the years they have built up an efficient infrastructure. The trail network is well-mapped and maintained, as are the purpose-built mountain lodges or *gîtes*. The adventure sport potential has been developed to the full. Other than trekking, organisations and facilities for mountain biking, climbing, horse riding, canyoning,

Fans of Hindi cinema have a good chance of glimpsing their screen idols in Mauritius, where Bollywood films are almost constantly in production.

Anse Ally Beach on Rodrigues.

canoeing, caving, even bungee-jumping can be found all over the island

Réunion has also countered its shortcomings with the marketing of its colonial heritage, which it seems to have preserved far better than its neighbours. Plantations and colonial houses have been faithfully restored and opened to the public. In contrast, despite the opportunities for cultural heritage tourism that the rich history and diverse population of Mauritius offer, museum development and tours of cultural and historic sites remain unsophisticated. The marketing of the island's cultural heritage, particularly around gastronomy, will be a strong focus for the Mauritius Tourism Promotion Authority in the coming years.

THE FORGOTTEN ISLAND

Rodrigues, granted regional autonomy in 2002, is the minuscule and often forgotten partner in the twin-island Republic of Mauritius. Until not so long ago, the island could be reached only by a cargo vessel which docked at Port Mathurin just once a month and only the most determined travellers reached its rugged shores. Nowadays, the *Mauritius Trochetia* makes the 36 hour crossing two or three times a month, bringing in islanders and the odd tourist on short breaks.

Tour operators are beginning to turn their attentions to Rodrigues, but tourism is still very much in its infancy here and further development seems to be hampered by the difficulties of air access, water shortages and concern about its infrastructure. Light aircraft make regular flights to and from Mauritius and visitors from Réunion have to fly via Mauritius before continuing to Rodrigues.

The Association of Rodrigues Tourism Operators is a body of guesthouse and hotel managers, tour operators, car hire companies and shopkeepers who, in conjunction with the Mauritius Tourism Promotion Authority, are promoting cultural and niche tourism, with some success. Their organised activities include staying in islanders' homes, going to folklore shows, walking, game fishing, diving and kitesurfing. The gigantic lagoon for which Rodrigues is famous is an unspoilt haven for divers, and is currently the subject of detailed research by scientists studying the Indian Ocean's unique coral islands.

Rodrigues remains uncrowded and unspoiled. There are no high-rise hotels or malls, and chickens still roam the capital's streets. Interestingly, the island is visited mostly by Mauritians looking for a relaxing weekend break and small numbers of European and South African tourists travelling from Mauritius who are keen to discover another facet of life in the Mascarenes.

It was hoped an extended airport runway, built in 2002 with European funding, would attract more flights, increasing Rodrigues' popularity as another Indian Ocean destination, but little has changed. Developers will one day home in on its beaches, but hopefully with the sensitivity to the natural environment that is essential to the survival of such a small island.

SEYCHELLES' TOP TEN

With its soft crescents of white sand lined with palms and backed by dramatic granite boulders, it's little wonder Seychelles regularly appears on lists of the world's best beaches.

In 1987, the film *Castaway* – nothing to do with the later Tom Hanks-vehicle, *Cast Away* – was released. It was based on the true story of two Londoners who dreamed of living for a year on a tropical island, but the beaches on the real island, which lies between Papua New Guinea and Australia, weren't photogenic enough. The director, Nicolas Roeg, looked around the world for the perfect tropical paradise. He settled on the perfect arc of white sand at Anse Kerlan on Praslin, lapped by crystal-clear blue waters and surrounded by lush tropical vegetation. The film starred Oliver Reed and Amanda Donahue, but according to one review: 'The real star was the beach.'

The beaches of Seychelles are legendary. When German travel magazine *Reise & Preise* conducted a survey to rate the world's most fabulous beaches, thousands of its readers responded to the 'Beach Test', rating sand, surf, sunbathing, accessibility, water quality and so on. Many beaches and many countries were listed, and Seychelles emerged the clear winner, with six of the top 12 beaches in the world. In a supplementary list of insider tips for those beaches rarely mentioned in the guidebooks (this one excepted), Seychelles again dominated with two of the world's top five. No other country had more than one slot in the same category. 'There is no doubt,' concluded the magazine, 'that the best beaches in the world can be found in Seychelles.'

Top of the league table is **Anse Lazio**, followed at number two by its close neighbour **Anse Georgette**, both on Praslin. La Digue also had two entries, **Anse Source d'Argent** at number five and **Grande Anse** at 12. Frégate Island's **Anse Victorin** was rated at number seven and Mahé's **Anse Intendance** at nine. In the supplementary rankings, **Anse Soleil** on Mahé and **Anse Cocos** on La Digue completed the roll of honour. Seychelles is never absent from similar polls. Anse Source d'Argent was rated number one beach in the world for wow factor in a 50 best beaches of the world feature in the Guardian newspaper, while *Condé Nast Traveler* magazine highlighted Anse Lazio as one of the world's best as did American cable TV station the Travel Channel.

The stark white sands, swaying palms and emerald seas of these and other idyllic coastal stretches are the answer to many a film-maker's, not to mention advertiser's, dream. Roman Polanski chose to shoot scenes for his swashbuckling adventure film *Pirates* on Frégate. Take a closer look at the classic paradise backdrop to any fashion shoot, TV or glossy magazine ad, and there's a good chance you'll recognise a Seychelles hotspot.

Anse Lazio's acolade-winning beach.

The truth is, when beaches are this good it is difficult to choose. There are beaches for every mood. Romantic beaches to wander along, surf-lashed beaches to frolic on, fish-rich waters to snorkel in, child-friendly beaches on the edge of sleepy lagoons, lively beaches with water sports and restaurants, and beaches where you'll not see a soul all day except perhaps for a fisherman. Mahé's **Beau Vallon**, though the most developed beach in Seychelles, retains a majestic beauty. It remains uncrowded and unspoilt relative to most destinations. At the other extreme of sophistication are the remote **Outer Islands**. The little-visited islands of St François, Desroches, Alphonse, Farquhar and Assumption all have stunning beaches. Small resorts and live-aboard cruising are slowly opening up this corner of Eden.

A dream setting for a tropical wedding at Sugar Beach Mauritius, Wolmar, Flic-en-Flac.

THE WEDDING INDUSTRY

Weddings and honeymoons in the Indian Ocean are increasingly popular, and affordable. Forward planning is the key to their success.

The lure of Mauritius and Seychelles comes in many guises for brides and grooms to be. (As Réunion operates under French rule, European visitors are forbidden by its residency laws to marry here.) More often than not, it's the desire to escape all the hassle and cost of a formal white wedding at home that tempts couples overseas. Apart from an idyllic setting and perfect climate, these islands offer the freedom to kick off your shoes and tie the knot barefoot in the sand if the mood takes you.

Mauritius and Seychelles have so far managed to avoid the tackiness to which other destinations have succumbed. Unlike many Caribbean resorts, where newlyweds often bump into each other, most hotels here prefer to limit ceremonies to one a day.

TYING THE KNOT

Weddings are generally civil, the ceremony held either under a gazebo beside the beach, on the jetty or in a hotel garden. Church weddings are possible, but they involve a little more organisation and often an extra cost for hiring the church. However, provided the hotel or tour operator is willing to make the arrangements, there's nothing to stop more adventurous couples getting married anywhere they choose. In Mauritius, couples can helicopter into the highlands for a ceremony at the Varangue Sur Morne near the Black River Gorges with awesome views of the dramatic landscape and turquoise ocean. Or they can board a luxury catamaran for a wedding on the water, or get married in the grounds of a romantic château. In Seychelles, at resorts such as Denis or Frégate Island Private, you can have your own exclusive island wedding, providing your budget stretches that far.

Honeymooners on Denis Private Island.

The key to a successful Indian Ocean wedding is finding the right tour operator (see Travel Tips, Transport, for a list of reputable organisations) and making sure you have complied with all the legal requirements (see Travel Tips, A–Z). Then there is little or nothing to organise except the provision of the necessary documents, and the arrangement of a few details like hair appointments, flowers, wedding cake and choosing between, say, a sunset cruise or a romantic dinner.

Mauritius has a sophisticated wedding scene, with its four- and five-star international resorts well equipped to organise ceremonies, many with dedicated wedding co-ordinators who guide couples through all their arrangements.

Seychelles may not be as slick as Mauritius when it comes to organising weddings, but in many ways this adds to its charm. With its pristine beaches, dramatic peaks and rainforest, not to mention the notorious coco de mer 'love nut', Seychelles is just as seductive.

Trends show that weddings abroad are on the increase and more and more couples are accompanied by friends and family. The beauty of the Indian Ocean is that once the wedding is over, guests can stay on for a holiday while newlyweds can honeymoon on another island, take an island-hopping cruise, go on safari in Africa (not a long plane journey away) or go for a spell on Réunion – a great contrast to Mauritius or Seychelles, with its dramatic volcanic scenery and intensely French culture.

The average two-week wedding and honeymoon in the Indian Ocean costs in the region of £4,500 (US$5,900) per couple. If the wedding party is big enough, some of the larger hotels may waive the cost of the wedding package (usually £350–£600/US$525–$900) – but you'll need to book well in advance.

A wedding at Lemuria Luxury Hotel on Praslin.

⊘ WEDDING DOS AND DON'TS

Do book well in advance and plan your wedding date at least three days after your arrival so you can acclimatise and get all the details and legal paperwork completed. (Check the latest regulations for how many days before the wedding you need to be on the island.) Hang your wedding dress or suit in a steamy bathroom on arrival to remove creases. Check exactly what's included in your wedding package and whether you want any extras such as live music. Take out wedding and travel insurance. Don't wear new or tight shoes, as your feet will expand in the heat. And remember – formalities often proceed at a slower pace in a hot climate.

TOP MAURITIAN WEDDING VENUES

Foreigners marrying in Mauritius can incorporate elements of traditional weddings into their ceremonies if they wish, but must advise the hotel as to what they want.

Six hotel groups – Beachcomber, Sun Resorts, LUX* Resorts, Veranda Resorts, Heritage Resorts and Attitude Hotels – dominate the island. All are geared up for weddings and take care to make couples feel special. Most of the other upmarket hotels on the island, such as The Résidence Mauritius, The St. Regis Mauritius Resort, Shangri-La's Le Touessrok Resort & Spa and Constance Prince Maurice, also cater for luxury weddings. LUX* Resorts even offers the possibility of getting hitched on its Robinson-Crusoe-style private island, Île des Deux Cocos.

SEYCHELLES WEDDINGS

In Seychelles there are registrars on the main islands of Mahé, Praslin and La Digue. However, resorts on the other islands can also assist with wedding arrangements, including photography if required.

Foreign couples can marry anywhere they want to, although strictly speaking they are not supposed to marry on the distinctive white

stunning shots. Some of the best-known hotels for weddings on Mahé are the Four Seasons, the Berjaya hotels, Coral Strand Smart Choice

Couples wanting to marry in Mauritius and Seychelles send their requests as much as 18 months in advance. November and December are particularly popular months, so book early to avoid disappointment.

The perfect place for a classic honeymoon – Sainte Anne Island Beachcomber.

sand beaches. However, hotels such as Four Seasons have pavilions or gazebos beside the beach. Favourite beach wedding settings are Anse Source d'Argent on La Digue and Anse Lazio on Praslin, proclaimed the best beaches in the world by many glossy travel magazines, is equally idyllic. Foreigners can also marry in church, but for an extra charge.

Most hotels in Seychelles welcome weddings. As they tend to be smaller than in other destinations, they lend themselves to intimate gatherings. Coco de Mer Hotel & Black Parrot Suites on Praslin decorates its wooden pier with local flowers and banana leaves to create a wedding venue over the water. A ceremony just before sunset allows the photographer to capture some

Hotel and Banyan Tree. Over on Praslin favourites include Coco de Mer Hotel & Black Parrot Suites, Le Domaine de La Réserve, Raffles Resort and the Constance Lemuria Resort. On La Digue couples can arrive by ox cart for their wedding at La Digue Island Lodge. As there are so many islands to choose from, it's worth considering marrying on one island, such as Mahé or Praslin, and honeymooning on another, or even island-hopping by air or sea.

Those who really want to get away from it all can make arrangements on several of the small outer islands: Denis has its own tiny wedding chapel; Desroches, Alphonse, Cousine and Frégate Island Private all fit the tropical paradise bill.

Myriad small fish surround a red sea fan on a Seychelles coral reef.

MARINE LIFE

Not far beneath the surface of the Indian Ocean lies a fascinating world, teeming with life and easy to explore.

For many people the 'Underwater World' is a strange and inaccessible place, full of mystery and danger. While it is true that most of the submarine environment will remain an area that few have the opportunity to experience, the temperature and generally favourable conditions here make the shallow waters easy to explore. The most popular holiday destinations in the Indian Ocean are on the coast and have easy access to the sea. Mauritius is encircled by an almost continuous reef barrier, interrupted only to the south between Le Souffleur and Souillac; many of the Seychelles islands support fringing coral reefs, while some experts maintain that Rodrigues' corals are even better than those of the Seychelles.

Many parrotfish sleep in a mucus 'bubble', which they blow around themselves as an early warning system of approaching danger.

School of Moorish idols.

TIDAL ZONE

The first type of terrain you are likely to come across is the tidal zone. Here at sea level, rock pools host a number of small fish species adapted to the inter-tidal way of life. Prominent among these are the rock skippers, small brown blennies and gobies which have modified fins that act as suckers, allowing them to cling to the rocks as the surf sweeps back and forth.

Many species of crustaceans are found only in these refuges. Most striking of the rock pool treasures are the crabs that scurry nimbly from rock to rock, such as the aptly named Sally Lightfoot. Barnacles spend their life attached to rocks. From their cone-shaped structure, they extend hairy paddle-like legs that beat to create a current, bringing nutrient-rich water to their mouths.

SANDY AREAS

As you wade into the sea and peer through the water, the sand beneath the surface looks like a submarine desert when compared to the busy reefs beyond. But look a little closer and you'll spot some interesting sea creatures. Often the most obvious are the slow-moving crawlers such as crabs, sea urchins and sea cucumbers, the long sausage-like objects littered around many sandy bottom areas. These creatures are the caretakers of the sea bed and feed on detritus and algae in the sand's surface layer. The small submarine 'volcanoes' characteristic of some areas are built by marine worms, generally hidden from view.

Flat-fish species, such as the peacock flounder, are difficult to see. Generally well camouflaged, they only give themselves away when they glide off in search of another resting spot. Various types of ray also inhabit sandy bottom areas, especially in the shallow lagoons. They can be quite large, measuring up to 2 metres (6.5ft) across their wide wing-like disc. You have to look quite hard to spot a resting ray as they often cover themselves with a coating of sand, but their whip-like tails, which

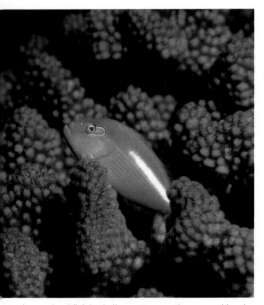
Arc eye hawkfish in shallow waters, resting on coral heads.

tend to stick out of the sand like flagpoles, often give them away. While the sting ray is indeed well equipped with a sting mechanism in his barbed tail, it is used purely for defence and divers and snorkellers should have no fear of attack unless they provoke the animal or tread on it. A few minutes spent watching a sting ray hunting through the sand for molluscs and crabs can be very rewarding. Manta rays are among the biggest Indian Ocean fish and feed on plankton and small fish. They are quite harmless and a joy to watch as they sail gracefully through the water.

A number of the unique animals inhabiting the sandy sea bed are often mistaken for plants; sea pens, for example, have a feather or plume-like structure on a fleshy stalk that protrudes from the sand. The 'plume' is in fact an intricate structure of arms that is rotated to face into any water currents and strain out plankton and other particles of food.

Look out for areas of algae or sea-grass which provide food and shelter for a number of animals. Wrasse are often found feeding here and you may even come across a charismatic little seahorse clinging to the grass with his tail.

Sea-grass beds are also visited by larger algal browsers, notably the green turtle, the larger of the two turtle species found in this region. Watching the turtles feeding is one of the rare opportunities you will have of observing them at close quarters. The other prime time for a good sighting is when the female turtles come up the beach to lay their eggs.

ROCK REEFS

Rock reefs are another easily accessible and productive zone in the Indian Ocean and provide the habitat for a profusion of marine life. The rocks themselves are often covered in a variety of marine plants and creatures ranging from subtly coloured encrusting hard corals, barnacles and limpets to brightly coloured sponges and soft corals, so much so that little of the actual rock surface may be visible. Each of these encrusting structures is itself host to a number of other creatures and provides a micro-ecosystem on the reef. In soft coral formations look out for small fish such as gobies and blennies that often mimic the colour of the coral for protection. They actually nest on the corals and feed on zooplankton. The hard coral formations are home to a number of brightly coloured fish species including hawk-fish, damselfish and small scorpion or rock-fishes, all benefiting from the protection that the branching structures provide. Various crabs also use the branching corals for shelter, such as the red-spotted crab and hermit crab, which hides in its borrowed shell for protection.

Many fish species hide in the gaps and crevasses between the rocks of the reef for protection from predators and can be found feeding above the reef during the day. Along the reef you are sure to see brightly coloured surgeonfish that graze algae off the rocks, often just below the wave zone. Their name derives from the sharp spines found at the base of their tail, which is why fishermen are extra careful when handling them.

CORAL REEFS

Coral reefs are the submarine equivalent of the rainforest and have the greatest diversity of marine life. They are formed by tiny animals, coral polyps, which secrete a hard external casing of calcium. Successive generations build on top of each other to form the limestone of the reef with just the outer surface covered with the living corals.

There are a vast number of hard coral formations. The real reef builders are known as 'massive' corals. They form enormous rounded coral heads which coalesce to form reefs. Other

of these stings are harmless to humans, but the one coral to learn to recognise and avoid is the so-called fire coral. If you brush against one, the potent sting it inflicts on your skin feels like the burn from a stinging nettle.

SEA ANEMONES

Related to the corals are the sea anemones – a bit like giant coral polyps without the external shell. These creatures are generally hidden within cracks and ledges of the reef but a few species are conspicuously stuck to the surface of the rocks.

Snorkelling in clear water above coral, Seychelles.

hard corals are highly branched, with delicately ornate structures, giving rise to such evocative names as staghorn and elkhorn.

While the stony corals secrete a calcium casing, many of the soft coral species grow on even more complex structures. Some – the colourful tree corals, for example – support their bodies with a latticework of tiny calcium needles. Others produce a horny resilient material called gorgonin and develop into long spiral whip corals or intricate fans. These grow at right angles to the current and act as living sieves, filtering out food particles as the water flows through.

All corals are really predatory animals and their polyps have tentacles that are armed with stinging cells that stun microscopic prey. Most

Cone shells, with their beautiful intricate designs, are among the most attractive shells in the world. But beware! Never pick one up by the thin end, for its poison is deadly.

They are mostly host anemones and are almost always associated with the anemone fish, also known as the clown fish. Theirs is a classic symbiotic relationship: the anemone fish gains shelter and protection from the anemone, and in return the anemone gets scraps of food from the resident fish. Although the anemone fish is able to develop a protection against the anemone's stings, they are still a powerful deterrent to a would-be predator. The exact mechanism of the anemone fish's immunity is not clearly understood but it is thought that the mucus coating covering the scales of the fish, which it wears like a coat, absorbs small amounts of the anemone's sting; the anemone begins to accept this coated fish as being itself and thus no longer tries to sting it.

COLOURFUL TROPICAL FISH

For many snorkellers, and even divers, it is the brightly coloured and most visible fish which

Butterfly fish swim over a Seychelles reef.

⊙ CORAL BLEACHING

During 1997–8, a rise in sea temperatures in the western Indian Ocean (attributed to climate change and the El Niño effect) killed many corals, bleaching them white. In areas of good environmental conditions a natural cycle of colonisation by algae was triggered, allowing re-colonisation by coral larvae. In Seychelles, the reef life was further protected by the underlying granitic structure that gave shelter to displaced species. Long-term prospects for Mauritius' reefs, which endured another bleaching in 2009, are good. Meanwhile a 2011 Wildlife Conservation Society (WCS) study praised Réunion for its reef protection programme.

gather in the shallower waters around and above the reef that leave the strongest impression. Many of these fish are in fact deep water species which come into the shallows to feed. Colourful schools of fusiliers, known locally as mackerel, have the characteristic 'fishy' shape of a torpedo-like body with small fins, and feed on phyto-plankton above the reefs. Most of the common species have bright blue body colourings with a mixture of stripes and flashes ranging from yellow through to pink, which shimmer in a vivid colour display as the school moves.

On the reef itself the two most colourful species are the angelfish and butterfly fish, both of which have bodies which are flattened from side to side when viewed from ahead and are almost circular when viewed in profile. Butterfly fish are generally small, around 8–15 cm (3–6ins) across the disc and are predominantly algal and coral grazers; most have body colours that are yellow, black or white. Angelfish species are larger in size, up to 25cm (10ins), and display a wide range of markings. They also have different patterns in juvenile forms compared to the final adult phases and so add enormously to the colour of the living reef.

A larger visitor to the coral reef is the hawksbill turtle; this is probably the most commonly found marine turtle species in this region and takes its name from its hooked, hawk-like beak which it uses to carve chunks off sponges and soft coral formations. In some areas of Seychelles these turtles may be found nesting on the beaches in daylight – a very unusual sight.

Just like a rock reef, the coral reef offers shelter and protection to a vast number of species as well as being a food source for some of its residents. Some fish are especially adapted to feeding on coral polyps, such as certain butterfly fish and filefish; others feed on small shrimp and other invertebrates that shelter between the branches, such as the razor or shrimpfish.

Molluscs are frequent residents; the most obvious of these are the brightly coloured nudibranchs, or sea slugs. Despite their small size they are the most apparent because of their bright coloration that warns would-be predators that they do not taste good and might be poisonous. A number of shelled molluscs can be found during the day as well but many have highly camouflaged shells to conceal them so they can be difficult to spot.

Other animals actually live within the limestone of the coral colony; these include the tube or 'feather-duster' worms that are evident from their coloured fans which extend above the surface of the coral colony to trap particles. Some are spectacularly formed into twin spiral cones, as in the Christmas-tree worm, and these pretty structures are often brightly coloured. All fan worms are sensitive to changes in light and therefore will disappear into their tubes on the sudden appearance of a snorkeller or diver.

DEEP WATERS

The open ocean is a very different and much more inaccessible environment. The deep waters and their currents support marine life from microscopic plankton to some of the largest creatures on the planet but often the concentration of individuals is very low. Due to the constraints of deep water activities, most people will only get the chance to see these creatures when they come to the surface. Luckily, some places seem to have special properties that encourage deep water species to aggregate at the surface; in these areas it is possible to find whales and dolphins at specific times of the year.

Dolphins are one group that visitors are likely to come across on boat journeys around the islands, although in-water encounters are unfortunately a rare occurrence. There are a number of species in this area and the larger bottlenose and common dolphins are most often seen. In more remote areas there are local populations of the smaller species, notably spinner dolphins, which are readily recognisable by the habit of the youngsters to leap out of the air performing aerial twists and acrobatics. In some instances these places are special feeding or breeding areas and although the animals may appear to be easily approachable in organised encounter programmes, there are strict codes of conduct to ensure the safety of visitors and the protection of the animals concerned.

Within the last decade Réunion has seen increasing numbers of migrating humpback whales visit its waters. These marine mammals make the long journey up from Antarctica between June and September to mate, give birth and nurse their young in the warmer waters around the island. Scientists can identify each whale from its tailfin, the colour and shape of which is unique to each creature. They breach frequently and spectacularly, allowing visitors a chance to admire them.

Some deep water species are generally only seen when landed by fishing boats; these big

> *Many molluscs secrete chemical substances which, without being poisonous, are distasteful enough to put off a would-be predator.*

Leaping humpback whale at St Paul's Bay Cap la Houssaye.

game species such as sailfish, marlin, wahoo and dorado are relatively abundant but are seldom seen in their natural environment. Other deep water creatures are sometimes washed ashore by the ocean currents. These include several varieties of medusa or jellyfish; characteristically these have a clear gelatinous bell-shaped body and like their coral cousins they have a ring of stinging tentacles. While some jellyfish are harmless, others can deliver a powerful and possibly lethal sting and so contact should be avoided.

The Indian Ocean offers a huge diversity of life. Whether you choose to scuba dive, snorkel or take a glass-bottom boat trip, a glimpse into this magical underwater world will most certainly be a highlight of your trip.

📷 TROPICAL ISLAND BLOOMS

From delicate orchids and hibiscus to vibrant bougainvillaea and flaming red flamboyants, the richness and variety of plant life are astounding.

When the first explorers set eyes on the Indian Ocean islands, it was the luxuriant forests and sweet-smelling colourful plants that led them to believe they had found Eden. In Mauritius, four centuries of human habitation have brought plantations, roads and logging, and destroyed many of the island's plants. In Seychelles, the shorter human history, absence of plantations and mountainous islands have helped preserve the environment. Réunion, too, was fortunate: its rocky and mountainous landscape is more inaccessible, so swathes of natural forest remain untouched.

Although many species are still endangered, the islands' flora remains rich: Mauritius has 670 native species, of which 315 are endemic; Réunion has over 700 indigenous species, of which 161 are endemic; Seychelles, too, has a remarkable flora. Of around 1,500 species, over 400 are native, with 75 endemic and a further 43 found only in the Aldabra group.

BOTANICAL GARDENS

All the islands have botanical gardens where visitors can admire and learn about the abundant plant life. Mauritius has the famous Pamplemousses Botanical Gardens near Port Louis, the Curepipe Botanical Gardens and Le Pétrin Native Garden in the Black River Gorges area; Réunion has the Conservatoire Botanique National in St-Leu and the Jardin de l'Etat near St-Denis; and in Seychelles there's the Botanical Gardens and the Jardin du Roi spice gardens, both on Mahé.

With its dense canopy of bright red flowers, the flamboyant tree in bloom is an impressive sight. It flowers between November and January.

Luxuriant passion fruit vines grow all over Seychelles. The fruit is used for juices.

Frangipani (plumeria) flowers in Mauritius.

Dried vanilla pods, Réunion.

La vanille bourbon

Vanilla was introduced to Réunion from Central America in 1819, but attempts at natural pollination failed. Then, in 1841, a 12-year-old orphaned slave called Edmund Albius discovered that its flowers could be pollinated by grafting. (Edmund had been raised like a son by botanist Ferreol Beaumont Bellier, who was cultivating vanilla in his garden.) By the end of the 19th century Réunion was churning out 100 tons a year, using the techniques of drying and fermentation of vanilla beans practised by the Aztecs. In its heyday in the 1930s, Réunion accounted for three-quarters of the world's vanilla production.

Annual production has dropped significantly since then, but the island remains one of the world's leading producers. Cultivation is concentrated on the lush eastern side of the island where the warm, wet conditions are ideal. The pods are harvested between June and September, about eight months after pollination. Still green, they are scalded in boiling water, fermented, then laid out in the sun to dry. Now brown, the pods are then left in airtight containers for two to three months, during which time they develop their strong aroma.

...otus blossom, one of around 500 plant species you can ...ee in Mauritius famous pampli-mousses Gardens, not for ...om the capital, Port-Louis.

...opical Réunion orchids are often epiphytic, meaning ...ey lend to grow on other plants such as trees. They ...ten bloom in the wet season.

The delicate hibiscus flower comes in myriad colours, but the bloom only lasts for one day.

Hikers in Belouve forest
on Réunion.

Paddling on Blue Bay beach near
Mahebourg, Mauritius.

THE MASCARENES

The Mascarene Islands may form a whole, but each offers very different landscapes and completely different experiences.

Get ready to water-ski.

Named after the Portuguese admiral Pedro Mascarenhas, whose fleet anchored by these uninhabited islands more than 500 years ago, the Mascarenes had lain undisturbed since they rose from the sea in a series of volcanic eruptions millions of years earlier. Even so, their discovery hardly led to a mad rush to colonise. And as far as tourism is concerned, they were a dot on the map until a trickle of visitors arrived in the 1970s.

For most people, Mauritius is the best known island, a favourite with both honeymooners and families, but the French have been holidaying in Réunion for years. If you're in Mauritius, the 35-minute hop to Réunion's capital St-Denis is easy and you can see some of the best of the island in just two or three days if time is limited. For Mauritius regulars, the short hop to Rodrigues is becoming an increasingly attractive proposition, and shouldn't be missed if you've got a few days to spare.

Mauritius is, in many ways, the archetypal romantic idyll, with gorgeous fine-sanded beaches lined with exclusive luxury hotels – sporting world-class golf courses, top-notch spas and gourmet restaurants – whose high standards of service attract the rich and famous.

A local Creole cook.

Rodrigues, an autonomous part of Mauritius, lies 560km (350 miles) east and is markedly different from the motherland in character and culture. This is the place to come for a taste of authentic, remote island life: just rugged beauty, a warm and welcoming people and serenity.

Just 160km (100 miles) southwest of Mauritius is Réunion Island, where the first thing that strikes you is the awesome nature of the landscape, whose volcano and massive cirques force most islanders to live along the coast – and gives visitors the urge to pull on their hiking boots. Wherever you go you will be beguiled by the mixture of classic Frenchness and local Creole culture.

Few people discover all the islands of the Mascarenes in one trip, but whichever you choose, you're unlikely to be disappointed.

DECISIVE DATES

EARLY DISCOVERERS

10th–12th centuries
Arabs sight the Mascarenes.

15th century
Arab names Dina Arobi, Dina Margabim and Dina Moraze for Mauritius, Réunion and Rodrigues appear on early world maps.

1505–7
Portuguese navigator Diogo Fernandes Pereira names Mauritius the Ilha do Cirne, probably after one of his ships.

1513
The islands are named after Portuguese admiral Pedro Mascarenhas.

1528
A Portuguese seaman Diogo Rodrigues visits Rodrigues and gives the island his name.

THE DUTCH YEARS

1598
First Dutch landing on Ilha do Cirne. The island is annexed to Holland and renamed Mauritius after Prince Maurice of Nassau, son of William of Orange.

1601
First Dutch landing in Rodrigues.

1638–1710
Dutch settle at Port South East, Mauritius, but abandon it after several attempts to colonise. The first slaves are imported from Madagascar. Sugar cane, deer and pigs from Java are introduced.

1642
The French take possession of Rodrigues and Réunion, which

Declaration of the abolition of slavery on Réunion, 1848.

they name Mascareigne and later Bourbon.

1646
First French settlers occupy Bourbon.

1688
Last recorded sighting of dodo on Mauritius.

1691–3
François Leguat and crew become Rodrigues' first settlers.

THE FRENCH PERIOD

1715
France annexes Mauritius, naming it Île de France; it is controlled by the French East India Company.

1721–1810
French occupation of Île de France. Slaves from Madagascar, Africa and Asia are imported to work on sugar cane plantations.

1735
Labourdonnais becomes governor of the Mascarene

Islands, based on Île de France. He expands Port Louis.

1756–63
The Seven Years' War so seriously affects French interests in the Indian Ocean that by 1764 the French East India Company is forced to officially hand Île de France to the French crown.

1790
News of the French Revolution reaches the Mascarenes and provokes a rebellion.

1793–1805
Indian Ocean privateering reaches its peak. The French Revolution leads to the creation of colonial assemblies in all the islands. Fear of losing their slaves provokes local resistance to French political emissaries. Bourbon is renamed Réunion.

1799
General Decaen restores order to Île de France in the name of Napoleon after islanders had enjoyed years of autonomy. Slavery continues.

THE BRITISH PERIOD

1810
Weakened by Napoleonic wars, Île de France and Réunion capitulate to British naval forces. Île de France reverts to its former name Mauritius.

1814
The Treaty of Paris places Mauritius, Rodrigues and Seychelles under British ownership, while Réunion reverts to France.

Statue of Sir Seewoosager Ramgoolam.

1835
The British abolish slavery in Mauritius and introduce Indian indentured labourers, or 'coolies'.

1848
Slavery is abolished in Réunion.

1885
Mauritians William Newton and Virgile Naz found the Reform Movement, leading to the introduction of the country's own constitution.

THE MODERN AGE

1909
Indian immigration ceases and political and social reform begins in the Mascarenes.

1936
The Labour Party is formed in Mauritius.

1946
Réunion becomes an overseas French *département*.

1968
Mauritius achieves independence, with Sir Seewoosagur Ramgoolam elected its first prime minister. Rodrigues becomes a dependency of Mauritius.

1982
Sir Seewoosagur Ramgoolam is defeated by a political alliance. Anerood Jugnauth becomes prime minister.

1992
The Republic of Mauritius is declared, with Cassam Uteem as its first president. Rodrigues becomes part of Mauritius.

1995
The Labour Party wins elections in Mauritius under Navin Ramgoolam.

2002
Rodrigues is granted regional autonomy.

2003
Paul Bérenger becomes Mauritius' first non-Indian prime minister.

2005
Navin Ramgoolam returns as prime minister and leader of the Social Alliance Party.

2008
Le Morne Brabant becomes a Unesco World Heritage Site.

2008–10
Construction of Sino-Mauritian Economic and Trade Cooperation Zones at Riche Terre.

2010
The Pitons, Cirques and Remparts of Réunion, covering 40 percent of the island's interior, become a Unesco World Heritage Site. Navin Ramgoolam is re-elected prime minister of Mauritius.

2014
A surprise shake-up at the Mauritius elections sees Anerood Jugnauth return as prime minister.

2015
Debris from the missing Malaysia Airlines flight MH370 washes up on the shores of Réunion.

2016
The Economist Intelligence Unit rates Mauritius as a full democracy.

2017
In January, the 86-year-old prime minister, Anerood Jugnauth steps down, appointing his son, Pravind Jugnauth as his replacement.

2018
Mauritius celebrates its Golden Jubilee – 50 years of Independence on 12th March, with a year-long calendar of events.

2019
Mauritius hosts the prestigious Indian Ocean Games at Côte d'Or on the Central Plateau in July.

Debris discovered on Réunion belonged to missing flight MH370.

An early map of Île de France.

SAILORS AND EXPLORERS: DISCOVERERS OF THE MASCARENES

From Arabs to Europeans, the history and culture of the Mascarenes has been determined by traders, explorers, colonisers and corsairs.

The Mascarenes were all uninhabited until the arrival of European colonisers in the 16th century. Ever since, these islands have been subjected to the whims of European taste and ambitions which have determined their population, their pursuits and, to a large extent, their politics.

The Mascarenes are oceanic islands – they did not break away from continental land masses but developed independently as a result of volcanic action. Mauritius is the oldest at about 8 million years, Réunion and Rodrigues are around 3 and 2 million years old respectively. The islands are affected by volatile weather conditions; and the vagaries of trade winds and cyclones, which blew countless sailing ships off course or onto reefs, meant that it was as likely accident and misfortune as intrepid exploration that provoked the first sightings of these small land masses in the southwestern Indian Ocean.

The earliest recorded proof of the identification and location of the islands is from Arab documents and maps. Writings dating back to the 12th century include descriptions of islands which may be the Mascarenes. In 1498, Vasco da Gama saw maps by Ibn Majid in which three islands southeast of Madagascar are named Dina Moraze, Dina Margabim and Dina Arobi, which roughly translate as 'eastern', 'western' and 'deserted' islands.

It was not until the early 16th century that Portuguese explorers became the first recorded European visitors to the Mascarenes. They named Mauritius 'Cirne', probably after one of their ships, Réunion 'Santa Apolina' after the date of its discovery and Rodrigues after the navigator Diogo Rodrigues, the only one of the islands to retain its Portuguese name. The Portuguese only occasionally used the Mascarenes

A scene from the 18th-century novel 'Paul et Virginie'.

route on their way to the Indies but it was a welcome place of respite for damaged ships and weary crews which found themselves blown towards these archetypal desert islands.

NATURE'S BOUNTY

Still uninhabited in the early 17th century, the fertility and unspoilt nature of the Mascarene Islands were extolled by Dutch, French and English visitors. Samuel Castleton, who first set eyes on Réunion in 1613, described thick forest, cascading waterfalls, fat eels in the rivers and plentiful turtles and birds. In homage to its natural beauty, he named the island 'England's Forest'. The Dutchman, Mandelslo, wrote that Mauritius teemed with figs, pomegranates, partridges and pigeons. There were no cats, pigs, goats, dogs or even rats – at least not until some escaped from ships wrecked near Mascarene shores.

> The Mascarene Island group is named after the Portuguese navigator Pedro Mascarenhas. Like Columbus, he has probably been given more credit than his due, as he did not discover any of them.

COLONISATION BEGINS

The Dutch occupied Mauritius twice, between 1638 and 1658, and again from 1664 to 1710. Their first settlement was around the southeast harbour (where present-day Mahébourg is now situated). The garrison and commander, along with a small group of free farmers, brought convicts and slaves from Southeast Asia and Madagascar to help them with wood-cutting and crop cultivation. Runaways from these groups combined with soldiers and sailors who deserted from the garrison and visiting ships'

The Dutch settlement at Vieux Grand Port.

These early visitors brought back drawings of a strange flightless bird, indigenous to Mauritius and Réunion. It was described as fat, clumsy and bigger than a turkey. In 1628, Emmanuel Altham sent a live specimen of this 'strange fowle' home to his brother in Essex. This was the dodo (see page 61) whose relative, the solitaire, was found on Réunion and Rodrigues.

The ebony forests on Mauritius, and its two natural harbours, made it a colonial prize for European traders and explorers. Annexed for the Netherlands in 1598, the Dutch felled much of the valuable black wood on the island, until a glut in the European market slowed the destruction.

crews to form a counter-settlement in the forested interior. They launched frequent raids and arson attacks on the fort and farmers. The difficult conditions of the earlier settlers were made worse by seasonal cyclones, which ripped through their fragile wooden homesteads, and by the depredations of rats which ate the crops and stores. The ruins of the Dutch fort at Vieux Grand Port can be seen to this day, having only been excavated by archaeologists in 1977.

While the Dutch were establishing their settlement on Mauritius, the French had annexed the other Mascarene islands. Both nations supplemented piecemeal colonisation by sending unruly settlers from their bases at the Cape, Batavia and Madagascar into exile on the Mascarenes.

Bourbon, later renamed Réunion, was given its royal name by the French governor at Madagascar after hearing from a group of returned exiles of its beauty, abundance and healthiness. In 1654, the French attempted a permanent settlement of the island with a mixed group of French and Malagasy. They left four years later and Bourbon remained unoccupied until 1663.

The next group of settlers included three women, but disputes over them led to the creation of rival camps of French and Malagasy men. Attempts to send volunteers from France met with mixed results – many died en route.

Two events then proved a turning point for Bourbon: firstly the French were massacred on Madagascar, forcing the abandonment of that base, and secondly war with Holland closed off the Cape to French ships. Bourbon now became an important post for them on the Indies route. A governor was appointed from France, and, in a series of efforts to boost the size of the population, Indian convicts were imported, Indo-Portuguese women were induced to settle, and pirates, tired of a life of plunder, were invited to marry into the growing Bourbon community.

ECOLOGICAL DESTRUCTION

The glowing description of Bourbon made by its first forced inhabitants had also inspired a group of Protestants, persecuted in France, to set up their Eden on the last remaining desert island of the Mascarenes. François Leguat was one of eight males who settled on Rodrigues until the effects of solitude and the lack of women led them to escape in a small boat to Mauritius.

The reality of life on a tropical desert island was far removed from the visions of recuperating sailors and persecuted Protestants. The small settlements, peopled with prisoners and pirates, neglected by the trading companies, presided over by frustrated commanders and weakly defended, found survival a struggle. Geographical constraints – isolation and unreliable weather – had been revealed to be major determinants of Mascarenes history.

The impact of these visitors from across the seas was immense. The fragile island ecologies were irreparably damaged by human settlement and by the animals they imported that upset the natural balance. The coastal palms and the ebony forests were depleted. Eventually

30 species of birds, including the dodo and solitaire, and some of the large tortoises and turtles with whom they cohabited, would become

> The Mascarenes were legendary refuges. Mandelslo's description of a man marooned on Mauritius in 1601 is one of many such tales said to have provided Daniel Defoe with inspiration for his tale of Robinson Crusoe.

Maurice of Nassau.

extinct – casualties of the fragility of unique small island populations.

The Mascarene Islands have become the archetypal example of the destruction of ecological systems by outsiders. Once this process began, it took only a few decades for these small island 'Edens' to change irrevocably.

THE FRENCH CENTURY

Between 1710, when the Dutch left, and 1810 when the British took control, the French had a century of uninterrupted supremacy in the Mascarenes. Over this period the islands served several purposes: as a rest and refuelling point for European ships on the Indies route, where goods could be traded and ships repaired; as cultivating grounds for spices and coffee; and as good vantage points for the study of astronomic phenomena.

Already established on Bourbon, in 1721 the French sent a party of colonists from there to settle on Mauritius, renamed Île de France. A governor and several hundred soldiers and colonists were also sent from France, arriving the following year with 30 Malagasy slaves they had acquired en route. They settled in the southeast of the island, building on top of the Dutch ruins. Administered from Bourbon, both islands struggled to master their environment. One visitor to Île de France at

The Mahé de La Bourdonnais statue in Port Louis.

⊘ MAHÉ DE LABOURDONNAIS

Mahé de Labourdonnais is fêted in Mauritius and his statue stands in the centre of Port Louis, its capital, because in a few short years he transformed this natural harbour into the beginnings of a flourishing port.

Some of the works he undertook are still in evidence today, including the renovated mill and granary on Port Louis waterfront. Labourdonnais also built a hospital, established a road network and imported the first primitive sugar processing equipment to be used in Mauritius, now seen in the grounds of Pamplemousses Botanical Gardens, formerly the site of his estates.

this time sarcastically renamed it 'Kingdom of the Rats', describing the discomfort of nights spent trying to ignore them crawling over his body.

A decisive change occurred in the administration of the French Mascarenes in 1735, with the arrival of Mahé de Labourdonnais, and the decision to transfer the seat of government to Île de France. For the rest of the 18th century, Bourbon was relegated to what its colonists believed to be the inferior position of 'granary', supplying food for its sister island, and watching as the latter developed into a substantial trading and naval repair post.

Labourdonnais aimed to transform Île de France into a flourishing colony, but his ambitious plans could not be achieved without labour, and from this period, the trickle of West Africans and Asians arriving with visiting ships was regularly supplemented by the organisation of slave trading voyages to East Africa and Madagascar, and the importation of skilled workers from India and France. With serious food shortages threatening the increased population, Labourdonnais introduced manioc to the Mascarenes, which became a staple food of slaves, and began the systematic plunder of tortoises from Rodrigues. This marked the beginning of the irreversible decline of its endemic land and marine fauna, a process accelerated by the periodic presence of naval squadrons.

By 1764 the French East India Company, suffering severe financial losses occasioned by years of warfare, gave up control of the Mascarenes to the French king. Port Louis was able to expand its trading activities, which had been limited by the company's monopolistic practices, and developed an air of prosperity and style which led to its designation as the 'Paris of the Indian Ocean'.

But this facade of culture, elegance and profit concealed an economy based on speculation and a society in which the presence of celebrated intellectuals and naturalists could not prevent the continuing destruction of nature and the differentiation of men by colour and chains.

The French had hoped to use the Mascarenes to further their interest in the spice trade and to cultivate tropical produce. Colonists were encouraged to grow coffee, cotton, indigo, sugar cane, cinnamon, tea and pepper. Cloves and nutmegs were introduced. Many crops failed – eaten by birds, rats and monkeys or destroyed by adverse weather conditions. Coffee and spices grown on Bourbon nevertheless became the principal exports of the Mascarenes, while sugar cane was found to resist the onslaught of the elements best on Île de France. Its cultivation, expanding towards the end of the 18th century, was to become the defining feature of the Mascarenes in the 19th century.

> The French author of Paul et Virginie, Bernardin de Saint Pierre, observed: 'I do not know whether coffee and sugar are necessary to the happiness of Europe, but they have certainly made much of the world miserable.'

REVOLUTION AND REBELLION

French rule in the Mascarenes had instituted a kind of social apartheid which subjected slaves to the provisions of the Code Noir – a famous law the French applied to their colonies which prevented the free coloured population from marrying white colonists. After 1789, the revolutionary fervour emanating from France swept away such laws and unleashed a chain of events in the French colonies that culminated in the breakaway of Haiti and provoked a rebellion in the Mascarenes.

News of the French Revolution did not reach the Indian Ocean islands until the following year, but once ships bearing the tricolour arrived, Colonial Assemblies were set up on the islands and the royal name of Bourbon was changed to Réunion. The revolution was not very bloody in the Mascarenes, although one notable victim was MacNamara, a royalist naval officer who was hacked to death by a mob in Port Louis. Restrictions on mixed marriages between white and coloured colonists were lifted and the gulf between social groups was briefly narrowed.

In 1796, however, the Revolutionary government in France took matters too far for the liking of the colonists. Having proclaimed the abolition of slavery, France sent two representatives to the Mascarenes to put this into effect – they were thrown out within three days. For a while the islands ruled themselves but not without serious disagreements which almost led to Réunion separating from its sister island.

The arrival of Napoleon on the political scene led to the re-establishment of slavery

and in 1803 he sent General Charles Decaen to rule, granting him absolute power over the Mascarenes. Réunion was briefly named Bonaparte Island but, once again, did not flourish in the shadow of Île de France. The rigid social and fiscal legislation introduced by Decaen was designed for, and discriminated in favour of, the latter.

PIRATES, TRAITORS AND SPIES

For Portuguese and particularly British ships plying the route to the Indies, the French Mas-

Slaves carrying a palanquin, Ile de France, Mauritius, 1817–1820.

carenes were by now chiefly known for being a 'nest of pirates'. Between 1793 and 1802 more than a hundred captured ships were brought into Port Louis, where the booty on offer attracted neutral peoples like the Danes and Americans. The port was also popular with sailors: the increasing cultivation of sugar cane meant that one of its by-products, rum, was widely available, and it was one of the few places on the Indies route, outside the Cape, where men did not heavily outnumber women.

This privateering (led by the king of the corsairs, Robert Surcouf) was one of the reasons why the British decided to target the Mascarenes. In 1806 they blockaded Île de

France, where the celebrated British explorer and naturalist Matthew Flinders was then imprisoned. The British sent an armada from Bombay and the Cape, which regrouped at Rodrigues and took Réunion in July 1810 without much struggle.

Île de France was not so easy a conquest. In August, the British were defeated after a three-day naval battle in Mahébourg bay, known as the battle of Grand Port. In November 1810 they returned to attack with 70 ships and 10,000 troops, landing on the north coast and marching to the capital. Both sides recognised the numerical superiority of the British and General Charles Decaen therefore negotiated an honourable capitulation.

After the conquest, Île de France reverted to its former name, Mauritius. The British retained control of Réunion until 1814, when the Treaty of Paris returned the island to French rule. Louis XVIII is supposed to have commented to the British minister who negotiated the deal: 'You are leaving us the volcano and you are keeping the port.'

Indian labourers.

⊙ FRIENDLY ENEMIES

Despite the relentless conflict between the two nations during the Napoleonic wars, Anglo–French relations remained chivalrous. When the wife of the English officer commanding the squadron blockading the islands between 1803 and 1810 gave birth to a child on board ship, the French Governor, Decaen, sent her a boatload of fresh produce.

After the battle of Grand Port in 1810 – the only Napoleonic victory over the British that is inscribed on the Arc de Triomphe – the wounded leaders of both forces were treated side by side in what is now the National History Museum of Mahébourg.

ABOLITION OF SLAVERY

The British conquest of Mauritius and Rodrigues, undertaken for strategic motives, did not lead to a large influx of British settlers, and the Francophone character of the Mascarenes has consequently never been lost.

Early British colonial officials not only had to deal with a largely French settler class, but had to implement unpopular slave amelioration laws. The abolitionist movement, which had a massive following in Britain at this time, turned its attention to Mauritius at the worst possible moment for that colony. The island was in the process of converting itself into a plantation society and needed extra labour to clear land and plant canes. When John

Jeremie, a known abolitionist, was sent to the island in 1832 to take up an important legal post, the colonists gave him a 'welcome' akin to that received by the delegates from France during the Revolution. A general strike was organised which paralysed the capital and the fearful British governor ordered Jeremie to re-embark almost immediately. In response, the British built the Citadel (Fort Adelaide) on a hill overlooking the capital – a striking symbol of colonial power designed to quell its unruly inhabitants. The colonists were appeased by a £2 million compensation package given to slave owners (including those whose slaves had been illegally introduced) and the day of emancipation passed without incident in 1835.

IMMIGRANT LABOUR

From 1835 the British decided to make Mauritius the site of a 'great experiment' to see whether free labour could produce sugar as cheaply as slaves, by allowing the colony the first opportunity to import Indian workers under the indenture system. Almost half a million indentured workers were introduced in the 19th century, making Mauritius the largest recipient of Indian labour in the empire and helping the island to achieve the position of Britain's premier sugar colony within a decade.

> In 1811 a slave revolt on Réunion led to the execution of 30 ringleaders. A later uprising in Mauritius was also snuffed out. But for as long as slavery was in force, the Mascarene mountains remained a refuge for runaways.

Both Réunion and Mauritius had turned increasingly to sugar production as falling supplies from the British and French West Indies encouraged the newer colonies to fill the gap. Réunion was given the go-ahead to import British Indian labour from 1860, and both islands continued to recruit smaller numbers of Chinese, Malagasy, Comorian and Mozambican workers. Africans rescued from slave ships by British naval cruisers were also offloaded at Mauritius and the Seychelles

from the mid-19th century and 'liberated' into lengthy apprenticeships with local employers.

Réunion adapted to socio-economic change at a more gentle rate than Mauritius. It was slower to abolish slavery (abolition was declared in 1848, 13 years after Mauritius), and slower to develop into a monoculture economy. Both islands, nevertheless, underwent a revolution of sorts, as mechanisation and centralisation of estates transformed them into plantation societies where plantocracies confronted increasing ranks of

Robert Surcouf captures the British vessel, Kent, in 1800.

immigrant labour. Only Rodrigues remained primarily an agricultural colony and did not experience the vast influx of Indian labour which had transformed the demographic characteristics of its neighbours. Administered from Mauritius, Rodrigues was only rarely visited by British governors.

Indentured labourers were contracted to work at a fixed wage for a number of years. Breaches of contract or an inability or unwillingness to work were punishable by imprisonment, and the physical chastisement and limited mobility of Indian workers made their treatment akin to that of slaves. In 1872 and 1877 Commissions of Enquiry were sent to

Mauritius and Réunion to compile reports on the conditions of these workers, and they found much evidence of malpractice.

DISEASE AND DISASTER

When sugar prices began to fall in the last quarter of the 19th century, the distress of the enormously enlarged populations of the islands increased their vulnerability to outbreaks of such deadly diseases as smallpox, cholera and malaria. In 1892, a fierce cyclone hit Mauritius, killing 1,260 people, and making 50,000 home-

A labourer working in the cane fields in 1956.

less, while Réunion experienced periodic eruptions of its active volcano. But the sequence of disasters did not end there – rats once again wreaked devastation on the Mascarenes as bubonic plague struck, and in 1902 a fly-borne parasite necessitated the slaughter of thousands of horses, mules and cattle in Mauritius. The islands were at their lowest ebb and were a far cry from the idyllic Edens encountered barely 200 years before.

With the sugar economy still in a state of depression, the flow of labour immigration had all but ended, but traders, principally Chinese and Gujarati, continued to settle in the Mascarenes, and gradually took over the retail and wholesale sectors. On the other

hand, emigration began to take place from Réunion to Madagascar and from Mauritius to South Africa as colonists sought opportunities elsewhere.

Politically, progress was swift in Réunion, which moved from a system of absolute government to one of universal suffrage, and was given the right to be represented in the French Parliament from 1870. Mauritius, by contrast, did not have an elected legislative council and a constitution until 1885. In both islands, however, a few wealthy planter families continued to wield disproportionate influence.

POST-WAR MASCARENES

World War I brought an increase in sugar prices and a degree of prosperity was restored to the Mascarenes, but by the 1930s the disaffection among labourers had transformed into widely orchestrated strikes on both Mauritius and Réunion.

> *Mark Twain, who visited Mauritius in 1896, noted a local saying about new settlers: 'The first year they gather shells; the second year they gather shells and drink; the third year they do not gather shells.'*

World War II affected the islands much more directly. The British hurriedly set up naval and air bases on Mauritius, while the Vichy regime, installed on Réunion, isolated the island and brought it to the verge of famine. Following the war, both islands were supplied with a regular air service, becoming increasingly accessible to visitors.

Réunion was given the status of a *département* or district of France in 1946 (along with Martinique, Guadeloupe and French Guyana). The flow of capital from France produced a socio-economic power shift from the planter class towards the growing public and commercial sectors of the economy.

Departmentalisation entailed a process of assimilation, which Réunion, little touched by the 'negritude' movement of the French Caribbean to assert 'black power', seemed initially disinclined to resist. However, since 1959 when the Communist Party was set up, there has always been a movement on the island fighting for the recognition of a distinctively Réunionese identity. This was partly achieved in 1981 when the acknowledgement of a 'right to difference' produced a kind of cultural revolution to accompany the political departmentalisation revolution.

The 1980s was a period of political radicalism in Mauritius also, with the rise of the left-wing Mouvement Militant Mauricien, the MMM, which gained a huge following under

has become of increasing importance to them in Indian Ocean geopolitics.

The growing recognition that independence would lead to rule by the Indian majority led to fears of Hinduisation policies, and the 1968 celebrations were marred by ethnic violence and the emigration of disaffected minorities. Between 1968 and 1982 the ruling Labour Party did indeed become increasingly identified with its Hindu power base, but it was the combination of corruption scandals, overpopulation and high unemployment which swept the opposition

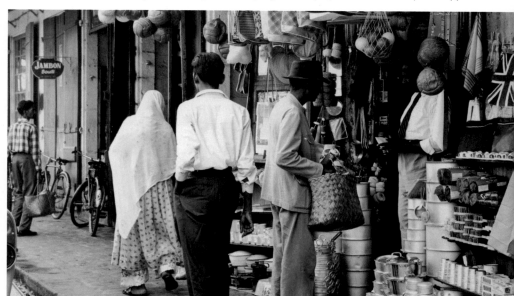

An Indian merchant's shop at Port Louis in 1955.

the banner of 'One nation, one people'. Both of these movements have ultimately been limited in their effects, and the struggle to create a sense of national identity – Réunion against the linguistic and cultural hegemony of France, and Mauritius against the competing claims of ethnic identity – goes on.

MAURITIAN INDEPENDENCE

Independence was something of a brokered affair in Mauritius, with Britain willingly divesting itself of the island in 1968 in return for the British Indian Ocean Territory created from a group of smaller, dependent islands. The Americans were promptly leased one of these – Diego Garcia – for use as a military base, which

The cutting of the Suez Canal robbed the Mascarenes of strategic significance. Ironically, the wife of De Lesseps, the man responsible for building the canal, was Mauritian and many of her compatriots worked on the construction.

MMM into office in the early 1980s. The shift to radicalism was short-lived. Since then, Mauritius has been governed by a series of coalitions of four principal parties – Labour, the MMM, the PMSD and the PSM – all of which have a pro-capitalist stance. The 2014 elections brought back former prime minister Aneerood Jugnauth, indicating that Mauritians were not quite ready for a change. And, in 2017, he stepped down so son Pravind could take his place, continuing the dynasty. Mauritius celebrated 50 years since independence in 2018, with the cry of 'lame dan lame' (hand-in-hand), continuing to forge its destiny as a multicultural island.

ECONOMIC WOES

In 1992, Mauritius became a Republic, and the Queen was replaced as head of state by a locally nominated president.

Anerood Jugnauth.

Rodrigues, formerly a dependency of Mauritius, is politically integrated with its sister island. In 2002 the island was granted regional autonomy.

Economically the islands remain fragile, although Mauritius has gone furthest down the road towards diversification with manufacturing and textile production. Until 2003 Mauritius earned more money exporting manufactured goods than from sugar exports. But changes to international sugar pricing agreements hit the sugar industry hard, and textile factory closures caused by cheap competition from India and China have increased unemployment.

Sugar barons are now turning their lands over to tourism and real estate development.

Tourism brings more than a million visitors annually, while it is hoped that financial services and communications technology – the latest additions to the economy – will provide new jobs to replace those lost in other sectors.

Some Rodriguans have sought a share in the development of their country's infrastructure by migrating to work on Mauritius, as their own island lags behind in resource-allocation – its economy remains largely agricultural and youth unemployment is high. The economic prosperity which has kept ethnic frustrations at bay in this two-island Republic has been unfairly redistributed, with the Afro-Creole populations on both islands feeling increasingly aggrieved. In 1999 widespread rioting on Mauritius constituted a clear signal that socio-economic disparities were a source of tension. It remains to be seen whether the Mauritian political elite will respond effectively. As yet, little has changed.

Réunion inhabits a position midway between the developed and developing nations. Its health and education infrastructure are akin to those of 'first world' states, while its economy lags far behind. Unlike Mauritius, Réunion has not been able to develop a significant Export Processing Zone because wages are too high. The island has its own appeal for tourists, but lacks the plentiful beaches that have made the Seychelles and Mauritius internationally known as holiday destinations. The Chaudron riots of February 1991 underscored the problems of social inequalities and high unemployment that persist in Réunion. Ironically, these disturbances occurred at a time when the French government had at last begun to address the demands of the overseas *départements* for social and economic parity. Réunion has also been active in forging a regional identity: taking part in projects of regional cooperation with its Indian Ocean neighbours.

The Mascarenes constitute one of the few regions where Francophony continues to make advances against the worldwide dominance of the English language. The French have clearly returned to their 18th-century bastion in the Indian Ocean, ready to stand their ground in the 21st century, less in military than in political and cultural terms.

DEATH OF THE DODO

The most famous of Mauritius' unique wildlife might be the dodo. The island's national emblem, it continues to fascinate the world 400 years after its destruction.

This giant, flightless bird, which developed from the pigeon family and was killed off in the 17th century, has become a byword for stupidity and a symbol of man's destructiveness, throughout the world.

The dodo was first seen in Asia and Europe in the 17th century when Dutch sailors brought live specimens from Mauritius to the world's attention. Their name for the bird is thought to derive from Dutch words meaning 'round arse'. The Dutch described the bird as fearless of man, ungainly, so fat that it could not run, and so foolish that it did not recognise danger. In pre-Darwinian days, the dodo was seen as an example of a mistake made by God, and later as an evolutionary failure. In Grant's *History of Mauritius* published in England in 1801 it is described as a 'feathered tortoise' which was an easy target for hunters.

For many years, contemporary paintings and written descriptions of the birds were practically all that were known of them – only a disputed claw and other remnants having survived from the birds brought to Europe: Naturalists began to argue that the dodo was a figment of sailors' rum-fuelled imagination. In the mid-19th century, however, dodo bones were dug up at Mare aux Songes and models of the bird were constructed and placed in museums throughout the world. Lewis Carroll saw one such model at the University Museum in Oxford, which evidently sparked his imagination – the flightless bird was immortalised in *Alice in Wonderland*.

With the reality of the dodo's existence, and its fame now firmly established, naturalists turned their attention to the bird itself. Travellers' accounts and cultural artefacts were re-examined along with the skeletal evidence unearthed in the 20th century. Bones excavated in Rodrigues were found to belong to a similar bird with longer legs, named the solitaire. These findings vindicated the account of French Huguenot, François Leguat, two centuries before.

The overweight dodo was rehabilitated when it was discovered that the bird ate seasonally and was both fast and trim at other times of the year. The new slimline model of the dodo is now on display in several museums. Naturalists also absolved the Dutch from the ignominy of killing the last dodo. While men were the catalyst of its destruction, it was the pigs, rats and monkeys they introduced to Mauritius that ate the eggs and chicks.

Some facts about the dodo remain to be elucidated. Travellers' accounts speak of a grey dodo in Mauritius and a white dodo in Réunion. Others assert that the dodo in Réunion was more like a solitaire. It is clear that a similar large bird to the dodo and solitaire was found on Réunion but no bone discoveries have been

An artist's impression of the dodo, which was extinct by 1661.

made to confirm the various theories. Scientists in the UK are now attempting to use new genetic techniques to re-create the dodo, so we may one day see the bird back in what remains of its natural habitat. Until then, the dodo remains the world's most famous example of extinction, food for thought when we visit today's examples of rare species in Mauritius.

Île aux Aigrettes, off the southeast coast of Mauritius, is thought to be the site of the dodo's extinction. Since 1987, the MWF (Mauritius Wildlife Foundation) has been working on restoring the island's original ecosystem. Obviously it's too late for the dodo, but the pink pigeon has been saved from the same fate and can be seen here. Most hotels organise day trips to the island and some the cost goes towards wildlife conservation.

Graviers beach on Rodrigues.

Livestock for sale at Port Louis's Central Market.

MAURITIUS

Mauritius, as its people will tell you, is a tropical paradise, but there's more to the island than beaches and hotels.

Sega dancer.

Bounded by a coastline littered with glittering beaches, protected by a virtually unbroken coral reef, Mauritius fulfils fantasies of a tropical island paradise. Furthermore, its excellent hotels offer everything most visitors could possibly want, from plentiful water sports to gourmet restaurants, top-notch golf courses to world-class spas. The quality of the service you will receive is not due simply to good training, but also to the genuine good nature of the people of Mauritius. And, with ice-cold drinks served to your sun lounger, it can be hard to drag yourself away to explore inland.

Mauritius has its fair share of traditional tourist attractions, notably Pamplemousses Botanical Gardens, some wonderful old plantation houses, and museums – not forgetting the eco-adventure tours, animal parks and colourful local markets. It is an island ripe for exploring: take a scenic drive among coastal fishing communities or discover the verdant plateau at the heart of the island, once the floor of a gigantic volcano which blew its top and left behind the jagged peaks and rock formations that now characterise Mauritius' scenery. Rainfall on the plateau feeds many rivers and streams, providing abundant irrigation for the sugar cane fields that cover most of the island's arable land, as well as waterfalls to visit.

Mauritius is a multicultural society, with a diversity of races and cultures living side by side. Brightly coloured Hindu temples and shrines glisten in the sun, and some Mauritians of Indian descent wear the traditional clothes of their forbears, while Creole fishermen still set sail in traditional wooden pirogues. Hardly a week goes by without some celebration or religious ritual taking place, from Tamil fire-walking and Hindu body-piercing ceremonies to Catholic pilgrimages and Chinese dragon dances.

Windsurfer at the Paradis Beachcomber Golf Resort & Spa.

But, in reality, although you'll be pleasantly surprised by the attractions of this island and its people, you will always be drawn back to the sea. Whether you end up lazing by a lagoon or diving over the coral reef, it is probably the delectable coast that will remain imprinted on your mind long after returning home.

THE MAURITIANS

The complexity of ethnic groups in Mauritius is bewildering, but Mauritians are happy to explain the intricacies of their nation.

It is said that Mauritians only consider themselves such when abroad – at home they are first and foremost members of a community. Descended from immigrants from Europe, Asia and Africa, the ethnic mix of the island population is both fascinating and incredibly complex. Racism does not exist in Mauritius – or so its political leaders claim – but colour, creed and language continue to divide its people.

ORIGINS, RELIGIONS AND CULTURES

The French colonial period, which lasted just under a century, until 1810, has left an enduring legacy in Mauritius. The Franco-Mauritians are a distinctive community who trace their ancestry to the early white settlers and, while numerically very small, remain important in economic terms. Slaves and free labourers from Africa and Asia who also arrived in the 18th century are now mostly subsumed into the Creole population. Within this group, characterised not by ethnic homogeneity but by a shared religion – Catholicism – an old hierarchy that favoured those of mixed origin and lighter skin still persists.

In the 19th century, during British rule, large-scale Indian immigration transformed the island's demography. Two-thirds of the population is now of Indian origin. These Indo-Mauritians are not a homogeneous group, but are divided on regional, caste and religious lines. About 15 percent of the population are Muslims, mostly from Bihar – known, confusingly, as Calcuttyas, to distinguish them from the smaller, endogamous groups of mainly Gujarati Muslims. The Hindus, who constitute around 50 percent, also differentiate themselves along regional lines with a larger Bihari Hindu component and smaller Tamil, Telegu and Marathi minorities. The Bihari Hindus play a key

Clothing stall proprietress, Port Louis's Central Market.

⊘ FORMS OF ADDRESS

Human interaction in Mauritius is a compelling mix of the formal and the endearing. Old habits of deference linger in the custom of politely addressing even the children of influential people as *Mamzelle* and *Misié (Monsieur)*. A middle aged person might be hailed as *tonton/tantine* (uncle/auntie). Once on friendly terms, you might be jokingly referred to as a *cousin* or *cousine*. Indo-Mauritians have specific terms for relatives on the paternal or maternal side, some in common use. For example, the first prime minister of Mauritius, Sir Seewoosagur Ramgoolam, is affectionately termed *chacha*, or uncle.

role in politics – every prime minister since Independence, apart from Paul Bérenger, has been a member of this community.

Other small minorities include the 3,000 or so Chinese, who mostly came during the mid-19th century to engage in commerce, and still run many of the shops, while now also important in the professions and other sectors of the economy. The Chinese have embraced Catholicism, but many continue to practise Buddhist traditions in the home. Even today, most Mauritians marry within their community, and although Indo-Mauritians can only converse in Bhojpuri, a regional dialect based on Hindi, while the older generation of Chinese are more proficient in Cantonese or Hakka than their adoptive tongues. The so-called 'ancestral languages' of Mauritians of Asian origin are actively promoted by members of these communities, and state controlled television and radio are obliged to broadcast in all the community languages. The island's cinemas show either Hollywood films dubbed in French, or Bollywood productions in Hindi.

Visitors to Mauritius will find that most island-

Hindu ladies preparing to make temple offerings.

mixed weddings are becoming more common, shared religious belief remains a strong element in the choice of a life partner.

Despite Mauritius being a British colony between 1810 and 1968, the English did not settle in large numbers, and those who have remained have generally intermarried, mainly into the Franco or Creole communities. The most visible legacy of British rule is on the roads, where the British system of driving and signage is used.

A MULTILINGUAL SOCIETY

The mother tongue of most Mauritians is Kreol. The language of education and government is English, and that of the media overwhelmingly French. To add to this linguistic complexity, some ers are reasonably proficient in English, though they are more at ease with French. Official forms at customs/immigration or at police stations are in English. Indo-Mauritians generally have at least a basic knowledge of Hindi, and if you attempt a few words in the island's lingua franca, Kreol, you will be sure to raise a smile (for a short list of Kreol words and phrases, see page 360).

RELIGIOUS LIFE

Religion is a way of life in Mauritius, and mosques, churches and temples have full and thriving congregations. The islanders put as much effort into the preparations for Hindu, Muslim or Catholic festivals as other societies do for their annual carnivals. The biggest crowd-puller in Mauritius is

still a pilgrimage and all the major religions organise such events. The island's public holidays take
account of the different communities, so at least
one festival of every ethnic group is celebrated.
Non-participating Mauritians may organise a family picnic at the beach on such occasions.

Weddings are another common weekend activity
on the island. Hindu nuptials take place over several
days, and innumerable sittings are organised in mar-
quees for guests, who are served vegetarian curries
on a banana leaf. The bride will wear a traditional red
or cream sari, and her groom – probably for the only

immigrants brought to the island, have persisted
into modern-day Mauritius. There are all kinds of
quirky customs and taboos, ranging from cutting
your toenails only at certain times of day to leaving out food to pacify malevolent spirits. Chinese
Mauritians are partial to the number nine, as their
car number plates testify.

Local sorcerers, known as *longanistes* or *trai-
teurs*, have followers from diverse backgrounds,
and are called in to settle quarrels, exact revenge,
reverse bad luck and administer love potions.
When one's spouse or lover loses interest, a rival

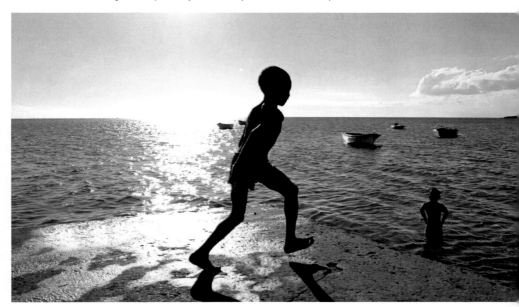

Young boys on the dock.

time in his life – will don an ornate turban, and slip-
pers. Muslim weddings are characterised in Mauritius by the serving of a biryani meal, accompanied by
a soft drink, generally Pepsi. The ceremony, or *nikah*,
is shorter than that of Hindus, and at some gatherings male and female guests are accommodated in
separate areas. Weddings of Catholics, be they Chinese, Creole or Franco-Mauritian, generally involve
a ceremony at the local church, followed by a reception. Sooner or later, at most functions, the sega will
be played and guests of all ages will join the dancing
(see page 73).

FOLKLORE AND SUPERSTITION

Diverse beliefs and practices, some originating
in the popular customs which African and Asian

may well be suspected of having used the services
of a sorcerer. Cemeteries are powerful sites for
such practitioners of magic, and they can often
be seen at midday, sacrificing a small chicken,
breaking coconuts, and lighting candles or cam-
phor sticks on the graves, surrounded by a small
knot of followers.

The phenomenon of the loup garou, or werewolf, is a good example of how a popular belief
can become a serious issue in Mauritius given
propitious circumstances. In 1994 a serious
cyclone, Hollanda, brought down most of the
island's electricity pylons, leaving many areas
without power for several weeks. During this
time, the notion that a loup garou was on the
loose took hold of the popular imagination.

Women claimed to have been raped by the creature, and there were daily sightings. The loup garou became front page news for several weeks, and hysteria mounted daily, with women and children barricading themselves indoors. The police issued a communiqué, assuring people that it was tackling the problem, and only when the issue took on a communal dimension, with Muslims asserting that the werewolf was hiding in a Catholic shrine, and inter-religious tensions increased, did the president intervene, disputing the existence of such a creature.

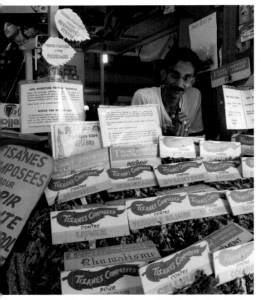

Herbal teas for sale at the Central Market in Port Louis.

⊙ KAYA

Joseph Reginald Topize was born in Roche Bois in 1960 and began his singing career in the early 1980s. He called himself 'Kaya' after one of Bob Marley's albums and his 'seggae' (a fusion of reggae and sega), dreadlocks and pot-smoking gained him a following among young islanders. In 1999, Kaya's death in police custody sparked off communal riots on a scale not seen since Independence. He has become a symbol of discrimination against Afro-Creoles. The president, sensing that things could turn ugly, pleaded with the nation to form a human chain around the island to symbolise solidarity among Mauritian ethnic groups.

COMMUNITY, CLASS AND GENERATION

It is one of the peculiarities of Mauritian society that any seemingly insignificant object can become an ethnic signifier. Here, the company you work for, the kind of car you drive, even the type of soft drink you buy, is often a decision governed by communal factors. The reason may simply be that the importer of a certain make of vehicle or product is a member of your community, influencing your decision. There is a popular saying in Mauritian Kreol, *'sak zako bizin protez so montan'* (each monkey must protect his mountain), which refers to the tendency to put members of one's own ethnic group before others.

That tensions sparked by the prevalence of favouritism and nepotism do not erupt into more serious violence can be attributed to the pragmatism of most Mauritians and to the elaborate balancing act performed by all governments. In fact, ministerial posts are assigned in cabinet so that members of competing caste and ethnic groups each have at least one representative. Alongside relatively recent strategies of ethnic lobbying, the old demon of racial discrimination still exists, however. Widespread rioting in 1999, following the suspicious deaths of a number of Afro-Creoles in police custody, highlighted the frustrations of this group, who are most affected by the persistence of racial stereotyping.

The generational differences in Mauritius are also marked, but may ultimately be an antidote to the long-standing divisions based on community and colour. School is a bastion of cultural mixing in a society with a large youth population, and increasing exposure of teenagers to Western media is impacting on old preconceptions. While most Mauritian girls still do not have the freedom of their Western counterparts, or even of their male peers, dance clubs provide a means of socialising that was not available to their mothers.

Mauritius today is a fascinating blend of the spiritual and the material. A place where the accountant working in the booming offshore sector will take a day off to participate in a religious pilgrimage, maybe buying a herbal infusion from a stallholder at the Port Louis bazaar – who claims to know the remedies for all the world's ailments – which he will sip as he browses the internet, effortlessly combining 'olde worlde' beliefs with an enthusiasm for all that modern technology has to offer.

SEGA

The sensual dance unique to the Mascarenes and Seychelles may have its roots in Africa, but it is performed by all island communities at celebrations today.

Sega goes back at least to the early 18th century, when it evolved as the soul dance of the African slaves as a form of escapism from the harsh reality of their daily lives. After a long week toiling in the cane fields, they would gather around a fire drinking alembic (home-brewed rum) and singing and dancing what became known as the sega.

Sega has been described as 'an erotic dance that leaves little to the imagination', as 'provocative in the extreme' or even as 'a simulated sexual act'. The movements are sensuous and the flirtation real, but however tempestuous it becomes, the sensuality is controlled and it is never obscene.

The original sega instruments were made from anything the slaves could find. The *ravan* (a goatskin tambour), *maravan* (a hollowed out tube filled with dried seeds) and *triang* (a triangular-shaped piece of old iron) were played, along with anything else that could produce a sound – pots and pans, empty bottles and spoons. The *ravan*, *maravan* and *triang* are still played, but modern *ségatiers* also use guitars and keyboards.

The accompanying songs, often scattered with double entendres and sexual overtones, are today an added amusement. In the past, they were also a way for the slaves to express their pent-up feelings and vent their ire on their masters, whom they mocked in the lyrics.

Although its roots are in Africa, sega in its present form is found only in Mauritius, Rodrigues, Seychelles and Réunion, and each place has its own particular version. In classical Mauritian sega, or *sega typic*, the women begin the dancing. They hold out their bright, long skirts in both hands and sway to the rhythmic music, swinging their hips to reveal a glimpse of leg, enticing the men to join them. As more and more dancers join in, shuffling their feet and swaying to the powerful beat of the drums, the dance develops into a sort of courtship drama. Both men and women try to attract a partner of their choice. The women are teasing and

provocative, changing partners, until they single out their man. The men stretch out their arms as if to catch a dancer they admire or to prevent their chosen partner from escaping. When at last a pair form, the woman leans backwards while the man extends his body over hers, at which point the singers may encourage the dancers by shouting *'enba! enba!'*, literally 'get down!' Then they swap positions and the woman dances above the man while he lies on the floor inviting her to come lower and lower. The drumbeats become more frenzied as the dancers move closer to each other – they never touch. Onlookers may be forgiven for thinking that anything could happen next. But the crescendo of the drum reaches a dramatic climax and, on a last beat, ceases.

Nowadays, classical sega in Mauritius is mostly associated with the Rivière Noire area on the west coast. Public holidays are the best time to try to catch

A traditional sega dance.

authentic performances; you may be lucky enough to see locals gathered around a fire on the beach, drinking rum and spontaneously breaking into dance.

However, if the only sega performance you get to see is at your hotel, you may well wonder what the fuss is all about. 'Sega hotel', as the locals call it, is a refined, formalised version of the dance. The men wear tight breeches or trousers rolled up to the knee with *corsair* shirts knotted at the waist. The women wear full, colourful skirts and short bodices. It makes a pretty sight but is often nothing to get excited about – though you may be asked to join in.

📷 CEREMONIES AND CELEBRATIONS

This multicultural society's festival calendar is full all year, but the colourful Hindu and Tamil celebrations draw the biggest crowds.

So many festivals are celebrated in Mauritius that visitors are bound to see one or more in any month of the year. The majority emanate from the Indian communities and they are great and colourful occasions of religious celebration.

Cavadee (Thai Poosam) is a Tamil festival which is celebrated in January or February. It is an amazing if blood-curdling sight. Tamil devotees pierce their bodies with needles; some also partake in fire-walking ceremonies. The Cavadee – a wooden arch decorated with flowers with a brass pot of milk attached to each end – is carried in a procession to the temple, where it is placed before the Tamil deity, Muruga.

Holi is a raucous two-day festival held in February or March. It begins with a bonfire on which an effigy of the evil demon Holika is burnt. Men, women and children then all join in squirting coloured water and smearing red and purple powders on each other's faces and hair.

Divali is the Hindu's happiest festival. Celebrated in October or November, at the darkest period of the autumn months, it marks the victory of Rama (an incarnation of Vishnu) over the demon Ravana and also commemorates Krishna's destruction of the demon Narakasuran. Candles and simple earthen lamps are lit around houses, gardens and even at business premises to brighten the moonless night.

Women making offerings during a Hindu ceremony at Beau Champ on Mauritius's east coast.

The festival of Holi is characterised by red, the colour of joy for Hindus. Be careful not to get caught in the line of fire during the water and powder battles – unless, of course, you want to join in the fun.

On the day of Thai Poosam several processions are held in the major towns. They usually start from a river and end at the temple.

Devotees immerse a huge statue of the Hindu elephant god Ganesh in the sea at Belle Mare, eastern Mauritius.

Pilgrimage to Grand Bassin

In 1972 sacred water from the Ganges was poured into Grand Bassin lake, which is some 550 metres (1,800ft) above sea level, after which it became known to the Hindus as Ganga Talao – the Lake of the Ganges. It is the most sacred spot on the island for Mauritian Hindus, presided over by a statue of Shri Mangal Mahadev. Candy-coloured temples are scattered around, along with altars where islanders come at weekends to lay fruit and flowers as offerings, burn incense and pray. One of the most important festivals for the Mauritian Hindu community is Maha Shivaratree (February/March) which is celebrated in honour of Lord Shiva, also known as the upholder of the sacred Ganges. Following an all-night vigil, Hindu pilgrims, dressed in white, make their way to the lake carrying bamboo structures decorated with flowers and multicoloured bells. At the lake, devotees offer prayers to Lord Shiva and other deities. Some bathe and many take the sacred water home. The whole colourful scene is reminiscent of the great rituals on the banks of India's holy Ganges.

s an act of penance, some Tamil devotees pierce their
ces and bodies with skewers and needles during
avadee; some cover the whole torso, front and back.

elebrating Divali.

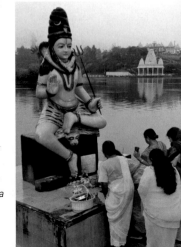

Praying at a statue of Shiva at holy lake Grand Bassin, for the Hindu festival of Maha Shivaratree.

CUISINE OF THE MASCARENES

Local cuisine is an inspiring combination of Indian, Creole, French and Chinese influences, using local produce with great flair.

The people of the Mascarene Islands, whose ancestors came from Europe, Africa, India and China, are dab hands at throwing together a bit of this and a bit of that and turning out a cuisine as richly diverse as its people. Ever since Mauritius was discovered in the 16th century, colonial powers popped in and out, each leaving their own gastronomic legacy. The Portuguese brought pigs and monkeys, the Dutch introduced deer and sugar, the French brought fruit trees and spices. Indian and Chinese incomers brought rice, while African slaves utilised the lands' natural bounty of fruit, greens and wild animals. Out of this cultural melting pot came a unique cuisine.

KEY INGREDIENTS

Rice is at the heart of both Mauritian and Réunionnais cuisine. Whether you dine in upmarket restaurants or gather round en famille you'll find mountains of it – whether it's plain boiled, fried or steeped in saffron. Noodles are a popular alternative and come in all shapes and sizes, from the vermicelli-like meefoon, ideal for a light bite, to the gut-busting fried version, mine frite. As versatile as a plain pizza base, you can ring the changes with chicken, meat or seafood (the 'mine frite special' comes with a bit of each).

Seafood here is as good as you would expect on a tropical island. It is prepared in a mouthwatering range of ways – fat shrimps and octopus, firm and flaky cordonnier (surgeon fish), cateaux (parrotfish) and the close-textured licorne come stewed, curried and fricasseed. Carangue (trevally fish), bourgeois (red snapper) and vieille rouge (grouper) are marinated in

A fresh octopus salad.

lemon juice, oil and spices and simply grilled. Capitaine (white snapper) is good in a bouillabaisse or oven-baked.

Meat appears in similar guises. Beef, chicken and even the humble sausage are thrown into casseroles and curries. Venison, usually curried or served in a thick sauce, and cochon marron (wild boar), traditionally served with sweet potato, are seasonal foods, reserved for special occasions.

EATING OUT

There are scores of restaurants, bars, cafés and fast food outlets to choose from. Restaurants usually close by 11pm and booking is rarely necessary. Generally, the atmosphere is relaxed, the service good and, compared to hotel dining, prices are very reasonable.

Nearly every restaurant menu lists Indian, Creole, Chinese and European dishes. Standard fare includes the spicy Indian *vindaye* curry and *briani*, a typical Muslim dish made with beef, venison or meaty fish; *bol renversé*, literally 'upturned bowl', a quirky Creole rice dish with slivers of pork, spicy sausage and chunks of chicken; *fooyang*, a Mauritianised Chinese omelette, filled with lobster, crab or prawn; *rougaille*, a Mediterranean type of stew made with

Barbequeuing fish on a hot grill in Port Louis.

any meat or fish cooked in a mixture of fried tomatoes, onions, garlic, herbs and ginger; and *daube*, a smoother version of *rougaille*. Among the many exotic vegetables you'll come across are heart of palm *(coeur de palmiste)* or 'millionaire's salad', *gros pois* (fat butter beans), *brèdes* (fresh greens), *lalo* (lady's fingers) and a variety of pumpkin and marrow.

Mauritians often pick up their lunch from street vendors who serve spicy snacks such as *gâteaux piments* (fried lentil and chilli balls), curry-filled *samousas* and *dal puris* (lentil-based pancakes filled with vegetables and sauces), along with a variety of soups and noodle dishes, all eaten piping hot. A word of caution for newcomers: it's a good idea to give yourself a couple

of days to acclimatise before sampling any roadside snacks, which can cause tummy upset.

HOME COOKING

If you are lucky enough to be invited to someone's home, go with an open mind and an empty stomach. You could be offered anything from smoked marlin or a spice-packed meat *massala* to Indian-style pancakes (known as *puri*, *roti*, *chapati* and *farata*, depending on how they're cooked). Few islanders serve Creole food without rice. The Japanese 'rice cooker' is as common in the Mauritian kitchen as the microwave is in Western homes. Another key utensil is the wok, into which just about anything edible is thrown and stir-fried to perfection. Less common in an age of supermarkets and ready-made spices is the curry stone, the Indian equivalent of a pestle and mortar, which is used to make *massala*, a curry paste made of ground turmeric, coriander, black pepper, nutmeg, ginger, garlic and as many chillies as the cook or guests can stand. Chillies turn up everywhere, either in a dish or as an accompaniment. Strengths vary, so be warned – they can set the unsuspecting mouth on fire.

Mauritians buy their bread fresh every day. In addition to crusty French-style loaves, most bakeries offer a choice of croissants, choux buns and sweet or savoury puff pastries, but other than the rich milk-based Indian sweetmeats, you won't find a great variety of cakes and puddings, which are reserved for special occasions. Fruit is the most common dessert and home cooks are experts at throwing together fruity creations from their own back gardens: pawpaws, mangos and lychees parade alongside sweet pineapples, tiny gingli bananas, watermelons and guavas.

DRINKS

Some very palatable white and rosé wines are made in Mauritius from imported grape concentrate and labels to look for are Château Bel Ombre, Eureka and Saint Nicholas. The purist can buy imported South African and Australian wines at reasonable prices. French wine does not always travel well and is more expensive. The best beer brands to go for are the locally brewed Phoenix and Stella, and the slightly stronger Blue Marlin. Better still are craft beers produced by The Flying Dodo, the island's own microbrewery. Mauritian men drink imported or local whisky, and neat rum. Rum cocktails and punches are popular with women who drink alcohol. The best local rum brands are Penny Blue and New Grove, although it's the island's artisanal rums, from St Aubin, Chamarel and Chèteau Labourdonnais, that are making waves on the world stage.

Of the usual range of fizzy drinks on offer, Pepsi reigns supreme. Fresh fruit juices are popular and Indian *lassi* is a refreshing yoghurt and water drink. For something more Mauritian, try alooda, a Persian import comprising of coconut milk, basil seeds, rosewater and gelatine.

Tea comes in a variety of vanilla-flavoured strengths, with the Bois Chéri brand a favourite. If you prefer vanilla-free tea, a choice of other exotic flavours and local brands, including black and green tea, is available. Most hotels and restaurants offer filter coffee, cappuccino and espresso. The locally produced Chamarel coffee is palatable, but pricey because it is produced in small quantities. The smaller restaurants and snack bars tend to serve instant coffee.

RODRIGUAN SPECIALITIES

Rodrigues is famous in Mauritius for its food. Octopus fishing is one of Rodrigues' greatest industries so it's hardly surprising that this cephalopod turns up as a tasty fried, grilled, casseroled or curried tit-bit on most of Port Mathurin's restaurant menus. The massive lagoon is Nature's larder, from which lobster and crab are simply steamed; prawns are served plain or smothered in chilli-rich tomato sauce. *Cono-cono*, similar to the whelk, makes a light lunch when mixed with salad, while freshly caught fish, cooked Chinese style in ginger and garlic, wakens tired taste buds. But for a typical Rodriguan meal, try *carri de poulet aux grains*, organic chicken curry with red beans and mashed maize served on fluffy white rice.

There is no such thing as genetically modified vegetables in Rodrigues and the meat, poultry and fish are additive-free. Onions, limes, lemons and chillis form the basis of the famous mind-blowing *chatinis* (chutney) and *achards* (sun-dried pickles). Some of the hottest chillies on earth are grown in the back gardens of

Rodrigues; crammed into bottles and preserved for posterity, the tiny green ones are so ragingly hot that Mauritians and Réunionnais make special trips to bring them home.

The little luxuries of life may be absent in Rodrigues, decent coffee being one of them, but there's no lack of sticky puddings. Many of these are creolised versions of old-fashioned stodgy puddings, such as *pain frit* (fried bread sprinkled with sugar), *gâteau patate* (sweet potato cake), *gâteau manioc* (manioc pudding) and *pudding maïs* (maize pudding).

Piles of red and green chillis for sale.

⊘ MONKEY BUSINESS

The monkeys that inhabit the forests of Mauritius are not protected, and are seen as a pest. They are still hunted for their meat, though the practice is becoming rare and the meat isn't for sale anywhere. However, some enterprising hunters are well paid for their troubles by licensed exporters and 6,000 live monkeys a year are shipped to overseas labs. Other local delicacies you won't find on the average tourist menu include curried tenrec, or hedgehog, curried *chauve-souris* or fruit bat, and *mouches jaunes*... crispy fried wasp larvae! However unappealing this may sound, people risk life and limb to shake them from their nests.

A Rodrigues flying fox, native to the island, roosting.

BATS, BIRDS AND BANYAN TREES

With the help of conservationists, the native wildlife is starting to flourish in the protected parks and reserves of Mauritius and Rodrigues.

For the naturalist, tropical oceanic islands are akin to a Pandora's box of the unique and strange. Once upon a time, Mauritius and Rodrigues were home to flightless birds, giant tortoises and dwarf lizards, but today there are other species, equally remarkable in their own way, that still live on these islands and surrounding islets isolated in the Indian Ocean.

Originally, wildlife had to get here by flying, swimming or hitching a ride and many species are now endemic. But since the nearest land mass is Madagascar, 855km (550 miles) away, the only mammals that made it over on their own were bats and sea mammals. Due to the lack of land predators, reptiles evolved from the latter and birds had no problem establishing themselves here, bringing seeds from other lands which grew up into hardwood forests. In the 17th century, humans arrived, triggering the demise of many species of flora and fauna.

CONSERVATION EFFORTS

During the past 50 years, conservationists have been hard at work, and their endeavours can now be witnessed in small protected areas, such as the Black River Gorges, Île aux Aigrettes, La Vallée de Ferney and Ebony Forest Reserve Chamarel, supporting the remaining original forests that are home to the island's wildlife.

Giant fruit bats include the Mauritian fruit bat, a truly stunning animal with a wingspan of about a metre (nearly 4ft) and a furred body that varies from dark brown to a gorgeous golden orange, now endangered due to culling. Around 50,000 of these bats range over the island at night and feed on fruits in gardens and forests. By day they sleep in gorges or on mountain sides hanging on trees in huge colonies of up to a thousand. A roost can

A Mauritius lowland forest day gecko.

☉ WILDLIFE WATCH

Forests in the Black River Gorges National Park shelter a large proportion of Mauritian endemic wildlife. Go to the Black River Visitor Centre, or the Pétrin Information Centre (near Grand Bassin) for details of walking trails and sites to explore.

The forested Île aux Aigrettes nature reserve off Mahébourg is gradually being restored to its pristine state and is home to a population of pink pigeons that are easily spotted. The more accessible La Vallée de Ferney offers a guaranteed sighting of the Mauritius kestrel at feeding time, and glimpses of the paradise flycatcher from a raised walkway at Ebony Forest Reserve Chamarel.

be seen beneath the Black River Peak Viewpoint, or spot them at La Vanille Nature Park. The Rodrigues golden fruit bat can be seen flying overhead in many parts of Rodrigues at dusk.

MAMMALS AND VERMIN

Most of the mammals on Mauritius have been introduced. The Javan deer and the black feral pigs are common in the forest and are hunted for food. Both are also farmed, as the meat is very popular. One of the most interesting of the introduced mammals is the tenrec, a nocturnal insec-

Bassin where they are fed by visitors, and sometimes at Black River Peak Viewpoint.

The black rat, feral cat and mongoose have contributed the most to the demise of the endemic wildlife. The rats climb the trees and raid birds' nests and damage the fruit on native trees. Similar to the African wildcat, the spotted tabby cat with russet orange ears has an appetite for birds.

The lesser Indian mongoose, most common in the dry lowlands, was introduced in 1900 to control the rats. The founding population of 16 males and three females quickly multiplied and

A cheeky monkey hitches a ride on the back of a deer in Gazela Park.

The Rodrigues fruit bat, known as the blonde bat due to a pale tuft of fur on its head, was saved from extinction in the 1970s by the late naturalist Gerald Durrell.

tivore similar to a hedgehog, from Madagascar, although it is rarely seen. Monkeys, long-tailed macaques from Java, abound in the forests and woods. About 60,000 in all, they are a terrible pest, damaging native plants and destroying bird nests. Nevertheless they are very interesting and intelligent animals and a good place to see them up close is next to the sacred lake of Grand

soon wiped out several populations of game birds. Their diet is eclectic, including insects, lizards, rats and birds but a favoured food is the toad, which most animals find poisonous. The discovery of a young endangered Mauritius kestrel in the stomach of a mongoose also revealed that they played a large part in the falcon's struggle for survival.

ROAMING REPTILES

Since pristine Mauritius had no land mammals, many of the reptiles evolved to fill their niche. Two species of giant tortoise have gone but have been replaced by the Aldabra giant tortoise (see page 257), which roam in the parks. Queen Victoria had them brought to Mauritius after

Charles Darwin advised that the last population on Aldabra should be protected in captive herds. Some may even be original immigrants.

Out of the island's many native and endemic geckos and skinks (a smooth, shiny lizard), the nocturnal house gecko is the most common and the Phelsuma day gecko the most spectacular. A group of bright green and red lizards, the latter lives on coconut palms and banana plants, avoiding the greedy eye of mynah birds.

The house gecko can also be seen in gardens, along with the common Agama lizard, known erroneously as a chameleon. There are some real chameleons in Mauritius, but not many.

Contrary to popular belief, snakes do live on the main island of Mauritius, although none of them are poisonous. There are two species of blind, worm-like, burrowing snakes and a larger wolf snake, which bites if handled but as it rarely reaches half a metre (2ft) in length it does little harm.

Free from rats, Round Island is home to a whole community of native reptiles, including three species of skinks and two Phelsuma geckos, one of which is a Durrell's night gecko, named after the late naturalist Gerald Durrell, who made Round Island famous in his book *Golden Bats and Pink Pigeons*. Two rare types of endemic boa live here as well, but one of these, the burrowing boa, has not been seen since 1975. This island is so important that visits can only be made with special permission. However, a population of the Round Island or Telfair's skink has now been introduced on Île aux Aigrettes.

SURVIVING BIRDS

There are 11 surviving species of land birds endemic to the islands of the southwest Indian Ocean, and seven of them are endemic to Mauritius. The best known are the Mauritius kestrel, pink pigeon and echo parakeet, for these have been the subjects of a conservation programme since the mid-1970s (see page 85). The remaining survivors are the Mascarene cave swiftlet, Mascarene swallow, Mauritius cuckoo shrike, Mauritius black bulbul, Mauritius fody, paradise flycatcher and two types of white-eyes. The swiftlet breeds in lava tunnels but has been in decline for many years on Mauritius as its nest is considered a delicacy for bird's nest soup. There are 2,000–3,000 birds today, which can be seen flying in flocks over the island. The heavily built swallow keeps to the dry southwest of Mauritius and is most active in the late afternoon when it feeds on flying insects. The only other endemic bird that you are likely to see around and about is the grey white-eye, a tiny grey bird with a white rump that travels in small flocks and is known as a *pic-pic*. You would be lucky to see any of the other birds, which are all perching songbirds (passerines), unless you specifically go to look for them in the forests of the Black River Gorges and Bassin Blanc.

Echo parakeet.

The woods along Cascade Pigeons River and at Solitude on Rodrigues are home to two of the world's rarest birds: the endemic warbler, which only has about 25 pairs left, and the striking yellow and orange fody, with about 200 pairs.

The colourful birds commonly seen around the hotels and houses have mostly been introduced to Mauritius. Many of these may seem very familiar since they are common cage birds that long ago escaped from captivity and established themselves in the wild. The most prolific are the mynah bird, the elegant, crested red-

Spinner dolphins.

whiskered bulbul, the bright red Madagascar fody and the yellow village weaver.

COASTAL CREATURES

Nesting on the small islands around Mauritius, and most easily seen on Île aux Cocos on Rodrigues, are boobies, sooty terns and noddies, as well as several species of petrel. A wonderful sight to see is the elegant, rare red-tailed tropicbird which nests in cliffs on Gunner's Quoin, Flat Island and Round Island. But its more common smaller cousin, the white-tailed tropicbird (paille-en-queue) can be watched from the Black River Peak Viewpoint.

Fourteen species of whales and dolphins have been recorded around the Mascarene coasts.

Spinner and bottle-nose dolphins can often be seen from the shore and in Tamarin Bay, beyond the reef. The chances of seeing dolphins on a boat trip are high and you may also see sperm whales off the west coast. A school of humpbacked whales returns to the waters between the mainland and Round Island during July and August most years, probably to breed.

At one time dugongs, or sea cows, lived in the lagoons around Mauritius and Rodrigues feeding on sea-grass. These sea beauties are believed to have been the creatures sea-weary sailors mistook for mermaids, but it didn't stop them from being hunted. Luckily, some still survive off Madagascar in the Mozambique Channel.

FASCINATING FLORA

The native hardwood forests of Mauritius are now largely limited to the mountain tops and deep in gorges, where they could not be exploited for their timber. Only 5 percent of the island is forested, and only small areas of that are in good condition. Nevertheless, Mauritius has 685 species of native plants of which 311 are endemic and most are endangered.

> The beautiful boucle d'oreille (Trochetia boutoniana), meaning earring, is the national flower of Mauritius. However, it can only be seen in cultivated sites or on the slopes of Le Morne Brabant.

It is a sobering thought that Mauritius has some of the rarest plants in the world. The palm *Hyophorbe amaricaulis* is down to its last plant, surviving in the Curepipe Botanical Garden. Rodrigues is hanging on to its last specimen of café marron (*Ramosmania heterophylla*) but we are too late for the *Pyramid pandanus*, which succumbed to Cyclone Hollanda in 1994.

Many of those that haven't survived have been supplanted by alien plants, such as the Chinese guava and *Lantana camara* that have run riot, suffocating seedlings. The familiar casuarina tree seen lining the beaches was brought from Malaysia as a windbreak and the mighty banyan tree with dangling roots, so typical of tropical forests, comes from India.

MAURITIUS' ENDANGERED BIRDS

Mauritius' most celebrated bird may be dead, but the island is still home to some of the rarest birds on earth, including the famous pink pigeon.

The dodo is the best known of Mauritius' extinct birds, but there are many others that have vanished, including a large black flightless parrot, the largest parrot ever known, a blue pigeon, some ducks, owls, more parrots and others. Indeed scientists still argue about the numbers of species that have disappeared. However, since the mid-1970s three birds – the Mauritius kestrel, the pink pigeon and the echo parakeet – have been rescued from the edge of extinction by a group of conservationists, led by the ornithologist Carl Jones along with Gerald Durrell's Jersey Wildlife Preservation Trust (JWPT).

The Mauritius kestrel *(Falco punctatus)* is a small falcon that lives in the forested gorges and mountains, feeds on bright green day geckos and nests in cliff holes. In 1974 there were only four wild birds, and only one pair were breeding. The rescue operation was started by breeding birds in captivity. Over several years, eggs were harvested from the last pair – every time a clutch of eggs was taken from the wild kestrels, they would lay again, increasing their productivity. Many of the young reared from harvested eggs were released back into the wild together with birds that were bred in captivity. These were fed and provided with nest boxes and protected from predators. The released kestrels began to breed well and between 1984 and 1994, 331 birds were put back into the Black River Gorges and tracts of forest that had not had kestrels for decades, including La Vallée de Ferney, with guaranteed sightings at feeding time. Today it is believed there are between 500 and 800 birds.

Almost as rare as the kestrel, the pink pigeon *(Nesoenas mayeri)* was believed by some to be extinct. But in the 1970s a population was found in an isolated pocket of woodland near Bassin Blanc. These birds were slowly declining because rats and monkeys were stealing their eggs or they were being caught by feral cats. By 1990 there were only 10 birds left in the wild but a small population had been established in captivity and since then the captive-bred birds have been released into the wild, boosting the numbers. A programme controlling the introduced predators has also been put in force. The pigeons have responded dramatically to these initiatives and the population has increased to more than 470 birds, but the pink pigeon still has a way to go before it is safe.

The work with the kestrel and pigeon may have been tough but the problems were minor compared to those encountered rescuing the echo parakeet *(Psittacula echo)*. This emerald green parrot – distinguishable from the introduced ring-necked parakeet by its shorter tail, more rounded wing and darker green – was the world's rarest parrot, until recently. In 1987 there were thought to be only eight left, with only two females. The problem

Pink pigeons.

was their low breeding rate. Working under the auspices of the MWF (see page 83), conservationists tried rearing the young and eggs taken from nests that seemed doomed to failure. Many died until it was learned how to nurture them with a good diet, filtered water and scrupulous hygiene. The wild parakeets were provided with extra food and their nest sites in hollow trees improved. The nesting birds were guarded against predators and their nesting cavities regularly cleaned out and treated with insecticide, to kill the nest flies that sucked out the babies' blood. The population increased slowly and now the future looks good, with around 550 echo parakeets flying free along the Macchabee Ridge in the Black River Gorges National Park, and in the Bambous Mountains, around La Vallée de Ferney.

Divers explore a coral reef.

INTO THE BLUE

The sea is never far away in the Mascarenes, with plenty of activities on offer on, in or beside it.

The Réunionnais surf on it, the Rodriguans fish in it and the Mauritians love to sit, eat and chat beside the sea, which is central to leisure time in the Mascarenes. At weekends huge parties of Mauritians head for the beach armed with picnic hampers, curry pots and all the necessary accoutrements for a day or two's relaxation beside the lagoon.

Tourism has brought new and exciting activities to these translucent Indian Ocean waters. Most hotels offer free windsurfing, water-skiing and boating, although scuba diving, big game fishing and parasailing come at a price. If you don't want to go as far as learning to dive, the tranquil lagoons are perfect for snorkelling. Otherwise there are plenty of kayaks, canoes and pedalos to keep you amused and rides in glass-bottom boats for views of life in the lagoon without getting your feet wet.

Beyond the reef is the game fisherman's sporting ground, where wahoo, shark, marlin, tuna and other big fish prowl the depths of their deep blue domain. They have few enemies, but even the great speed and strength of a blue marlin requires some cunning to outwit that most determined of ocean predators – the deep sea fisherman. The business of sport fishing is bigger, bolder and more macho in Mauritius and Rodrigues than in Réunion or Seychelles (see page 91).

THE BEST DIVE SITES

The waters around Mauritius offer some exciting diving experiences. There are dozens of sites to choose from where shoals of small reef fish, such as blackspotted sweetlip, humpbacked snapper and squirrel fish, play hide and seek; or you could venture further out for sightings of hammerhead shark, ray and barracuda.

Windsurfing fun.

The best dive sites, no more than an hour's boat ride away, are found off the west coast near Flic en Flac (see page 139) and include some wonderful wrecks. Well worth exploring are *Kei Sei 113* and *Tug 11*, sunk in the late 1980s to form artificial reefs and now inhabited by giant moray eels and a vast community of colourful reef fish.

On the east coast, organised diving is rather more limited due to prevailing winds and exposed seas and nearly all diving takes place in or around passes through the reef. However, the region has excellent facilities at the major hotels, many of which have PADI dive centres. When weather conditions become too unpleasant for diving in this area, clients are transported to Grand Baie in the north, where nearly a dozen sites – including the wreck *The Silver Star*, sunk in 1992 to form an artificial reef – can easily be reached by boat.

Diving conditions in the south of the island are best in the sheltered lagoon at Blue Bay where

The best time for catching marlin is from October to April, although big game fisherwoman Birgit Rudolph says 'You never know when a big one is coming.'

See shoals of fish just below the water's surface.

you can dive all year round in complete safety for sightings of weirdly shaped corals and dancing reef fish. Experienced divers can choose from several sites beyond the reef where caves and tunnels attract shoals of kingfish, crayfish and black-tip sharks.

SNORKELLING

While authorities argue that safeguards and restrictions are in place to protect the lagoons, such as a ban on dynamite fishing, collecting shells and corals from the seabed and spear fishing, many islanders complain of increased pollution and impaired visibility. However, there is still an amazing marine world to be discovered just below the surface. Snorkelling is just as popular as diving. Hours of pleasure can be had gliding silently over shallow reefs to observe the many creatures which live there. Hotel boathouses provide free snorkelling trips to the nearest best spot and equipment for their guests, though this is not always in tip-top condition. If you've been bitten by the snorkelling bug, you might want to invest in your own equipment. Good quality masks, fins and goggles are on sale everywhere. The best destination for snorkelling on the island is down south, at Blue Bay Marine Park.

A WALK ON THE WET SIDE

An alternative way of discovering the seabed is to take an undersea walk or 'helmet dive'. Undersea walking began in the Bahamas in 1948, but the idea was patented and brought to Mauritius in 1990. Following the success of

⊘ TAKE THE PLUNGE

Mauritius' warm waters and rich marine life make it the perfect place to learn to dive. Dive centres attached to hotels are affiliated to CMAS (World Underwater Federation), PADI (Professional Association of Diving Instructors), NAUI (National Association of Underwater Instructors) and BSAC (British Sub-Aqua Club) and operate under strict safety rules, providing all the equipment you need and multilingual instructors.

Most dive centres offer a brief resort course designed to test your affinity with the sport. For more in-depth training, you can enrol on an intensive five-day course leading to a PADI Open Water

One certificate, followed by a number of qualifying dives. Children are specially catered for, with themed dives introducing them to the wonders of the ocean.

Experienced divers can expect to pay up to R1,400 for a day dive and R2,000 for a night dive, although packages of six and 10 dives are better value.

Diving accidents are rare but if you get into trouble, arrangements are quickly made to convey you to the island's recompression chamber at the paramilitary Special Mobile Force (SMF) Headquarters at Vacoas (tel: 686 1040), about an hour's drive from the coast.

the first company, Solar Undersea Walk (which started as Captain Nemo's Undersea Walk) in Grand Baie, others followed, including Aquaventure in Belle Mare.

Undersea walking attracts people of every age and ability, including non-swimmers and children over seven. A boat ferries you to a floating dive platform inside the reef where a glass fronted steel helmet is placed over your head and rests loosely on your shoulders. Initially it feels heavy but once you are under water it becomes relatively weightless. Compressed air is then pumped into the helmet and filtered out through valves ensuring a fresh air supply and preventing the water from seeping up to your face. You can even chat to your fellow undersea walkers, and wearers of contact-lenses or glasses need not worry. Experienced guides stroll with you through a garden of spectacular coral inhabited by giant clam and flowering anemones, and let you hand-feed the shoals of zebra fish. A version of this, for children over eight and the less mobile, is a 30-minute ride on an enclosed motorised aqua scooter. This cross between a scuba bike and a mini submarine chugs along at around 3 knots, some 3 metres below the surface in Trou aux Biches.

SUBMARINE SAFARI

To observe the colourful corals teeming with fish, and stay dry, join an hour-long submarine safari from Grand Baie with Blue Safari Submarine (see Travel Tips, Activities). You can also hire the submarine for a private party, a night dive, or even as the venue for an underwater wedding.

Unmissable for families with young children is a trip in *Nessee*. This semi-submersible boat can be booked through hotels and tour operators and guarantees viewings of marine life gliding through a riot of ornamental vegetation, in the comfort and safety of an air-conditioned compartment attached to the hull.

SAILING

Most hotels offer free use of Hobie cats, windsurfing boards and kayaks for pottering about inside the lagoon. But to experience the real McCoy, you could spend a day sailing along the coast with an experienced crew in a luxury catamaran or yacht. Join in pulling a few ropes or just relax on deck and watch the shapes and shadows of miniature mountains unfold. Full-day tours cost around R2,500 per person including lunch and soft drinks. Mauritius is a favourite with kitesurfers, with 'One Eye' at Le Morne, in the southwest, cited as the world's third best kitesurfing spot. Le Morne Bay is one of the safest spots for beginners and improvers to learn, and kitesurfing is also found at nearby Bel Ombre, and around Île aux Benitiers, offshore from La Gaulette, which offers the cheapest places to stay. Professional operators certified by the IKO (International Kiteboarding Organisation) include ION Club (www.ion-club.net).

A Blue Safari submarine.

⊘ LETHAL WEAPON

The stone fish *(synancea verucosa)*, known locally as the laff, lurks like a barnacle of basalt in mud and rock, clamping its upturned mouth on whatever takes its fancy. Hollow dorsal spines emit a highly toxic poison causing excruciating pain and swelling, and days of incapacity to anyone unfortunate enough to step on one. In some cases the injury can even prove fatal.

Wearing plastic water shoes when wading through mud and rocks is essential to protect your feet from the laff's noxious spines (and to avoid cutting yourself on rocks and corals). If you fall victim to the laff, clean the wound and seek medical help immediately.

MOTORISED WATER SPORTS

Sea-karting is the latest craze, from Fun Adventure (www.fun-adventure.mu), based in Black River. A cross between a jet-ski and a speedboat, and with room for four people, sea karts can reach 100kmh (62mph). You can take to the helm with an hour's tuition (over 16s only) or ride as a passenger (minimum age of 8 years) to Flic en Flac, with a barbecue lunch on Île aux Benitiers and views of Le Morne.

UNSPOILT RODRIGUES

When it comes to corals, many experienced divers maintain that Rodrigues wins over Seychelles. In *Islands in a Forgotten Sea*, author T.V. Bulpin refers to the scenery outside the lagoon as 'dreamlike jungles of coral reefs', while Jacques Degremont, instructor at Jacky Diving, Tekoma Hotel, believes the island's waters are far superior to anything he has seen in Mauritius, especially since 1998, when many Indian Ocean corals died because of the rise in water temperature caused by El Niño. Because of its southerly location, Rodrigues escaped the worst of the El Niño effect. (The 2004 tsunami had little or no impact on the waters around Mauritius bar flooding in Port Mathurin, but an early warning tsunami system for the Indian Ocean is now in place.) Today pristine sites in crystal-clear waters can be enjoyed for most months of the year outside the cyclone season.

One of the best sites for both divers and snorkellers is The Aquarium, inside the lagoon near Cotton Bay Hotel, where you need only slip over the side of the boat to see beautiful coral outcrops infested with brightly coloured reef fish. Just beyond the reef, at Aquarium Passe, lie canyons inhabited by shoals of king and unicorn fish. You may even spot some turtles.

Two hotel dive centres at Cotton Bay Hotel and Les Cocotiers Hotel provide equipment and instruction with qualified PADI instructors. Both are affiliated to international dive associations. Rates here are slightly higher than in Mauritius, but groups tend to be smaller and more intimate. As the island does not have a recompression chamber, dives deeper than 30 metres (100ft) are never undertaken and precautionary decompression stops are compulsory for dives deeper than 12 metres (40ft).

The range of other water sports on offer in Rodrigues is similar to Mauritius, though there is no parasailing or water-skiing because the lagoon is too shallow. Kitesurfing is excellent here, and centred on Mourouk Ebony Hotel in the southeast. Big game fishing was only introduced to Rodrigues in 1997, and is still in its infancy, but the unpolluted waters attract yellow fin tuna, dog tooth tuna, skipjack, dolphin fish, blue, black and striped marlins and sizable sailfish. With just five big game fishing boats to choose from and an entire ocean to play in, your chances of hooking 'The Big One' are high.

Kitesurfing.

⊘ THE SHOALS OF CAPRICORN

Initiated by the Royal Geographical Society (www.rgs. org), the Shoals of Capricorn marine science research programme ran from 1998 to 2001 and studied the marine environment of the Mascarenes plateau, comprising Seychelles, Mauritius and Rodrigues. Larger than the Great Barrier Reef, longer than the Red Sea and covering around 115,000 sq km (44,000 sq miles), it is one of earth's few submerged features clearly visible from space. Findings included the expansion of the species list in the Rodrigues lagoon from 45 to 1,000 – with more than 100 species new to science – and new coral growth on Seychelles' reefs.

THE BIG ONES

World record-breaking Blue Marlin put Mauritius firmly on the game fishing map, and it's still there for the taking for those who like a challenge.

Big game fishing is big business in Mauritius all year round. It's no secret that the numbers of fish in Mauritian waters have dropped in recent years. Nevertheless, the seas are still rich in game and some of the top big fishing grounds in the world are around here.

The best season for black and blue marlin is usually from October to the end of March or April, although the World Cup Blue Marlin Championship is held in Black River each July. For 16 years, Mauritius held the world record for blue marlin at 648kg (1,430 lb). Yellow fin tuna traditionally migrate in massive shoals to Mauritian waters between March and April. They can weigh anything between 63 and 90kg (140–200 lb). Then in September the ocean sees prolific runs of wahoo (reputed to be the fastest moving fish in the sea), sailfish (averaging around 45kg/100 lb), which literally fly through the air when hooked and furiously fight for their freedom, not to mention bonito, better known to the supermarket shopper as skipjack tuna. Then, of course, there are the different species of shark, from blue, hammerhead, mako and tiger to black fin and white fin.

Most of the big hotels have their own boats and there are a number of boat clubs that operate fishing excursions for tourists. The largest fleets are based at the Corsaire Club at Trou aux Biches and JP Henry Charters at Black River, which is the centre of the deep-sea fishing scene. If you're staying at Paradis Beachcomber Golf Resort & Spa at Le Morne in the southwest, you can get to the fishing grounds from the fishing centre at the hotel jetty, just a 20-minute ride away. Luxury craft are all equipped with ship-to-shore radio, trolling equipment for live and artificial lures, life-saving rafts and jackets and everything you would expect from an experienced skipper and deck hand.

If you're up to flexing your muscles with a marlin, just sit back in a fighting chair, strap on your harness and wait for the big moment. There really is nothing quite like the thrill of the chase to get the adrenalin levels pumping when a marlin strikes. These majestic, hugely powerful fish don't give themselves up easily and if they are hooked and landed, the winners pose for pictures alongside their catch.

You may prefer just to sit back and scan the ocean for signs of marlin or shark fins while the professionals prepare themselves for a fight. If you're just going along for the ride, the sun deck of any big game fishing boat is designed for a long sultry day at sea. You need do nothing more strenuous than cover yourself with high factor suncream and equip yourself with a cool drink.

Tamarin fishermen carrying a yellow-fin tuna.

As for the catch, professional operators encourage tag and release, especially for marlin. Smoke houses in the Black River area process and package marlin, which is similar in taste and texture to smoked salmon and is perfect served with a twist of lemon and black pepper. If you want to taste your own catch then smaller fish, such as bonito, can be cooked to order by the chef at your hotel.

If your luck is out and you're keen to get a glimpse of a marlin, there's a fine specimen hanging from the rafters of the Blue Marlin Restaurant at Paradis Beachcomber Golf Resort & Spa.

Most boats take up to six passengers and a half day's hire is from R15,000.

Sailing from Île des Deux Cocos in Blue Bay, Mahébourg.

Cavendish Bridge over
La Chaux River, Mahébourg.

MAURITIUS: PLACES

A detailed guide to Mauritius and Rodrigues, with principal sites clearly cross-referenced by number to the maps.

Shangri-La's Le Touessrok Resort & Spa.

Although just a speck on Indian Ocean maps, Mauritius is a large island, so it is important to think carefully about where to base yourself. The most established tourism centre is on the northwest coast – in particular Grand Baie, the island's only conventional resort, with a wide choice of hotels and excursions, and evening entertainment. Nearby Trou aux Biches and Mont Choisy are quieter, with beautiful beaches, and further down is the exclusive enclave of Baie aux Tortues (Turtle Bay).

The sheltered west coast resorts, Flic en Flac and Wolmar, renowned for year-round fine weather and magical sunsets, offer some of the finest beaches, best diving and water sports, and are well located if you are keen to explore. Within easy reach is the forested Black River Gorges National Park, a perfect place for walking, with the chance to glimpse Mauritius' endangered birds. The rugged south coast is the site of the newest development, with leading hotels, a golf course and tourist trails. It's best to hire a car to travel the quiet roads past isolated fishing communities, lonely beaches and a windswept coast. At Mauritius' tip, Le Morne Peninsula, known as the 'five star strip', is arguably the island's most exclusive address.

For some, the east coast may feel too isolated. People come here to enjoy the established top-class hotels, the superb Belle Mare beach and the picture-postcard islands off Trou d'Eau Douce.

Smaller hotels and guesthouses at Pointe d'Esny, Blue Bay and the former capital Mahébourg, in the historic south-east, are handy for the airport, and for exploring the quiet south and east coasts.

Canyoning on the Black River Gorge.

It's possible to go to Mauritius and not even visit the capital, Port Louis, especially as the airport is on the opposite side of the island – but you'd miss out on the real Mauritius.

Likewise, few people make it across the water to Rodrigues. Yet what this island lacks in sophistication is compensated for by the warmth of its residents; and it offers a simple, no-frills insight into remote island life.

PORT LOUIS

The capital of Mauritius may lack obvious appeal, but the busy streets, the jumble of new and old buildings, and the market are worth exploring.

Port Louis

Not so long ago, when office workers chorused 'pens down at 4pm' and left the stifling heat of the capital for the cooler uplands, Port Louis simply shut up shop and went to bed. The city was as dead as a dodo and, save for late-night gambling with Sino-Mauritians and newly arrived sailors in the casino, there was nothing else to do. Since then, Port Louis has undergone something of a transformation – or, as the locals would say, a 'lifting', a hand-me-down expression acquired from the British, meaning a face-lift. This is thanks largely to the development of the Caudan Waterfront, which, with its trendy designer shops, alfresco cafés, cinemas, museums and 24-hour casino, has become the focal point of the city – and is generally considered the main attraction for tourists.

But anyone not interested in shopping is likely to find more of interest in the rest of the city, with its jumble of new and decrepit old buildings, mosques, churches and temples, Chinese and Muslim quarters, racecourse and, above all, the lively, attractive market. There is enough to keep you busy for half a day at least, and fun and informative street food walking tours are a popular way to explore. Choose from cultural tour specialists My Moris (tel: 57 23 17 55, https://mymoris.mu/en), or newcomer Taste Buddies (tel: 266 7496, www.tastebuddies.mu), which also

has a China Town food tour. Remember, though, that between November and April the city can be uncomfortably hot.

HISTORY OF PORT LOUIS

Port Louis started out in 1722, when the infant French East India Company transferred its headquarters from the old Dutch settlement at Warwyck Bay (now Mahébourg) to what was then North West Harbour. It was renamed Port Louis after Louis XV of France. From its early days, fortune seekers descended on the city, prompting an

⊙ **Main attractions**
The Waterfront
Blue Penny Museum
Natural History Museum
Central Market
Aapravasi Ghat
Chinese Quarter
The Citadel

Map on page 98

Port Louis's city skyline.

18th-century traveller to note that it contained 'a sort of scum of bankrupts, ruined adventurers, swindlers and rascals of all kinds'. Those characters have long gone, but, for all the modernity of air-conditioned shopping malls and fast food outlets, the past has not been completely erased.

Under the British, Port Louis developed into a major port for sailing ships, but by the late 1800s, with the introduction of the steamer and the opening of the Suez Canal, the city had lost much of its appeal, while outbreaks of disease, cyclones and fire caused many of its folk to flee to the healthier climate of the uplands.

A look across the Caudan Basin today, with its cargo and freighter ships, reminds you that Port Louis is still very much a working port and commercial centre. Many thousands pour into the city each day to work, congesting the roads with traffic and adding to the resident population of 150,000 – all packed into 10 sq km (4 sq miles). It is no surprise that Port Louis, like most modern capitals, is crowded, dirty and noisy. But the Moka Mountains behind, and the sea in front, provide a resplendent setting.

THE WATERFRONT

The waterfront development is officially divided into two sections – the large, privately run Caudan Waterfront and the smaller, government-run Port Louis Waterfront. A good place to start a walking tour of the city is from the **Port Louis Waterfront Ⓐ**, where you'll find several cafés and L'Astrolabe shopping mall.

The most curious sight in this area is the **Windmill Museum** (Mon–Fri 10am–noon and 1–3pm; free). A windmill was first built on this spot by the French in the 18th century, and it was France that donated the mechanism inside the modern reconstruction and which also supplies the grain used in occasional demonstrations. The collection of old photographs and the video focus on the transformation of the waterfront.

Over on the **Caudan Waterfront Ⓑ**, beyond the complex of shops and restaurants, rises the vast **Labourdonnais Hotel**. Patronised mainly by

Le Caudan Waterfront promenade is lined with bars and restaurants.

international businessmen, the hotel is not a bad pit stop in the evening – particularly if you're flush with rupees from the nearby casino.

Kwan Tee Pagoda, on the roundabout south of the Caudan Waterfront, is the oldest Chinese temple in town and is dedicated to the Chinese warrior god who fought for justice.

One of the best views of the city is from the sea, and you can take a **harbour cruise** from just outside the Labourdonnais. The pleasure boat chugs past a panoramic view of a delectable landfall of peaks and knolls. Looking inland, from right to left, the bulk of Signal Mountain dominates the city. Next, Le Pouce (The Thumb) rises from the south wing of the Moka Range in a 'thumbs up' sign. The most distinctive peak of all, whose pinnacle looks like the cloak-shrouded shoulders of a man, comes in the form of **Pieter Both**, named after the Dutch Admiral who drowned off the coast. Closer to the city to the north is a knoll known as La Citadelle, named after the ruin of a fortress at its crest.

Looking out over the Champ de Mars racecourse.

A museum well worth calling into is the **Blue Penny Museum** (tel: 210 9024; www.bluepennymuseum.com; Mon–Sat 10am–5pm). Home to a rich collection of national treasures, it exhibits fine art, old maps and sections on philately and postal history, coins, paper money, postcards and photography. Many items were formerly in the possession of private collectors.

PLACE S. BISSOONDOYAL

If you cross by the subway beside the waterfront you reach the **Place S. Bissoondoyal** (often still referred to by its previous name, **Place d'Armes**), where you'll be greeted by the most famous landmark of the city, the bronze statue of Bertrand François Mahé de Labourdonnais. He arrived in 1735 as the newly appointed French governor-general of the Mascarene Islands and went about transforming shambolic Port Louis into a thriving sea port and commercial centre.

Some local people seem to enjoy having a chat beneath the royal palms that line the square, but the constant buzz of cars around the edge does not make the Place S Bissoondoyal a peaceful place. At the top stands **Government House**, the official centre of government. It started life as a ramshackle wooden hut, was enlarged by Labourdonnais in 1738 and later embellished by the British. In the courtyard, secured by wrought-iron gates, is a rather severe marble statue of Queen Victoria, shaded in summer by brilliant red flamboyant trees. Beyond it stands a statue of Sir William Stevenson, British governor from 1857 to 1863. To the right, on the corner of Chaussée, the old Treasury Buildings (1883), refurbished in 2004 as the prime minister's office, provide good cover if you get caught in a downpour.

Along La Chaussée is the Mauritius Institute, home of the **Natural History Museum** Ⓔ (tel: 212 0639; www.mauritiusmuseums.mu; Mon, Tue, Thu, Fri 9am–4pm, Wed 11am–4pm, Sat 9am–noon). This museum used to be an apology for what was once a priceless collection of flora and fauna; it underwent a successful redesign in 2009, complete with a new dodo gallery, but then closed for further renovation until further notice in January 2017 so check the website for reopening times. It's the only place on the island where you can see a skeleton of Mauritius' iconic bird. The **Company Gardens** next door is busy at lunch time, when city workers take a break beneath giant banyans and bottle palms, to eat a *dal puri*. On Chaussée Street is **l'Amicale Casino** (tel: 210 9713; daily 10am–2am), built to replace the original, which rioters reduced to a heap of ruins in an arson attack in 1999 during which seven people lost their lives. Today's smoke-filled, seedy den is open to tourists but is mainly patronised by male hopefuls huddled around blackjack and roulette tables or trying their luck on the gaming machines. Further down the road, turn right for the **Mauritius Tourism Promotional Authority (MTPA) office** (tel: 203 1900; www.tourism-mauritius.mu; Mon–Fri 9am–4pm, Sat 9am–noon), on the fifth floor of Victoria House, St Louis Street.

Ⓔat

At the Café du Vieux Conseil, virtually opposite the Museum of Photography, you can enjoy a drink and a snack or lunch, shaded by trees and away from the bustle of the city streets. It is open in the daytime only.

⌚ A DAY AT THE RACES

In Mauritius, it is said that there are three seasons – summer, winter and the racing season. The Mauritius Turf Club, the second oldest in the southern hemisphere, was founded by Colonel Draper in 1812. He had friends in high places on both sides of the divide and, being a passionate punter, thought it only gentlemanly to bring the French and English together in an atmosphere of leisure.

Today, most horses come from South Africa and Australia and are trained in one of the island's eight stables. Race meetings are held every Saturday afternoon from the first week in May to the end of November. Spirits run high, with screams of *'Allez, allez!'* following the horses as they gallop round the course. Music is played between races as punters press round bookies to place their bets or collect their winnings, and food sellers do a roaring trade.

Many Mauritians are well versed in the international race scene. They follow the progress of individual horses closely and the use of starting stalls, photo-finish systems and adherence to Newmarket disciplines attracts jockeys from all over the world. There are even professional gamblers who try to make a living from picking a winner; most of them will have a 'hot tip', but remember, despite what some may tell you, there is no such thing as a 'dead cert'.

Shopping for fresh produce at the Central Market.

FROM INTENDANCE STREET TO THE RACECOURSE

A quick stroll south from Place S. Bissoondoyal along Intendance Street takes you past the city's other main historic buildings. First is the **Municipal Theatre**, which was built in 1822 and is the oldest theatre in the Indian Ocean. If it is open during the day, ask the caretaker to show you the beautiful painted dome and crystal chandeliers. During the 1930s, the citizens of Port Louis were entertained by old favourites like *Madame Butterfly* brought to them by visiting troupes from France. The theatre had virtually shut down by the 1950s but re-opened in 1994 after a massive face-lift. Seats now sell fast for modern jazz gigs, sega, operas and plays, but it's also the hotspot for weddings and prestigious functions, when big shots get invited by moneyed Mauritians.

Opposite the theatre, cobbled Rue du Vieux Conseil (Old Council Street) leads to the **Museum of Photography ⑤** (tel: 211 1705; www.museedelaphotomaurice. com; Mon–Fri 10am–3pm), where you'll find one of the island's oldest displays of cameras and prints, which includes daguerreotypes as well as photographs of colonial Mauritius. All these have been collected by photographer Tristan Bréville, who fights a constant financial battle to keep his museum open.

Heading east, you reach the austere **St Louis Cathedral**. The original French church was reduced to rubble by cyclones in the 1800s. It was rebuilt twice before the present version was consecrated in 1932. To the left is the **Episcopal Palace**, a fine 19th-century colonnaded mansion. The other important church in the city is **St James Cathedral**, nearby in Poudrière Street, which looms over gardens shaded by palm trees and tumbling bougainvillaea. It was once a gunpowder store and prison under the French, before the British turned it into a church, and also saw service as a refuge centre when Port Louisiens would abandon their wooden houses on the approach of a cyclone for the security of its 3-metre (10ft) walls.

From these two places of worship, it is only a short diversion to the **Champ de Mars Racecourse ⑥** (also known as the Hippodrome; tel: 212 2212; www.mauritiusturfclub.com; May–Nov), cradled by the Moka Mountains at the eastern edge of the city. Once the training ground for French soldiers, today it is often used for Independence Day celebrations on 12 March – and the nation's most popular sport: horse racing. An invitation to the members' enclosure on classic race days, like the Gold Cup or the Maiden Cup, should not be refused; you get a bird's-eye view of the paddock, free rein of all facilities, which include bars and comfortable terraces, and an unmissable opportunity to rub shoulders with those in the know. On non-race days, joggers replace the horses.

THE CENTRAL MARKET

If there is one place no one should miss in Port Louis, it is the covered **Central Market ⑪** (daily 6am–6pm), known as the Bazar Central in Kreol, two blocks north of Place S. Bissoondoyal. Built in 2004 to replace its old tumbledown predecessor, where traders from all continents had converged for more than 150 years, this attractive building accommodates over 300 stalls in rather more hygienic and pleasant conditions, yet manages to retain its traditional charm and atmosphere.

On the ground floor you can follow the locals picking out the best from the mounds of tropical fruit and vegetables, or picking up herbal remedies claiming to cure everything from diarrhoea to diabetes. Upstairs, Indian, Creole and Chinese traders sell T-shirts, basketware, spices and cheap clothing, and there are good views from the gallery of the bustle below. You can pick up spicy pancakes *(dal puris)*, curry-filled *samousas* and other popular Mauritian snacks for just a few rupees, perfect for a mid-morning snack or light lunch. Those with a more sensitive constitution may want to steer clear of *bombli*, the dried salt fish with a stench that defies description.

POSTAL MUSEUM AND AAPRAVASI GHAT

After the bustle of the market, you can find solace in the calm of the **Postal Museum ❶** (www.mauritiuspost.mu/postal-museum; Mon–Fri 9.30am–4.30pm, Sat 9.30am–3.30pm), which lies across the busy road from the market in the former General Post Office. This well laid-out museum contains 19th-century postal equipment such as telegraph and stamp-vending machines and a fine collection of stamps, postal stationery, original artwork and printing plates. For serious collectors there are stock books, stamp albums, mounts, magnifying glasses and tweezers, and first-day covers and commemorative sets of stamps, such as the 400th anniversary of the Dutch landing that was issued in 1999.

A short walk north alongside the busy road takes you to the gardens of the **Aapravasi Ghat** (tel: 241 0386; www.aapravasighat.org; Mon–Fri 9am–4pm, Sat 9am–noon; free), a Unesco World Heritage Site with guided heritage trails available. Once known as the Immigration

The Chinese Quarter is a bustling part of the city.

Depot or Coolie Ghat, it housed the first Indian immigrants who were brought here before being farmed out to the sugar estates. Look for the 11 bronze murals showing scenes of immigrant life, including one depicting a pair of hands breaking free from chains. A poem dedicated to the Unknown Immigrant recalls how 'He... turned stone into green fields of gold', a reference to sugar cane.

THE CHINESE QUARTER

The **Chinese Quarter** ⓙ, encompassed in several streets to the east of the market, is the most colourful part of the city with its specialist food and spice shops and herbal remedy stores. There are plenty of eating houses too, where fast cheap meals, such as the ubiquitous noodles *(mines)*, can be slurped from bowls. A variety of snacks, such as *gâteaux piments*, crispy *samousas* or the more unusual combination of fresh pineapples with hot red chilli sauce, are also sold from mobile food wagons on street corners.

The **Jummah Mosque** ⓚ in Royal Street is open to tourists only at certain times, but one of its most striking features is the beautifully carved teak doors and the ornate decorations of the outer walls. Built in around 1853 for the growing Muslim community and subsequently enlarged, it is the island's most impressive mosque. Plaine Verte, the Muslim Quarter to the north of Port Louis, is home to the annual Ghoon festival, but other than its small teahouses and tumbledown textile shops, it has little to interest the visitor.

THE CITADEL AND LINE BARRACKS

The only reason for going to **The Citadel** ⓛ (La Citadelle; Mon–Sat 8am–8pm), also known as Fort Adelaide, is the panoramic views of the city's amphitheatre of mountains, the Champ de Mars racecourse and the harbour. The basalt fort was named after Queen Adelaide, wife of William IV, and must rank as Port Louis' greatest white elephant. Apart from the occasional concert and a few small shops selling local arts and crafts, it never seems to wake

Port Louis street life.

from its apathy, even when the silence is broken by the babble of tourists.

For some Mauritian quirkiness, wander down to **Line Barracks** Ⓜ (*caserne*), home of the Mauritian Police Force, which contains fine examples of 18th-century colonial architecture. Inside, look out for learner drivers taking their tests. See the prison dubbed 'Alcatraz' and the Golden Gates at the main entrance, which caused a stir because they cost a fortune. Nearby is an incongruous blue-tiled archway marked 'Gateway of Discipline' which leads to the old drill square.

ATTRACTIONS AROUND PORT LOUIS

The Church and Shrine of Père Laval at Sainte-Croix in the foothills of Long Mountain to the northeast is only a 10-minute drive from the city centre. Père Laval, known as the black apostle, arrived as a missionary in 1841 and was soon revered for his work with the poor. When he died in 1864 his body was buried at Sainte-Croix and became the object of pilgrimage. The church was renovated in 2014 to mark the 150th anniversary of his death. Many Mauritians still believe in his special healing powers and every day hundreds of people of all faiths file past the stone sarcophagus that contains his remains, topped by an effigy framed with flowers, and pray for the sick. He was beatified by the Catholic Church in 1979 and is one step away from being canonised, so it won't be long before Mauritius has its very own patron saint. An annual pilgrimage to the church takes place during the nights of 7 and 8 September. The curate's residence nearby is a superb example of colonial architecture.

Breathtaking views of Port Louis can be enjoyed from the peaceful setting of the Marie Reine de la Paix monument on the flanks of Signal Mountain, southwest of the city. In 1989 this place of pilgrimage swelled as thousands of islanders gathered for Mass held by Pope John Paul II. In the foothills of Signal Mountain, on the southeast edge of town, is **Thien Thane**, Port Louis' best Chinese temple for its pagoda architecture and serene location.

Thien Thane temple.

Fun in the sun at Pereybère.

THE NORTH

The beach-lined north coast is the most popular on Mauritius, and has the island's only proper resort town, Grand Baie. The Pamplemousses Botanical Gardens lure people away from the sea.

Port Louis

Most visitors to Mauritius head for the hotels north of **Port Louis ❶**. Tourism is well established between the resorts of Balaclava and Grand Baie, which act as bookends to one of the loveliest stretches of beach on the island, with an unbroken chain of powder-white beaches and gentle, crystal lagoons. Hotels, guesthouses and private villas and bungalows are plentiful in this area, and more hotels are also sprouting up in the less accessible areas between Balaclava and Port Louis. The coast's best-kept beaches are attached to hotels with beach loungers reserved for residents' use, but if you want to mix with the locals the public beaches at Balaclava, Mont Choisy and Pereybère are lively, particularly at weekends.

Away from the coast, the sugar-swathed plains of the north are not as scenic as the mountainous interior of the south, but the flat terrain, broken up by the gentlest of hills, is ideal for cycling, and there's something exciting about getting lost in the maze of sugar cane fields and asking for directions – only to get the reply back in Kreol, French, English or a combination of all three.

BAY OF TOMBS

The fastest route to the northern beaches is to take the motorway – either straight to Grand Baie or Trou aux Biches, or to the turn-off for the

resorts further south – but if you are in no hurry, you could opt for the longer coastal route. The Terre Rouge–Verdun Link Road, which bypasses the capital, opened in 2013 and has cut travel times from the south to the north.

Just beyond Port Louis' suburbs is **Roche Bois ❷**, where the mass of headstones in the Chinese Cemetery are bright red, the colour of good luck, and bear witness to the island's Sino-Mauritian population. But Roche Bois is also a poor Creole suburb and a byword for poverty on the island. In

Main attractions
Maheswarnath Temple, Triolet
Grand Baie and Pereybère
Cap Malheureux
Northern Islands
Goodlands
Pamplemousses Botanical Gardens

Map on page 108

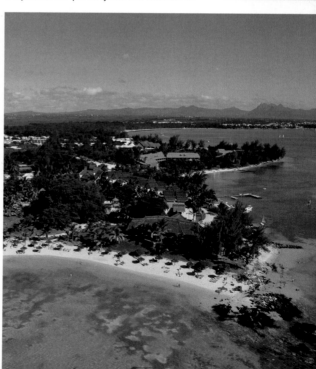

Canonnier Beachcomber Golf Resort & Spa.

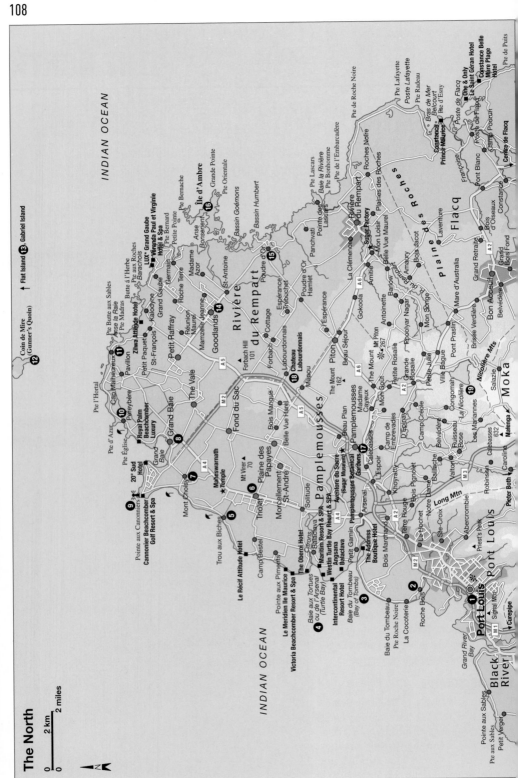

1999, one of its sons, a Creole singer called Kaya, was arrested for smoking cannabis at a pro-pot public demonstration and next day died in a police cell (see page 72).

In 1615, four Dutch East India Company ships were swept on to the reef during a cyclone and sunk at nearby **Baie du Tombeau ❸ (Bay of Tombs)**. Everyone died, including the Dutch Admiral Pieter Both who was on his way to Holland after a spell as the governor of the company. The sleepy village of Baie du Tombeau lies on the bay's southern flank, apparently turning its back on the world, and blocking its lovely, deserted beach from view. Access to the beach is not easy – to find it look out for the ruin of an old French fort partially hidden in shrubbery nearby. The Address Boutique Hotel, with Mediterranean-style architecture overlooking the sea in Port Chambly, is just 20 minutes by shuttle from Port Louis.

You link up again with the Grand Baie road at the crossroads near **Arsenal** (named after a French ammunition store nearby), where you can also turn inland towards the Pamplemousses Botanical Gardens (see page 116).

TURTLE BAY AND POINTE AUX PIMENTS

Beyond residential **Balaclava**, reached through sugar fields on the B41, is an area that is fast being developed – though passers-by will see nothing but the entrances to private drives leading to hotels such as The Westin Turtle Bay Resort & Spa, The Oberoi Mauritius, Ravenala Attitude and Maritim Resort & Spa. These neighbouring hotels flank the banks of the River Citrons, which enters the estuary forming the **Baie aux Tortues ❹ (Turtle Bay)**, also known as Baie de l'Arsenal, where great armies of turtles once swam. The Maritim Resort & Spa occupies grounds that formed part of a French arsenal at nearby **Moulin à Poudre**,

where ammunition for ships was supplied for expeditions to India.

A cluster of high-class hotels surrounds the bay and they are doing their best to restore the health of the coral with replanting schemes. The bay once contained 90 percent live coral, but sadly the current figure is just 20 to 25 percent.

The road finally hits the coast at **Pointe aux Piments**, where filao trees rustle in gentle breezes and life chugs on slow and unhurried on the beaches. If you can leave the pristine paradise fronting Victoria Beachcomber Resort & Spa, Le Meridien Île Maurice and Recif Attitude hotels, then take a stroll outside and surrender to the magic of a Mauritius sunset and watch wellie-booted fishermen wading in a shallow lagoon. Alternatively, visit the Mauritius Aquarium (tel: 261 4561; Mon–Sat 9.30am–5pm, Sun 10am–4pm; feeding times 11am and 3pm) on the Coastal Road.

TROU AUX BICHES

The small resort of **Trou aux Biches ❺**, with its gently shelving sands and deep blue lagoon, is a mecca for beach-lovers.

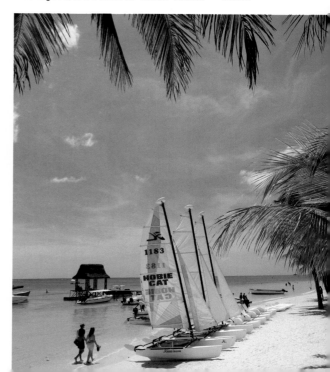

Sailboats lined up on Trou aux Biches's beach.

It is much more sedate than its northern neighbour, Grand Baie, particularly mid-week when you can glimpse snapshots of how life used to be, and still is in parts of this former fishing village. At the start of the 3km (2-mile) beach, beside the fish landing station, fishermen huddle beneath casuarina trees talking in Kreol. Here you'll find a couple of restaurants and Chez Popo's supermarket, where you can hire bikes and, if self-catering, buy a wide range of essentials.

The hotels all have facilities for water-skiing, windsurfing, diving and snorkelling, and will also arrange sailing and glass-bottom boat trips. At weekends the tranquillity of the lagoon is broken by the roar of an increasing number of speedboats, but the beach remains a retreat for relaxation and beach games. Old boys on bicycles sell freshly caught fish and touts sell seashells, pareos and trinkets, keeping you amused with gentle banter. There's no shortage of fruit sellers wandering along the beach and to watch them peel pineapples with their machetes is quite a spectacle.

The private beach at the Royal Palm Beachcomber Luxury.

TRIOLET AND MONT CHOISY

Triolet ❻ can claim to be the largest and longest (and perhaps plainest) village on the island. It has played a lively part in Mauritian political life since Independence, and is the constituency of Mauritius' first prime minister. The village also has the highest population of Indo-Mauritians, and is home to the biggest Hindu temple in Mauritius (just inland from Trou aux Biches police station). Built in 1857, the Maheswarnath Temple complex (daily 6am–5pm) is a kaleidoscope of colour. It stands beside an enormous banyan where a placard welcomes all pilgrims.

At weekends and holidays it seems that everyone from the area toddles off to **Mont Choisy ❼** beach, where turquoise seas meet a long strip of sugar-soft sand backed by a forest of casuarina trees. Matronly Indo-Mauritian mums make for the shade and unpack pots of rice and curry from great baskets *(tentes)* around which families gather to eat. Children play on a former landing strip, now a grassy football pitch, where a monument celebrates the first ever flight made by French pilots from Mauritius to Réunion in 1933. Midweek, Mont Choisy is a perfect spot for a quiet dip in the warm lagoon or a trip in a glass-bottom boat and has recently become a favourite for water-skiing.

GRAND BAIE

Grand Baie ❽ is the island's hub of tourism, where not only hotels and restaurants but also bars, clubs and designer shops are strung around a huge horseshoe-shaped bay. Dubbed the 'Creole Côte d'Azur' and, by Mauritian standards, brash, busy and boisterous, Grand Baie's development from a tiny fishing village to a large holiday resort seems to have dealt a fatal blow to the village atmosphere. Many shops have become supermarkets, property development is haphazard and islanders often complain of the lack of pavements, congested coast road and a rise in petty crime. Yet it remains popular with local residents, many of whom have second homes here, as well as with tourists who can find plenty of places to eat and drink. From here

you can book island tours, including to Rodrigues, find self-catering accommodation and hire a car through tour operators, such as Mautourco, and many other smaller travel agents.

Much of the activity centres around **Sunset Boulevard** (www.sunsetboulevard.mu), a modern waterside shopping mall (closed Sun) opposite a cluster of supermarkets, restaurants and fast food stalls. You'll find a centre for big game fishing on the waterfront and facilities to book undersea walks, undersea safaris and parasailing trips over the lagoon. The bay, which at times is crowded with small pleasure craft and catamarans, has no decent bathing beach; for peace and relaxation take a short stroll to the soft wide sands of La Cuvette public beach to the north of the bay, which has modern facilities including showers, toilets and changing cubicles. Just beyond the black basalt rocks to the right of the beach is the luxurious **Royal Palm Beachcomber Luxury** but be aware that casual beach strollers are not welcome unless they have a reservation for lunch or dinner. A good place to shop is

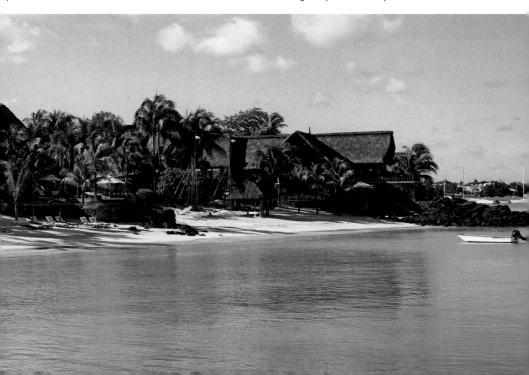

at Super U complex, a short stroll inland from Sunset Boulevard. Here, a large supermarket provides everyday items, and you'll find good-value restaurants, such as Happy Rajah. Opposite, is state-of-the-art shopping mall, La Croisette, with leading western brands.

Grand Baie has more nightclubs (boîtes de nuit) than any other resort on the island (which draws quite a few local prostitutes to the area). For a spot of balmy nightlife try Banana Beach Club for drinks and live music or let your hair down at the Buddha Bar & Club, which attracts a trendy, young crowd.

POINTE AUX CANONNIERS

Enormous flamboyant trees, emblazoned with deep red flowers in summer, flank the road leading to **Pointe aux Canonniers** ⑨, a beach-belted headland at the northern end of Grand Baie which was once used as a garrison by the French and later turned into a quarantine station by the British. Eighteenth-century cannons and a ruined 19th-century lighthouse watch over the reefs (which have caused the

Temple detail in Pereybère.

doom of dozens of ships) from the gardens of the **Canonnier Beachcomber Golf Resort & Spa**.

Hotels and shady villas house tourists and locals attracted by the tranquillity of the area. At the opposite tip of the headland from Canonnier is the **20° Sud Hotel**, a colonial-style boutique hotel, complete with planters' chairs and faded pictures, overlooking a swimming pool and a private sandy cove.

PEREYBÈRE

Just 2km (1 mile) to the north, **Pereybère** ⑩ seems to be merging with Grand Baie. But the pace of life is much slower, providing a foil to the sometimes brash atmosphere of its sister resort as well as cheaper day-to-day living. Traditionally a holiday retreat for the Chinese community, Pereybère is changing rapidly to accommodate increasing numbers of foreign self-caterers, as well as holidaymakers from Grand Baie who come for a change of scene, and to stretch out on the lovely casuarina-fringed beach or snorkel in the lagoon.

⊙ COLONIAL MANSIONS

For a touch of bygone French glamour, wander around the island's colonial plantation homes and gardens, stopping for an elegant lunch on the veranda. Most of the colonial mansions on Mauritius were created during the French colonial period and date back to the 18th and 19th century. With a style adapted to the tropics, they were constructed from wood, with lime-washed walls and rain-resistant *armagasse* roof tiles, over a vaulted roof. A wide, long *verangue* (veranda) helped keep the house cool and dry, doors replaced windows for ventilation and lacy wooden or metal fringes, or *lambrequins*, decorated the roof. The kitchen and bathrooms were in an outside building.

Some of these elegant plantation homes are living museums, open to the public, with decent restaurants for a lunchtime stop. Three lie in the island's north: Eureka at Moka, perhaps the best example of colonial architecture on the island, with turreted windows, a wrap-around veranda and 109 doors; Château Labourdonnais at Mapou, whose famous orchard once supplied the island's fruit and now produces artisanal gourmet rum; and Demeure de Saint Antoine near Goodlands, with paintings from celebrated Mauritian artist Malcolm de Chazal. Other colonial houses worth visiting are Domaine les Aubineaux, in Curepipe, on the central plateau, with pretty turquoise shutters, and Saint Aubin, near Rivière des Anguilles, as part of The Tea Route.

A smaller version of Mont Choisy (see page 110), Pereybère is swamped at weekends by islanders, who come to picnic, chat under the trees, swim, go for glass-bottom boat trips, and maybe even round off the day with an impromptu sega party. Food stalls sell hot snacks, drinks and fresh fruit (conveniently cut up into small pieces and sold in bags) and, if you're lucky, there'll be an ice cream van, too. Away from the beach, small shops provide basics and simple restaurants serve slap-up meals at knockdown prices. And if you're after a pareo, the tree-lined catwalks along the main road offer plenty of choice; prices are lower than those offered by both shops and beach hawkers.

CAP MALHEUREUX AND GRAND GAUBE

Taking on the appearance of a country lane lined with casuarinas shading shallow bays and rocky coves, the coast road swings east to **Cap Malheureux** ⓫, 6km (4 miles) beyond Pereybère. This, the island's most northerly point, probably got its name – Cape of Misfortune – from the number of ships that foundered here. It offers a stunning view of the Northern Islands. Nothing much goes on in this tranquil beauty spot, though if you get there around 4pm you will see the village wake up momentarily when fishermen bring in their catch to sell to islanders congregating beside the striking red-roofed church of **Notre Dame Auxillatrice** (daily 6.30am– 5.30pm; free). There is a small beach where local kids play, just one restaurant, a general store and petrol station.

A 5km (3-mile) drive east through sugar cane emerges at the sparkling white beaches of the fishing village **Grand Gaube**, where the luxurious LUX* Grand Gaube, recently redesigned by Kelly Hoppen, overlooks the curvaceous bay. Next door is the cute, revamped, Veranda Paul & Virginie. Or you could enjoy tasty snacks and drinks at the Caribbean-style restaurant and bar Di Sab on the main road, or become 'an islander' at Zilwa Attitude in Kalodyne, the newest, funkiest hotel on the block, whose bar overlooks the Northern Islands.

Notre Dame Auxillatrice.

Tip

Those interested in learning more about sugar cultivation and its history should visit L'Aventure du Sucre Museum on the Beau Plan Sugar Estate near Pamplemousses (tel: 243 7900; www.aventuredusucre. com; daily 9am–5pm).

At Historic Marine.

THE NORTHERN ISLANDS

Gunners Quoin (Coin de Mire), Flat Island (Île Plate) and Gabriel Island (Îlot Gabriel) all make good day trips. Depending on weather conditions, you can have a fun day out sailing around the islands, being pampered by experienced crew. Full-day tours from Croisières Australes with lunch in the luxury catamaran cruiser *Le Pacha*, accommodating 20 to 30 passengers, leave from Sunset Boulevard in Grand Baie. It drops anchor in sheltered bays with plenty of opportunity for snorkelling and swimming or sunbathing on deck. Other operators in Grand Baie lay on similar tours.

Coin de Mire ⑫, the closest island to the shore, is composed of layers of crumbling volcanic sandstone, making landing difficult, but on calm days, offers some of the islands' best snorkelling, in its shadow. Getting on to **Flat Island** ⑬ is worth the effort just to pad along the lovely beaches ringed by coral reef. The same coral reef encircles neighbouring **Gabriel Island**. These last two islands once served as quarantine stations for immigrants during the cholera epidemic of 1856, which nearly wiped out the population of Port Louis. Picnic parties to Flat Island are popular and you can spend the whole day exploring the little pathways that meander round its lighthouse and cemetery.

You need permission to land on Round and Serpent islands, 24km (15 miles) north of Mauritius, which are both designated nature reserves; but they are difficult to land on anyway because of their sheer cliffs. **Round Island (Île Ronde)** is home to many endangered species, including the rare Telfair skink, two species of snake and the *paille-en-queue* – the tropicbird that graces the tail fins of Air Mauritius planes. Serpent Island (Île aux Serpents) is a bird sanctuary, but there are no snakes. And in case you were wondering, **Pigeon House Rock (Le Pigeonnier)**, north of Flat Island, doesn't have any pigeons either.

GOODLANDS AND AMBER ISLAND

From Grand Gaube the road finally draws you away from the coast and swings south to **Goodlands** ⑭. The streets in this densely populated town are usually heaving with people, who frequent the high street shops and the daily **market**. Goodlands is also home to the largest model sailing ship factory in Mauritius, **Historic Marine** (tel: 283 9304, https://historic-marine.com; Mon–Fri 9am–5pm, Sat–Sun 9am–noon; guided tours). There is a large showroom downstairs (with many wooden objects other than ships), while upstairs you can watch the craftsmen patiently working on these mini master-pieces (weekdays only). Colonial mansion **La Demeure de Saint Antoine** (tel: 282 1823; https://lademeuresaintantoine.com; Tue–Sat lunch, afternoon tea and dinner by reservation only; guided tours), tucked behind a high wall on the outskirts of town, was built by a relative of painter and poet Malcolm de Chazal, and has a room scattered with his paintings.

The road southeast of Goodlands hits the coast at **Poudre d'Or** ⓰ (Golden Powder), an appealing village where you can linger on the headland opposite the reef where, in 1744, the *Saint Géran* foundered in a storm, a tragic incident that inspired French novelist Bernardin de Saint Pierre to pen his famous love story *Paul and Virginie*. Some objects rescued from the wreck are on display in the National History Museum in Mahébourg. Take a guided bike tour with cultural tour specialists My Moris (tel: 57 23 17 55, https://mymoris.mu/en) for an insight into Mauritian village life. (see page 124). **Île d'Ambre** ⓰ (Amber Island), an uninhabited island, is just 30 minutes' boat ride from here, and if you ask around, you should find a local fisherman to take you from the jetty at Poudre d'Or; arrange for him to pick you up later so that you can enjoy the excellent swimming and snorkelling. Or take a guided kayak excursion from Goodlands with Yemaya Adventures to learn about the island's history and ecology. A picnic lunch is included.

The headland marking the boundary between the north and east coasts is dominated by the wild and windy beaches of Roches Noires and Poste Lafayette, studded with black volcanic rocks. They are often deserted but for men fishing in the shallows or landing their catch from boats. Be careful if you want to swim as the seas can be rough.

Poudre d'Or.

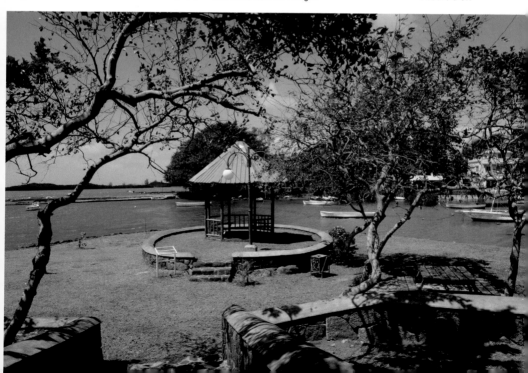

PAMPLEMOUSSES BOTANICAL GARDENS

From Poudre d'Or the road heads inland to the **Botanical Gardens** 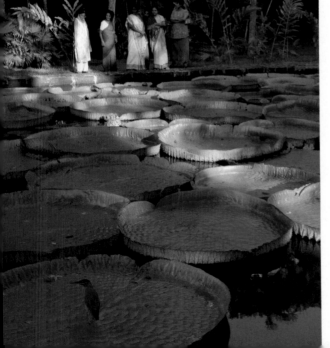 at Pamplemousses (tel: 243 9401, http://ssrbg.govmu.org; daily 8.30am–5.30pm), a 30-minute drive from Port Louis or Grand Baie. They are well worth a visit, the best time being between December and April.

The 25-hectare (62-acre) gardens were renamed the Sir Seewoosagur Ramgoolam Botanical Gardens in 1988 in honour of the late prime minister, but they are still known by everyone as Pamplemousses (French for grapefruit). The village was named after a variety of citrus plant, imported from Java by the Dutch in the 17th century and which once grew in the area.

You should allow a couple of hours to explore the maze of palm-lined avenues. Tour operators often combine a visit with a shopping spree to Port Louis and tend to lead groups on lightning-quick tours. The official guides will also whisk you around rather quickly for a fixed fee of R100, but they do point out the main attractions and provide interesting nuggets of information about some of the more unusual species; try to collar one of the older guides, who are likely to have worked in the gardens for years and are usually more informative. If you want to explore independently, it's a good idea to buy the guidebook (available at the main entrance), which contains a map as well as an authoritative explanation of the plant species – only some are labelled – and other attractions. There are no refreshment facilities inside the gardens, so stock up on water from the food stalls by the car park (near the motorway turn-off).

Wrought-iron gates (exhibited at the 1851 Great Exhibition at London's Crystal Palace) mark the original entrance to the gardens but the main entrance is now by the big car park on the other side. From here, guides will lead you along shaded avenues named after botanists and benefactors and show you trees such as the bastard mahogany (Andira inermis), marmalade box (Genipa americana), chewing gum (Manilkara achras) and sausage tree (Kigelia pinnata).

In all, there are about 500 plant species out of which 80 are palms and 40, such as ebony, mahogany and pandanus, are indigenous to the Mascarene Islands. Among the most impressive sights are the **Lotus Pond**, filled with yellow and white flowers, and the huge **Lily Pond**. Half concealed by the floating leaves of the giant Amazon water lily (Victoria amazonica), this is everyone's favourite photo opportunity. The flowers of the lily open white, fade to a dusky pink by the end of the second day and then die; the unmistakable flat leaves can reach as much as 1.5 metres (4.5ft) in diameter. The talipot palm is another remarkable species. It waits 40 to 60 years to flower, then dies. Ginger, cloves and cinnamon are among the many spices you can sniff out.

The gardens' origins go back to 1735, when Mahé de Labourdonnais bought a house in the grounds, which he called Château Mon Plaisir. In 1768 it became the residence of the French horticulturist

The Lily Pond at Pamplemousses Botanical Gardens.

Pierre Poivre, who planted the seeds for the specimens seen today (see page 242). The present **Château Mon Plaisir**, a 19th-century British legacy, is now used as an administration office, although it is crying out to be transformed into a museum and restaurant.

CHÂTEAU DE LABOURDONNAIS

An impressive tree-lined driveway leads to the colonnaded **Château de Labourdonnais** ⑱ in Mapou (tel: 266 9533; http://domainedelalabourdonnais.com; daily 9am–5pm). Modelled on Versailles, this colonial mansion was built in 1859 and opened to the public in 2010. Its orchard once supplied fruit to the island and the château is now known in international circles for its gourmet artisanal rum – visits include a rum tasting. Informal restaurant Le Table du Château, with home-made condiments, is really rather good, and a new holistic health centre, WellnesSenses, opened in 2018.

SCENIC ROUTE TO PIETER BOTH

For a scenic drive – where a foreground of sugar cane is framed by the quirky peaks of the Moka Mountains – take the A2 from Pamplemousses towards Centre de Flacq and the east coast. En route you pass **Grand Rosalie**, where the first sugar estate was established in 1743. The plantation house is closed to the public, but you can get an idea of the lay of the land from the nearby **La Nicolière Reservoir** ⑲. The road winds uphill, giving bird's-eye views of the luscious landscape, and descends through woods and sleepy villages. If the light is right, stay a while at the welcoming hamlet of **Malenga**, the nearest you'll get to **Pieter Both**, whose pinnacle resembles a man's head perched precariously on cloak-shrouded shoulders. They say that the day the head comes off some great catastrophe will destroy the island, but even the worst cyclones of 1892 and 1960 have failed to shift it. From Malenga you can watch the mountain change colour and shape as sun and clouds cast shadows across its face. From here, the B34 joins the motorway at Terre Rouge. The more direct route to Malenga is along the Verdun to Terre Rouge bypass.

Château de Labourdonnais.

An inviting hammock at Shangri-La's Le Touessrok Resort & Spa.

THE EAST

The east – with its glorious beaches, secluded hotels and sleepy villages – is tranquil and uncrowded, despite the presence of the airport.

Port Louis

Tourism development has been slow in the east compared to the north and west coasts, though hotel developments are starting to monopolise the white beaches to the north and south of Belle Mare. Some of the island's best hotels are already well established here, including the world-famous Constance Le Prince Maurice, the One&Only Le Saint Géran and the Shangri-La Le Touessrok Resort & Spa. There are few local excursions to tempt you away from the beach, and due to the relatively poor road links, access to the north and west coast isn't particularly speedy. If you are eager to do a lot of exploring, it's best not to base yourself on the east coast for your entire stay.

FLAT FLACQ

The northern area of the east coast lies in the district of Flacq, which derives from Groote Vlakte (Great Plain), the name given to the area by the Dutch when they arrived in the 17th century. The flat terrain is perfect for the cultivation of sugar, and much of the land is owned by sugar estates, including FUEL (Flacq United Estate Limited), the largest in Mauritius. This is the most rural area in the country, and the vast sugar cane fields are interspersed with crops of onions, tomatoes, chillies, peanuts and aubergines, grown for local consumption.

A sugar cane plantation located at the foot of craggy mountains.

When the French arrived they called the main town **Centre de Flacq**, now dominated by a 19th-century British-built District Court House. Apart from a small lively Sunday market *(foire)* and stacks of shops there are few other attractions, but if you want to get around independently, you'll find plenty of buses and taxis to take you to Port Louis, Mahébourg and the east coast villages.

BELLE MARE PLAGE

The main concentration of beaches and hotels is around **Belle Mare** ❶, about

Main attractions
Île aux Cerfs
Fort Frederick Hendrik Museum, Vieux Grand Port
Mahébourg and its National History Museum
Blue Bay
La Vallée de Ferney
Île aux Aigrettes

Map on page 120

La Nicolière

Pamplemousses
Maré d'Australia

Brisée Verdière

Nicolière Mts

Bon Acceuil

Grand Retraite
A 2
Belvédère

Salazie

Bois d'Oiseaux

Grand Bois Fond

Constance

St-Rémy

Belle Vue Allendy

Centre de Flacq

Camp Garreau

Union Flacq
A 7

F.U.E.L.
Sugar Factory

Camp
Bonnemère

Françoise

Poste de Flacq
Pont Blanc

Camp Poorun

Providence

Poste de Flacq

One & Only
Le Saint Géran Hotel

Constance Belle
Mare Plage
Hotel

Long Beach
Mauritius

INDIAN OCEAN

Pte de Puits

The Residence
Mauritius Hotel

Belle Mare
1

Pte du Puits des Hollandais

LUX* Belle Mare Hotel
Veranda Palmar
Beach Hotel
Ambre Mauritius
C Mauritius
Salt of Palmar

Mare
du Puit

Camp Bouillon

Mare la Chaux

Isidore Rose

Bramsthan

Quatre Cocos

Camp Ithier

Palmar

Mare Tatos

St-Julien

Rich Fund

St-Julien d'Hotman

Mont Ida

Medine

l'Unite

Bel Étang

Camp de
Masque Pavé

West Peak
433

Camp
de Masque

Fayence Mountain

Mare Jacot

Queen Victoria

Ecroignard

Flacq

Île Vacoas

Pte Quatre Cocos

Quartier Militaire

Providence
A 7

Moka

Petite Cabane

Hermitage

Clemence

Belle Rose

Trois Îlots

Petit Bois

La Caroline

Bel Air
(Rivière Sèche)

Ernest Florent

Trou d'Eau Douce
2
Île de la Batterie

Îlot Lievres

Shangri Le Touessrok
Resort & SPA

Île de l'Est

Bubble
Lodges
Île aux Cerfs
3

Melrose

Petit Paquet

Montagne
Blanche

Mt Blanche
532

Blanche Mountain

Pellegrin

Lesur

Sebastopol

Beau Champ

Deep River

Deux Frères

Otentic River
Experience

Grande Rivière
Sud Est

Pte
Grand Vacoas

Île aux Chats

Île Camisard

Anse
Cunat

Pte de la Batterie

Françoise ou du Boucan

Sans Souci

Clavet

Olivia

Quatre Soeurs

Pte St-Lain

Pointe aux Feuilles

Grande Rivière Sud-Est

L'Étoile

La Commune

Bois d'Oiseaux

Marie Jeanne

Pte aux Feuilles

Kewal Nagar

Grande Rivière Sud-Est

Pic Grand Fond
521

Bambou Mountains

Mt Bambou
626

Grand
Sable

Anse du
Grand Dable

Pointe aux
Roches

Otentic Mountain
Experience

Pte aux Roches

Anse du Petit Sable

Petit Sable

Pointe du Diable

Pte du Diable

Îlot Flamants

Île aux Oiseaux

Domaine
du Chasseur
Reserve

Anse Bambou
Pte Corail

Bambous Virieux

Anse Jonchée

Pte Bambou

Providence

Anse Jonchée
Pte Masulipatan

INDIAN OCEAN

Le Val

La Vallée de
Ferney
7

Ste-Madeleine

St-Hubert

Cent Gaulettes

Eau Bleue
(Rama)

St-Hilaire

Mare Chicose

Astroea

Riche en Eau

Camp Jardin

Monument to
the Dutch
1

Ferney

Le Vallon

Vieux
Grand Port

Anse
Colas
4

Pavillon du Grand Port

Bois des Amourettes

Lion Mt
480

Salles d'Armes

Treize Cantons

Île aux Singes

La Terre Rouge
Trou Beloute

Rivière des Créoles
Pte Brocus

Île Marianne

Rocher des Oiseaux

Île aux Fous

Deux Bras

New Grove

La Rosa

Mare d'Albert

A 10

La Rampe
le Moint

Grand Port

La Chaux

Rau Copeau

Petit Bel Air

Rault Biscuit
Factory

Grand Bel Air

Mahébourg
National History
Museum
5

Pte de la Colonie

Ville Noire

Anse des
Courants

Île du Hangard

Île aux Aigrettes
8

Preskil Beach Resort Hotel

Îlot Vacoas

Île aux Fouquets

Île de la Passe

Port Louis

Gros Bois

La Rampe
le Moint

M 1

Plaine Magnien

A 10

Sir Seewoosagur Ramgoolam
International Airport

Beau Vallon

Pte D'Esny

Pointe D'Esny

Pte des Deux Cocos

Union Vale

Trois Boutiques

Mon Trésor-
Mon Désert

Shandrani Hotel
Resort & SPA
6

Blue Bay

Blue Bay
Marine Reserve

Île des Deux Cocos

Le Chaland

Pte Vacoas

N

The East

0   2 km
0   2 miles

10 minutes' drive from Centre de Flacq. There is a better-than-average public beach, backed by casuarina forests where old kilns remain as monuments to the once thriving coral burning industry; from the top of them you get lovely views of coast and cane fields. The public beach is a mere extension of the more pristine, regularly swept ones fronting the nearby **Constance Belle Mare Plage**, newly refurbished **LUX* Belle Mare** and chic **Long Beach Mauritius** resorts. Newly refurbished four-star hotels Salt of Palmar and C Mauritius at Palmar Beach, have more of a hip, playful vibe, with Salt of Palmar offering 'humanistic hospitality for the culturally curious traveller', and while serious about creature comforts, C Mauritius features a musical shower.

As you head south, keep an eye out for brightly painted statues of Hindu gods, peeking out of the thick vegetation. The string of hotels continues with **The Residence Mauritius**, an imposing, plantation-style place, and **Veranda Palmar Beach**, with its distinctive thatched roofs, and several newer four-star contenders, including the all-inclusive resort **Ambre Mauritius**.

TROU D'EAU DOUCE

Arriving in the village of **Trou d'Eau Douce ②** (Hole of Sweet Water) after the string of hotels further north, you may feel jolted back to reality. The reason for visiting for most is to reach what lies across the water, and there's a small car park and a refurbished waterfront where enthusiastic operators are happy to ferry you to Île aux Cerfs. Many tourists stop at the handful of souvenir shops and simple restaurants, which make a welcome change, especially if you've been holed up in a resort for a few days. Beyond the village the pace of life has barely changed despite the proliferation of visitors to the area.

ISLAND-HOPPING IN THE EAST

The **Île aux Cerfs ③** is a long-time favourite with Mauritians and foreign visitors. It is managed by Sun Resorts, and is open to the public (unlike Îlot Mangenie, where an enclave is restricted to residents of Shangri-La's Le Touessrok Resort & Spa only). The free car park inside the grounds of Shangri-La's Le Touessrok Resort & Spa is reserved for golfers with a reservation at the golf course on the island, who can take a shuttle direct from there. If you don't have your own transport you could join one of the full-day excursions (including by catamaran) offered by tour operators in tourist centres around the island. Otherwise a couple of companies in Trou d'Eau Douce run a regular ferry service from the waterfront.

The island is covered by 285 hectares (700 acres) of woodland and has a golf course, lovely beaches and limpid, blue waters. You can swim and snorkel from the shore. A boathouse near the jetty provides equipment for water-skiing, windsurfing and boating, and scattered among the trees (and even in the trees) nearby are open-air shops and restaurants. The atmosphere is relaxed, but it can get very crowded. If you want

Shangri-La's Le Touessrok Resort & Spa's spectacular location.

solitude, there are quieter beaches close by, and enjoyable walks can be made round the island along marked paths. From 2018, you can enjoy a night under the stars in an exclusive Bubble Lodge, a semi-transparent eco-dome – one cradled in the Banyan Tree and two others by the beach, beside the golf course, with butler service, complimentary golf and gourmet meals in the clubhouse.

Catamaran trips to Île aux Cerfs stop in the deep estuary of Grande Rivière Sud-Est, the longest river in Mauritius, where at a small but pretty waterfall you can often see bold young islanders diving into the water from the basalt cliffs, hoping to be rewarded with a few tourist rupees. Nearby is the islands' first glamping site, Otentic Ecotent River Experience (tel: 5941 4888) https://otentic.mu/en), with a free daily shuttle to Île aux Cerfs, and which can be combined with a stay at Otentic Ecotent Mountain Experience above Bambous Virieux, with trekking in the Bambou Mountains.

Colourful pirogues in the bay by the islet of Mouchoir Rouge.

THE OLD DUTCH COAST ROAD

The drive from Trou d'Eau Douce south along the B28 or Old Coast Road to Mahébourg is one of the loveliest on the island. Head inland to Bel Air where the road veers towards the coast, hitting the sea at the gorge of **Grande** Rivière **Sud-Est**. From here, it barely manages to keep a toehold on land as it contrives to avoid the steep foothills of the Bambou Mountains. Fishing hamlets and picturesque villages are scattered along the route.

The **Grand Port** district in the southeastern corner of Mauritius is full of historical connections since this is where the French and Dutch began their colonisation of the island. There are many ruins in the area, some dating from the 17th century, but most are in a poor state of repair. Lying in the shadow of Lion Mountain, **Vieux Grand Port ❹** is of particular historical interest as it was the first base established by the Dutch, in the 17th century. The original Dutch fort disappeared beneath defences built by the French in the 18th century. Now all that remains are a few blackened and disintegrating walls, but in 1997 archaeologists unearthed beakers, pottery, glass and Chinese porcelain from the 17th century. These and other finds are displayed in the adjacent **Fort Frederick Hendrik Museum** (tel: 634 4319; www.mauritiusmuseums. com; Mon, Tue, Thu–Sat 9am–4pm, Wed 11am–4pm, Sun 9am–noon; free), along with a model of the fort, while audiovisual displays explain the history of the Dutch East India Company and its role in Mauritius. Explore Nou Zil's ('Our Island's) circular ride by electro-bike of Grand Port, from Mahébourg, takes in 400 centuries of island history.

Along the water's edge are the caves of **Salles d'Armes**, where French gentlemen once fought duels. They are best approached by sea with a local fisherman, but you can make your own way by zigzagging through the cane fields at the northern end of Vieux Grand Port village.

Further north, the **Bois des Amourettes** was a favourite haunt of French soldiers and their sweethearts. During World War II the British built a naval lookout post but all that remains are some old concrete bunkers poking through the sugar cane on the shore.

Between Vieux Grand Port and Mahébourg, you pass two memorials: one commemorating the first Dutch landing in 1598 and another marking their introduction of sugar in 1639. These memorials sat unnoticed for years, but were spruced up for the royal Dutch visit in 1998, when Mauritius celebrated the 400th anniversary of the Dutch arrival.

MAHÉBOURG

Named after the first French governor of the Mascarenes, Mahé de Labourdonnais, **Mahébourg** ❺ (pronounced Ma-y-bourg) lies on the southern shores of the immense Vieux Grand Port Bay. Under the French, Mahébourg was a busy, thriving port, which the British later linked by rail (now abandoned) to Port Louis. The names of the neatly laid out grid-style streets reflect the influence of European settlers, and there is a historical feel here that is absent in many Mauritian towns.

These days Mahébourg is a dusty, rather run-down place, crammed with grocers' and fabric stores. Yet it has an appealing, laid-back bustle, and is photogenic. The seafront Rue des Hollandais is done no favours by the sprawling presence of the bus station, but the area benefited from a facelift in 2003. The waterfront, with its memorial to the Battle of Grand Port, makes for a pleasant stroll. Fisherrnen still ply the harbour in their traditional pirogues around the islet of Mouchoir Rouge (Red Hanky island), while, in the backstreets, life trundles slowly by; women still scrub clothes on the stone sinks at Le Lavoir, the outdoor washhouse off Rue des Hollandais. There is a lively daily market, best on Mondays, worth visiting for its exotic fruit, vegetables, herbs and spices, and street food stalls. Explore it on a food tour with Taste Buddies (tel: 266 7496, www.tastebuddies.mu), or on a photographic

⊙ BATTLE OF GRAND PORT

In August 1810, British ships arrived in the Bay of Grand Port to capture Île de France (present-day Mauritius) from the French. The superior British navy expected an easy victory as they waited on Île de la Passe for French ships returning from a voyage. They intended to trick them by flying the French flag, before opening fire. But then gunpowder exploded on the island, causing injury and confusion, and two British ships ran aground on the reef, allowing the French to regroup and defend their territory.

This historic three-day Battle of Grand Port, which ended in a British surrender, is the only naval battle the French won against the British in the Napoleonic era, and is commemorated on the Arc de Triomphe in Paris.

An old colonial building in use as a hardware shop in Mahébourg.

safari with Clique Photography (tel: 5250 6990, www.clique.mu/en/gallery/5/photographic-safari).

NATIONAL HISTORY MUSEUM

Mahébourg's **National History Museum** (tel: 631 9329; Mon, Tue, Thu–Sat 9am–4pm, Wed 11am–4pm, Sun and public holidays 9am–noon), on the southern outskirts of the town, is housed in an 18th-century building. Its original owner, Jean de Robillard, turned the house into a hospital where the commanders of the French and British forces who had fought in the Battle of Grand Port convalesced side by side. The museum contains an eclectic display of exhibits from the Dutch, French and British periods. Portraits line the walls, among them Prince Maurice of Nassau, Pieter Both, botanist Pierre Poivre and 'king of the corsairs', Robert Surcouf, who donated the dagger he seized in 1800 from Captain Rivington of the English ship *Kent* following an attack in the Bay of Bengal. One of the most famous relics is the ship's bell from the ill-fated *St Géran*, which sank off the northeast coast in 1744. A newspaper cutting recalls the fate of the British steamer *Trevessa*, which sank hundreds of miles from Mauritius in 1923. The survivors landed at Bel Ombre on the south coast after 25 days in a lifeboat with nothing to eat but ship's biscuits. You can see the remains of the biscuits and the cigarette tin they used to measure water rations. Other exhibits include Mahé de Labourdonnais' four-poster bed and two wooden palanquins in which slaves would carry their masters.

AROUND MAHÉBOURG

The approach to **Blue Bay** ❻, south of Mahébourg, isn't promising as you drive past some very poor housing, but Pointe d'Esny is considered a desirable place to live, and high-walled private bungalows dot the coast. En route you pass **Le Preskil Island Resort** hotel; a nice enough spot, on its own small peninsula with views of the mountains, but unless you want easy access to the airport, it's rather an isolated place to stay. The public beach at Blue Bay, however, is worth an excursion. You can hire a glass-bottom boat here to view wonderful corals in the Blue Bay Marine Park and sail past the islet of **Île des Deux Cocos** (tel: 698 9800; www.iledesdeuxcocos.com; daily 10.30am–3.30pm), an exclusive luxury retreat that can be visited for the day and hired for weddings and private functions. On the other side of the bay, the **Shandrani Beachcomber Resort & Spa** is the height of luxury. It stands on its own peninsula in 30 hectares (74 acres) of gardens, just 6km (4 miles) from the airport. To the west of Shandrani Beachcomber Resort & Spa, at Mare aux Songes, an almost intact set of dodo bones was discovered in 1865 and the skeleton is on display in London's British Museum. In 2006 Dutch scientists unearthed more dodo bones, which will enable them to understand more about this extinct bird, and in 2019, Mare aux Songes will open as a historic tourist attraction.

Taking a boat trip around the picturesque area of Blue Bay, near Mahébourg.

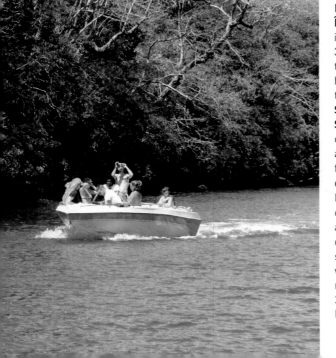

From **Ville Noire**, north across La Chaux River from Mahébourg, signs point the way to the **Rault Biscuit Factory** (tel: 631 9559; http://biscuitmanioc.com; Mon–Fri 9–11am and 1–3pm), where you can take a guided tour to see women baking *biscuits manioc* made from the cassava that grows in the nearby valley.

The B7 from Ville Noire runs through cane fields to the village of **Riche en Eau**. The area, literally 'rich in water', was home to small family-owned sugar estates, where isolated chimneys, now listed as national monuments, mark the sites of early factories. Signs in the area lead to **La Vallée de Ferney** ❼ (tel: 5729 1080; www.valleedeferney.com; daily 10am–6pm), where the former Ferney sugar factory has been converted into a visitors' centre. Wall maps and information boards highlight conservation issues, and guided walks through the 200-hectare (494-acre) valley reveal rare birds – including the Mauritius kestrel, with guaranteed sightings at feeding time – bat-watching at sunset and indigenous plants thriving amid mountain-backed landscapes and bubbling streams. Also part of La Vallée estate and a short shuttle ride away is Falaise Rouge, a simple restaurant perched on the red cliffs (hence the name) overlooking the bay nearby. Serving traditional Mauritian specialities, it is an atmospheric place for lunch.

ÎLE AUX AIGRETTES

Ecotourism is developing at **Île aux Aigrettes** ❽ (tel: 631 2396; www.mauritian-wildlife.org; Mon–Sat 9.30am–2.30pm, Sun 9.30–10.30am), a nature reserve that opened to the public in 1998. It's a 20-minute ferry trip from Pointe Jérôme near the Preskil Island Resort. A guide from the Mauritius Wildlife Foundation (MWF) leads no more than 20 visitors at a time along marked paths. Look out for bands of pink pigeons (see page 85) breeding among flora found nowhere else in the world. The MWF has been active in regenerating the island, its main aim being to re-create a microcosm of the original coastal habitat. It has introduced Aldabra tortoises, seen lumbering under the canopy, Telfair's skink and the Mauritian fody. During World War II, much of the native forest was cleared to make room for British troops, who installed guns (still in place) as defences against a Japanese invasion. Old hands remember waiting for the enemy which never came. The old generator room has been converted into a museum and if you climb to the rooftop viewing platform panoramic views unfold across the sweeping bay and **Île de la Passe** beyond.

Among the historic ruins on this islet off Vieux Grand Port are the remains of French defences, an old reservoir and a beautifully preserved 18th-century powder magazine, complete with a harp etched into its wall. This was probably engraved by a homesick soldier of the 87th Royal Irish Fusiliers, stationed here in the 1830s. Both islets make a wonderful half-day excursion.

A distinctive pink pigeon on Île aux Aigrettes.

Rochester Falls.

THE SOUTH COAST

The rugged south coast is the island's wilder side, far from well-trodden shores, and is easily explored in a day's drive.

Port Louis

The south coast from Bel Ombre to Riambel is currently undergoing major development to increase tourism and revive the economy of this forgotten region. The lack of tourist amenities is offset by gorgeous scenery and the sense that you are witnessing Mauritius as it used to be. Great stretches of rugged basalt cliffs assaulted by strong southeasterly winds lie against a backdrop of hills and undulating sugar fields that are part of century-old plantations. The old estates, built to withstand the southern winds, have survived better here than elsewhere. Apart from a scattering of luxurious hotels dominating sandy beaches in the west, there is scant evidence of the 20th century, let alone the 21st. Yet although still a far cry from the north, changes are afoot in the south, heralded by the 2004 Heritage Resorts development at Bel Ombre in the southwest, which has plans for further villa development, and the strip of hotels which followed nearby. Among them are Shanti Maurice Resort & Spa, with its spacious beach-side accommodation at St Felix, midway along the south coast, and the redevelopment of the Movenpick Hotel into Outrigger Mauritius Beach Resort. Le Morne, on the southwestern tip, is the recipient of the latest development, with 500 beds added in 2015, courtesy of Rui hotels.

Walking through sugar cane near Rochester.

Rivers flowing from the central uplands to the ocean have, in many places, prevented coral reefs from gaining a foothold, depriving the area of the gentle lagoons reminiscent of the north, and swimming, except from designated beaches, can be dangerous. In the west, the Savanne Mountains (which give the district its name) rise steeply from deep coves, relegating the coast road to a narrow strip west of Souillac. The east is flatter. Here, the roads run through cane fields and over bridges spanning rivers and

 Main attractions
Robert Edward Hart Museum
Rochester Falls
Le Gris Gris
Saint Aubin and Le Bois Cheri Tea Factory
La Vanille Réserve des Mascareignes

Map on page 128

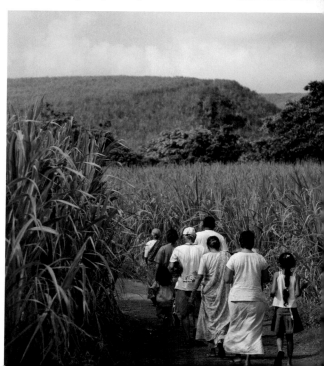

⊙ Tip

In Heritage Nature Reserve look out for the relics of an old mill standing on the site of a former sugar factory, indigenous plants and trees, plantations of edible palms and herds of deer. Book at tel: 623 5615, www.heritagenature reserve.com).

streams, linking shanty villages. Not a lot of tourists pass this way.

If you're driving, the south coast can easily be explored in one leisurely day – less if you're based at one of the hotels on the west coast or on the southeast coast near Mahébourg. If you have a full day to spare, you might even consider making a circular drive by taking in the route through the Black River Gorges National Park (described in The West chapter, see page 137). Most hotels offer full-day tours of the south coast, which usually include lunch in an old sugar estate house.

AROUND BEL OMBRE

Our tour begins at the western end, just east of Le Morne. Here you'll find a quiet rock-strewn beach, where fishermen sit mending their nets and children play among the trees. The first significant hamlet is **Baie du Cap ❶**, typical of many villages along the south coast: there are just a few Chinese-run *boutiks* (and a police station built by a local sugar magnate from a ship that sank offshore in the 19th century), although Andalaba, a new villa development under construction, has now reached this quiet backwater.

A short distance beyond is **Bel Ombre ❷**, where at certain times of the year lorries laden with sheaves of sugar cane are seen, bound for St Aubin and Savannah factories further east. Bel Ombre has long been the heartland of the south coast's sugar industry. Back in 1816, philanthropic businessman Charles Telfair, after whom the hotel nearby is named, bought the factory. Newly arrived from England, he immediately set about turning Bel Ombre into a model sugar estate, only to incur the wrath of local slave owners who did not agree with his idea of providing proper food and shelter for slaves.

Adjoining the colonial-style Heritage Le Telfair Golf & Wellness Resort is the 18-hole Heritage Golf Course; all that is left of the factory is the chimney, with a second Championship course opening in 2019. Guided nature tours, 4x4 excursions and quad-biking trails into **Heritage Nature Reserve**, coupled with elegant haute cuisine in the evening at the splendid 19th-century Heritage Le Château, attract golfers, 'green' tourists, gourmets and wellness seekers. Other contenders offering

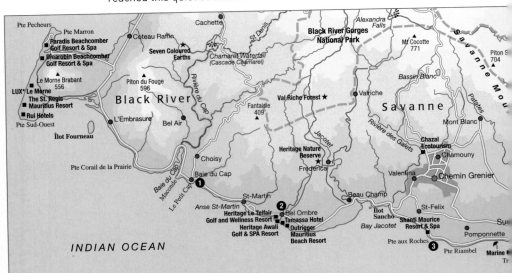

grand-scale sanctuary, serenity and space are the Heritage Awali Golf & Spa Resort, with its enormous African-village style spa, and Heritage Villas, nestled on the hillside with spectacular views across the estate. A nudge east along the coast is the sumptuous Outrigger Mauritius Beach Resort and the red-roofed Tamassa Hotel.

BEAU CHAMP TO RIAMBEL

The 'unspoilt' southwest, where the lush foothills of the Black River Gorges National Park merge with the forests of Bel Ombre, is a natural place for ecotourism. Driving east through swaying fields of sugar cane, a mile or so east of Beau Champ, the B10 branches inland to **Chemin Grenier**, where a minor road runs north to the water-filled crater of **Bassin Blanc**. Here, with a little patience, you may be able to spot the brilliant green echo parakeet and Mauritius kestrel.

The B9 coast road to the west of **Pointe aux Roches** ❸ fringes a public beach; the area to the east is dominated by the Shanti Maurice Resort & Spa. If you would like to combine beach activity with 'green tourism', Chazal Ecotourism at the 2,400-hectare (6,000-acre) St Felix Sugar Estate offers speed zip wire rides and river trekking on the Rivière des Galets. More sedate activities on offer include archery and guided nature tours through the estate, and camping.

Meanwhile, the coast remains beautifully rugged, although it is not without its dangers due to an absence of coral reef. Further east, **Pomponette** is known for its treacherous currents, and most locals head for the safer **SSR Public Beach** just before the peaceful hamlet of **Riambel** (from the Malagasy word meaning 'beaches of sunshine'), where the well-established Green Palm restaurant provides delicious south Indian meals. Perhaps the most interesting place to visit here is **The Vortex** (tel: 736 9038, http://www.lumieresdelaudela. com; daily 9am–5pm; by donation) a tranquil clearing in a coastal forest said to be one of the world's 'energy' hotspots, with intense vibratory levels for healing. Lie in one of the meditation cabins, and recharge your chakras.

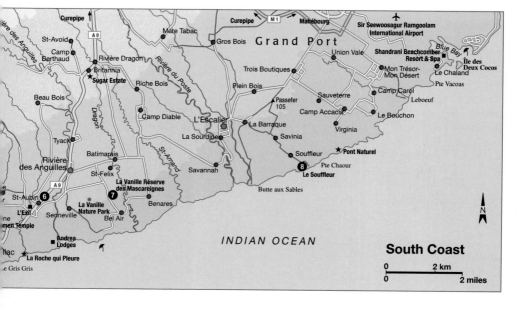

SOUILLAC

The largest settlement on the south coast is **Souillac ❹**, which lies on an inlet where the rivers Savanne and Patates form an estuary (about 30 minutes' drive from Le Morne on the west coast). At the height of sugar production in the 19th century, steam ships loaded cane from nearby estates and shunted along the coast to Port Louis, but the port fell into decline when road and rail replaced the steamers. In the 1990s, substantial improvements were made to the old port area, prompting the town's designation as a 'tourist village'. While such a billing owes more to optimism than reality, it is worth stopping off to explore the handful of sights that are scattered around the bay.

On the western side a road turns off to Souillac's **Marine Cemetery**, one of the most beautiful in Mauritius. Who knows what graves were washed out to sea over the years, but in 1957 people reported seeing hundreds of skulls and human bones littering the cemetery as a result of a tidal wave. Meanwhile, constant erosion of the sea wall threatens even more damage to graves, many of which date back to the early 19th century. One of the oldest tombs is that of Thomas Etienne Bolgerd (1748–1818), a Souillac bigwig and owner of 500 slaves who was captured by the British in 1809 and released in exchange for some goats. The most famous member of the d'Unienville family, Baron Marie Claude Antoine Marrier d'Unienville (1766–1831), is also buried here, as is Robert Edward Hart (1891–1954), the country's most celebrated poet and writer.

Next stop is the old **port** area, where the most evident improvement is the restoration of a 200-year-old sugar warehouse, part of which is now occupied by **Le Batelage** restaurant, where tourists on organised trips are often fed and watered. The shady terrace on the quay at the front provides good views over the river, now so tranquil after years of inactivity.

The **Telfair Gardens** are just across the road from the bus station.

⊙ AIN'T NO MOUNTAIN HIGH ENOUGH

Mauritius' 28 quirky-shaped mountains, reminders of its volcanic past, may be miniature compared to those in Réunion, but the climbing is easier and you are rewarded with spectacular views. Follow in the footsteps of Charles Darwin on a three-hour return climb up Le Pouce (812 metres/2,663ft), 'The thumb', protruding from the Moka mountain range, for views of Port Louis. Hike up independently along a well-marked trail from Le Dauget village, or take a guided climb with Yemaya Adventures (tel: 5752 0046; www.yemayaadventures.com). For the highest views on the island, take a straightforward three-hour hike along a forested path in the Black River Gorges National Park to Mauritius' highest mountain, Piton de la Petite Rivière/Black River Peak (828 metres/2,716ft). The two-hour return climb up Lion Mountain (480 metres/1,574ft) with Vertical World (tel: 697 5430; www.verticalworldltd.com) is brought alive with stories of myths and legends, and affords sweeping views over the historic southeast.

A dramatic climb, for those of moderate fitness, is up the iconic monolith Le Morne Brabant (556 metres/1,824ft) with Yanature (tel: 5785 61177; www.trekkingmauritius.com), with inspiring views of forested estates and coral gardens in a translucent lagoon. Its poignant slave past earned this mountain Unesco World Heritage status in 2008, and it's the only place to find the large, red *trochetia boutoniana*, the island's national flower, in the wild.

Shaded by gigantic Indian almond trees and banyans, the gardens are a favourite spot among the locals who come here to pass the time of day while kids, quite oblivious to the skull-and-crossbones signs, swim off the rocky coast. The cemetery is visible across the bay.

From here it is a 10-minute stroll to the **Robert Edward Hart Museum** (tel: 625 6101; Mon, Wed–Fri 9am–4pm, Sat–Sun 9am–noon), the former home of Souillac's most famous son. The half-Irish, half-French poet and writer lived alone in a charming little coral-built bungalow, known as La Nef (The Nave), which contains manuscripts, books and personal belongings. Hart churned out work in English and French and his efforts were recognised in both English and French literary circles, with an OBE and a gold medal from the Académie Française. He was obviously inspired by the beauty of his surroundings, and you can understand why when you see the golden beach pounded by ferocious seas at the rear of the house.

ROCHESTER FALLS

Not far from Souillac's seafront, a road runs 5km (3 miles) inland through cane fields to the **Rochester Falls**, which tumble from the Savanne River from a height of 10 metres (33ft). Constant erosion has fashioned the basalt rock into upright columns, and young boys enjoy scaling the jagged cliffs before diving into the cold fresh water. It's also a great place for a swim. Taxi drivers will take you there (and wait to take you back), but you can also hoof it. The track weaves uphill for about 15 minutes before descending to the falls. However, it is an isolated spot and at the time of writing there have been reports of intimidating behaviour from locals, so visiting it alone is discouraged.

On the way, you pass **Terracine**, one of the island's earliest factories, dating back to 1820. It closed down in 1947 but the chimney, a national monument, stands as a reminder of its sugar-producing days. Right next to it, the colourful Mariamen Temple, which

Wild terrain at Le Gris Gris.

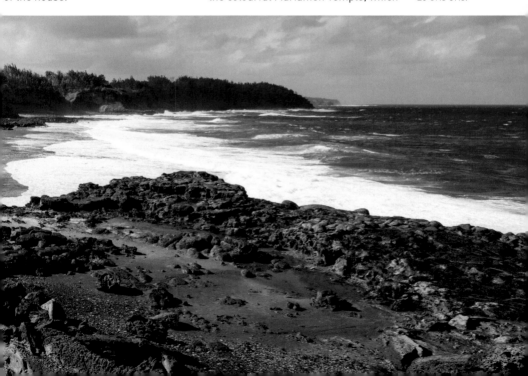

⊙ Eat

The Hungry Crocodile restaurant in La Vanille Nature Park has an interesting menu. If you're not tempted by the idea of crocodile croquettes, you can always opt for a croc-free *croque monsieur*.

remains quiet for most of the year, bursts into life in December and January when it is taken over by Tamil fire-walking and body-piercing Cavadee ceremonies (see page 74).

THE WILD SOUTH

If you continue along the road from La Nef you reach **Le Gris Gris ❺**, the most southerly point of Mauritius, more like the windswept coast of Scotland than the gentle shores of a tropical island. Some say it is called Gris Gris because black magic (*gris gris* in Kreol) used to be performed here. If you walk along the yawning sandy beach and allow your imagination to run riot, you can pick out the figure of a sorcerer scored out of the rock, who appears to be holding a cauldron. Up on the headland, where weather-beaten casuarinas attest to the ferocity of the winds, a 15-minute walk along a small path leads to a rocky outcrop called **La Roche qui Pleure** (The Crying Rock), so named because the sea which cascades around it gives the impression that it is weeping. (A monochrome photograph in La Nef illustrates the uncanny similarity between the silhouette of this rock and the profile of Robert Edward Hart.)

THE TEA ROUTE

One of the highlights of a south coast tour is a visit to the area's colonial homes. Many are off-limits to the public but local tour operators offer The Tea Route, a full-day guided tour that starts at Domaine les Aubineaux, a former tea planter's residence in Curepipe, with tea tasting in the attractive tearoom, and finishes with lunch at the residence of **Saint Aubin ❻** (tel: 626 1819; http://www.saintaubin.mu/fr/route_du_the.aspx; Mon–Sat 8.30am–4.30pm), built in 1870, on the A9 5km (3 miles) northeast of Souillac. The visit provides a leisurely glimpse of colonial life, with relaxation on the broad verandas, a tour of the vanilla and anthurium plantations, rum tasting at the distillery and a stroll through spacious grounds.

It also includes the **Bois Chéri tea factory**, 10km (6 miles) inland. Although tea is no longer produced in large quantities, the factory is worth visiting to

Saint Aubin.

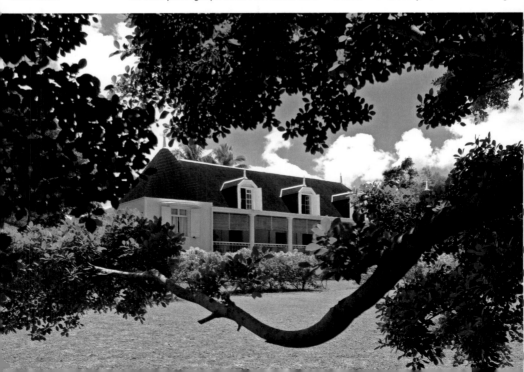

see how it is processed and packaged. You will also be driven to a hilltop tea pavilion overlooking a lake surrounded by neat tea fields. Here, you can sample plain, vanilla or even passion fruit flavoured tea, and go for a stroll on the hillside, with magnificent views of the coast. You can now stay the night under the stars here, in an exclusive Bubble Lodge, a luxurious semi-transparent eco-dome, either nestled by the crater lake, or overlooking it on the hilltop. Boating on the lake, a romantic dinner at the Bois Chéri hilltop restaurant and guided walks on the estate are included in the package.

OFF THE BEATEN TRACK

If you head north along the A9, you pass the manicured lawns and pineapple plantations of the **Britannia Sugar Estate**, the south's last significant sugar plantation. It is still very active, with a pristine estate village of stone-built homes and a school.

THE CROCODILE PARK

You don't need to be on an organised tour to visit **La Vanille Nature Park** ➐, still known locally as The Crocodile Park (tel: 626 2503; http://lavanille-naturepark. com; daily 8.30am–5pm), signposted right off the road running through the large village of **Rivière des Anguilles** (on the banks of the river of the same name). The park occupies a valley that features about the closest thing you'll get to tropical rainforest, which is why Owen Griffiths, an Australian zoologist, chose the area to farm Nile crocodiles. The stud of the estate and four females were brought from Madagascar in 1985, and the mating process produced little critters that grew into man-eating monsters. They are kept in secure enclosures, waking only at feeding time to snap mighty jaws with a sickening thud on freshly killed chicken.

A nature trail meanders through the forest, past squads of giant Aldabra tortoises at all stages of development,

wide-eyed Mauritian fruit bats, wild boars, macaque monkeys, an insectarium, a host of luminous green geckos and chameleons, and even lemurs to pet; it's also one of the few places to see echo parakeets. (Be sure to douse yourself with plenty of insect repellent before you visit.)

LE SOUFFLEUR

If you are heading towards Mahébourg, you can follow the little-used B8, which branches east from Rivière des Anguilles. About midway, at **L'Escalier**, a road runs south to **Le Souffleur** ➑, a blowhole fashioned in a dramatic outcrop of rock (due to erosion it is now more a cloud of spray than the fierce jet of water that shot skywards until the 1970s). If you walk along the coast you'll get a clear view of the break in the coral reef that allows the sea to rush up against the cliffs. There's also a striking *pont naturel* (natural bridge), which formed when the roof of a sea cave collapsed. Le Souffleur is accessed via the grounds of the Savinia sugar estate (turn right at the L'Escalier police station).

Some of the residents of the Crocodile Park.

📷 SUGAR PRODUCTION

Despite rapid developments in the tourism and textile industries, the giant sugar estates are still the country's third biggest employer.

Until recently, over 90 percent of arable land in Mauritius was given over to the cultivation of sugar. With the diversification of agriculture and expansion of the tourism and textile sectors, sugar production is no longer the country's number one earner. Many sugar workers have opted for more comfortable employment in offices, factories and hotels. Nevertheless, mechanisation has ensured that sugar production continues to play a major role in the economy and there are perks for those who have remained in the industry. Sugar estates provide housing, hospitals and free medical facilities, free school transport and leisure and sporting activities. Many have scholarship schemes and sponsor the training of workers and their families in technical schools.

Mauritius produces the best unrefined sugar in the world and most of it is exported to the European Union. One important by-product is *bagasse* or cane fibre, which is used to fire boilers in the factory and any excess burned to generate additional electricity for sale to the national grid. Another is molasses, used in the production of vinegar, drugs and perfumes, while cane spirit is used to make rum. Nothing goes to waste; even the scum from the purification process contains essential nutrients which are fed back into the soil, and the long green leaves of the cane are used for animal feed.

Between June and December the air is thick with the sweet scent of molasses as cane is cut and loaded into lorries.

Although much of the work traditionally undertaken by labourers is now being done by machine, teams of cane workers toiling in the fields are still part and parcel of the Mauritian landscape.

Just over half of Mauritius is owned by several giant sugar estates; the rest is shared among 30,000 individual farmers or "planters"

Mechanic equipment is now increasingly being used for the sugar cane harvest.

Crumbling giants

The island's sugar industry has had an impact on everything from the landscape to the economy, politics and population. Sugar cane was introduced to Mauritius by the Dutch, who brought it over from Jakarta in 1639, and the French expanded the plantations. By the time the British came in 1810 thousands of acres had been planted with sugar cane. For generations sugar was the lifeblood of Mauritius. People got rich on it, fought over it and died for it. It wasn't until the 1980s, with the progressive centralisation of the sugar industry, that the number of sugar estates began to dwindle. Of the hundreds of factories that once thrived across the island, only a few are left. But the ruins of the old sites remain, and the chimneys – which have been designated national monuments – are dotted all over the countryside.

To see how the brown sludge from the crushed canes was transformed into sugar crystals, before mechanisation took over, visit the early sugar mill reconstructions at l'Aventure du Sucre or at Domaine les Pailles, a 10-minute drive south of the capital.

Old rum distillation machine at Chamarel Rum Distillery in Mauritius.

essing sugar cane for the distillation of rum at Domaine Saint Aubin.

is rum distillery at Chamarel makes a refined rum om the surrounding sugarcane fields, where garcane is not burnt, thus ensuring the purest of ice extracts for distillation.

The beach at Dinarobin Beachcomber Golf Resort & Spa, Le Morne Brabant.

THE WEST

The west's draw is beautiful beaches – and for nature lovers the Black River Gorges National Park is on the doorstep.

Soon after leaving the uninspiring suburbs and industrial installations of Port Louis, the quirky angles of the Corps de Garde, Rempart and Trois Mamelles mountains and, in the distance, the solid hammer head of Le Morne Brabant peninsula stay with you as you travel southwards, offering a range of rewarding views unmatched in other parts of the islands. The A3, which runs the length of the 50km (30-mile) coast, meanders inland south of the capital, with side roads periodically offering access to the sea, but from Tamarin the road hugs the coast. The glistening beaches of Flic en Flac, Wolmar and Le Morne and their turquoise lagoons remain tantalisingly hidden from view.

PORT LOUIS SUBURBS AND BEYOND

It is all too easy to speed through the suburbs of Port Louis as you make a beeline for the obvious attractions of the coast, reachable in about 30 minutes, but there are a few places that might attract your attention along the way.

Heading out of Port Louis along the A1, before the A3 branches off to Flic en Flac, you pass through **Grande Rivière Nord-Ouest**, notable for the iron bridges that span the river of the same name, and for the ruin of an 18th-century hospital. There are splendid views over the river at the point where the B31 leads

Chamarel Waterfall.

coastwards to **Pointe aux Sables ①**. The beach here is mediocre by Mauritius's standards, but attracts a crowd due to its proximity to the capital. Note that the resort has a seedy reputation due to its popularity with local prostitutes; the beach and overall scene is more pleasant at the point than in the village itself.

The B31 links up with the B78 (just before it rejoins the A3), which veers west to **Pointe aux Caves ②**. A climb to the top of the early 20th-century Albion lighthouse, which features in the 2019 Hollywood movie *Serenity*, here

Main attractions
Casela World of
  Adventures
Tamarin Bay
Tamarind Falls
Black River Gorges
  National Park
Seven Coloured Earths
  Geopark, Chamarel
Grand Bassin
Le Morne Brabant

Map on page 138

West Coast and Plateau

0 _____ 2 km
0 _____ 2 miles

N

INDIAN OCEAN

Grand River Bay

Port Louis

Abercrombie

Priest's Peak

Signal Mtn

P o r t   L o u i s

Les Guibies

Pointe aux Sables **1**

Pte aux Sables

Petit Verger

Pailles

Pieter Both 823

Domaine Les Pailles/ Swami Vivekananda Conference Centre

Le Pouce 811

La Laura

Pte aux Caves

Albion Lighthouse **1 2**

Petite Rivière

Roselyn Cottage

L'Agrement

L'Avenir

Pte Petite Rivière

Eureka **19**

Moka **18**

St-Pierre

Mont Fleury

Camp Creoles

Gros Cailloux

Belle Étoile

Richelieu

Chebel

Mount Ory

Bagatelle Shopping Centre Complex

Folk Museum of Indian Immigration

A 7

Circonstance

Verdun

Petite Rivière Bay

Albion

Canot

A 1

Beau Bassin **16**

Chateau du Réduit

M o k a

Telfair

Pte Moyenne

Plaisance

Stanley

Rose Hill **17**

Ebene Cyber-City

Belle Terre

Côte d'Or

L'Assurance

Pte Sud Flic en Flac

St Martin Cemetery

La Ferme Reservoir

Corps de Garde

Ebène

Bagatelle

Bambous **3**

Eau Bonne

Corps de Garde 720

A 8

Cinq Arpents

Mt St-Pierre 446

la Source

Quatre Bornes **20**

Petit Camp

Mauritius Glass Gallery

Highlands

Hermitage

St-Antoine

Flic en Flac **4**

Cascavelle Shopping Mall

Beaux Songes

Palmyre

Casela World of Adventures **6**

Carreau la Liane

Valentina

Phoenix **22**

Mesnil

Camp Fouquereaux

Sugar Beach Mauritius Resort

La Pirogue Mauritius

Wolmar Nature Reserve

Cascavelle

Palma

La Caverne

Vacoas **21**

Engrais Martial

A 10

M 1

Sofitel Mauritius L'Imperial

Wolmar **5**

Hilton Mauritius Resort & Spa

Rivière du Rempart

Quinze Cantons

P l a i n e s   W i l h e m s

Engrais Cathan

Maradiva Villas Resort & SPA

Mt du Rempart 545

Holyrood

Floreal

Sands Suites Resort & Spa

Trois Mamelles

Curepipe **23**

Domaine des Aubineaux

Barachois

Tamarina Golf & Spa Boutique Hotel

Tamarin Estate

Papares

Glen Park

Camp Caval

Forest Side

Baie du Tamarin

Veranda Tamarin Hotel

Tamarin **7**

Tamarin

Camp Roches

Camp la Savanne

Les Casernes

Pte du Tamarin

B l a c k   R i v e r

Vacoas Mountains

Camp Mapou

Yemen

Henrietta

La Marie

Riverland Sports Club

Tourelle du Tamarin 548

Simonet 632

Seiziéme Mille

A 10

La Preneuse

Boucan

Curepipe Point 686

Martello Tower

Ruisseau Creole

Grand Rivière Noire **9**

La Mivoie

Grande Rivière Noire Bay

Tamarind Falls Reservoir

Tamarind Falls **8**

Tamarin

Mare Longue Réservoir

Mare aux Vacoas

G r a n d   P o r t

Les Salines

Îlot Fortier

Grande Rivière Noire

Black River Visitor's Centre **10**

Petite Rivière Noire Bay

Petite Rivière Noire

Îlot Malais

Petite Case Noyale

Gorges de la Rivière Noire

Le Pétrin Information Centre

Le Pétrin **13**

Kanaka Crater

Rivière du Poste

Piton de la Petite Rivière Noire 828

Grande Case Noyale

Plaine Champagne

Black River Gorges National Park

Grand Bassin 702

Bubble Lodges

Grand Bois

Bois Chéri

Île aux Bénitiers

La Gaulette

Chamarel **11**

Black River Peak Viewpoint **12**

Alexandra Falls

Tea Factory

Rivière des Anguilles

Ebony Forest Reserve Chamarel

Cachette

Rhumerie de Chamarel

S a v a n n e

Coteau Raffin

Curious Corner of Chamarel

Chamarel Seven Coloured Earths Geopark **15**

St Denis

Mt Cocotte 771

Piton Savanne 704

Le Morne Brabant

Piton du Fouge 596

Chamarel Waterfall (Cascade Chamarel)

Rivière du Cap

Bassin Blanc

Savanna Mountains

Valriche

Patates

provides good views of the mountains and coast. A mountain bike ride along the cliffs with Yemaya Adventures (tel: 5752 0046; www.yemayaadventures.com) ends with a swim in a rock pool.

Back on the A3, the road continues southwards bisecting a wide and fertile plain and separating the plateau towns from a picturesque coast of low cliffs. At the busy village of **Bambous ❸**, with flamboyant tree-shaded avenues and pretty dwellings, ask for directions to **St Martin Cemetery**, nestling in cane fields north of the village. Here, 127 identical tombstones are the final reminder of 1,580 Jewish wartime refugees from Eastern Europe. Having been refused entry to Palestine by the British in 1940 because they were considered 'illegal immigrants', they were transported to Mauritius. They were well received, but conditions in their refugee camp, where they were kept until the end of the war, were poor. After the war, many started new lives abroad but their families still return to Mauritius to pay their respects to those who never made it back home. There are also some beautiful Tamil tombs in the cemetery.

FLIC EN FLAC

The name of the village **Flic en Flac ❹** is Dutch in origin and is thought to derive from 'Fried Landt Flaak', meaning 'Free and Flat Land'; later, under the influence of the French, this evolved into Flic en Flac. Most visitors don't waste too much time wondering about etymology but head straight for the beach.

If Grand Baie is the Creole Côte d'Azur then Flic en Flac is the Creole Costa del Sol, with a concentration of small seafront hotels, shops, restaurants and bars backed by concrete apartment complexes spreading inland to replace the sugar plantations of yesteryear. But it's a popular choice for self-caterers, independent travellers and islanders themselves (many of whom have weekend homes here), lured by the nightlife, a superb beach

and public transport giving easy access to Port Louis, the Plateau Towns – just a 45-minute bus ride away – and the Black River Gorge National Park.

At the entrance to Flic en Flac is a small clutch of bars and cafés, together with the resort's main hotel, **Villas Caroline**, which overlooks the northern reaches of the enormous beach. Soft, powdery sands shelve into the lagoon, where people windsurf and swim. Further along the main road ubiquitous casuarina trees back the beach, where the sand is packed hard enough for cars to drive on. Sunsets here are often a hypnotic vision of feathered clouds flecked with silvery-peach hues. On weekdays it is quiet, with just a couple of food stalls. But on weekends, the resort springs to life as locals descend from all around, and at the end of the day, great groups of islanders wait in orderly queues for the homebound bus.

Flic en Flac is a haven for divers, windsurfers and snorkellers. Unlike Grand Baie, no speedboats disturb the waters with wash thrown up from their bows, and the best dive sites in Mauritius lie

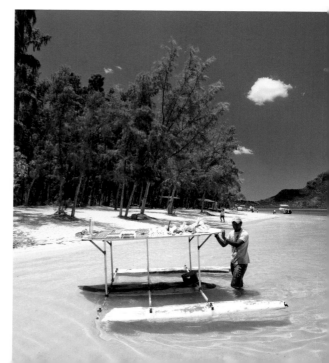

Flic en Flac hosts a range of water sports and activities.

off this part of the coast (see page 87). One of the best places in Mauritius to learn is **Sundivers** (www.sundiversmauritius.com), based at La Pirogue, while more experienced divers will find interesting opportunities with Exploration Sous Marine (www.exploration-sous-marine.com) at Villas Caroline.

Less than 2km (1 mile) south, past the Cascavelle Shopping Mall on the edge of town, **Wolmar** ❺ is really an extension of Flic en Flac. The original hamlet has now been completely swamped by a handful of very smart hotels, which include the Sugar Beach Mauritius Resort, La Pirogue Mauritius (complete with casino), the Sofitel Mauritius L'Imperial, the Hilton Mauritius Resort & Spa, Maradiva Villas Resort & Spa, the most luxurious on the west coast, and sister hotel Sands Suites Resort & Spa. These hotels certainly have better facilities than anything you'll find in Flic en Flac.

SOUTH TO TAMARIN

Casela World of Adventures ❻ (tel: 401 6500; www.caselapark.com; daily 9am–5pm)

focuses on fun and 'green tourism'. Sitting on the flanks of Rempart Mountain on the A3 just south of Flic en Flac, the extensive grounds include walkways over delightful ponds, a petting farm, dozens of aviaries containing 142 species of birds from all over the world – including the rare pink pigeon and Mauritius kestrel – fishing and a restaurant overlooking the west coast's rolling, cane-clothed countryside. Guided tours include photo safaris for sightings of antelope, ostrich, deer, zebra, wild boar, hyena, white rhino and hippopotamus, exciting nature escapades by camel, quad bike, buggy and Segway, and rock climbing, ziplining and a canyon swing. Animal interaction includes tortoise, giraffe and rhino feeding. Unmissable for a humbling and exciting experience is the popular attraction of walking in the wild with Casela's lions and cheetahs, accompanied by expert guides.

Pressing southwards, the massive mound of Le Morne Brabant appears to rise over Tamarin Mountain, while inland the horizon is dominated by the bulk of Rempart and the Black River mountains. Some 6km (4 miles) south of Casela you hit the coast and **Tamarin** ❼. The village, overlooking a tranquil bay, is showing encouraging signs of development as a quieter alternative to Flic en Flac and its *pensions* provide a good base for exploring the southwest.

The Veranda Tamarin Hotel right on the beach has jazz nights and a number of other nightspots have opened here in the last five or so years. The Riverland Sports Club (tel: 269 6051; www.riverland.mu), with its large pool, tennis courts, golf course, gym and pleasant restaurant, welcomes day visitors. The area was also the focus of Mauritius's first Integrated Resort Scheme (IRS) and an example of how sugar barons are turning their lands over to real estate development. Under the scheme foreigners can buy property – albeit in designated areas and for a minimum investment of US$500,000 – making it a popular place

⦿ MARTELLO TOWERS

Overlooking the public beach of La Preneuse, 2km (1 mile) or so south of Tamarin, is the best-preserved Martello Tower in Mauritius. The tower is one of five such fortifications that were constructed on the coast of Mauritius by British soldiers in the 19th century; three remain, all on the west coast: one in Pointe aux Sables (see page 137), another at La Harmonie and one at Les Salines just south of Grande Rivière Noire. The tower at La Preneuse is open as a museum (tel: 493 6648; Tue–Sat 9.30am–5pm) and is worth visiting for the guided tour and rooftop cannon.

The towers were built to withstand gunfire and have walls that are an impressive 3 metres (11ft) thick on the seaward side. They included a powder magazine and store, living quarters for 20 men, and revolving cannons on the roof. They were veritable fortresses, entrance to which could be made only by a ladder that was let down from high up the building so that attackers would find it almost impossible to enter.

The name comes from Mortella Point in Corsica, where British soldiers first came across such a tower during the French Revolution. Between 1796 and 1815 the British went on to build around 200 Martello Towers in Britain and throughout the Empire – in places as far flung as Bermuda, Ireland and the Ascension Islands.

for South African expats to live. In 2007, luxurious villas and an 18-hole golf course were completed at Tamarina Golf Estate, with the four-star Tamarina Golf & Spa Boutique Hotel, right on the water, making Tamarin a fashionable resort.

There is a good unspoilt beach but the coral reef is subdued by fresh water that flows from the central highlands via the Rempart and Tamarin rivers. The waters are famous for the black and long-beaked dolphins, and local people run dolphin-spotting tours from the bay. Between June and August waves can reach over 2 metres (6ft) and the bay is also popular with surfers.

The area around Tamarin is one of the west coast's most scenic. In summer the River Tamarin is lined with scarlet-blossomed trees, and at any time of year, especially in the late afternoon, there's definitely a romantic feel about the place. If you're a photographer this is the best time to capture the reflections of Tamarin Mountain on the river and watch the pencil-thin surf rolling in.

The River Tamarin starts at the **Tamarind Falls ❽**, where a reservoir near the small village of Henrietta on the central plateau (see page 151) supplies water for irrigation and to a hydro-electric power station some 250 metres (820ft) below. Also known as The Seven Cascades, the main falls tumble over seven stepped cliffs through a deep narrow gorge and are the tallest falls in Mauritius. The best way of getting there, particularly if you're an adrenalin junkie, is with Vertical World (tel: 697 5430; www.verticalworldltd.com), who offer trekking and canyoning trips, where they provide ropes and harnesses to abseil your way down. Beginners are first given lessons on how to abseil on dry cliffs before taking the plunge. Intermediate and hard-core enthusiasts can try their skills negotiating 45-metre (145ft) drops into ponds and smaller waterfalls followed by a strenuous hike back to the top.

Other ways of getting to Tamarind Falls are from a rough track from Henrietta or hiking from Le Pétrin in the Black River Gorges National Park (see page 142), but neither option is recommended unless you go with a

Braving a Vertical World trip.

qualified guide, such as Yanature (tel: 5251 4050, www.trekkingmauritius.com). As one the island's most beautiful walks, it's worth the trip.

BLACK RIVER AREA

Vast rectangular pans, where salt is extracted from sea water by solar evaporation, lie alongside the A3 south of Tamarin en route to **Grande Rivière Noire ❾**, at the estuary of the eponymous river that tumbles through some of the most rugged areas of Mauritius. The Rivière Noire (Black River) area is sparsely populated, with no proper towns, only small villages and hamlets. Once regarded as the poorest region in Mauritius, with a predominantly Afro-Creole population, the area now has an influx of cash-rich expatriates building luxurious homes and villa developments aplenty.

Contrasting sharply with the laid-back lifestyle of Grande Rivière Noire village and its traditional eateries and stores, which are strung out along the A3, is the gleaming Ruisseau Créole complex and the newer La Place, Cap

The Seven Coloured Earths Geopark at Chamarel.

Tamarin, with their designer shops and restaurants. Just a stone's throw from the main road of Grande Rivière Noire village is the west coast's centre for big game fishing, where trips can be arranged through **JP Henry Charters** (tel: 5729 0901; www.jph.mu). If staying elsewhere, your hotel should also be able to arrange a trip for you. Between September and March, marlin, sailfish, yahoo, yellow fin tuna and various species of shark migrate to the warm waters around Mauritius (see page 91) and feed just beyond the reef where the seabed falls abruptly to a depth of 600 metres (1,970ft).

BLACK RIVER GORGES NATIONAL PARK

Much of the beauty of the west lies inland, and nowhere more so than in the southwest corner of Mauritius, where the rugged mountains once provided a hideaway for marrons (runaway slaves), who lived in isolation, safe in the knowledge that their masters would never find them. The good news for visitors is that these mountains are now easily accessible via the **Black River Gorges National Park**, which was officially opened in 1997 in an attempt to preserve what is left of the island's disappearing native forests. The 6,575-hectare (16,250-acre) park offers something for everyone, from dedicated walkers to those who just fancy a scenic drive and a break from the beaches. This green heart of Mauritius is not a place to spot wildlife on a grand scale, but you could spend days tracking down the 150 endemic species of plants and nine endemic species of birds, including pink pigeons and Mauritius kestrels. While you may be lucky enough to spot these two endangered species, you are more likely to see the graceful white tropicbird, cuckoo shrike and Mauritius blackbird.

From the west coast you can access the northern area of the park by taking the new road which leaves the A3 just south of Grande Rivière Noire village. This leads through sugar fields to a picnic and parking area just 5km (3 miles) inland, where the **Black River Visitor Centre** ⑩ (tel: 258 0057, http://npcs.govmu.org; daily 9am–5pm) provides walking maps and information on the condition of the trails. From here you can explore the lower slopes of the park or follow the boulder-strewn Grande Rivière Noire for a strenuous 16km (10-mile) uphill trek on the 'Parakeet' and 'Macchabee' trails, which link the Gorges area with the Plaine Champagne.

The other way to get to the Black River Gorges is to drive south from Black River village to Grande Case Noyale, and then turn inland and upwards to the forested plateau of **Plaine Champagne**, named after the creamy white flowers of the privet that call to mind the white froth of champagne. This route leads to Le Pétrin, the park's other visitor centre (see page 144), but is also better suited to those interested merely in a scenic drive.

THE HIGHLANDS

From Grande Case Noyale the road winds steeply through the forested foothills to the village of **Chamarel** ⑪, offering glorious views down to the coast; if you are heading downhill, be sure to test your brakes first. The fertile Chamarel area is known for its coffee, but the reason most people come here is the waterfall and the curious geological phenomenon the village is famous for. However, with added attractions in the last five years, it is easy to spend the day absorbing the 'Spirit of Chamarel'.

Chamarel Waterfall (Cascade Chamarel) tumbles from the St Denis River into a large crater, and at 83 metres (272ft) it is the most accessible high waterfall in Mauritius. About 1km (half a mile) further is the **Chamarel Seven Coloured Earths Geopark** (tel:

483 4298, www.chamarel7colouredearth.com; daily 8.30am–5.30pm). Geologists are fascinated by this unique rolling landscape of multicoloured terrain, thought to have been caused by the uneven cooling of lava, now fenced off and beautifully landscaped with viewing platforms and timber walkways. Interestingly, the colours never fade in spite of torrential downpours.

Just beside this celebrated attraction, is the **Ebony Forest Reserve Chamarel** (tel: 460 3030, http://ebonyforest.com; daily 9am–5pm), a small patch of native forest on a hillside which opened in 2017. A steep jeep ride takes visitors for guided tours along a raised walkway, with a chance of spotting the Mauritian bulbul or paradise flycatcher among ebony trees and other rare endemic plants and trees. So far around 140,000 endemic species has been replanted here, with an aim to restore 50 hectares (123 acres) to preserve endangered flora and fauna. It's worth a visit alone for the views from Sublime Point of Le Morne (with a snack stall). At the entrance is a small but informative museum, and a restaurant.

The picturesque falls at Chamarel.

Just opposite the entrance is the **Curious Corner of Chamarel** (tel 483 4200; www.curiouscornerofchamarel.com; daily 9.30am–5.30pm). Although it has little to do with Mauritius, this house of illusions – with stairs made of piano keys, an upside-down kitchen and a mirror maze in the basement – is well run and entertaining. There's a café in the garden serving 'pyramid pizza', among outdoor curiosities.

East of Chamarel village, nestling in a verdant valley, is **La Rhumerie de Chamarel** (tel: 483 4980; www.rhumerie dechamarel.com; Mon–Sat 9.30am– 5.30pm). Bundles of cane are cut daily and brought to this state-of-the-art distillery where *fangourin*, a sweet non-alcoholic juice, is extracted, fermented and turned into high-quality Chamarel rum. Guided tours include rum tasting and the shop sells unusual Mauritian-made handicrafts and gifts, such as candles, honey, salt from Tamarin and a range of designer clothing and accessories. The popular gourmet restaurant, L'Alchimiste, serving local specialities is worth a visit – book ahead.

From the waterfalls, you can continue southwards through sugar cane via a tortuous road to the south coast emerging at Baie du Cap (see page 128), or backtrack to Chamarel village and push eastwards.

BLACK RIVER GORGES VIEWS AND WALKS

The road east of Chamarel running high up across the Plaine Champagne is narrow and lined with scrubby vegetation, offering fleeting chances to admire the scenery. It has no verge and only the occasional stopping place, though there are a couple of designated viewpoints. Most people stop at the **Black River Peak Viewpoint** ⑫, where there's usually a snack van and a man selling freshly cut fruit in the car park – the only source of refreshments for miles – among the souvenir stalls. A few miles east, a track runs a short way to the **Alexandra Falls**, with less extensive views down to the south coast, and you can hear the falls more than you can see them.

Just east of the Alexandra Falls the road veers suddenly north taking you to **Le Pétrin Information Centre** ⑬ (tel: 471 1128, http://npcs.govmu.org; Mon–Fri 9am–3pm, Sat–Sun 9am–4pm), the first port of call for those approaching the Black River Gorges area from the plateau towns and the best access point to all areas of the park. Next to the Information Centre is the **Pétrin Native Garden**, a mini showcase of native species, including many medicinal plants. Among the plants are the national flower, the *boucle d'oreille* (earring), the quirkily named *patte poule piquant* (prickly chicken legs), used for stomach upsets and liver problems, the *pots de chambre du singe* (monkey chamber pots) and the umbrella-shaped *bois de natte* tree, often draped with tree ferns, wild orchids and lichens.

GRAND BASSIN

Located 2km (1 mile) east of Le Pétrin and surrounded by forests infested

Paradis Beachcomber Golf Resort & Spa.

with monkeys, the water-filled crater of **Grand Bassin** 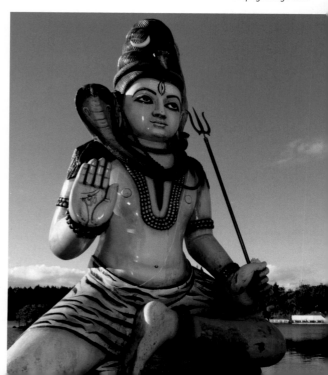 attracts crowds not so much for its natural beauty but for its religious significance. The volcanic crater is known among Hindus as Ganga Talao, and is dominated by Mauritius's tallest sculptures, of the Hindu god Shri Mangal Mahadev (Shiva), which stands 32 metres (108ft) high, and Maa Durga (Shiva's wife, Pravati in one of her nine forms), riding on a golden lion. Legend has it that the lake contains nocturnal fairies, but it was after a Hindu priest dreamed that it was linked to the sacred River Ganges that Grand Bassin became a place of pilgrimage for the annual Maha Shivaratree festival. In February/March, thousands of Hindus dressed in white walk (or bus in) from all parts of the island and converge on the lakeside to make offerings at the colourful shrines as a sign of devotion to Shiva. Bus lanes and vast car parks designed to cope with the crowds are empty the rest of the year.

To see a classic example of a volcanic cone, head 5km (3 miles) further east through tea fields to **Kanaka Crater**. Only the determined should make the challenging trek to the 180-metre (590ft) high rim for views into the choked up crater.

LE MORNE BRABANT

The peninsula of **Le Morne Brabant** ⑮ is the most westerly point of Mauritius. It is named after the 555-metre (1,820ft) mountain that rises from its centre. Runaway slaves used Le Morne as a hiding place. In 1835, soldiers were sent here to announce the abolition of slavery, but the slaves, thinking this was just another attempt to hunt them down, are said to have flung themselves to a watery grave.

The isolated spot, which was added to the Unesco World Heritage list in 2008, is now an upmarket tourist area with just seven hotels – Paradis Beachcomber Golf Resort & Spa, Dinarobin Beachcomber Golf Resort & Spa, LUX* Le Morne, St. Regis Mauritius Resort and three Rui hotels – overlooking the idyllic beach. The silence is broken only by the arrival of helicopters whizzing tourists to and from the airport and motorised caddies speeding across the golf course. Lagoons fronting the luxury hotels lure water lovers to try scuba diving, snorkelling, windsurfing, water-skiing and boat trips to the uninhabited Benitiers Island nearby. It is also the island's kitesurfing centre, with beginners' lessons offered in the protected Le Morne Bay and experienced kiters aiming for 'One Eye', with some of the best wave conditions in the world. The main lure of this romantic spot is the 5km (3 miles) of powdery beach – undoubtedly the best on the island.

You can also enjoy some fine hiking on this private mountain reserve with an experienced guide from Yanature (tel: 5251 4050, www.trekkingmauritius.com), and the island's best horse riding, either on the mountain's lower slopes or into the surf, with Haras du Morne (tel: 450 4142; www.harasdumorne.com).

⊙ Tip

At Le Pétrin Information Centre you can pick up walking maps, ask advice about the condition of the trails and the difficulty of the walks, or arrange a guided walk. There is also a large trail map outside describing several walks, each graded for ability.

Grand Bassin is a Hindu pilgrimage site.

Curepipe as viewed from Trou
aux Cerfs crater.

PLATEAU TOWNS

The heavily populated towns in central Mauritius aren't attractive, but they offer shopping bargains and an insight into ordinary Mauritian life.

In the early days of settlement, you had to be mad, bad or indifferent to live in the interior. The area was unexplored and full of runaway slaves who booby-trapped the unwary, but over the years one or two adventurers, such as German wanderer Wilhem Lechenig, settled in the uplands. When the French replaced the vacuum left by the Dutch in 1721 they found Lechenig leading a reclusive life and named the district of Plaines Wilhems after him.

Today, **Plaines Wilhems** contains all the island's significant towns other than Port Louis – that is, Beau Bassin-Rose Hill, Quatre Bornes, Vacoas-Phoenix and Curepipe. With about 30 percent of the population, it is the most densely populated district of Mauritius. The towns grew as a result of several migrations from Port Louis after fire, disease and cyclones sent people scurrying to the healthier uplands. For Mauritian professionals, they are desirable places to live, offering better facilities and housing and more shops.

While for Mauritians the plateau towns have a distinct identity, for visitors passing through they tend to merge into one and, in truth, have no immediately obvious appeal. Indeed, most tourists come here only to shop (all tour operators arrange shopping trips). However, anyone interested in discovering the 'other' Mauritius

should come here. There are pockets of architectural interest and a few minor attractions to seek out, while the cooler climate makes a change from the sultry temperatures of the coast. Getting to (or away from) the plateau towns is easy, either by taking the motorway or the Royal Road (A1), but avoid rush hours if possible. Download the free My Mauritius app from Mauritius Tourism Promotion Authority (MTPA) with an interactive map of the island (and zoom in to key towns) to help you explore.

Main attractions

Eureka
Mauritius Glass Gallery
Shopping bargains in Curepipe and Floreal
Trou aux Cerfs
Domaine des Aubineaux

Maps on pages 138, 148

Church of St Jean, near Quatre Bornes.

Tip

To get away from the noisy towns head east along the sugar cane-lined Moka road and look for the signpost indicating Le Pouce Mountain, just before Roselyn Cottage. Great walks can be had here and climbing the thumb-shaped peak is not too difficult as long as you go in dry weather.

BEAU BASSIN-ROSE HILL

Like Vacoas-Phoenix further south, Beau Bassin and Rose Hill are not so much sister towns as joined towns. **Beau Bassin** 16, the less frenetic of the two, has one or two sights worth visiting. The backstreets contain some beautifully preserved colonial houses. One such is **Le Thabor** (entrance on Swami Sivananda Street), in an area that once attracted the English aristocracy and diplomats, whose love for gracious living, horse riding and gardening earned it the name of the 'English Quarter'. Le Thabor, now a pastoral centre for the Catholic Church, has seen some famous faces in its time. During a visit here in 1836, Charles Darwin noted 'How pleasant it would be to pass one's life in such quiet abodes'. Pope John Paul II dropped in on an official visit in 1989.

In the same street are the **Balfour Gardens** (Thu–Tue 6am–6pm), giving wonderful views of the Moka Mountains across a ravine and to a waterfall that tumbles into the Grande Rivière Nord-Ouest.

You may be lucky enough to catch one of the rosy sunsets (after which **Rose Hill** 17 got its name) over Corps de Garde Mountain, which served as a lookout post for runaway slaves. Concrete, rain-stained office buildings juxtaposed with brightly painted tin-roofed shops and eateries contrast with a modern infrastructure of roads leading east to Ebène, home to the Cyber City complex, a gleaming 21st-century symbol reflecting the island's desire to become a leader in information technology in the Indian Ocean. For a local shopping experience cross the road from the Victorian post office to **Arab Town**, named after the original Muslim traders who gathered here, where Mauritian housewives barter for household goods. Back on the Royal Road, you can pass the time browsing through the jumble of wares, from statues of Hindu gods and Virgin Marys tucked between bottles of shampoo and underwear, to swathes of sari fabric.

The **Plaza Theatre**, housed in Rose Hill's Town Hall (on the right-hand side of the Royal Road as you approach from

Port Louis, and before the town centre), rarely stages plays these days but is worth noting for its Creole architecture.

DIVERSION TO MOKA

Just north of the A7, less than 4km (2 miles) east of Rose Hill, is the university town of **Moka** ⑱. The Mahatma Gandhi Institute here is home to the **Folk Museum of Indian Immigration** (tel: 403 2000; Mon–Fri 9.30am–3.30pm), which traces the life and times of the Indian cane workers brought to the island in the mid-19th century. It is popular with locals wanting to trace their ancestors, but attracts few tourists.

The president's official residence is in Moka. The magnificent **Le Château du Réduit** was built in 1748 as a country residence and retreat for wives and children of the French East India Company in the event of an invasion. Situated on a peninsula isolated by two ravines, the château overlooks lawns and is surrounded by exotic trees and shady pathways. The house is open to the public only twice a year, on specially allocated days in March and October.

Just north of Moka is the splendid Creole house of **Eureka** ⑲ (tel: 433 8477; Mon–Sat 9am–5pm, Sun 9am–3pm). It was built in 1856 by an Englishman and bought a few years later by the wealthy Franco-Mauritian Leclézio family. Apparently, Henri Leclézio, who devoted his life to restoring the mansion, cried 'Eureka' when his bid was accepted at auction. The house and birthplace of many more Leclézios has been known as Eureka ever since. The property comprises two houses and three pavilions. The main house, built of wood, is filled with colonial-style furniture. In the external stone-built kitchen, crammed with original Creole cookware, a traditional Mauritian lunch is prepared, which you can enjoy on the veranda. A path through the gardens deposits you unexpectedly by a deep ravine, and there is usually a guide waiting by the small waterfall – a lovely picnic and swimming spot – if you want to explore further down the ravine.

Moka is also home to the island's most popular shopping mall, **Bagatelle**

An interior at Eureka Plantation House.

⊘ PETER PEPPER

Eureka's esteemed neighbour was the French horticulturist Pierre Poivre (Peter Pepper; 1719–1786), who lived across the valley for a time and was most famous for the design of Pamplemousses Botanical Gardens. Born in Lyon, he travelled throughout the Far East as a missionary in his 20s, before, on a journey to the East Indies on behalf of the French East India Company in 1745, he was hit by a British cannonball on the wrist, which led to a partial arm amputation. Pierre became intendant of Île de France (Mauritius) from 1749 to 1772, assigned with wrestling the monopoly of the spice trade from the Dutch. The spice trees that he shipped from India and ornamental trees brought from the colonies were planted in Pamplemousses Botanical Garden (see page 116).

(tel: 468 8555; www.mallofmauritius.com; Mon–Thu 9.30am–8.30pm, Fri, Sat 9.30am–10pm, Sun 9.30am–3pm), set against the backdrop of the Moka Mountains. With 130 shops, a food court, bars and restaurants, locals flock here at weekends.

QUATRE BORNES

On leaving Rose Hill you enter **Quatre Bornes ㉒**, named after four sugar estates which marked the original boundaries *(bornes)*. To the west rises the Corps de Garde mountain, to the south Candos Hill, a firing range for SMF officers but also a venue for fêtes, cross-country running and other sporting events. In February, the Indian temples on the flanks of Corps de Garde come alive when Tamils undergo a remarkable ritual of body piercing at the most dramatic of festivals, Cavadee (see page 74). Little exists here to lure tourists from the beach. There's nothing grand about the Grande Route Saint Jean, which slices through town, but wander into the streets behind and you'll find a maze of bamboo-clad avenues with some

Busy stalls at Curepipe's bus station.

lovely old villas set in large gardens. Elsewhere, numerous little restaurants and snack bars provide a taste of local life. On Thursdays and Sundays traders converge for the market or *foire*, where they sell just about everything beneath multicoloured canopies.

VACOAS-PHOENIX

Vacoas and Phoenix, traditionally occupied by expats, diplomats and Franco-Mauritians because of the cooler temperatures, are essentially one big urban sprawl. Other than an animated bus station and market, there seems to be no heart to **Vacoas ㉑**. The old HMS building, once occupied by the British, now houses the Special Mobile Force headquarters. It's a fine example of colonial architecture: formerly a Scottish Presbyterian church and then a rum store in Port Louis, it was dismantled stone by stone and rebuilt in its current spot.

Phoenix ㉒ is an industrial area famous for its glassworks, the **Mauritius Glass Gallery** (tel: 696 3360; https://phoenixbev.mu/index.php/en/glass_gallery-50; Mon–Fri 8am–5pm, Sat 8am–noon; free). See artisans hand-blowing products out of recycled glass in the workshop, from ashtrays to swans, which can be purchased in the adjoining shop. This is where the glass from the town's largest drinks processing company ends up: **Phoenix Beverages** (formerly Mauritius Breweries), produces the local Phoenix Beer.

CUREPIPE

Curepipe ㉓ is the highest plateau town at 550 metres (1,840ft), and is traditionally the stronghold of the white Franco-Mauritian community, who live in grand houses hidden behind high hedges in nameless streets around the centre and in the suburbs of **Floreal** and **Forest Side**. Curepipe has the dubious distinction of having the highest rainfall on the island, and on rainy days, which is most of the time, the buildings look depressingly grey. The town's most attractive public buildings are clustered in a compound on Elizabeth Avenue near the market. Of most interest are the 1920s **Carnegie Library** Ⓐ and the impressive Creole-style **Town Hall**, which overlooks a statue of *Paul et Virginie*, central characters of the 18th-century romance inspired by a shipwreck off the Île d'Ambre. **La Sablonnière**, the Chazal family home in rue Bernardin de St-Pierre, is a classic example of colonial architecture, complete with miniature Eiffel Tower.

Most people come to Curepipe to shop. **Currimjee Arcades** (on the corner of Royal Road and Chasteauneuf Street) is not particularly large, but has a few good clothes shops downstairs. A couple of designers have outlets here, and a recent luxury addition to the scene is **L'Antiquaire** on Sauzier St, which offers a mixture of antiques and interior home design, with a café to ponder over objects d'art on site. For serious clothes shopping, you'd do better to go to Floreal shopping complex, where you can purchase quality garments made from raw imported materials, such as cashmere, cotton and silk.

Curepipe Botanic Gardens Ⓑ, in the west of town, are not as big or as impressive as the Botanic Gardens at Pamplemousses, but are perfect for a quiet stroll (daily, Oct–Apr 7am–7pm, May–Sept 8.30am–5pm).

The most famous local attraction is **Trou aux Cerfs** Ⓒ, a 300-metre (980ft) diameter crater. Formed as a result of volcanic activity millions of years ago, it is now choked with silt, water and dense vegetation. The crater is a 15-minute walk or a short taxi ride from the centre of town. The view stretches beyond the blanket of buildings to the spectacular mountains, which so far have remained untouched by developers.

To the southeast of Curepipe, along the A10 at Forest Side, **Domaine des Aubineaux** (tel: 676 3089; www.saintau bin.mu; daily 9am–5pm), the turquoise-shuttered 19th-century family home of

tea plantation owners which opened as a museum in 2000, is one of the prettiest, and least visited, colonial mansions on the island. Rooms are filled with furniture imported from around the world, old photographs and antique paintings, and visitors can enjoy a stroll through its camphor-scented gardens and a traditional lunch on the terrace.

HEADING SOUTH

The plateau towns are a good starting point for a drive south through the Black River Gorges National Park. Either take the B3 from Quatre Bornes south through Glen Park and La Marie to Le Pétrin, or the B70 from Curepipe to La Marie, where you turn left for Le Pétrin. If you're short of time, you can get a taste of the area by driving just past the village of Henrietta, where touts will show you a viewpoint overlooking Tamarind Falls (see page 141), a 15-minute hike along a rough downhill path. It's better to go with a specialist operator, such as Yemaya Adventures (tel: 5752 0046; www.yemayaadventures.com) to see the falls up close.

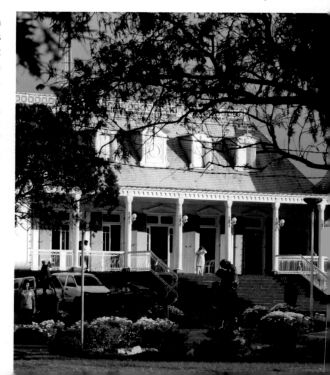

Curepipe's Town Hall is housed in an Old French-style château.

A tropical idyll at Île aux Cocos's beach lagoon.

RODRIGUES

This island is remote, laid-back and rugged. Its charm lies in its simplicity and eco-friendly credentials – and its marine environment is hard to beat.

Hidden in a lagoon almost twice its size, Rodrigues is the smallest of the Mascarene trio. Lying 560km (350 miles) east of Mauritius and shaped like a plump fish, the island is just 18km (11 miles) long and 8km (5 miles) wide. A hilly ridge runs along its length, from which a series of steep valleys extend to narrow coastal flatlands. The appeal of Rodrigues, as discovered by Prince William and friends during a holiday in 2004, lies in its rugged and simple beauty. There are stunning coves and deserted beaches. You can fish in shallow lagoons, dive and snorkel the reefs and enjoy magnificent walks through casuarina forests. The Creole people are warm and welcoming, in spite of being cut off from the rest of the world.

Rodrigues welcomes visitors who are unbothered about swift service and five-star trappings. The island has just a handful of hotels and a growing number of guesthouses. Tourists from Réunion and Mauritius often come here on three- or five-day packages that include the flight and half-board accommodation. Those who have more time can take a cabin on the *Mauritius Trochetia*, which makes regular crossings to Rodrigues (see Travel Tips), but it's not for the faint-hearted.

A PINT-SIZED CAPITAL

Rodrigues was occupied in 1726 by the French who established a tiny settlement at **Port Mathurin** . They imported slaves from Mozambique and Madagascar and settlers from French-occupied Mauritius, increasing population to just over 100 in 1804. The town, laid out in grid style in 1864 by the British, had many streets named after local administrators. After the island became autonomous in 2002, they were officially renamed, but people still use the old names.

At last count, Port Mathurin numbered around 6,000 inhabitants. The capital may be bereft of monuments,

Main attractions
Port Mathurin
Caverne Patate
François Leguat Giant
    Tortoise and Cave
    Reserve
Île aux Cocos

Map on page 154

Port Mathurin.

but a wander round will give you a taste of Mascarene Island life at its most leisurely. A good place to start is the jetty where a memorial stands to Rodriguan volunteers who fought in both World Wars. It's worth hauling yourself out of bed early for the **Saturday market** in Wolphart Harmensen Street (formerly Fishermen Lane). Many of the islanders set off from their villages in the hills at midnight to set up stalls (trading starts at around 6am) or to be the first to bargain for the best fruit and vegetables. By 10am most people have packed up and gone home. Parts of the market are given over to touristy knick-knacks, but bottles of home-grown chilli and chutneys and fruit and vegetables sell like hot cakes.

There is no tourist strip as such and most shops, no more than corrugated iron shacks with handwritten nameplates nailed to the door, are concentrated in the block bounded by Rue François Leguat, Rue de la Solidarité and Rue Hajee Bhay Fateh Mamode. A few shops in Rue Max Lucchesi sell more unusual gifts and lethal

home-bottled chillies, but for a great range of island handicrafts call at the **Careco Workshop** (tel: 831 1766; email: careco@intnet.mu; Mon–Fri 8am–4pm, Sat 8am–noon, shop only) at Camp du Roi at the back of town. Careco employs 30 people with disabilities, who make and sell original souvenirs. An apiary also produces the clear and distinctly flavoured Rodriguan honey. The workshop is a tourist attraction in its own right and tour operators feature it on every itinerary of Port Mathurin.

The main artery of the town is Rue de la Solidarité (formerly Jenner Street), one block back from the waterfront, that starts from the island's only petrol station to the west and continues over a footbridge, built to replace the Winston Churchill Bridge which collapsed in 2006, to the bus terminus in the east. At the western end of Rue de la Solidarité, tucked between shops, is the tiny six-minareted **Noor-ud-Deen Mosque**, built for the few descendants of the first Muslims who arrived in 1907 as textile merchants. In the same street is **La Résidence**, the former Island Secretary's house, with the original wide veranda shaded by a gnarled Indian almond tree. It is opposite the Rodrigues Tourism Office (tel: 832 0866; www.tourism-rodrigues.mu).

A short stroll east leads to the Anglican **St Barnabas Church**, surrounded by gardens and trees. Most Rodriguans are Catholics and the little **St Cœur de Marie Church** in Rue Mamzelle Julia sees a regular congregation. Crossing the footbridge over the River Cascade you stumble across the spot where Rodrigues' first settlers, led by François Leguat, set up camp in 1691.

Further up river towards Fond La Digue, the latanier huts of the 1940s once occupied by 'women of easy virtue' have been replaced by Port Mathurin's main hotel, the simple, Creole-style **Escale Vacances**, set in a deep-wooded valley overlooking the river. There are some lovely walks from here (some uphill) along jungly boulder-strewn tracks – sturdy shoes are advisable.

AROUND PORT MATHURIN

In 1761 a British fleet arrived and camped on a strip of beach at **Anse aux Anglais ➋** (English Bay) east of Port Mathurin and, meeting with little opposition from the handful of French inhabitants, stayed for six months. The Englishness of Rodrigues was compounded in 1901 when cablemen from the Eastern Telegraph Company (later Cable & Wireless) laid a submarine telegraph cable linking the island with Mauritius, thus completing the line of communication between Australia and Europe. There are good views across Port Mathurin from the headland where French and British astronomers recorded the Transit of Venus in 1761 and 1874.

A cluster of small guesthouses overlooks the beach at Anse aux Anglais and at low tide the lagoon is a favourite haunt of groups of fisherwomen, known as *piqueuses ourites*, who make a living spearing octopus, which they hang out to dry in the sun. A stiff uphill climb from Anse aux Anglais, via the tranquil beachside bungalows of well-to-do Rodriguans and Mauritians at Caverne Provert, leads to a fairly flat area where acacia trees border the road. From the headland are resplendent views over **Grand Baie**. You can follow the road up from Grand Baie beach until it peters out to a narrow uphill track towards the sweeping deserted beach at **Baladirou**. A less strenuous way of getting there is to take a 40-minute boat ride along the coast from Port Mathurin.

Just 2km (1 mile) west of Port Mathurin is **Baie aux Huîtres ➌** (Oyster Bay), an enormous bay surrounded by hills and thick casuarina forest. For the best views, drive up to **Allée Tamarin**, a hamlet at the back of the bay.

INLAND FROM PORT MATHURIN

Port Mathurin's bus station and taxi stand are a boon for independent travellers and a handy location to start a journey inland, around fearsome hairpin bends, to the spine of the island where little villages overlook the north and south lagoons.

A vegetable seller at Port Mathurin's market.

You can jump on a bus, thumb a lift or drive yourself to the Meteorological Station on the windswept **Pointe Canon** for panoramic views over Port Mathurin and the lagoon. Here a cannon, erected by British troops during World War II, points out to sea and is oddly juxtaposed beside a white statue of the Virgin Mary, La Reine de Rodrigues. If you're around on 15 August, the approach road and hills are a riot of colour with islanders trekking towards the statue to celebrate the Feast of the Assumption.

The forest at **Solitude** is 2km (1 mile) south of Port Mathurin on the Mont Lubin road. Bounded by deep valleys and thick with eucalyptus trees, the forest also has small copses of jamrosa and mango trees, which provide food for the Rodriguan fruit bats that swoop down to feed on them at dusk.

Mont Lubin ❹, a busy little village of tumbledown shops, gives the impression of being at the top of the island, but the highest point is actually nearby Mont Limon at 398 metres (1,289ft). Most visitors drop in at the **Women's Handicraft Centre** to watch women weaving baskets from vacoas leaves and perhaps buy one of the finished articles on display, before making their way to Pointe Coton and the beautifully isolated beaches of the east.

Heading westwards on the Mont Lubin road, it's worth making a detour to Rodrigues' biggest church at **St Gabriel**. The church was built by locals in 1939 under difficult conditions. Specially trained donkeys carried most of the sand from the coast to the heights of St Gabriel and voluntary helpers, including women and children, brought cement, lime, blocks of coral, corrugated iron and timber up narrow mountain paths. It can be visited any time, but for a splash of colour, music and singing, get there in time for 9am Mass on Sunday.

The 5km (3-mile) stretch of twisting road between the hamlets of Petit Gabriel, Quatre Vents and Mangues is peppered with glimpses of translucent blue lagoons and scenes of rural life.

The next main settlement after Mangues is the large and noisy village of **La Ferme**, which has a small stadium where Pope John Paul II held mass

A vacoa basketwork weaver on Rodrigues.

during his visit to Rodrigues in 1989. You need to pass through La Ferme to reach **Cascade Pistache** (2km/1 mile west of the village), an enormous crater hewn out of granite surrounded by grassy hills. The waterfall that tumbles into Rivière Pistache is particularly beautiful after heavy rains. Alternatively, take the road northwards from La Ferme to Baie du Nord for a scenic 9km (5-mile) coastal drive back to Port Mathurin, passing isolated homesteads swathed in poinsettias, hibiscus and marigolds, and causeways filled with mangroves at Baie Malgache.

IN SEARCH OF THE SOLITAIRE

For an invigorating walk (not for the faint-hearted or claustrophobic) through dark passages studded with stalagmites and stalactites, head for the coral caves in the southwest corner of the island at **Caverne Patate** ❺ (tel: 832 1062; daily 9–11am and 1–3pm). The caves, some 18 metres (60ft) below ground, have fascinated naturalists ever since the first official exploration in 1786 when bones, believed to

be those of the dodo, were found by a French captain. Later searches by British naturalists in 1894 led to more bone discoveries and comparisons with earlier findings proved that they belonged to the solitaire, described by François Leguat back in 1691. According to early accounts the caves contain 'superb petrifications of an infinite variety of shapes all different from each other', but modern visitors can, depending on their imagination, discern carved rock lookalikes of Winston Churchill and the Great Wall of China. The tour takes around one hour, with professional guides who issue visitors with hard hats and torches. Do come with sturdy shoes. You complete the 500-metre (550-yd) circuit and emerge at the exit where locals stand waiting to sell coral-carved solitaires and souvenirs.

Better caves containing impressive formations of stalactites and stalagmites, some sprinkled with a yet to be identified quartz-like substance, can be explored with guides at the nearby **François Leguat Giant Tortoise and Cave Reserve** ❻ (tel: 832 8141, http://www.

The view from Mont Limon.

⦿ VOYAGES AND ADVENTURES

The first settlers on Rodrigues were a band of Huguenots (all men) led by François Leguat. Fleeing religious persecution in France, they set sail from Holland in search of their own island paradise. Travellers' tales drew them to the Mascarene archipelago and, in 1691, they landed on the uninhabited island of Rodrigues. They lived for the next two years on 'very wholesome and luxurious foods which never caused the least sickness'.

During his stay, François Leguat wrote the island's first guidebook, *Voyages and Adventures*, a classic tome documenting the island's unique flora and fauna. In it he describes how the beaches were covered with tortoises weighing over 136kg (300 lb) so that he literally used their shells as stepping stones to reach the sea. Leguat's name would have sunk into oblivion were it not for the opening in 2007 of an amazing reserve named after him, the **François Leguat Giant Tortoise and Cave Reserve** at Plaine Caverne. Conservation programmes to restore Rodrigues' native habitat are paying off here with the planting of thousands of endemic plants plus a colony of more than 1,500 giant Aldabra tortoises shipped over from Mauritius. Explore caves with qualified guides and visit the only museum devoted to Rodrigues' history, fauna and flora.

tortoisescavereserve-rodrigues.com; daily 9am–5pm). Well-lit timber walkways and handrails make this a safer, easier option for most people, especially children. Visitors also get the chance to stroke a giant tortoise grazing on the plains outside.

For the active, the **Tyrodrig Zipline Adventure** on Montagne Malgache (tel: 499 6970; email: worldcanopy@yahoo.fr; daily 9am–5pm) is a 30-minute ride across deep ravines stuffed with thirsty plants – the highest is 100 metres/328ft above the ground. They also have a Nepalese bridge across Cascade Pistache, which opened in 2017, with a pendulum swing jump for those who dare.

THE SOUTH

The 6km (4-mile) journey from Mont Lubin to Port Sud-Est must rank as the most beautiful in the entire island. The road snakes its way down hillsides, twisting and turning along a series of hairpin bends, each giving way to vistas of the lagoons around Port Sud-Est, dotted with small coral atolls. Your journey's end is the **Mourouk Ebony Hotel** (https://www.mourouk-ebony-hotel.com), sitting atop

Sundown over Cascade Pistache.

a gentle cliff and as isolated as Rodrigues itself. It has good diving facilities and is a centre for wind- and kitesurfing. The nearest shop, a crimson-red shack, sells basics such as bread, water, sweets and cigarettes; the nearest village is at Songes, where cyclone-proof houses are scattered on the hillsides like dominoes.

Were it not for fishing, life around **Port Sud-Est** ❼ would grind to a halt. As it is, it's pretty inert except in the mornings, when fishermen wade out to the lagoon to retrieve cages they've left out for a couple of days, which they hope have trapped lobster, prawn and crab. Now and again they venture out in pirogues and an opportunity to go with them (for a small fee) should not be missed.

Hikers might enjoy the walking trails, native plants and views of the south coast, including the pretty beach of Petit Gravier, in the **Grande Montagne Nature Reserve**. The Information Centre (tel: 831 4558, http://www.mauritian-wildlife.org; Mon–Fri 8am–3pm, Sat 8am–10.45am; guided tour at 9.30am, other times by arrangement) at Grande Montagne provides maps and there is a museum displaying solitaire and giant tortoise bones.

POINTE COTON AND THE EAST

Cotton Bay Hotel ❽ overlooks the island's best swimming beach and is flanked by low coral cliffs. The hotel, popular with holiday-makers and honeymooners, makes a comfortable base for walks to **Roche Bon Dieu**, a sandstone outcrop said to have fallen from heaven. For more superb beaches you could pant your way south along cliff-top pathways to **Anse Ally**, **Saint François** and **Baie de l'Est**. The walk veers inland from here into the protected forest at **Tasman**. The area is fenced off to prevent grazing cattle from eating young shoots, but the watchman will let you in. The pathway, bounded by great forests of casuarina trees and acacias, runs parallel to the coast, crossing a plateau of dead coral where massive white rollers pound the reef. From here the paths rise and dip into the lovely coves and bays of **Grand Anse**, **Trou d'Argent** and **Anse Bouteille** before linking up to Port Sud-Est. Looking out to sea from this, the most easterly point of Rodrigues, the nearest landfall is the western coast of Australia 5,500km (3,400 miles) away.

SLEEPY LAGOON ISLANDS

Île aux Cocos ❾ (11km/7 miles from Port Mathurin) is the last refuge of the fody and brush warbler, which have virtually disappeared from Rodrigues. This idyllic island, one of 18 floating inside the lagoon, promises an all too short experience of desert island living. Softspoken fishermen ferry you to sugary white beaches where the only resident, a government watchman, leads a Robinson Crusoe existence in a large bungalow. You can camp out for the day beneath the trees. To visit the island you need a permit from Discovery Rodrigues (tel: 832 1062; email: discoveryrodrigues@intnet. mu) in Port Mathurin, which most tour operators will arrange for you (see Travel Tips, A–Z).

Fishermen from Port Sud-Est make trips to equally beautiful **Cat Island**, ideal for swimming and snorkelling, and **Hermitage Island**, one of the most picturesque of all Rodrigues' satellite islands.

A coconut grove under a stormy sky at Port Sud Est.

Belouve forest lodging.

St-Denis from La Montagne.

A waterfall and peaks along the Mat River.

RÉUNION

This may be a Gallic outpost, but you won't find scenery or a local culture like this in France.

Chillis at Marché de Saint Paul.

Réunion, born three million years ago as a result of an undersea volcanic eruption, consists of two great volcanic mountain masses. The oldest, in the northwest, covers two-thirds of the total area of the island and rises to form the Piton des Neiges, which, at 3,070 metres (10,072ft), is the highest peak in the whole southwest Indian Ocean. Over time, the Piton des Neiges, an extinct volcano, collapsed and eroded to form three caldera-like valleys, or cirques. Piton de la Fournaise (2,632 metres/8,635ft), one of the most active volcanoes in the world (but well-monitored), formed the more recent mountain mass, in the southeast around 530,000 years ago. Almost half the island has been designated a Unesco Natural World Heritage site.

Réunion has its share of popular beaches, but the biggest thrill for tourists is taking in the beauty of the verdant cirques and the eerie landscape of the volcano. The island cannot compete with Mauritius in terms of beaches and luxury hotels, but it has many more conventional sightseeing opportunities in the shape of museums, sugar factories and well-preserved colonial and Creole architecture. Many people come just for the adventure sports, which are the big thing here – from trekking, mountain biking and horse riding, to kayaking, canyoning and paragliding.

Eighty percent of Réunion's visitors are French. They see the island as an extension of the motherland and feel comfortable with the left-hand drive Renaults and Peugeots, the smooth roads, the out-of-town hypermarkets, and the bistros and boulevards. They feel at home with euros and in the mountain gîtes, can even bring their dogs with them, and of course everyone speaks French.

Local gecko.

The tropical warmth and breathtaking scenery are intoxicating and the Réunionnais are an attractive, gentle people. Ethnically a fascinating mélange of Malagasy, African, European, Chinese and Indian, they are taking inspiration from their counterparts in Mauritius and rediscovering their heritage.

Réunion remains little-known in the English-speaking world and, for the discerning traveller, in many ways it is the most fascinating of the Mascarene trio.

An old Creole gentleman.

THE RÉUNIONNAIS

The melting-pot phenomenon is seen more clearly in Réunion than anywhere else in the Western Indian Ocean.

The culture and people of Réunion can be defined in two words – 'melting pot'. The over-riding importance of the French language and culture throughout most of the island's history has meant that religious and ethnic differences were always subordinate to the notion of integration with the mother country. The assimilationist tendency that characterised the period from 1946 to 1981 hindered the emergence of a separate Réunionnais identity, but today the inhabitants happily juggle several identities and recent years have seen a cultural and religious resurgence among Réunionnais of Tamil, Muslim and other non-Christian minorities.

THE FOUNDATIONS OF SOCIETY

The first inhabitants of Réunion were a few exiled Frenchmen and a handful of Malagasy. The birth of their Franco-Malagasy children heralded the beginning of a process of *métissage* (ethnic mixing) that has always characterised Réunionnais society.

In the 17th century, more settlers arrived in dribs and drabs from Europe and Asia, and pirates relocated to what was then called Bourbon from their old haunts in Madagascar. With the development of coffee cultivation, and the importation of slaves from East Africa and Madagascar, 18th-century Bourbon became a society where blacks outnumbered whites. During this period the Kreol language was in its formative stage. Some whites, however, became pauperised as the subdivision of landholdings between siblings forced the less fortunate to the higher regions, to farm the inhospitable terrain of Les Hauts. In 1830 land concessions were made for Salazie, and in 1840 for Cilaos, but Mafate, the largest of the cirques, was still too difficult to access.

Divali in St André.

The 19th century saw the arrival of sugar cane culture in Réunion – Charles Desbassyns introduced the first steam-powered machinery – and other *grands blancs*, or powerful white families, joined him to form the island's plantocracy. By mid-century cane had become the island's principal crop. On 20 December 1848 slavery was abolished, and many of the new free men established themselves in Les Hauts as blacksmiths and charcoal makers. Among the indentured workers subsequently imported to Réunion were Malagasy, Indians and Chinese. A few Comorians and Yemenis were also brought.

Towards the end of the 19th century, free immigrants began to arrive from Cantonese- and Hakka-speaking regions of China. They gravitated into hawking and shopkeeping in the north and south of the island respectively, establishing community networks for themselves and

> The term zorèys ('ears'), used for the French living on Réunion, is said to originate from the habit new arrivals had of cupping their hand behind their ear as they attempted to understand the Kreol language.

Réunion's demographics reflect its varied background.

schools for their children. Traders arrived from Gujarat and Bombay over the same period. This last wave of chiefly commercial immigrants adopted a dualistic pattern of socialisation: absorbing one culture while retaining another. To this day, these communities are perhaps the most self-enclosed and distinctive within a largely integrationist culture.

SOCIAL REALITIES

Today, roughly three-quarters of Réunion society is composed of métis – persons of mixed origins. There are few signs of racial antagonism, although a few white families still wield an economic influence disproportionate to their numbers. They are the remnants of the large landowning class, some of whom have moved into banking and import/export businesses. Professionals and senior civil servants, including many recent arrivals from France, have swelled their numbers. Their luxury homes are in the best quarters of St-Denis and St-Pierre, and they keep holiday villas in cool Cilaos or Hell-Bourg for the summer and often have a beach house at St-Gilles that they use in winter.

The less well-off whites, or petits blancs, who have been living in Les Hauts for generations, have evolved into a tight-knit but distinctive community, attached to the traditional agricultural and handicraft occupations of their forebears.

The Réunionnais today are differentiated less by colour than by creed. The descendants of Indian traders, most of whom are Muslims, are known as Zarabs. Almost a quarter of all Réunionnais are of South Indian descent; their forebears were mostly Tamil-speaking Hindus. Freed from the enforced Catholicism of the colonial period, many Tamils are rediscovering their religious roots. This group are also called Malbars. The largely Catholic Chinese of Réunion are increasingly intermarrying, and may not be a distinctive community for much longer.

The newest constituent of society are the zorèys from mainland France, who help to run the modern state as civil servants, teachers and the like. The status of Réunion as a département of France means that any EU national can apply to work and live on the island, just as the Réunionnais have the right to travel to, work and stay in France. The plum posts occupied by zorèys sometimes provoke resentment among the Réunionnais, just as the mainland French occasionally give vent to less than charitable assessments of the laid-back approach of the islanders.

Despite the preponderance in Réunion of individuals of mixed ethnicity, the African origins of a significant proportion of the population are clearly evident. Descendants of these Afro-Creoles are sometimes known as kafs (from the Arab kafir or heathen); a woman is a kafrine.

Society as a whole is characterised by dependence: the population (totalling 850,000 in 2015) is young – about 40 percent is below the age of 25 – and unemployment in Réunion currently stands at 29 percent. A significant proportion of the population relies on social security payments. The evident disparities between the haves and have-nots have created latent tensions that occasionally erupt: in February 1991 riots in Chaudron, a disadvantaged suburb of the capital, brought these social problems into sharp relief.

Many of these problems are structural – the high living standards that the French have fostered in Réunion mean that entrepreneurship of the kind that has given neighbouring Mauritius a dynamic economy is untenable in a society where wage rates price the islanders out of the market. The political relationship with France is not often questioned and is presumably sufficiently important to the French to make the prospect of jettisoning what must be a financial burden unthinkable. But as long as this is the case, Réunion has little prospect of becoming an economically viable entity.

Culturally, Réunion benefits greatly from membership of the Francophone world. Sophisticated media links bring French television into every home and reinforce the commonality of the French–Creole diaspora through the diffusion of French Caribbean rhythms and style.

CULTURE AND RELIGION

Hindu beliefs and practices on Réunion date from the settlement of plantation labourers of Indian origin who built small temples near the sugar estates, some of which can still be seen. The goddesses Draupadi, Mariammen and Kalimai are celebrated in annual festivals, and several Hindu temples in Réunion regroup all three. The monkey-god Hanuman used to be celebrated with an annual dance through the streets led by a devotee painted in bright colours, known as the *jacot* (monkey). Traditional funeral rites, or *samblani*, continue to be performed by Tamils.

The older generation of Chinese in Réunion still celebrate their own rites of passage, and they have built a number of pagodas on the island. Ancestor worship is practised on small altars in the home, and the pagoda at St-Pierre is used by Hakkas for honouring the souls of the dead in an annual ceremony. Distinctive Chinese tombs can be found in several of the island's cemeteries.

There are 38 mosques and prayer rooms on the island, the oldest of which dates from 1905. Most Muslims here regularly attend Friday prayers and practise fasting during the month of Ramadan. Many also pay *zakat* (tithes) to the mosque. Most women of Islamic faith in Réunion wear Western dress, although a minority have adopted a head-covering or the veil.

The African and Malagasy cultural heritage is omnipresent – in the faces, music, language and place names of the island. The *maloya* is a former dance of slaves, and many Kreol words derive from Bantu and other languages associated with East Africa. Malagasy place names in Réunion are particularly evocative. Cilaos is said to mean 'the place where cowards do not go' and Cimendef, at Mafate, is so named after a Malagasy who escaped – it means 'he who cannot be

Local entertainment.

Ⓞ DANCING THE MALOYA

Maloya and sega music are the two major traditional music genres that evolved among slaves and developed into contemporary forms in Réunion. While Réunion's sega resembles the sega typical of Mauritius and the *moutya* of Seychelles, *maloya* retains a unique Réunionnais sound, and was inscribed on the Unesco list of Intangible Cultural Heritage of Humanity in 2009. The word 'maloya' is said to come from a Malagasy expression meaning 'fed up', and employs instruments that reflect its African roots: the large *roulèr* barrel drum, flat *kayamb* rattle and *piker* bamboo percussion. French Caribbean *zouk* can also be heard on the airwaves.

a slave'. A few families of Malagasy origin continue to practise traditional funeral rites, known as *velasa*, and ancestor worship.

A MULTITUDE OF FAITHS

For many years, the practice of non-Christian religions was frowned on in Réunion and, partly as a result of this, some Hindu traditions have been absorbed into Christian celebrations. The cult of Mariammen, for example, is often assimilated with worship of the Virgin Mary, while Krishna's birthday is associated with that

Chinese New Year in St Denis.

of Jesus Christ. The veneration of St-Expédit (nominally Catholic, but not recognised by the Vatican) is symbolic of the confluence of religious practices found in Réunion, for the saint is also identified as a manifestation of Kali.

Catholicism itself has developed a particular style in Réunion where Christians visit shrines such as that of the Black Virgin at Notre Dame de la Salette to honour a promise made in exchange for a request exacted, in a striking resemblance to Hindu practices. This is just one of hundreds of shrines to the Virgin scattered around the island, always bedecked in flowers and ceramic *remerciements* (thank you notes).

Chinese Catholics continue to adhere to Buddhist rituals in the home, and to venerate

their ancestors in the colourful pagodas dotted around the island.

Many folk practices and superstitions brought by immigrants have survived the centuries of French acculturation. Hindus believe that prayers made to specific gods and goddesses can cure certain diseases, while Muslims trace some forms of illness to possession by evil spirits, or *djinns*. The word for an Indian sorcerer is *pusari* in Réunion, and given that Tamil priests are known as *pujaris*, this suggests a crossover of religious and magical practices. A sorcerer of Malagasy origin is called an *ombiasy*.

Formulas for casting black magic spells have circulated in Réunion for many years. *Petit Albert*, the collection of magic spells imported to the region from Europe, and the brand of African black magic known as *gris gris* in the islands, still have many practitioners.

The belief in wandering, troubled souls is also very common in Réunion and may originate in the Malagasy concept of the *matoatoa*. People who have died of the plague or of other epidemic diseases are believed to be possessed of special powers and cemeteries in St-Denis and at Le Port, where such graves are found, are frequented by believers at auspicious times.

PUBLIC HOLIDAYS AND FESTIVALS

The first Hindu festival of the year, Pandyale, takes place in early January when fire-walking ceremonies are held. Cavadee, the spectacular body-piercing festival, takes place in January/ February, when fire-walking is also part of the proceedings. Hindus honour Mariammen, a goddess associated with Tamils, in May each year. Kali's festival in August is marked by the sacrifice of cockerels and goats. Chinese New Year is also celebrated in Réunion, in February/March, and in September the mid-autumn festival provides an opportunity to taste moon cake. The Muslim trader families, or *zarabs*, celebrate Eid ul Fitr and Eid ul Kebir, when animal sacrifices are made. Some rituals are grounded in very real, local fears: on 15 August each year pilgrims go to the shrine of the Madonna with a Parasol, Ste-Rose, to pray that there will be no volcanic eruption. The abolition of slavery in 1848 is commemorated annually by a public holiday on 20 December.

CASES CRÉOLES

Réunion, Mauritius and Seychelles are home to a number of diverse colonial-era buildings, all of which reflect the islands' histories and ways of life.

The architectural heritage of the Indian Ocean islands is fast disappearing, as the once ubiquitous delightful wooden homes, with their long verandas, are being replaced by modern concrete buildings that have little of their predecessors' appeal. Do take the opportunity on your visit to appreciate the charm and ingenuity of the remaining colonial homes, from the humble *case créole* to the grandiose plantation house.

The design of the typical *case créole* dates from the 18th century when settlers employed marine carpenters to build their houses from local wood. The *bardeaux*, or shingle roof, still a feature of many Creole houses, and the plank-lined outer walls were clearly inspired by boats. Local weather conditions also played an important role in the development of building styles. The triangular and porch roofs were designed to protect from heavy tropical rains, while the *varangue*, or veranda, was airy to combat the humidity and heat of the tropics and formed an extension of the main living area. The inhabitants added their own decorative touches, which over time have given the Creole house its distinctive style. The designs of the *lambrequins*, mantle decorations that help to shield the house from the elements, often have a unique motif which was the owner's cultural trademark. One of the finest examples of a *case créole*, complete with a type of garden extension known as a *guetali*, can be seen at Villa Folio, in Hell-Bourg (see page 224).

In the 18th century wealthy merchants built more grandiose versions of the *case créole* close to centres of commerce, and enclosed them within ornate railings. Some of these stylish and historic houses can still be seen in the backstreets of Port Louis and in Rue de Paris in St-Denis. As the middle classes moved to new residential areas, Creole architecture became more refined and was complemented by elegant lawns and gardens. The towns of the Mauritian central plateau, from Rose Hill to Curepipe, are still dotted with the well-maintained former residences of affluent 19th-century colonists.

The most impressive of the island residences are the grand homes built by the sugar barons and planters of valued export crops such as vanilla and spices. The plantation houses, with their turrets, columns and balustrades, manage to harmonise the classic features of Creole design with the evident pretensions of their owners. The verandas are enclosed by colonnades and extend around the house. The delicate lacework *lambrequins* above the numerous windows alleviate the solemnity of these 18th- and early 19th-century châteaux. Most are still privately owned, but visitors to Mauritius can take a guided tour of the Maison Eureka in Moka, to see how the plantocracy really lived, or dine at stately St Aubin in the south. Holiday-makers in Mahé, Seychelles,

A Creole house in the village of Cilaos.

can stay at La Résidence Bougainville, which has been converted into a guesthouse with a sea view, or at the Château St-Cloud on La Digue, a vanilla plantation house dating from the Napoleonic period.

The seats of government of the French administrators, much enlarged and restored over succeeding years, particularly Le Réduit (the Mauritian president's official residence), retain the simple beauty of colonial architecture, while providing an appropriately stately venue for visiting dignitaries. At the other end of the scale, look out for the quaint stone post offices that the British built in Mauritius and Seychelles. One enduring and endearing feature of the insular landscape is the Creole corner shop, with its gaily coloured walls, hand-painted hoardings and corrugated roof.

RÉUNION CUISINE

French cuisine is the norm at most hotels and restaurants, and Chinese, Indian and Italian food is on offer in the bigger centres, but traditional home cooking is Creole.

The food may appear to have a strongly French influence – *café au lait* and croissants for breakfast, *croque monsieur* (toasted cheese and ham sandwich) for lunch and *civet* (a type of stew) for supper are all standard fare. Nevertheless, even in Réunion Creole cuisine holds sway. Its absence from some of the bars and bistros of St-Denis or St-Gilles-les-Bains may send you searching, but head for the cirques and you'll find local people living on *carris* (mild curries), as well as white rice or yellow rice (cooked with turmeric), pulses (red or white haricot beans, lentils or peas) accompanied by a variety of *rougails* (the hot and spicy chutney known as *chatini* in Mauritius) and *achards* (pickled spiced vegetables).

Meat curries are usually made with chicken, beef or pork, but one of the tastiest curries you'll find is *cabri masalé* (goat masala). The meat is cooked very slowly in a rich flavoursome sauce and melts in the mouth. Fish and seafood are also curried, *zourit* (octopus) and prawn being favourite ingredients.

VERSATILE VEGETABLES

Vegetarians are well catered for in the local markets, which are stocked with an enormous variety of fresh fruit and vegetables. However, ordering a vegetarian meal in a Creole restaurant is a little more tricky. Meat or fish features are central to many main dishes, but a number of starters and accompaniments are vegetable based. Vegetable or lentil *carris* can be made if requested and *salade de palmiste* (heart of palm) appears on some menus, but check before ordering any other salads, as they may contain pieces of meat or fish. *Tarte brèdes chou chou*, a creamy pie made from spinach-like greens on a crusty pastry base, is a filling alternative.

Chou chou (also known as *christophine*) is a very versatile vegetable, which tastes a bit like watery courgette. It is added to cakes, jams and

Measuring vanilla.

⊘ SWEET TREATS

Lots of interesting goodies exist to satisfy the sweet-toothed in Réunion. At St-Gilles-les-Bains there are several places just right for that sugary bite: two to look out for are Chez Loulou (86 rue Général de Gaulle) and Au Vieux Quimper (Place Paul Julius Benard). Try *macatias*, a local version of a butter-free brioche that can come plain or jazzed up with chocolate chips, coconut or both. Other sweet treats include *tartes*, made with pawpaw or mango, honey biscuit rings called *bonbons au miel*, Indian-style *goolab* glistening with sugary syrup and flour-based cakes called *napolitains*.

curries, served *au gratin*, as *brèdes chou chou*, or just plain boiled. The plant stems can be split and dried and used to make woven handicrafts.

VANILLA

Réunion is one of the world's leading producers of vanilla and it plays an important role in the island's cuisine. You'll find vanilla thrown into sweet and savoury sauces, rum-based liqueurs such as Pause Café and sometimes added to tea and coffee. If you want to see how it is grown and processed, visit the Vanilla Cooperative in Bras-Panon (see page 202).

crêpes (pancakes). Look out for *pâtisseries*, *croissanteries* and even 'sandwicheries' at out-of-town hypermarkets such as Jumbo or Super U, where you can take your pick from some mouth-watering displays of savoury Creole snacks; *bonbons piment* (spicy chickpea cakes), vegetable or meat *samousas*, stuffed chilli peppers and *brinjals* (aubergine fritters) are piled high and sold cheap.

RUM PUNCH OR WINE

Elements of Réunion's cuisine are found in drinks of all kinds. *Rhum arrangé*, literally, 'arranged rum', is a

Rhum arrangé.

HOME COOKING

For a taste of real Réunionnais cuisine, track down a *ferme auberge* (farmhouse inn) where you could try traditional offerings. A typical tourist menu at around €15 might consist of a set number of courses such as *gratin chou chou* for starters, followed by a fish curry or duck in vanilla sauce and finished off with *fondant au chocolat* – also with vanilla sauce. One of the most popular *ferme auberges* is in Bras-Panon at Chemin Rivière du Mat (tel: 0262 51 53 76), run by Madame Eva Annibal (booking is essential).

SNACKS AND SWEETS

There's no shortage of mobile food stalls along the popular west coast beaches selling filled baguettes and sweet and savoury Breton-style

mind-blowing concoction of rum and fruit that is left for months to macerate and mature in a mixture of spices. Marginally easier on the brain cells is *punch créole*, usually rum based, made from a range of fruits and berries, cane syrup and juice.

Grapes have long been grown in Cilaos and the region is the only wine-producing area in Réunion; you'll find some decent table wines there made from the Cot, Pinot Noir and Chenin grapes. In 1991 a small group of vine growers formed Le Chai de Cilaos Cooperative, which markets and exports the wines to France, but if you're in Cilaos then drop in for a winetasting session. The dry white wine goes well with grilled fish and cheese, the smooth sweet white is an excellent dessert wine and the fullbodied red from the Cot grape goes well with red meat.

Waterfall at Anse Des Cascades,
south of Piton Ste Rose.

VOLCANIC HABITATS

With large swathes of virgin rainforests still remaining, Réunion's dramatic volcanic terrain provides refuge for a wide variety of wildlife.

The high rugged mountains and deeply chasmed gorges of Réunion have ensured that, unlike on the other Mascarenes, much of the island's original forests still exist and are in good condition. Nevertheless, this hasn't stopped the demise of some spectacular wildlife, namely, as with Mauritius and Rodrigues, the giant tortoise, flightless birds and gaudy parrots.

Réunion once had a bird that was thought to be a white dodo or solitaire but recent discoveries have revealed that this creature, which was about the size of a turkey, was a flightless ibis. In the 17th century, before the advent of travel guides and bird books, the names of birds were not fixed and were sometimes used to indicate a complete species, hence the term dodo came to be used for any flightless bird.

Other birds lost to Réunion have been the crested starling, called the *huppe*, which was last seen in the middle of the 19th century, and a beautiful russet brown parrot with a lilac head that died out in the late 18th century. It is believed that these creatures' habitats had mainly been in the lowland rainforests, which had fallen under the settlers' axes for coffee, cotton and spice plantations.

A yellow-streaked tenrec.

IN THE COOKING POT

Considering the amount of high altitude rainforest Réunion has, it has long puzzled naturalists why the island should have lost its equivalent to the pink pigeon, kestrel, echo parakeet (see page 85), forest fody and fruit bat, the latter of which can be found in great numbers on the other Mascarenes. It has been suggested that extinction rates are higher on French-owned islands because much of the wildlife is heavily hunted for the cooking pot! Today, the best place to see specimens and models of Réunion's extinct wildlife is in the Natural History Museum at St-Denis.

NEWCOMERS TO RÉUNION

Many species of mammal were brought to the island by settlers mainly for food, including wild boar, lemurs, squirrels and hares, but most have died out, although not the boar. The Javan deer that arrived in 1761 had already been hunted to extinction by 1793. Regrettably, they were reintroduced in the 1980s to Plaine des Chicots and Bébour. They feed on the saplings of native trees, preventing natural regeneration of the forest.

One of the most interesting of the introduced mammals is the tenrec (*tenrec ecaudatus*), a hedgehog-like insectivore which comes from Madagascar and is known locally as *tang*. Brought over for the dinner table, it is still on the menu in some rural areas, although many meet their end flattened on the road. The female produces huge litters, the record being 34 young in one litter. Apparently only one egg has to be fertilised, which then divides repeatedly so all the young are the same sex and genetically identical.

The *musaraigne* or Indian house shrew, an omnivorous mammal that can also be found on Mauritius and Rodrigues, is common over much of the island and preys on reptiles and invertebrates. Apart from the rats and feral cats, similar to the spotted tabby African wild-cat, there are few mammals on Réunion and none that are indigenous.

ISLAND BIRDS

Despite the rats that steal birds' eggs and the cats that have catching birds down to a fine art, there are large numbers of native birds that should be easy to spot, especially in Roche Écrite or the Forêt de Bébour. The stonechat, or *tec-tec* (the exact sound of its call) is the most common, appearing everywhere except the low coastal areas of the north and west. You are more likely to see a paradise flycatcher – known locally as the *vierge* because it has a bluish-purple head and is believed to have seen the Virgin Mary – in Réunion than in Mauritius. The same goes for the island's black bulbul (*merle pays*) and two species of white-eye.

The Mascarene cave swiftlet lives here too and can often be seen feasting on clouds of flying insects. However, swallows are quite rare, keeping to the lowland east of the island and Cilaos. The bird you are least likely to see is the rare Réunion cuckoo-shrike (*tuit-tuit*), which hides in the forest of Plaine des Chicots above St-Denis.

Soaring or gliding over forests and in the cirques, the Réunion harrier or *papang* is the largest and most spectacular bird on the island. A bird of prey with a wingspan of more than a metre (3ft), the adult male is stunning in its grey, white and black plumage; the females are brown. They have a varying diet of tenrecs, rats, birds and invertebrates.

Manapany day gecko.

ESCAPED CAGE BIRDS

Many of the pretty perching birds you will see around the gardens are descendants of common cage birds that have escaped from captivity and are relative newcomers. These include yellow village weaver birds, waxbills, spice finches, the beautiful (more yellow than green) green singing finch and the not-so-pretty mynah bird.

The gentle cooing sounds are provided by the small grey barred ground dove and the Madagascar turtle dove, which was thought to have come from Madagascar but sub-fossil bones have since been found, proving that it is native. The bright red Madagascar fody can be seen everywhere.

Fortunately for the game birds, the mongoose has never been introduced to the island, so three species of quail, two of partridge, wild chickens and a button quail, thought to be a native, all live in relative peace.

IMPORTANT SEABIRDS

As well as the endangered Barau's petrel and Mascarene black petrel, Réunion is home to Audubon's shearwater, a small black and white seabird that nests in the cliffs and feeds on fish and squid; and several small colonies of wedge-tailed shearwater. Keep an eye open in the cirques, gorges and around cliffs for the spectacular white-tailed tropicbird *(paille-en-queue)*, which has a long, streaming tail and is the island's national bird. Petite Île, just off the south coast and Réunion's only satellite island, has a breeding population of at least 300 pairs of common noddies and up to 300 non-breeding lesser noddies, who have recently been joined by a fairy tern.

COLOURFUL GECKOS

Apart from the many nocturnal house geckos that you see darting about the gardens and houses, the island has two brightly coloured endemic day geckos that are worth looking out for. As the name implies, the only place you will see the stunning green, red and white Manapany day gecko is on a walk through Manapany on the south coast. There you will see them all over the place, basking on banana leaves, scuttling up coconut palms and the pandanus, or screw pine.

The Réunion day gecko, however, is a much more difficult species to find as it only lives high up in the forests of the northeast and east. A blue-green colour with red stripes down each side, its distribution has been split by lava flows from the volcano, creating different races of the same species. You can

sometimes spot them lurking around the tourist kiosks up there.

The beautiful green, blue and red panther chameleon from Madagascar is the only introduced species that is protected; it can be found all over the island.

TAMARINDS AND ORCHIDS

Cultivated land bearing sugar cane reaches as high as 800 metres (2,600ft) above sea level, then gives way to verdant mixed forest which becomes a dwarf heath as you

Tree ferns in the Bebour Forest.

move up to the higher elevations. There are more than 60,000 hectares (148,000 acres) of natural forest on the island, looked after by the Office National des Forêts (ONF), and the endemic tamarind of the acacia family, alongside an island bamboo called the *calumet*, is quite a common sight. Epiphytes, including a wide variety of orchids (seven of which are unique to Réunion), and ferns grow in abundance on trees that lend their physical support.

Some of the introduced plants are a menace, such as the *goyavier* from Brazil, which runs rampant in the forest undergrowth. But its small guava-like red berries are rich in vitamin C.

Taking in Réunion's landscape on horseback.

ISLAND OF ADVENTURES

The spectacular landscape of Réunion is punctuated by trails, craters, peaks, rivers, forests and waterfalls, tailor-made for a vast array of outdoor pursuits.

Experiencing the great spectacle of the interior uplands of Réunion can take as little or as much effort as you choose. Whether you take it easy and fly across the island in a helicopter or take a stroll along a nature trail, or prefer the challenge of hiking along a Grande Randonnée (see page 182), testing your nerve abseiling down a waterfall, or paragliding off a mountain ridge, you will discover mystery in its isolation, magic in its inaccessibility and power in its grandeur.

The cirques, mountains and plains providing the magnificent terrain for such activities were formed at different stages of the island's volcanic development over many thousands of years. Originally the Piton des Neiges (3,070 metres/10, 072 ft) was the summit of a massive volcanic dome that collapsed around it and then was eroded to form the three great amphitheatres of gorges, waterfalls and ridges known as the cirques – perfect for canyoning, white-water rafting, rock climbing, paragliding and tree-top adventures.

The High Plains (Les Hautes-Plaines), comprising La Plaine-des-Palmistes and the Plaine-des-Cafres, form an open landscape of forests and pastureland between the extinct volcanic landscape and the active Piton de la Fournaise. They are criss-crossed with mountain-bike tracks, hiking paths and horse-riding trails. The higher Plaine-des-Cafres is the gateway to the volcano summit (see page 213), while Le Grand Brûlé on the southeast coast offers the possibility of visiting some of the world's most recent lava tubes, dating from a 2004 eruption.

BE PREPARED

The best time to take on any arduous, lengthy activity, such as hiking, horse trekking or

A helicopter ride in Iron Hole canyon.

mountain biking, is during the cooler and drier months of May to November when mountain temperatures hover between 12°C (54°F) and 18°C (64°F) during the day but can drop to near zero at night. Weather conditions can change very rapidly so check online or, if you understand French, you can phone the meteorological office.

It's important that you are aware of your own level of fitness and stamina before starting any activity and stick to rules of basic safety. Helicopters frequently survey the cirques and should you be injured or in trouble you can send a distress signal by raising both arms in a V shape. Every year, scores of people, mostly suffering from broken bones or twisted ankles, are rescued in the cirques.

For overnight stays en route, there are several types of accommodation, ranging from *gîtes de montagne* (mountain huts or lodges), to *chambres d'hôtes* (B&Bs) and youth hostels. Campsites are infrequent, but there are a few *abris* (shelters) on trekking routes. The shelters consist of only a roof so you need your own tent and sleeping bag.

Many places provide meals and at several of the *chambres d'hôtes*, a *table d'hôte* is offered when all the guests sit down to a meal together with the host. Reservations must be made in advance for all accommodation through Réunion's tourist board. There is usually a grocer's shop *(épicerie)* in the villages *(îlets)* scattered around the interior, selling a basic range of foods, but not in all of them.

UP, UP AND AWAY

The cirques and mountains are an awesome sight, especially from the top, and you can experience the sensation of flying between the peaks in a helicopter (see page 217) or smaller still, in a microlight. One or two people can fly in a microlight round a choice of the lagoon, the cirques, Piton des Neiges

Gorge walking.

⊘ HEADING INTO THE MOUNTAINS

Whether you spend a day or a week in the cirques and mountains, Réunion's tourist board (tel: 0810 160 000; www.reunion.fr) can assist you with whatever you would like to do. Knowledgeable, English-speaking staff will advise on hiking routes, can arrange mountain accommodation and provide guides if necessary. They can also organise horse-trekking trips, canyoning, mountain biking, hang-gliding and many other mountain sports.

To ensure safety in the mountains, it is important to take some common-sense precautions. Never venture out alone, and if you don't know the mountains, take a guide. You must be fit to take full advantage of the mountains – plan an itinerary on a par with your physical capacity. For peace of mind, book a room and board in advance. Good shoes, and warm and waterproof clothing ensure comfort. Take enough water with you; do not drink water from rivers or pools. Do not light fires and always keep the mountains litter free.

To avoid accidents never take closed or unmarked paths; check the state of paths before setting out on a hike and always follow trail blazes. If you do get lost, stay calm and remember the distress signal – arms held up in a V. Never leave a wounded person alone. Wait for help.

or near the volcano. Alternatively you can skydive from a plane (south coast) or a helicopter (west coast), although once you've jumped you might not have much time to admire the scenery.

To fly like a bird with only the rush of wind in your ears has to be one of the greatest thrills, especially over, within and around such dramatic scenery as Réunion's. The most popular paragliding spot is from Colimaçons, above St-Leu, but hang-gliding and paragliding are also possible from Piton Maïdo on the edge of the wild and secluded Cirque de Mafate, from the top of Piton des Neiges and the Hauts de St-Paul, where protected from the strong winds, the conditions are perfect for beginners, too.

> The mountainous cirques of Salazie and Cilaos are sensational for hiking, rock climbing and canyoning. For rafting and kayaking, head to the south or east coast.

RIVERS WILD

Streams cascading over ridges and waterfalls powering off the mountains provide ideal conditions for the hair-raising sports of canyoning and gorge walking (randonnée aquatique). For daredevils only, in a well-padded wetsuit, canyoning means abseiling down waterfalls and torrents in the heights of the cirques, while gorge walking is slightly less physical. Try Rivière Langevin at St-Joseph, Îlet Fleurs Jaunes and Îlets du Bois Rouge in La Cirque de Cilaos, or Trois Cascades in La Cirque de Salazie. As the slopes become less steep, rivers, such as the Rivière des Roches, provide exciting conditions for kayaking; and there are plenty of rapids, such as those of the Rivière des Marsouins, for white-water rafting. Companies specialising in river sports often organise mountain climbing expeditions as well.

AT SEA

Sea-based activities are clustered around – but not limited to – St-Gilles-les-Bains. Scuba diving is the second most popular activity in Réunion after trekking, and there's something for everyone, whether you'd like a beginner's dive or are already certified. You don't need to dive to see the humpback whales who, every June, travel up from the Antarctic to reproduce and give birth in Réunion's sheltered waters, staying until September. Snorkelling, kitesurfing, big-game fishing, stand-up paddle and sailing are available too.

MOUNTAIN BIKE CHALLENGES

Seven large areas of the island's magnificent interior have been devoted to mountain biking (VTT), and marked tracks, approved by the French Cycling Federation, total nearly 700km (435 miles). These areas, each with their own steep challenges and beautiful views, include

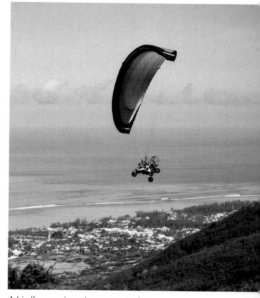

A bird's-eye view via paramotoring.

Maïdo, Entre-Deux, Cilaos, two at Hautes-Plaines, St-Philippe and Ste-Rose. Suitable bikes can be hired locally.

TREKKING ON HORSEBACK

Viewing the beauty of Réunion at your own pace from the back of a horse has to be an enriching experience – for an hour, a day or for several days, with tent and meals included in the price. Possibilities include a sunset ride at Cap La Houssaye, a three-day circuit through the Forêt de Bébour-Bélouve or a two-day ride to the volcano. The horses in Réunion are the gentle Mérens breed brought over from the Pyrénées in France, on which even a beginner will feel at ease.

HIKING ALONG THE GRANDES RANDONNÉES

Mysterious valleys, magnificent forests and soaring peaks are just some of the spectacular delights that await those who step onto Réunion's network of hiking paths.

Hikers trek the Rivière des Remparts.

Réunion is a walker's paradise, in spite of what novelist Walter Besant had to say about it when he walked to the Piton des Neiges in 1863. His tramp in the tropics may have been 'a time of bruisings, and barkings of the skin, of tearings and scratchings, of dirt, discomfort and disaster', but today there are more than 1,000km (620 miles) of well-marked trails across the island, mostly maintained by the Office National des Forêts (ONF) and ranging from an hour's easy walk to a challenging week-long hike.

There are several organisations that will help you plan your route, book accommodation in advance and provide guides, the main one being Réunion's tourist office (www.reunion.fr). If you are not familiar with the island, hiring a local *guide-pei* (native guide)

through the tourist office can be a good idea. Not only will you be in safe hands but they enjoy sharing their in-depth knowledge of their native land.

GRANDE RANDONNÉE TRAILS

The opening of GR R1 in 1979 made trekking less hazardous than in Besant's days. The 60km (37-mile) trail encircles Piton des Neiges through the three cirques of Salazie, Cilaos and Mafate. No visit would be complete without spending at least one night in the cirques, if only to wake at sunrise and gaze upon verdant valleys clothed in thick forests. The air is clear and sharp and rouses even the weariest walker to experience a world of lofty peaks. The 135km (84-mile) GR R2 crosses the island from the north to southeast, cutting through diverse landscapes of rugged mountains, fertile plains, volcano and humid forest to St-Philippe. The GR R3 was opened in 2005 and covers 47.5km (30 miles) in the remote Cirque de Mafate. The following are some ideas for hikes that take in the Grandes Randonnées and last from half a day to as long as you would like.

LA ROCHE ÉCRITE

One of the most popular walks, starting from St-Denis, takes you south to La Roche Écrite (2,277 metres/7,470ft). The trail passes through humid lowlands and tamarind forests with an abundance of rich flora to the almost denuded summit of La Roche Écrite itself. If you're on limited time, the return trip can be done in one full day, but overnighting at the *gîte* at Plaine-des-Chicots will enable you to wake early to complete the final ascent to the ramparts of La Roche Écrite, where you can experience the best views of Réunion's two highest mountains, Piton des Neiges (3,070 metres/10,072ft) and Le Gros Morne (3,019 metres/9,905ft) and the cirques of Mafate and Salazie to the right and left. The trail is clearly signposted from Le Brûlé in the highlands above St-Denis, rising gently through forests of cryptomeria and eucalyptus and lush areas of wild flowers and fruits and endemic bamboo (*Nastus borbonicas*). Continue southwards, crossing two ravines surrounded by forests of mixed evergreens or *bois de couleurs* and tamarinds to reach the *gîte* at Plaine-des-Chicots, where you can stop for the night. From here it is another 1.5-hour trek southwards to La Roche Écrite through landscape that changes to a plateau of lichen and moss. You'll pass two intersections on the way but you should ignore both and keep to the marked path; the first on the right after about 45 minutes leads to La Mare aux Cerfs, a small watering hole noted for dawn sightings of Réunion's deer, which you could visit on the way back. The second leads to Caverne Soldats. Continue on for another 25 minutes to La Roche Écrite.

MAFATE

The most isolated of the cirques, Mafate is wild and peaceful, only disturbed by the sound of the odd helicopter coming in for a closer look. It has plenty of trails, offering walkers anything from a simple but not so interesting three-hour walk along the Rivière des Galets to more difficult day- or week-long hikes. Alternatively, you can stay in Mafate trekking from *îlet* to *îlet* and overnighting in mountain *gîtes*, where breakfast and an evening meal are provided (booking ahead is essential).

The *îlet* of Dos d'Ane on the D1 is a handy starting point for a couple of days of trekking along the GR R2. This trail descends steeply for two hours, taking you down to the Rivière des Galets, which flows from the slopes of Le Gros Morne through a huge valley of *bois de couleurs* and meets the ocean at Le Port on the northwest coast. The trail crosses the river several times before it forks off to the left, leading to the *îlet* of Aurère, a good two-hour climb. The next day you can do a four-hour hike to Le Bélier on the edge of the Cirque de Salazie, along either the Sentier Scout path or the shorter, but more dramatic, direct path. This descends to the bottom of a ravine before climbing up to the top of the Grand Rein ridge, then down again and along the Route Forestière for the last leg.

Grand Place, past the turn-off to Aurère, is a good central *îlet* to use as a base for a few nights if you would like to spend several days exploring Mafate, as many of the trails pass through here.

SALAZIE

Hell-Bourg (see page 224), at the end of the D48, has plenty of places to stay and is where you can start a hike to the Piton des Neiges, lasting about 5.5 hours. The Gîte de la Caverne Dufour offers basic but hospitable dormitory-style

accommodation at the foot of the mountain. From there it is a 1.5-hour climb to the top, best started before dawn before the clouds descend.

CILAOS

The GR R1 winds and climbs its way west from Cilaos to Marla in the Cirque de Mafate. The six-hour hike goes via the Cascade de Bois Rouge and Col du Taïbit (2,142 metres/7,028ft). If you want to try to do it in a day, start from the trailhead on the Îlet à Cordes road, 6km (4 miles) west of, and accessible by bus from, Cilaos. Alternatively, you can hike

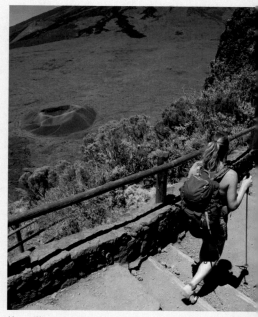

You will need the correct footwear and kit for a volcano trek.

up to Piton des Neiges (see page 225), or do a round walk to the Cascade de Bois Rouge waterfall in around two hours.

THE VOLCANO

Starting at Pas de Bellecombe or from the RF5, an alternative to climbing the Piton de la Fournaise (see page 184) is to follow the GR R2 along the southern ridge (l'Enclos) of the volcano to the Nez Coupé du Tremblet. This five-hour hike, which passes through the lunar landscape of Plaine des Sables (see page 215), has been graded as not too difficult but you could just go halfway by returning at Foc-Foc, where the trail forks.

📷 PITON DE LA FOURNAISE

In 1801, explorer Bory de St Vincent described the volcano as 'immense, tumultuous, bloody and majestic'. He was inspired by it, but many feared it.

Piton de la Fournaise ('Peak of the Furnace') is a 'Hawaiian-type' shield volcano and is one of the most active on earth. Since Réunion was first inhabited in 1640, it has erupted on average once every eight months. In 1778, it added notably to the size of the island by pouring millions of tonnes of lava into the sea; in 1786 the explosion was so loud that it was heard in Mauritius.

Piton de la Fournaise (2,632 metres/8,635ft) has two main craters. The highest, Bory, has been inactive since 1791, while the active Dolomieu manages, most of the time, to confine its eruptions to within the enclosure. On 8 April 1977 islanders witnessed the sheer power of their volcano when lava rolled down the mountainside destroying houses and a petrol station at Ste-Rose on the east coast, only to stop just before the doorstep of a church, since renamed Notre Dame des Laves (Our Lady of the Lava).

On 20 March 1986 an eruption extended the island's land mass by several hectares. On 9 March 1998 another spectacular eruption, this time lasting for 196 days – the longest in the 20th century – caused panic and excitement as blood-red fire fountains turned into rivers of lava.

April 2007 saw a major eruption that led to the spectacular collapse of the crater floor of Dolomieu, leaving it 300 metres (985ft) lower.

Any volcanologist will tell you that all live volcanoes, no matter how predictable, should be treated with caution and respect.

Just south of L'Étang-Salé les Bains, the RN1 cuts through a jagged expanse of black lava rock with views crashing waves and water jets, known as souffleurs.

The incredible sight of bright plants blooming out of cooled lava.

A helicopter tour reveals a clear view of a river of fire.

Fountains and rivers of fire

Like the volcanoes of Hawaii, Piton de la Fournaise is a shield volcano. It produces spectacular fire fountains and churns out rivers of basalt lava, which flow over great distances. Because the lava is so fluid it trickles easily downhill without piling up, which explains why shield volcanoes are not steep. During the 1986 eruption the lava flowed at a rate of 100,000 cubic metres (353,100 cubic ft) per hour, reaching temperatures of up to 1,160°C (2,120°F). Around the Piton de la Fournaise you'll find two types of solidified lava flow which have been given Hawaiian names: *pahoehoe* (pronounced pa-hoy-hoy) and *aa* (ah-ah). *Pahoehoe*, which looks like coils of rope, is smooth and easy to walk on. This type of lava cools slowly and remains viscous for a while, allowing the gases to ooze through a steadily solidifying 'plastic' skin. In contrast, *aa* flows quickly and solidifies into sharp chunks of lava called scoria, which make hiking slow and can ruin your shoes. Low-viscosity lava flows have led to the creation of lava tubes, which can be visited.

kkers hiking on Formica Leo.

aerial view shows how new land forms around
volcano.

A glowing rush of lava from the volcano's eruption in May 2015.

Vineyard by the roadside on Îlet à Cordes.

A trail in Belouve forest.

RÉUNION: PLACES

A detailed guide to Réunion, with principal sites clearly cross-referenced by number to the maps.

Natural arch on Piton Sainte.

If you've just flown in from Mauritius, the contrast in landscapes will come as a shock as you'll discover awesome volcanic craters, rugged coastlines and lush gorges. Most people head straight for the west coast, but no trip to Réunion is complete without a visit to the volcano and at least one of the cirques. There's no doubt that the island's greatest assets lie inland, and getting around is easy thanks to the good roads. At the heart of the island you'll find mysterious mountains, jagged peaks and gorges, rivers and waterfalls, extinct craters, isolated villages and a temperamental volcano.

It's possible, though not necessarily advisable, to get round the island in a day, which you can do either in a hire car or on the comfortable public buses. The capital, St-Denis, has some attractively restored buildings and a couple of interesting art collections, but there is not much to see or do here.

Most beaches can be found in the west, between St-Paul and St-Pierre. A good place to base yourself if you want to be by the sea might be St-Gilles-les-Bains, a lively resort with plenty of bars and restaurants and all the facilities you need for water sports, but it can get crowded. At the far end of the island's western beach stretch is the pleasant town of St-Pierre, another good base, being within easy reach of the southeast coast and about an hour from Piton de la Fournaise.

Volcanic eruption.

The east coast areas around the town of St-André and the sleepy corner of St-Philippe are often neglected, but deserve more than a brief stop to explore the inland forests, volcanic wastelands, rugged seascapes and walking trails.

For an altogether different experience, Hell-Bourg, in the Cirque de Salazie, is a popular base for trekkers and adventurers. From there you can climb the Piton des Neiges and admire some of the best-preserved Creole architecture on the island.

Cannons on the Le Barachois
waterfront, St-Denis.

ST-DENIS

Sometimes called 'Paris of the Indian Ocean', St-Denis is more like a provincial capital, but it's worth pausing to look at the lovely Creole architecture.

When French governor Regnault founded St-Denis in 1669, he chose a sheltered spot on the uninhabited north coast. Life for the first 77 inhabitants was dull and, save for the odd pirate or two who dropped by, fairly uneventful. Even when the headquarters of the French East India Company was transferred from the old capital, St-Paul, in 1738, the town still had little going for it, in spite of a hundredfold increase in population. Successive governors tried to turn the new capital into a maritime and military base, but it ended up as neither, and by the late 1950s the infrastructure was so poor that even tourists had a job finding a place to stay.

All that's changed, and St-Denis has transformed itself into a reasonably sophisticated capital of 200,000 people, and these days offers much that you'd expect from any major town in mainland France. The difference, of course, is the tropical setting. Splendid renovated Creole homes, often with grand wrought-iron gates and lush gardens, are one of the chief attractions for casual visitors. And while the restaurants may look typically French, you'll find *carri* (a local type of curry) and unfamiliar vegetables such as *chou chou* on the menu; as well as dozens of small Creole eateries offering all the local delicacies, such as *samousas* and *bonbons piments*.

St-Denis' 19th-century cathedral.

Spending a day in St-Denis will give you plenty of time to stroll the streets, visit the major sights, and book accommodation in the interior if you need to. But two words of warning: St-Denis is not a cheap city, and there are better things to do and see elsewhere. If you want to base yourself on the coast, you would do better to opt for St-Gilles, Boucan-Canot or St-Pierre.

THE WATERFRONT

Your first glimpse of St-Denis will most likely be from the air. The plane

Main attractions
Le Barachois
Villa Carrère
Musée Leon Dierx
Jardin de l'État
Musée d'Histoire Naturelle

Map on page 192

descends into Roland Garros airport, 11km (7 miles) east of the city, sweeping past dark mountains that must have struck awe into the hearts of the early settlers. Hemmed between the Rivière des Pluies and the Rivière St-Denis, the city spreads upwards onto the hill slopes, where modern apartment blocks and luxurious houses have replaced the shanty towns of the 1950s.

A good place to start is at the shaded waterfront promenade known as **Le Barachois Ⓐ**. The area, once an inlet for unloading ships, had an adjustable jetty affixed to the shore by a set of iron chains, which was raised or lowered above the sea to allow passengers to disembark; according to the writer T.V. Bulpin, they 'had to leap upon it with some display of acrobatics, with the thought of sharks if they slipped'. The contraption was rendered useless during cyclones, and the iron pier that later replaced it was equally ineffectual, so the inlet was eventually filled in and planted with palm trees. Nine cannons face out to sea, placed there to symbolise St-Denis' supposed days as a military base. They are among Réunion's many coastal cannons that were either salvaged from shipwrecks or bought for decorative purposes by various governors.

Le Barachois is as chic as St-Denis gets, overlooked from across the busy Boulevard Gabriel Macé by Hôtel St-Denis (now shut down and under new ownership; re-opening is planned) and a handful of cafés and restaurants.

Several former French East India Company warehouses survive here, in Place Sarda Garriga, with their facades still intact. One houses the town's oldest restaurant, the **Roland Garros** (tel: 0262 41 44 37), named after the famous aviator who was born in the capital.

AN ARCHITECTURAL TOUR

A walk inland, south along Avenue de la Victoire, leads to some of the city's finest buildings. First is **Hôtel de la Préfecture** , an attractive colonial mansion overlooking pretty gardens. It began as a humble coffee warehouse, grew into the headquarters of the French East India Company and later became the official governor's residence. In 1942 it was occupied by Free French Forces, who arrived to rid the island of its Vichy sympathisers. Later visitors have included General de Gaulle, Giscard d'Estaing and Jacques Chirac. The Préfecture is closed to the public.

In the adjacent square, now used as a car park, a **statue of Mahé de Labourdonnais** stares solemnly out to sea. It was here that important announcements from the motherland were made, including the abolition of slavery in 1848 by Sarda-Garriga. Labourdonnais is best remembered in Réunion for treating the island as a rather forgotten satellite when he was governor of the Mascarene Islands.

Three blocks beyond, past an uncharacteristically unobtrusive branch of McDonald's in a converted warehouse, is the 19th-century **Cathédrale** ⒞. It has some interesting bas-reliefs of St-Denis, but is not a beautiful building. The square at the front, with vast, twisted trees and a 19th-century iron fountain, is more attractive.

As you head south, on the right in quick succession are several more notable colonial buildings, including the Business School of the **Université**, built in 1759, but the best old buildings are still to come. The towering **Monument aux Morts** ⒟, which commemorates the death of over 1,000 Réunionnais who fought in World War I, marks the start of **Rue de Paris**, lined with some of the capital's grandest Creole homes.

⏺ **Drink**

To order a bottle of the local Bourbon beer, ask the barman for 'une dodo'.

Monument aux Morts by the town hall.

⏺ HOW THE OTHER HALF LIVED

Engineers of the French East India Company designed St-Denis' draught-board layout in 1720. At the time, the town was divided into sections – business, residential and defence. These areas blended over time but their organisational structure didn't change. Mansions were located in an upper middle class district in which only the richest could live.

All the houses on Rue de Paris shared the same layout as Villa Carrère. The front part of the house, which includes the *baro* (gate) and garden, was spotlessly maintained, while the rear part consisted of scruffier outbuildings and a backyard. The *varangue* (veranda), at the front of the house, was open to all visitors, but not every room would have been open to guests – in fact, the further you entered a house, the more intimate the rooms became.

Importing elements of the house – such as the gate at Villa Carrère – was common practice for Reunion's upper middle class families, as it indicated their wealth. Another sign of opulence would have been a pond; some gardens would have had three!

Whether a *varangue* was closed depended on the prevailing wind. If it faced east it would have been enclosed to protect against the wind, but if it faced west it was open. In either case, families gathered there daily to play, knit, read and gossip.

Villa Carrère Ⓔ (14 Rue de Paris; tel: 0262 41 83 00; Mon–Sat 9am–6pm) is a typical 19th-century Creole house (the only one open to the public in St-Denis) and is also home to the tourist office, which is on the veranda. Built in 1820, the house had fallen into disrepair until it was renovated in the early years of the 21st century. Only a few rooms have been restored, based on pictures, sketches, historical information and original elements. They're not exact replicas, but offer an approximate idea of the furnishings and style of the past. At the tourist office you can ask for advice, plan walking itineraries, book gîtes and so on.

Poet and landscape artist Léon Dierx (1841–1912) was born in one of the houses on Rue de Paris, and the **Musée Léon Dierx** Ⓕ (tel: 0262 20 24 82; Tue–Sun 9.30am–5.30pm), in a fine colonnaded mansion, displays his work alongside original sculptures and engravings of rather more famous artists such as Cézanne, Gauguin, Renoir and Picasso, as well as work by other Réunionnais artists. Unfortunately, the

The Three Graces in Jardin de l'Etat.

museum earns money by lending its best works to foreign museums, but there is normally at least one Gauguin or Picasso piece on show. Next door, in another superbly restored 19th-century villa, regular exhibitions of modern art are held in the former Maison Mas, now **L'Artothèque** (Tue–Sun). At 49 rue de Paris is the Saint-Denis extension of the **Musée des arts décoratifs et du design de l'océan Indien** (Wed–Mon 9am–12pm, 1–5pm), a decorative arts museum based in St-Louis (see page 207). Themed exhibitions are on display in the beautiful rooms of a Creole mansion, and there's a small gift shop too.

JARDIN DE L'ÉTAT

Rue de Paris ends at Place de Metz and the **Jardin de l'État** Ⓖ. A golden age blossomed under botanist Nicolas Bréon, who came to Réunion in 1817 with a collection of European trees. From his continued expeditions to far-flung places, he brought back the seeds with which to produce one of the most interesting botanical collections in the Indian Ocean. Two busts of green-fingered giants attest to the gardens' importance: Pierre Poivre, who founded the Pamplemousses Botanical Gardens in Mauritius (see page 116), and Réunion-born botanist Joseph Hubert, who brought back some useful spices from his travels. Labels cater to those interested in plants, while shady benches, the café and space for *boules* are the main attraction for most locals.

The centrepiece of the gardens is the **Muséum d'Histoire Naturelle** (Natural History Museum; tel: 0262 20 02 19; Tue–Sun 9.30am–5.30pm), in the former Palais Législatif. The themed sections inside show how fauna survived before the arrival of humans, how it suffered under them and the measures that can be taken to protect already threatened species. Upstairs, a separate room devoted to Madagascar includes displays of stuffed lemurs. Centre stage is a moulded

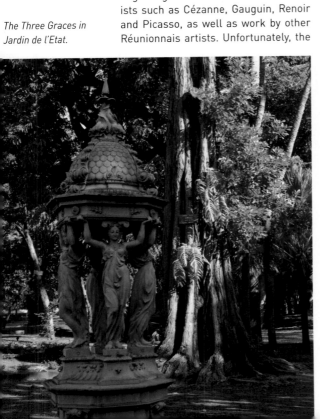

replica of a stuffed coelacanth, a prehistoric fish known only in fossil form until 1938, when a living specimen was caught off the Comoro islands. Other exhibits include stuffed specimens of the island's fauna, and reconstructed skeletons of extinct Mascarene birds, notably the solitaires of Réunion and Rodrigues, and the dodo.

ALONG RUE DU MARÉCHAL LECLERC

Rue du Maréchal Leclerc is the centre of the shopping scene in St-Denis – though this isn't saying much. Most popular among visitors is the **Grand Marché** (open daily) at the street's western end, on the corner of Rue Lucien-Gasparin. This craft market caters mainly to tourists and lacks the buzz of most tropical markets, including the Petit Marché further east. But don't let this stop you trying to bargain with the traders, many of whose prices deserve to be reduced. You can't miss the tablecloths which are draped above many stalls, while down below you'll find *tentes* – shopping bags made from the dried leaves of the vacoas tree – T-shirts and crafts, mostly from Madagascar.

East of Rue de Paris, the Rue du Maréchal Leclerc is partially pedestrianised and lined with shops catering to the everyday needs of the local people. Nestled among the shops, near the corner of Rue Jules Auber, is the **Grande Mosquée** (daily 9am–noon, 2–4pm); the minaret is easier to locate than the entrance. For fruit and vegetables, people head east to the **Petit Marché**, at the end of Rue Ste-Anne. Just opposite the market is the **Chinese pagoda** (Pagode Bouddhiste) and on the other side of the market is the Tamil **Kalikambal Temple** (Temple Tamoul), a madly colourful confection with lovely bas-reliefs of deities. To complete the religious medley, visit the 19thcentury Gothic **Church of St Jacques**, in the street of the same name nearby, just off Rue du Maréchal Leclerc.

Heading back to the waterfront from Rue du Maréchal Leclerc, you'll see some delightful Creole homes along **Rue Juliette Dodu** and nearby streets. There are several shops, restaurants and hotels in this area.

☉ Tip

You may be lucky enough to find a parking space in Place Sarda Garriga or by the Jardin de l'État. Otherwise there's a car park in Rue Félix Guyon (between Rue de Paris and Rue Jean Chatel), and two near the Grand Marché on Rue du Maréchal Leclerc and on Rue Lucien Gasparin.

Enjoying a horse-drawn carriage ride.

◎ Tip

Golfers can enjoy the mountain views and a challenging enough course at the Colorado leisure park. For information and reservations, www. golfclubcolorado.fr.

CIMETIÈRE DE L'EST

You could take a detour to the seafront **Cimetière de l'Est** (Eastern Cemetery), about 3km (2 miles) east of the Barachois, with early tombs and the communal graves of the thousands who died during the Spanish flu epidemic of 1919. In a separate section are the unmarked graves of sentenced men, including one containing the head of Mr Zett, who was decapitated in Salazie in the early 1900s for taking part in an orgy of rape and pillage. Right-thinking citizens of the day, afraid that his soul would rise again to terrorise the population, ensured it wouldn't by sending his head to St-Denis.

INTO THE HILLS

If you have time for just one short excursion from St-Denis, take a drive along the **Route de La Montagne**, a well-signposted road southwest of the capital on the D41. With enough switchbacks to make you dizzy, this scenic route gives a small taster of Réunion's winding roads, as well as panoramic views of the city: at night you'll see the light flashes of Bel Air lighthouse in Ste-Suzanne (see page 202).

About 15 minutes along the route is the **Jardin de Cendrillon** (48 Route des Palmiers, La Montagne; tel: 0692 86 32 88), a garden with over 300 varieties of orchid, a profusion of variously coloured anthuriums and a collection of medicinal plants and spices. Don't worry about the large but harmless armour-plated spiders (nephila inorata), known locally as the 'bib', spinning fine silky webs in the greenhouses. If they get too close for comfort, you can always sit outside, surrounded by bird-of-paradise flowers, and admire the views over St-Denis. The garden is in private hands and it is necessary to book a tour (minimum of four people) at the tourist office in St-Denis. The 1.5-hour tours are in French, but an English interpreter can normally be arranged.

Of more popular appeal is the enormous outdoor leisure park at **Colorado**, just beyond La Montagne and about 30 minutes by car from St-Denis. The park gets busy with local picnickers at weekends, but also offers a range of activities, from walking, mountain biking and horse riding to tennis and even golf (9-hole).

For a wilder experience, you should head south along the D42 up to the highland village of **Le Brûlé**, from where you can explore the surrounding cryptomeria forests. A well-marked trail runs 4km (2.5 miles) – it takes about 30 minutes – southwest to the lovely waterfalls of **Cascade Maniquet**.

A more challenging 18km (11-mile) trek leads southwards from Le Brûlé to the 2,277-metre (7,468ft) peak of **La Roche Écrite** for spectacular views over the Cirques of Salazie and Mafate (see page 221). Allow a full day for this excursion, starting from the car park at Camp Mamode (see IGN 1:25,000 4402RT Map St-Denis, Cirques de Mafate et de Salazie).

Route de La Montagne at dawn.

Tamil temple in St-Denis.

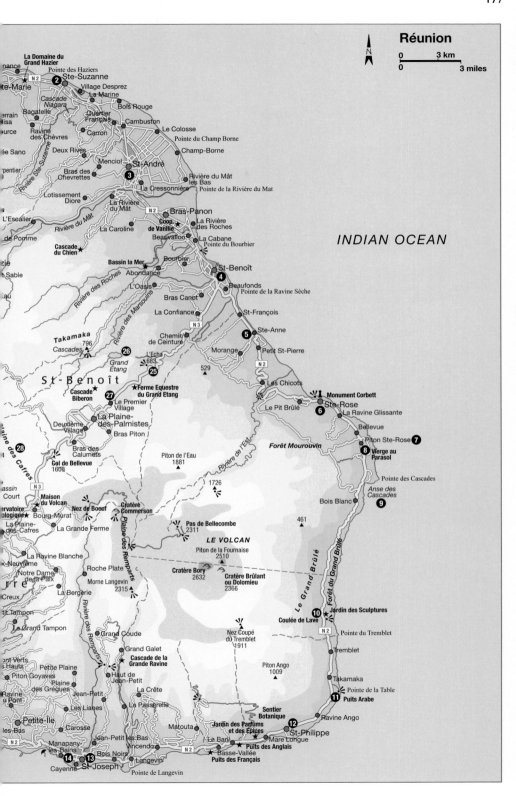

Réunion

N

0		3 km
0		3 miles

INDIAN OCEAN

La Domaine du
Grand Hazier
Pointe des Haziers
Ste-Suzanne
Village Desprez
La Marine
Bois Rouge
Cascade
Niagara
Bagatelle
Quartier
Français
Cambuston
Ravine
des Chèvres
Carron
Le Colosse
Pointe du Champ Borne
Deux Rives
Champ-Borne
Menciol
St-André
Bras des
Chevrettes
Rivière du Mât
les Bas
La Cressonnière
Pointe de la Rivière du Mat
Lotissement
Diore
La Rivière
du Mât
Bras-Panon
L'Escalier
Coop.
de Vanille
La Rivière
des Roches
de Pomme
Beauvallon
La Cabane
Pointe du Bourbier
Cascade
du Chien
Bourbier
Bassin la Mer
St-Benoît
Abondance
Beaufonds
Sable
L'Oasis
Pointe de la Ravine Sèche
Bras Canot
La Confiance
St-François
Chemin
de Ceinture
Ste-Anne
Takamaka
796
Morange
Petit St-Pierre
Cascades
L'Echo
683
Les Chicots
Grand
Etang
529
St-Benoît
Ferme Equestre
du Grand Etang
Monument Corbett
Cascade
Biberon
Le Premier
Village
Ste-Rose
La Ravine Glissante
Deuxième
Village
La Plaine-
des-Palmistes
Bras Piton
Bellevue
Piton Ste-Rose
Bras des
Calumets
Col de Bellevue
1600
Piton de l'Eau
1881
Forêt Mourouvin
Vierge au
Parasol
Pointe des Cascades
Maison
du Volcan
1726
Anse des
Cascades
Bois Blanc
Nez de Boeuf
Cratère
Commerson
Bourg-Murat
La Grande Ferme
La Plaine-
des-Cafres
La Ravine Blanche
Pas de Bellecombe
2311
461
Notre Dame
de la Paix
Roche Plate
LE VOLCAN
Piton de la Fournaise
2510
Creux
La Bergerie
Morne Langevin
2315
Cratère Bory
2632
Cratère Brûlant
ou Dolomieu
2366
tit Tampon
Le Grand Tampon
Grand Coude
Nez Coupé
du Tremblet
1911
Jardin des Sculptures
Coulée de Lave
Pointe du Tremblet
nt Verts
Hauts
Petite Plaine
Piton Goyaves
Plaine
des Grègues
Haut de
Jean-Petit
Grand Galet
Cascade de la
Grande Ravine
Piton Ango
1009
Tremblet
Ravine
u Pont
Jean-Petit
La Crête
Takamaka
Pointe de la Table
Petite-Ile
les-Bas
Les Lianes
La Passerelle
Puits Arabe
Carosse
Matouta
Sentier
Botanique
St-Philippe
Ravine Ango
Manapany-
les-Bains
Jean-Petit les-Bas
Vincendo
Jardin des Parfums
et des Epices
Mare Longue
Bois Noirs
La Baril
Puits des Anglais
Cayenne
St-Joseph
Langevin
Basse-Vallée
Puits des Français
Pointe de Langevin

An aerial view of Cap de la Houssaye.

THE COAST

Discover the extremes of Réunion's coast on the Route Nationale, from sugar fields and volcanic wastes in the east to coral-fringed beaches in the west.

There's little doubt that Réunion's main attractions lie inland: compared to the lush interior, the coastal area is dry and scrubby, particularly in the west and south. But it does have a handful of interesting towns and a few stretches of sandy beach. You can drive around Réunion's 207km (128 miles) of coast in a day thanks to one well-asphalted road, the Route Nationale (RN1), though it is worth spending at least two or three days exploring. Most of the towns have decent accommodation and tourist offices, and several are natural gateways to the cirques and other inland excursions.

The most popular coastal stretch is on the west coast between St-Paul and St-Pierre, where all the beaches are; but don't neglect the area around the eastern town of St-André and the southeast corner around the sleepy hideout of St-Philippe, whose inland forest, volcanic wastelands, rugged seascapes and walking trails deserve more than a brief stop.

Driving along the Route Nationale is reasonably straightforward, though it's perfectly possible to tour the coast on one of Réunion's comfortable public buses (see Travel Tips, Transport). There are stretches of dual carriageway, but this often reduces to single lane traffic through towns, when impatient local drivers tend to hang onto your tail, desperate to pass. If you are

planning to drive through St-Denis, try to avoid travelling at rush hour (7–9am and 4–6pm), when the road into and out of the capital is clogged up with commuter traffic.

ON THE SUGAR AND SPICE TRAIL

The gently sloping plains east of St-Denis ❶ were transformed into vast sugar plantations during the colonial era, and cane still smothers the area today. The other legacy of those early entrepreneurs are the grand houses

Boucan Canot.

Tip

About 2km (1 mile) south of Ste-Suzanne is the 30-metre (98ft) Cascade Niagara, a mini version of the Niagara Falls and a good place for a dip. Go midweek unless you are happy to share the pool with plenty of locals, for whom this is a popular picnic place.

that they built for themselves. One such abode is **Le Domaine du Grand Hazier** (tel: 0262 52 32 81; email: info@domainedugrandhazier.re; pre-booked guided tours only), just 3km (2 miles) west of **Ste-Suzanne** ②, which opened to the public in 1998. Concealed at the end of a palm-lined road, the 18th-century mansion contains original furniture and paintings and is surrounded by lush vegetable gardens and orchards. In the grounds is **La Vanilleraie** (tel: 0262 23 07 26; www.lavanilleraie.com; Mon–Sat 8.30am–noon and 1.30–5pm), where you can follow the stages of production of the precious vanilla pod; the plantation produces pods in sufficient quantities not only to stock its own shop but also to export. The tours (9am, 10am, 11am, 2pm, 3pm and 4pm) are informative, and the shop sells vanilla-flavoured everything.

Sugar production boomed in Réunion between 1815 and 1832, but when slavery was abolished in 1848 plantation owners had to source labour from India. Waves of immigrants arrived as contract workers, and today many of their descendants

Tamil Divali in Saint-André.

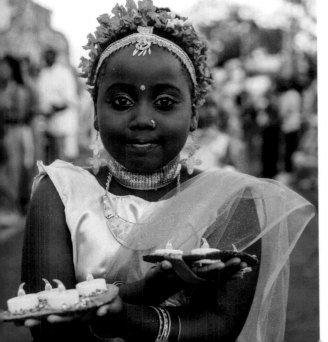

still live in the area between Ste-Suzanne and St-André. Some of these work at the sugar factory and distillery at **Bois Rouge** (tel: 0262 58 59 74; www.distilleriesavanna.com; Mon–Sat 9am–6pm, guided tours only). Several temples nearby catered to the spiritual needs of the Indian sugar workers, including an impressive **Tamil temple** tucked away in the fields beside the Rivière St-Jean, just west of Bois Rouge, and three others nearby at **Le Colosse** on the coast.

Quartier Français, just south of Bois Rouge, was home to some of Réunion's first settlers back in 1646 and to one of the oldest sugar factories, which once formed part of the vast Kerveguen sugar empire. The factory, in Avenue Raymond-Verges, closed in 1981 but is worth visiting for the finely preserved chimney.

St-André ③, 10km (6 miles) from Ste-Suzanne and about 30 minutes' drive from St-Denis, is the gateway to the Cirque de Salazie (see page 223). It is a pleasant enough town, with a buzzing main street but few interesting sights. Like Ste-Suzanne's La Vanilleraie, the **Vanilla Cooperative** (tel: 0262 51 61 74; http://provanille.fr; Mon–Sat 8.30am–noon and 1.30–5pm, guided tours only) in nearby Bras-Panon also offers tours of its factory and grounds.

On the ocean side of the Route Nationale, you can take Chemin Lagourgue to the coast. At the seafront turn right for **Champ-Borne**, where you can see the remains of a 19th-century church, seriously damaged by Cyclone Jenny in 1962 when huge waves swept inland and partially destroyed the cemetery.

ST-BENOÎT TO STE-ROSE

The next bead in the necklace of coastal towns, **St-Benoît** ④ is of scant interest unless you like ghost stories. The ghost of local mayor Louis Brunet (1847–1905), whose mausoleum is behind the town's 19th-century church, is said to wander through the town. For many people, St-Benoît simply marks the Route

Nationale's junction with the N3, which heads up to the high plains and volcano (see page 213). If all you want is a taste of the interior, you could take the D53, which runs 15km (9 miles) along the course of the **Rivière des Marsouins** to Takamaka and the lovely **Cascade de l'Arc-en-Ciel** (and hydroelectric complex).

Ste-Anne ❺, 5km (3 miles) beyond St-Benoît, would seem an unlikely place to feature in a film if it weren't for its church, whose intricate, Baroquestyle stonework must have appealed to François Truffaut: he used it in *La Sirène du Mississippi* (1969), starring Catherine Deneuve and Jean-Paul Belmondo. The church dates from the 19th century, but the extraordinary carving was done in the first half of the 20th century by a group of Tamil craftsmen.

From Ste-Anne the road winds inland to the foothills of the volcano, crosses a suspension bridge over the Rivière de l'Est, and then descends to the small fishing town of **Ste-Rose ❻**. In 1809, British men o'war tested the town's defences just before they took the island from the French; on the waterfront there is a monument to Commodore Corbett, second-in-command of the British fleet, who died in one of the skirmishes. Ste-Rose is constantly under threat from the volcano which, in April 1977, twice disgorged its molten lava into the next village of **Piton Ste-Rose ❼**, destroying some 20 houses. People watched entranced as the lava flowed around the church, now known as **Notre Dame des Laves**, without destroying it, and instead hardened to form a thick black girdle – still visible today – around the building. Newspaper cuttings inside the church reveal that some villagers saw their lucky escape as 'God's miracle'. Local artist Guy Lefèvre made the stained-glass windows, and pilgrims sometimes lay flowers at the **Vierge au Parasol ❽**. The shrine, which used to stand inside the caldera soon after **Bois Blanc**, was erected by a 19th-century landowner who believed it would protect his vanilla plantation from the fury of the volcano, until vandalism led it to being relocated to the church.

For the calm and quiet of a spectacular seascape, follow the signs

Notre Dame des Laves.

⦿ BEACON OF LIGHT

Bel Air lighthouse was built at Ste-Suzanne in 1845 and was the island's first lighthouse – it is the only one still standing. Constructed to prevent shipwrecks off this dangerous stretch of coast, it has long served as a landmark for sailors. With its base 40 metres (130ft) above sea level, it stands 20.25 metres (66.5ft) tall and was staffed until 1985 with keepers who had to wind the clockwork mechanism every four hours. It was automated in 1989 and fully restored in 1996. Come nightfall, three white flashes are emitted every 15 seconds, which are visible for 23 nautical miles. Now a listed building, Bel Air can be visited on the last Tuesday and second Saturday of every month. For more information contact the Ste-Suzanne tourist office, right next to the lighthouse.

south from Piton Ste-Rose for 3km (2 miles) to the turn-off for **Anse des Cascades** . Here, waterfalls tumble from towering cliffs into a shaded bay where fishermen sell their catch on the jetty. The secluded restaurant makes a perfect lunch stop and at weekends the cool forests of coconut trees are popular with picnickers.

VOLCANIC WASTELAND TOWARDS PUITS ARABE

Some of the most dramatic coastal scenery of Réunion can be seen along the next stretch of road to St-Philippe as the RN2 negotiates the southeast corner of the island, skirting an immense volcanic caldera known as **Le Grand Brûlé**, formed by the lava flow from Piton de la Fournaise and *Les Grandes Pentes* (The Steep Slopes). Every now and then, barren wastes of solidified lava indicate the progress of previous eruptions.

There are several red shrines to St-Expédit in the area, one of which lies right beside a **lava flow** *(coulée de lave)* which cut off the RN2 in 1998.

Vierge au Parasol.

If you stay on the coast road you'll be treated to more moonscapes of hardened black lava at **Puits Arabe** where information boards describe the sequence of events which resulted in the evacuation of 500 people as lava flowed in four stages between 19 and 30 March 1986, coating the slopes of **Takamaka** above the village before stabilising itself just 300 metres (980ft) from the road. You can scramble for 200 metres (650ft) over the solidified lava to **Pointe de la Table**, where another lava flow from the same eruption extended the island by 25 hectares (62 acres) into the sea; or opt for a lengthier 5km (3-mile) trek northwards towards **Tremblet**, crossing cliffs where an 18th-century lava flow is a good example of the structures of cooling.

ST-PHILIPPE TO ST-JOSEPH

Rugged, ragged and fierce best describes the south coast, where screw pines torn by warm winds watch over wild seas beating against black basalt cliffs. The sleepy little town of **St-Philippe** is a good place to break your journey through the volcanic wastelands of the east coast

⊘ ISLAND SAINT: ST-EXPÉDIT

St-Expédit is a relative newcomer to the world of sainthood and probably reached such heights more through folklore than by holy deeds. He started out as a Roman soldier, was made a martyr for his Christian beliefs and was revered in Germany and France for his power to produce fast solutions. In 1919 those powers were put to the test when a Réunionnais woman keen to leave Marseille prayed that a boat would appear to take her home. Whether or not it was thanks to convenient sailing schedules, she soon arrived clutching a statue of St-Expédit, and his reputation for prompt action spread. Since the 1930s, blood-red shrines to St-Expédit have appeared in cemeteries and caves, along the roadsides and beside statues of the Virgin Mary. The saint is portrayed as a Roman legionnaire; he holds a cross in his right hand bearing the inscription *hodie* (today) and with his left foot he crushes a crow, which utters the word *cras* (tomorrow). Viewed with suspicion by the Catholic clergy, St-Expédit has achieved cult status because many locals call upon him to do good or harm. The biggest shrine is at Mare Longue at St-Philippe in the south, but there are more than 300 elsewhere containing burned-down candles, *ex votos*, flowers, fruit or cigarettes as inducements to expedite a problem or to thank St-Expédit for his intervention. Some shrines contain beheaded statues, presumably the work of unhappy locals, but most bizarre are those draped in underwear.

and stock up on supplies if you need to. It has some interesting examples of Creole architecture and, in addition to a helpful tourist office, there are roadside eateries that provide ready-packed baguettes and other snacks – perfect fodder to take on a walk up into the hills.

West of town, tracks head inland from Mare Longue, Le Baril, Basse-Vallée and Langevin, some of them running all the way up the flanks of the volcano. If you aren't keen on the idea of a major hike, the forest inland from **Mare Longue**, just west of St-Philippe, is easy to explore. Here, the forest spreads over 70 hectares (173 acres) and includes pandanus and casuarina trees entwined with vanilla creepers, mixed evergreens *(bois de couleurs)* and tall edible palms. Rare plants can be seen along the Sentier Botanique, but if you have more time, ask the St-Philippe tourist office (41a Rue Leconte-Delisle; tel: 0262 97 75 84; email: otstphilippe@gmail.com; Mon–Sat 9am–5pm) to organise a visit to the **Jardin des Parfums et des Epices**, where orchids, moss and ferns grow wild among aromatic plants.

At **Basse-Vallée** tiny Creole houses in flower-filled gardens cram the roadside like cardboard cut-outs from a children's story book. A couple of kilometres east along the Route Nationale is **Hôtel Les Embruns du Baril**, one of the few places to stay along this remote coast. It is flanked by two lava wells, Puits des Anglais and Puits des Français. The story goes that one of them contains a treasure chest watched over by the spirit of a dead slave, but which one may be a matter for Anglo–French debate. Try asking the boss at the hotel, who might know the answer.

There's not much to see at the next town of **St-Joseph** ⓭, but it is the starting point for a challenging trek up the gorgeous valley of the **Rivière des Remparts** – the river that flows through the town and whose source is 30km (19 miles) north at **Nez de Boeuf** (see page 215). Experienced hikers only should try this two-day uphill trek along the Rivière des Remparts. The path from St-Joseph traverses some of Réunion's original lowland forest before the final, tough climb up to the Nez de Boeuf. A *table d'hôte* option in the isolated hamlet of **Roche Plate**, 19km (12 miles) along the way, provides meals and overnight accommodation (book ahead: tel: 0262 59 13 94).

If you want views without the effort, a road runs halfway up the valley, on the eastern side, to **Grand Coude**. You can also head to **Pointe de Langevin** on the coast to see Réunion's southernmost point. As Réunion is an outermost region of Europe, this also counts as the extreme southern point of the European Union territory.

The pebble beach at **Manapany-les-Bains** ⓮, 3km (2 miles) west of St-Joseph, and the sandy beach at Grande Anse, beyond, are often dangerous due to the fierce currents, but there are natural pools among the rocks where it is safe to swim. If you want to treat yourself to some fine Creole and seafood dishes, try **L'Etoile de**

⊘ **Tip**

Between May and December you can see (and smell) the vetiver plant, which grows around St-Joseph. The essential oil of the vetiver is used in the perfumery industry, and the leaves can also be dried to make thatched roofs. You can buy bundles of vetiver in some markets. Place among your clothes for a pleasant aroma.

In the Jardin des Parfums et des Epices.

Tip

In St-Pierre there is plenty of room to park under the trees right next to the old railway station.

Hôtel de Ville, St Pierre.

Mer at Basse-Vallée. Although pricey, this is one of the best restaurants on the island, and also offers spectacular sea views. You'll get more great views as you head west over the impressive Manapany ravine en route to St-Pierre.

FORGOTTEN ST-PIERRE

St-Pierre 15, which lies on a wide coastal plain at the mouth of the Rivière d'Abord, is the largest settlement in the south, with 80,000 inhabitants. It is one of Réunion's most pleasant towns and makes a good base, being well placed for reaching the southeast coast – as well as being just 45 minutes' drive from St-Gilles-les-Bains on the west coast, and about an hour from Piton de la Fournaise.

The town sometimes receives the full fury of cyclones raging in from the Indian Ocean. In 1989, Cyclone Firinga left it nearly in ruins, but a face-lift ensued: a new marina was built and an airport at Pierrefonds opened nearby, bringing in a fresh wave of tourists, mainly from Mauritius. St-Pierre's waterfront restaurants,

late-night bars and clubs, choice of hotels and adequate (but windy) beach attract islanders from as far away as St-Denis. The port is packed with fishing boats and pleasure craft and is fun to stroll around; on one side is the pretty **Bassin de Radoub A**, a small creek where boats were careened in the 19th century, now a historic monument. Just behind it is the recently renovated **Ancienne Gare** (old railway station) **B**, which spills out onto a sea-facing terrace. There are several restaurants on the other side of the seafront Boulevard Hubert Delisle where you'll also find the tourist office (email: saintpierre.tourisme@gmail.com; Mon–Sat 8am–6pm, Sun 8am–noon) directly opposite the port.

It is worth having a quick stroll around the town. The restored **Hôtel de Ville C**, a former East India Company building, is a fine example of colonial architecture, and further west on Rue Victor le Vigoureux you'll find a very attractive market – an unusual circular structure. The Marine Cemetery, at the western end of Boulevard Hubert

Delisle, is a lovely flower-filled cemetery that contains the grave of Sitarane, one of Réunion's most notorious bandits, said to have drunk the blood of his murdered victims. Each night, offerings of cigarettes and headless black cocks or fruits and flowers are left as an inducement to Sitarane to bring mishap, misfortune or even worse to enemies. Nocturnal visits are only for the courageous.

A few kilometres from the town centre is **La Saga du Rhum** (tel: 0262 35 81 90; www.sagadurhum.fr; daily 10am–6pm), in one of the island's oldest rum distilleries. This interesting and informative museum tells the story of Réunion's sugar and rum industry (in English and French).

Nestled between two rivers, the aptly named village of **Entre-Deux** ⑯ makes a pleasant side trip from the coast. Many of its picturesque Creole houses are decorated with *lambrequins* (filigree woodwork) – see how many different patterns you can spot.

St-Louis ⑰, the next town along the coast from St-Pierre, is home to the **MADOI, the Musée des arts décoratifs et du design de l'océan Indien** (Indian Ocean Decorative Arts & Design Museum; 17A Chemin Maison Rouge; tel: 0262 91 24 30; http://madoi.re; Tue–Sun 9am–5:30pm). The museum is in the renovated stables of the Domaine de Maison Rouge, a former coffee estate. You can wander around the grounds for free, and interesting bilingual information panels tell you about the history of the house and Réunion's ill-fated coffee industry.

At St-Louis you'll drive past one of the island's two sugar factories, Le Gol, and the town is also the starting point of the winding RN5 to the Cirque de Cilaos (see page 225). However, for a glimpse of the cirque without the long drive, you could take the D20, which runs 12km (7.5 miles) inland from St-Louis to **Les Makes** ⑱. This tiny village, situated at 1,000 metres

(3,280ft), is home to **L'Observatoire** (18 Rue Georges Bizet; tel: 0262 37 86 83; http://ilereunion.com/observatoire-des-makes; Mon–Fri 8am–1pm, Sat 8–11am), where you can study the stars on a guided tour at 9am or attend a special night show. Ten kilometres (6 miles) beyond Les Makes, along the wildly twisting RF14, you'll come to **La Fenêtre**, a natural window on to Cilaos cirque. If you arrive before the mid-morning mists you should get glorious views.

L'ETANG-SALÉ-LES-BAINS TO ST-LEU

If you've experienced the white beaches and lagoons of Mauritius you may find Réunion's coast disappointing. The beaches are clean but small and get crowded at weekends. Midweek, however, they are a delight, and at any time of the week there are several tourist attractions inland that are well worth a visit.

L'Etang-Salé-les-Bains ⑲ marks the beginning of the west coast beach stretch, but it is very quiet, with just a

St-Pierre's coastline.

> **Tip**

The Corniche, while generally well maintained, is susceptible to damage by rock fall and flooding. An alternative route back to St-Denis is the winding D41, La Montagne road from La Possession.

couple of hotels and restaurants, and the 5km (3-mile) black sand beach is not particularly picturesque. If you have children, you could take them 2km (1 mile) up the hill to the **Croc Nature Park** (tel: 0262 91 40 41; www.crocparc.re; daily 10am–5pm) in L'Etang-Salé-les-Hauts. In addition to the Nile crocodiles (brought from Madagascar and fed on Wednesdays and Sundays at 4pm), there are lemurs, iguanas, farm animals and peacocks, as well as a model Réunion village. A tour of the park takes about an hour; there is a snack bar and a shop.

The 2km (1-mile) trip south along the coast road from L'Etang-Salé-les-Bains to **Le Gouffre** is likely to be of more universal appeal. Here, you can witness the ferocity of the Indian Ocean as the waves crash against the basalt cliffs.

The RN1 slices through jagged black lava rock close to the shore for the next 22km (13.5 miles) to St-Leu. You'll pass a couple of laybys on the way where you can stop for spectacular views of *souffleurs* (blowholes): if the sea is

rough enough, tall jets of water spurt through these rocky crevices. For a different perspective, consider taking the high road (the D11) between L'Etang-Salé and St-Leu via **Les Avirons**. Known as the Allée des Flamboyants, this is a delightful route and also offers lovely views of the coast. Keep your eyes on the road, however, as it twists and turns and local drivers like to move at speed. Just before you rejoin the RN1, you'll pass the Stella Matutina museum (see below).

AROUND ST-LEU

The town of **St-Leu** ⑳ witnessed a slave revolt in 1811, survived a cholera epidemic in 1859, and has been hit by several devastating cyclones, but otherwise life here is reasonably uneventful and easy-going. The large, black-sand beach accommodates the weekend crowds reasonably well. When the conditions are right, experienced surfers flock here to ride what are reputed to be some of the best waves in the Indian Ocean (although at the time of writing, surfing has been 'temporarily' banned due to a rise in shark attacks). In addition to the beach there are several attractions in the vicinity of St-Leu, so it's worth devoting at least half a day to the town.

The church of **Notre Dame de la Salette** was built in the town in honour of the Madonna who the Réunionnais believe saved the lives of the people of St-Leu when the 1859 cholera epidemic swept the island. Every September there is a festival in her honour, which culminates in a pilgrimage to the church.

About 4km (2.5 miles) south of St-Leu along the Avirons road is the **Stella Matutina** (tel: 0262 34 59 60; http://museesreunion.re/stellamatutina; Mon 1–5.30pm, Tue–Sun 9.30am–5.30pm), a former sugar factory and now a fascinating museum devoted to the history of sugar production and agriculture on the island.

Zattes – a type of custard apple – for sale at St-Leu.

Kelonia (tel: 0262 34 81 10; www.
kelonia.org; daily 9am–6pm), 2km (1
mile) north of St-Leu on the RN1, is
a research and educational centre for
the study of hawksbill and green turtles. Visits include turtle spotting in
large tanks, but the centre itself is of
historic significance since it is home to
two of the oldest lime kilns in Réunion. Be aware that although commercial breeding of turtles was banned in
1998, you may still find turtle products
on sale, which manufacturers claim
were produced before the ban.

Virtually opposite Kelonia, the D12
runs uphill to Les Colimaçons and the
**Conservatoire Botanique de Mas-
carin** (2 rue du Père Georges; tel:
0262 24 92 27; www.departement974.fr/
actualite/mascarin-jardin-botanique-con-
seil-departemental-de-reunion; Tue–Sun
9am–5pm). This magnificent botanic
garden, which contains 4,000 botanical species, offers an insight into
Réunion's remarkable flora and is
landscaped into themed gardens of
rare indigenous and endemic plants,
plants introduced by early settlers, a
collection of palm trees, an orchard
of local fruits and an eye-popping
enclosure of cacti. But the pièce de
résistance is the 19th-century villa,
fully restored and filled with colonial
furniture. You can also visit the stables, hunting lodge and the old family
kitchen, which now serves as a restaurant, Le Vieux Pressoir. Next door
to the gardens is the church of Les
Colimaçons, which offers spectacular
views over the reef-fringed coastline.

To reach St-Gilles-les-Bains, you
can choose between the winding inland
route via St-Gilles-les Hauts (and the
fascinating Musée de Villèle: see page
210), the coastal route, or the faster
Route des Tamarins which links Etang-
Salé and St-Paul..

ST-GILLES-LES-BAINS

Dubbed the 'St-Tropez of the Indian
Ocean', **St-Gilles-les-Bains** ㉑ is

the hub of Réunion's holiday scene,
attracting local and French holiday-
makers. This is the best place on the
island in which to soak up the sun,
enjoy all the pleasure of the sea,
or just lie back and recover from a
hard mountain trek. If that's all too
sedate, then plenty of canyoning
and paragliding operators are on
hand to book the jump of a lifetime
down Réunion's ravines and gorges.
At night, the restaurants, bars and
clubs that line – and spill on to – Rue
Général de Gaulle come alive. The
cast of characters, from oldfashioned
hippies to trendy young locals, is
attracted by the blend of Gallic chic
and Creole insouciance that oozes
from the restaurants and bars.

One reason St-Gilles' broad, sloping beach is so popular is that it has
white, albeit rather coarse, sand. The
focus of activity is north of the Ravine
St-Gilles: it is here that most people
gather to watch the sunset, something of a local tradition. South of
the ravine, the more peaceful beach
known as **L'Hermitage** is backed by

On the "Sud Sauvage".

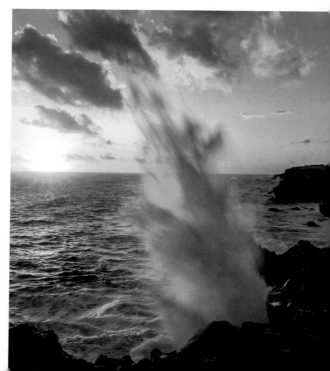

holiday homes and *pensions* rather than loud bars and restaurants. The port in the mouth of the ravine is packed with boats belonging to game fishing and scubadiving operators. Half a dozen game fishing boats depart on day trips to hook blue marlin, sailfish, tuna and sea bream; October to April is the best time. If you're a first-time diver, enquire at Bleu Marine Réunion (tel: 0262 24 22 00), which also offers special packages for children.

If you have a car, park first and then walk to the beach, which is hidden from view by the shops and restaurants along Rue Général de Gaulle. Parking is not always easy, though; there are a couple of small car parks on Rue Général de Gaulle, but they are often full. A good place is the patch of ground just before the bridge that crosses the ravine.

Just five minutes' drive north of St-Gilles-les-Bains, **Boucan Canot** ㉒ is a smarter, smaller and more laid-back resort than its neighbour. Unlike St-Gilles, most of Boucan

Chopped coconut at St-Paul's market.

Canot's cafés and restaurants are by the beach, so it's easier to potter off for a drink or snack in between stints on the sand. The sandy beach is clean but small, and can get crowded at weekends. Drivers should note that the main drag is pedestrianised, and that the only place to park is either at the north or south end of the seafront.

On the RN1 at Hermitage-les-Bains, just south of St-Gilles-les-Bains, the **Jardin d'Eden** (tel: 0262 33 83 16; www.jardindeden.re; daily 10am–6pm) is a beautiful oasis of calm away from the beach. Here, you can wander through lovely orchards of fruit trees and spices, learn how to cure a hangover with medicinal plants, or settle for some mysticism in the mini rice field surrounding the Zen garden.

ST-GILLES-LES-HAUTS

The **Musée de Villèle** ㉓ (tel: 0262 55 64 10; www.departement974.fr/actualite/musee-historique-de-villele; Tue–Sun 9.30am–12.30pm, 1.30–5.30pm, guided tours of the house, self-guided tours of the grounds and outbuildings), in St-Gilles-les-Hauts, is the former family seat of the Desbassyns dynasty. Built in 1787, the house's most famous resident was Madame Desbassyns, a coffee and sugar producer and notorious matriarch, who is said to have inflicted horrific punishments on her slaves. The local legendary figure Grand-mère Kal – a fiendish old woman who scares children – is said to be based on her. The colonial mansion now houses memorabilia and family portraits, maps of slave ship routes and fine French East India furniture. The slave hospital in the grounds was established not out of altruism but to conform to the law. Madame Desbassyns, who died in 1846, is buried in Chapelle Pointue, next to the ruins of the estate's sugar mill.

ST-PAUL: THE OLD CAPITAL

St-Paul ㉔ is a pleasant town less than 40 minutes' drive from St-Denis and well worth visiting. It is the island's original capital, and many historical buildings survive, such as the Hôtel de Lassays, now a fire station, and Grand Cour, the abandoned home of the Desbassyns dynasty on the Route Royale. There are vestiges of the old French East India Company, too, including the town hall, built in 1767. But most holiday-makers come to St-Paul not for a historical tour, nor to lie on its long, black-sand beach, but to visit the **seafront market** held on Friday afternoon and Saturday morning. The crowd that flocks here is a lively mix of tourists searching for crafts, spices, baskets and other souvenirs and locals buying fruit and veg, fish and other fresh produce. Numerous stalls and vans sell tasty snacks. Towards the end of the day, bands start playing, and people gather in the beach-side bars to watch the sun disappear into the sea.

Don't miss the **Cimetière Marin**, in a stunning position right by the beach just south of the centre. Here is said to lie the body of one of the Mascarenes' most notorious pirates, Olivier Le Vasseur, alias La Buse (The Buzzard), who was hung in St-Paul in 1730 (see page 240). His grave, right opposite the entrance, is marked by a simple skull and crossbones crudely etched on a basalt cross, and is still visited by followers. Presumably, they would not like the theory that La Buse's body isn't actually buried here – based on the fact that the cemetery did not exist in 1730.

LA CORNICHE

Driving north from St-Paul the RN1 crosses the enormous estuary of the Rivière des Galets, bypasses **Le Port** and emerges at **La Possession**, where Governor Pronis took possession of Réunion in 1642, before continuing to St-Denis. The 14km (9-mile) stretch of the Route Nationale from La Possession to St-Denis is, along with the Route des Tamarins, one of the busiest stretches of road in the Mascarenes. Known as **La Corniche,** or the Route du Littoral, it's a dramatic ride as you whizz beneath cliffs and through a tunnel only metres from the sea. However it can be subject to rock falls, and a major new highway is being built just offshore (partly on stilts and partly on an embankment). The current road runs alongside the old railway line and the only place you can stop is at **La Grande Chaloupe**, site of one of Réunion's original railway stations. The rail service stopped in 1963, but a Scafader 030T is preserved in the small **museum** (daily 9am–5pm) to remind you of the heavy locomotives that plied the route from St-Denis to St-Pierre. You can also visit the nearby **Lazaret** (tel: 0262 55 64 10; www.depar tement974.fr/actualite/lazaret-de-grande-chaloupe; see website for opening hours), a restored 19th-century quarantine building for indentured workers arriving from India.

On the beach at Boucan Canot.

A scientist examining lava at Piton de la Fournaise.

VOLCANO AND HIGH PLAINS

When Piton de la Fournaise trembles, fear and excitement lure many to witness the great natural phenomenon. Most of the time, however, the volcano is an awesome but peaceful sight.

The **Piton de la Fournaise** is one of the most active volcanoes on the planet; it has erupted at least 190 times since 1640 (the last eruptions were in 2018), and the lava flows have left trails of destruction. For modern visitors, however, getting a close-up view of the smouldering volcano is reasonably safe and easy to do, provided, of course, that you stick to the marked route.

Born on the flanks of the extinct volcano called Piton des Neiges, between 500,000 and 600,000 years ago, Piton de la Fournaise, a twin shield volcano known to volcanologists as a Hawaiian type, rises to 2,632 metres (8,635ft). It is surrounded by a horseshoe-shaped lava cliff enclosure, called Enclos Fouqué, which is 10km (6 miles) in diameter and has two craters; the higher one, Bory, has been inactive since 1791, while the active Dolomieu manages, for most of the time, to confine its eruption within the enclosure.

REACHING FOR THE TOP

Each year some 200,000 visitors make the journey up above the clouds to the top of the volcano. Most people drive to **Pas de Bellecombe** Ⓐ. Perched on the edge of the canyon-like Enclos Fouqué, it is a natural platform for spectacular views of Piton de la Fournaise across a wild and barren moonscape. Irrespective of whether you join an organised

Taking a helicopter to the volcano's crater.

tour or make your own way, you should aim to reach the caldera before 10am, when cloud often descends to mask the volcano's wild beauty. But don't despair if you can't see a thing on the way up – or even when you reach the top. The area is subject to sudden climate changes, which can go from swirling cloud and mist and sharp drops in temperature, to clear vistas across crisp blue skies. For this reason, you should also go equipped for all weathers. Good walking shoes are essential, and it can be chilly, so wear

Main attractions
Piton de la Fournaise
Cité du Volcan
Forêt de Bébour

Maps on pages 198, 214

long trousers, take a jumper and don't leave your hotel without a waterproof.

BOURG-MURAT

The gateway to Piton de la Fournaise is **Bourg-Murat ⓑ**, on the RN3, the only cross-island route, which links St-Pierre in the south and St-Benoît in the north. The journey there from the two coasts takes about 40 minutes and an hour respectively. More a large village than a town, Bourg-Murat is home to the **Observatoire Volcanologique**, set up in 1979 after the 1977 eruption (see page 184), from where eruptions can be monitored in complete safety. High-tech equipment records seismic activity so that these days the islanders have plenty of notice of an eruption. Bear in mind, however, that there was only a 45-minute warning of an eruption – albeit small – inside the Enclos Fouqué on 19 July 1999. If you're in Réunion to witness such a spectacle, expect to find the Enclos Fouqué closed and droves of enthusiasts and experts jostling with cameramen and reporters for the best positions.

Bourg-Murat's other main attraction is the futuristic building of the **Cité du Volcan** (tel: 0262 59 00 26; www.maisonduvolcan.fr; Mon 1–5pm, Tue–Sun 9.30am–5pm). Originally opened in 1991 and refurbished in 2014 with state-of-the-art technology, this fascinating museum owes much of its collection to French husband and wife volcanologists Maurice and Katia Krafft. Bilingual information panels, 'augmented reality' and interactive quizzes will teach you everything you ever wanted to know about volcanoes. There are also holographic projections, an art gallery and even a 4D cinema (French only). The shop sells all sorts of volcanic knick-knacks, from lumps of lava to posters, books and T-shirts commemorating particular eruptions. For a bite to eat try the nearby **Ti'Resto Lontan**, which serves tasty Creole *carri*.

VOLCANIC VIEWS ON THE ROUTE DU VOLCAN

Most people are too eager to get to the top to even pause in Bourg-Murat on the way up. From here, it's 23km (14 miles) and about 40 minutes' drive up to Pas de Bellecombe, but what an interesting route. The RF5 – or 'Route du Volcan' – which heads east from Bourg-Murat, becomes gradually more winding as you leave the town behind and head ever upwards, sweeping through pine woods, dairy farms, small villages and alpine meadows. The road is not in mint condition but is paved as far as Plaine des Sables.

As you get higher, you will enjoy new, and often astonishing, views at every turn. Some of the best of these are at established viewpoints. (However keen you are to reach the top, if the sky is clear on the way up, don't resist the temptation to stop, as you never know when the clouds are going to roll in.) The first of these viewpoints, 7km (4 miles) from Pas de Bellecombe, is at **Nez de Boeuf** C (2,070 metres/6,973ft), from where there are absolutely staggering views of the huge ravine of **Rivière des Remparts**. From these heights, the river appears as a thin pencil line flowing southwards to St-Joseph. A challenging Grande Randonnée (GR) trail runs along the banks of the river from the coast and links up with the RF5 just beyond the Nez de Boeuf viewpoint; the 30km (18-mile) trek is rather easier north to south than vice versa.

Next stop is **Cratère Commerson** D, where an observation platform perches over a 120-metre (380ft) deep crater, a few paces from the road. The extinct crater, named after French botanist Philibert Commerson, who discovered it by accident in 1771, is a dramatic sight. Most breathtaking of all, however, are the views across the crater's 200-metre (650ft) diameter towards the jagged ridge of Cilaos cirque.

However, the view that is likely to remain etched on your memory for longest is the one from the top of the Rempart des Sables ridge where the road begins its dramatic descent into the **Plaine des Sables** E. An information board describes the landscape that spreads below you – an utter wilderness of raw beauty and incredible wide-angle views of corroded lava, ground by the elements into fine black gravel and restrained by massive mountain ramparts and distant peaks. As the road descends across the eerie reddish-brown landscape, pockmarked with bizarre rock formations, the only signs of life are sparse bushes of gorse, heather and lichen and a trail of moving cars, before it climbs briefly to end at the parking area at Pas de Bellecombe. The track across the Plaine des Sables is unpaved and may be full of potholes if there's been recent heavy rain: drive slowly to avoid skidding, and be particularly careful in wet conditions.

A WALK AROUND EARTH'S FIRE

Pas de Bellecombe is also the starting point of several walking routes to and around Piton de la Fournaise. In a shelter by the car park some displays provide information on the geology and fauna and flora of the area. Most useful, however, is the relief model of

On the way to Piton de la Fournaise.

⊙ Tip

To witness a volcanic sunrise, make an overnight booking for the Gîte du Volcan, a short walk away from Pas de Bellecombe. Lovely topiaried gardens provide relaxing comfort and you can order drinks and snacks with mountain vistas thrown in for free. Book through www. reunion.fr.

the volcano, which shows the routes (and distances) of the various walking trails. You don't really need a map for the more well-trodden circuits, such as Pas de Bellecombe to Cratère Dolomieu, but for more involved trekking you should invest in the IGN 1:25,000 series map 4406RT Piton de la Fournaise. You can buy this in most bookshops or tourist shops, or pick it up at the Cité du Volcan in Bourg-Murat.

There is also a list of rules for walkers. The most important ones to heed are a) don't go alone, b) tell someone where you have gone, and c) take water and food. Light refreshments and toilets are available in the shelter. You can also walk to **Gîte du Volcan**, about 10 minutes away along a path from the car park. If you're driving, the track to the *gîte* branches left off the main track just before you reach the car park.

For the full experience you should consider doing the 13km (8-mile) circuit, a 'medium' classified trek, which takes about five hours. (Alternatively, you could choose to do just part of the route; for example, the return walk to Formica

Léo takes about 40 minutes.) Make sure you pack some energy-giving snacks and plenty of water. Provided you don't wander off the marked paths, and you heed the danger warning signs and wear the right clothes, you can't go wrong.

A stepped pathway winds its way down the 200-metre (650ft) cliff to the bottom. On the way down take a good look at the plants that grow on the cliff face – beyond there is nothing but layers of lava from across the ages decorated with splodges of white paint that mark the entire route. The first landmark on the volcanic floor is the rather undramatic scoria cone of **Formica Léo ⑤**. From here the path continues about 2km (1 mile) past what used to be the Chapelle de Rosemont, a hollow volcanic mound which was completely buried by an eruption in 2018. Here you have a choice of two paths. For the more strenuous route take the right-hand fork, which will lead you directly up a steep slope to the extinct 2,621-metre (8,599ft) high **Cratère Bory ⑥**. Caution should be taken on the potentially unstable paths. The left-hand fork leads you to an easier route that snakes gently northwards along the contours of the volcano to **La Soufrière** (2,530 metres/8,300ft), the northern wall of the active **Cratère Dolomieu ⑥**; you can sometimes smell sulphur emissions here. There is another choice of routes here: one carries on along the rim of both Dolomieu and Bory before heading back to Pas de Bellecombe; the other, shorter route cuts straight across to Cratère Bory.

There is a whole series of other walks to do. One of the easiest is the 9km (5.5-mile) walk north along the rim from Pas de Bellecombe to **Nez Coupé de Ste-Rose** and back. Another is the 8km (5-mile) circular route from the Rempart des Sables to **Morne Langevin** – you should allow about three hours for this relatively easy but scenic route.

Among the other much longer routes you could opt for are treks along sections

The road around Piton de la Fournaise.

of the Grande Randonnée R2, which crosses the island (IGN 1:25,000 series map 4406RT Piton de la Fournaise). One of these follows the southern edge of the volcano to **Nez Coupé du Tremblet** before descending to Pointe du Tremblet on the east coast. Another heads south from Pas de Bellecombe on the GR2, across the so-called Plateau de Foc Foc to link up with the **Vallée Heureuse** and the Gîte de Basse Vallée, before continuing all the way to the town of Basse Vallée on the coast.

THE HIGH PLAINS

The High Plains (Hautes Plaines) that separate Piton de la Fournaise and the three cirques may lack volcano-style drama but are still well worth exploring. Centred around La Plaine-des-Palmistes (named after a variety of palm trees of which only a few remain) and La Plaine-des-Cafres in the west, these upland areas reveal magnificent mist-enshrouded forests, waterfalls, lakes and mountains: in short, perfect terrain for tranquil walks, scenic drives and more active pursuits such as horse

riding and mountain biking. The route described below runs in a north–south direction from the coast. A number of villages on the way up from the south coast, such as Le Vingt-Troisième (23rd) and Le Dix-Neuvième (19th), have been named unimaginatively after their distance in kilometres by road from the sea, but at least they're handy landmarks.

From St-Benoît on the east coast, the RN3 meanders through sugar cane fields before hitting a series of switchbacks that lead to a viewpoint at **L'Echo ㉕**, which offers fine views north towards the coast and the ocean. Before the road winds up to L'Echo, about 12km (8 miles) from St-Benoît a track runs 6km (4 miles) west to **Grand-Etang ㉖**, a lake in a most stunning spot at the foot of an awesome ridge. To prolong the pleasure, you can follow the path right around the shores of the lake; there's a waterfall just off the path near the southern shore.

Beyond L'Echo, 20km (12 miles) from St-Benoît, you hit **Le Premier Village ㉗**, the first part of **La Plaine-des-Palmistes**, a popular holiday retreat, particularly in

A view of the volcano's dolomieu crater.

⊙ A BIRD'S-EYE VIEW

Réunion's scenery is awe-inspiring whatever angle you look at it from, but the aerial views you get from a helicopter of Piton de la Fournaise, and the Cirque de Salazie and Cirque de Mafate (see the following chapter), are hard to beat. These tours may be expensive, but they are worth every euro. Pilots fly in and out of deep ravines and hover precariously over isolated hamlets and the cirques, allowing plenty of time for photographs, before heading east to the volcano. Depending on weather conditions, helicopters, seating up to six or eight passengers, take off between 7 and 11am for flights lasting between 15 and 55 minutes. The price includes transfer from your hotel, individual headphones and commentary (in French unless all passengers are English speakers). Prices range from €95 to €320 per person, and you should try to book at least 72 hours in advance since these flights are extremely popular.

Hélilagon (tel: 0262 55 55 55; www.helilagon.com) flies from Roland Garros Airport or from l'Eperon heliport near St-Paul. Corail Helicopters (tel: 0262 22 22 66; www.corail-helicopteres.com) operates from St-Gilles or Pierrefonds Airport. Starting at only €40, microlight flights organised through Felix ULM (Base ULM de Cambaie, St-Paul; tel: 0262 43 02 59; www.felixulm.com) are a somewhat cheaper option. Tours, in specially equipped two-seater microlights, cover the cirques, volcano massif, and/or the lagoon.

☉ Tip

Tourist offices in the Hautes Plaines area are located at: Maison du Parc National, (258 rue de la République, Plaine-des-Palmistes; tel: 0262 41 17 70; Mon–Wed and Fri–Sat 9am–12.30pm, 1.30–5pm, closed Thursdays and Sundays) or Bourg Murat. (160 rue Maurice et Katia Krafft, Plaines-des-Cafres; tel: 0262 27 40 00; www.tampontourisme.re; daily 9am–5pm).

January and February when the weather on the coast is very hot. Even so, the area remains a comparatively untouched agricultural heartland where the red-berried *goyavier* (strawberry guava) fruit has become so important that every June there is a festival in its honour. Attractive wooden houses are very characteristic of this area; you'll see them featured on postcards and posters. La Plaine-des-Palmistes is a centre of operations and you may want to stop here to make use of the tourist office, which can supply details of accommodation and walks, ranging from gentle to strenuous, in and around the Forêt de Bébour, or for some souvenir shopping at the adjacent Domaine des Tourelles (tel: 0262 51 47 59; www.tourelles.re).

HORSE RIDING AND FOREST WALKING

To the northeast of Le Premier Village, a dozen gentle Merens horses wait at the **Ferme Equestre du Grand Etang** (RN3 Pont-Payet; tel: 0262 50 90 03; http://fermeequestredugrandetang.easyloisirs.com), to take even the most inexperienced rider

The Cascades de Takamaka.

for a pleasant half-day's trek. A morning with Rico Nourry, a former farmer who turned his love of the outdoors into a going concern, should not be missed. His enthusiasm is infectious as he leads groups of riders along rocky narrow pathways to the stunning lake of Grand-Etang where the horses take a break and splash about in the cool water. The trek takes you along a nature trail, passing through a garden of traditional medicinal herbs and citrus orchards where you can help yourself to fruit without getting out of the saddle. Rico believes in giving all his clients a hands-on experience, so you'll be expected to prepare the horses before the ride and hose them down afterwards. Four-day rides to the volcano can also be arranged.

For a gentle 2km (1-mile) walk, take the marked path from Le Premier Village, which passes through boulder-filled streams, leading to the 240-metre (787ft) high **Biberon** waterfall. There are a number of longer hikes through the **Forêt de Bébour**, noted for the endemic tree, *tamarin des hauts (acacia heterophylla)*, which contrasts in height and huge girth with the indigenous *bois de couleurs*, or mixed evergreens, and imported cryptomerias. For an in-depth look at this forest, which merges with the silvery tamarind forests of **Bélouve** and the rain-soaked gorge of Takamaka to the north, you'll need to spend a full day exploring the numerous trails and spend the night at the Gîte de Bélouve, about a two-hour trek uphill from Hell-Bourg in Salazie cirque (be sure to book well in advance at www.reunion.fr). Serious trekkers should equip themselves with the IGN 1:25000, 4405RT map.

PLAINE-DES-CAFRES

To see La-Plaine-des-Palmistes's luxuriant vegetation head southwards along the RN3, stopping after a 6km (4-mile) upward sinuous drive to a parking-cum-picnic viewpoint called **Col de Bellevue**. Continuing southwards along the RN3, the road straightens across **Plaine-des-Cafres** ㉘, once the hideout of runaway slaves, where the pasturelands, dairy farms and cattle give it an alpine feel. Although the area has less charm than La Plaine-des-Palmistes, there are some memorable walks and a range of *chambres d'hôtes* and restaurants dotted along the RN3 to neighbouring Le Tampon. As you enter La Plaine-des-Cafres from Col de Bellevue, look out for the pretty flower-bedecked shrine to St-Expédit, which seems strangely isolated as it stares across countryside towards Piton des Neiges. It's one of many dedicated to the Roman soldier (see page 204) who died for his beliefs, but this one is distinctly religious, unlike the dozens of other red-daubed shrines, which are often linked to black magic.

There's a lovely 5km (3-mile) walk that goes from the village church of La Plaine-des-Cafres (also known as Le Vingt-Troisième, or 23rd) north to Bois Court and a viewpoint over the waterfalls of Grand Bassin. They tumble into a deep gorge where three rivers – the Bras Sec, Bras de Suzanne and Bras des Roches Noires – meet along the southeastern foothills of the Cilaos cirque. Another possibility is to take a pleasant 9km (5.5-mile) drive along the D36 from Le Vingt-Quatrième (24th) through Notre-Dame-de-la-Paix to the picnic area, where you can explore the surrounding forests and botanical paths overlooking the Rivière des Remparts.

The tortuous RN3 then descends to Le Tampon (which possibly takes its name from the Malagasy word *tampony*, meaning 'peak') to St-Pierre on the coast. Since 1830, when the land was bought by Gabriel de Kerveguen and developed into a sugar-growing area, Le Tampon has remained primarily agricultural. It also used to be the centre of a thriving geranium-growing area, but in spite of Réunion essential oil being the best in the world for the perfume industry, production has fallen to 10 tonnes per year compared with 165 tonnes back in 1962.

Grand Etang riders.

Cirque de Mafate from
Piton Maido.

THE CIRQUES

Only one road penetrates each of the cirques of Salazie and Cilaos, and you need a helicopter for Mafate, but this dramatic landscape is a paradise for walkers.

The spectacular natural showpieces of Mafate, Salazie and Cilaos are huge caldera-like valleys that radiate north, east and southwest in a clover leaf pattern, with the extinct volcano of Piton des Neiges at its centre. The three cirques became the home of runaway slaves (marrons) in the mid-18th century and later of impoverished white settlers (petit blancs), who came up from the coast a century later. Here, they discovered awesome landscapes of jagged peaks, verdant gorges, rivers and waterfalls. As you take in the almost Dante-esque panorama, it is hard not to wonder how those first slaves and settlers ever survived in such an environment.

By far the easiest of the cirques to get to, if you're on limited time, is the waterfall-strewn Cirque de Salazie. Rains brought in by the southeast trade winds ensure that the area is lush and green all year round, unlike Mafate, which is much drier. Unsurprisingly, Salazie is the most visited of the cirques and in the tourist season can get relatively busy. If you're staying on the west coast, Cilaos appears deceptively close, but the drive from St-Louis is slow-going, and you should allow up to one and a half hours to negotiate the narrow and tortuous RN5. Whichever cirque you choose, weather conditions are very changeable, so go prepared for both sun and rain. Finally, make

sure you take enough euros with you as there are no banks there, and ATMs are few and far between, although most restaurants and hotels in Cilaos and Salazie accept major credit cards.

THE LOST WORLD OF MAFATE

With no cars, no roads and no large shops, the **Cirque de Mafate** is a happy escape from the maelstrom of the outside world. Runaway slaves knew that their masters would have a very hard job getting there, and even today tourists face similar difficulties. The

Main attractions
Mafate's îlets (villages)
Maïdo viewpoint
Villa Folio
Cilaos

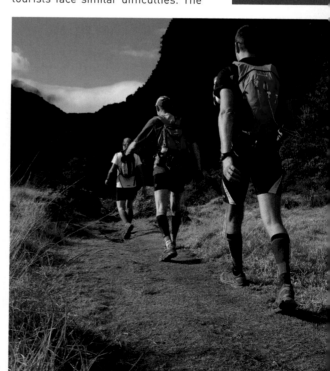

Trekking in Cirque de Mafate.

Map on page 222

cirque's seven hundred inhabitants live in a dozen scattered hamlets (îlets) linked by paths and tracks, and everyone, including the postman, walks.

Mafate is the least populated and least accessible of all the cirques, unless you take one of the dozens of hiking trails of the Grande Randonnée (see page 182). If you're on limited time, you can take a helicopter ride over hamlets and dizzying ravines before landing for an alfresco carri at La Nouvelle. Flights with Hélilagon (see page 217) leave every day from the heliport at L'Eperon, near St-Paul.

La Nouvelle ❶ is the most populated hamlet, with 130 inhabitants and three grocery stores, and has become the self-styled 'capital' of Mafate, relying on

tourism, small-scale cattle farming on Plaine des Tamarins, and geranium oil production, though the number of distilleries has dwindled over the years. It is well worth the effort to trek as far as **Marla**, Mafate's highest hamlet (1,600 metres/5,250ft), if only to overnight in a gîte and wake early to catch the spectacular cloudless views. An alternative – and comparatively easy – route for trekkers is from Le Bélier in Salazie cirque (see page 223).

If you're not a trekker, you can still admire Mafate from its western rim at **Piton Maido** ❷, sometimes known simply as Le Maido. It is worth making an early start in order to arrive before clouds descend between 10 and 11am. From St-Paul or St-Gilles, you should

Cirques

allow up to two hours to drive the winding 25km (16-mile) road to the top. The route takes you through the geranium-growing area of **Petite France**, and past numerous essential oil stills and picnic places. A stunning panorama spreads before you at the **Maido viewpoint**, at 2,203 metres (7,222ft). Looking from left to right you can see the peaks of La Roche Ecrite (2,277 metres/7,469ft), Le Cimendef (2,226 metres/7,301ft) and Le Morne de Fourche (2,195 metres/7,200ft), which separate the Salazie and Mafate cirques. The peaks of Le Gros Morne (3,019 metres/9,905ft) and the Piton des Neiges (3,070 metres/10,070ft) rise from the Salazie range of mountains marking the centre of the three cirques. To the south, Col du Taïbit (2,082 metres/ 6,832ft) and the peak of Le Grand Bénare (2,896 metres/9,499ft) divide Mafate and Cilaos cirques, providing another stunning spectacle. You can hike along the rim of the cirque to Le Grand Bénare, but it's tough going, and you'll need to allow six or seven hours to do the return trip.

For gentler walking, or a place to keep the kids happy, stop at **Parc du Maido** (tel: 0262 32 40 32; www.lugere-union.fr; Wed–Sun 9.30am–5pm), a recreational centre about 15 minutes downhill from the viewpoint. You can go tobogganing, mountain biking or pony trekking through the tamarind forests, which are dotted with picnic sites, or stay put and try your hand at archery.

EASY-GOING SALAZIE

The name Salazie comes from the Malagasy word *salazane*, which means a 'stake' or 'post', and probably stems from the three peaks of Le Gros Morne, which stand like sentries at the far southwestern corner of the cirque. Salazie's first European settler, a certain Monsieur Cazeau, lived in a home-made hut and made a name for himself by surviving on nothing but pumpkins during a 43-day period of rain. 'When it rains at Salazie,' noted one visitor in 1863, 'it does rain... in a steady, business-like European way.'

It still rains in Salazie, making it the most verdant of the cirques. These days the 25 villages carry on the farming traditions introduced in the 1840s, growing watercress, peaches, citrus fruit and an abundance of *chou chou*. The lime green, pear-shaped vegetable (see page 172) is fêted each May in a three-day carnival that attracts many visitors to the colourful stalls groaning with local produce. It's a jolly affair with local music groups and a Miss Chou Chou contest.

It does not take long, having left St-André behind on the coast, to get a taste of Salazie as you enter the luxuriant, tree-clad gorge of Rivière du Mât, where soaring peaks and dozens of pencil-thin waterfalls fill the space above you. Some of the latter are mere trickles of water – but not the **Voile de la Mariée ❸** or 'Bride's Veil', which positively cascades into the Rivière du Mât just beyond the village of Salazie. If you're driving take advantage of the handful of stopping places along the route to admire the scenery safely. The road is winding but mostly flat as far as Salazie; after that the climb is virtually

⊙ Fact

Geraniums were first brought from South Africa in around 1870 and became an economic lifesaver for the *petits blancs*, who made a living cultivating them for essential oil.

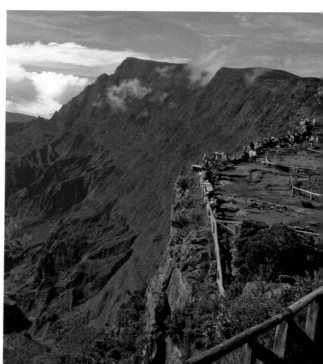

Cirque of Mafate from the Maido lookout.

continuous. There isn't much to Sala-zie, though it has a few shops and places to eat. For breakfast or lunch on the hoof, you can pick up freshly baked brioches, croissants and pastries at the *boulangerie* on the D48.

Close to the Voile de la Mariée, the D52 branches off west and snakes for 34km (21 miles) through the heart of the cirque to **Grand-Îlet** ❹, a hamlet overshadowed by the peak of La Roche Ecrite. This is a base for treks into Mafate cirque, and has a handful of cheap *chambres d'hôtes*. Most walks kick off from **Le Bélier**, a hamlet 3km (2 miles) south of Grand-Îlet (accessible by road), and follow the GR1 and GR2; one route penetrates south into Cilaos cirques (for details on long treks, see page 182). Alternatively, you can carry straight on to Hell-Bourg, a 30-minute winding drive above Salazie. There are two stunning viewpoints worth stopping at – one at **Mare à Poule d'Eau**, and the other at **Le Point du Jour**, just at the entrance of Hell-Bourg, at 892 metres (2,926ft). La Roche Ecrite is right in front of you

and you can see Le Bélier up in the hills to the left.

DELIGHTFUL HELL-BOURG

Hell-Bourg ❺ – named after a certain Governor de Hell rather than the domain of sinners – is a slow-paced, delightful village and a pleasant place in which to spend a couple of days. There are several things to see inside and just outside the town, and walkers can join up with the GR1 here, too. To cater for the steady flow of visitors, Hell-Bourg has a handful of small hotels, and there are a few small food shops and restaurants on the main street, **Rue Général de Gaulle**, as well as a helpful tourist office (https://visit.reunionest.fr).

There are some lovely Creole houses in Hell-Bourg, some of them brightly painted and with luxuriant gardens shaded by bamboo, orange trees and ferns like parasols. Note in particular the decorative little kiosks known as *guetalis*: strategically placed at the edge of gardens overlooking the street, they allowed the occupants to watch passers-by without being seen themselves. The name comes from the French verb *guetter*, which means 'to watch out for' or 'look at'.

For a close look at a traditional home, visit **Villa Folio** (tel: 0262 47 80 98; daily 9am–11.30am, 2–5pm for guided tours), almost hidden among its lush gardens opposite the church in Rue Amiral Lacaze. Built in 1870, the tiny villa is typical of the times and offers a rare insight into Creole life, when much of one's time was spent on the veranda. The two small pavilions at the back used to be the kitchen and servants' quarters and a reception area for friends who'd drop by for drinks made from the local rum and spices. The house contains original furniture, including a 19th-century English four-poster bed complete with canopy – hijacked, so the story goes, from an East India ship by privateers.

Cascade Blanche in the cirque of Salazie.

The discovery of medicinal springs near Hell-Bourg, in 1831, drew the sick to its healing waters for over a century. A landslide in 1948 reduced them to ruins, which you can see today by taking a pleasant 15-minute walk west of the defunct Hôtel des Salazes (a former military hospital), in Chemin du Cimetière.

Some of the casualties of the landslide were buried in the **Cemetery**, at the north end of Chemin du Cimetière. This is a very picturesque cemetery, framed by luxuriant bamboo and verdant cliffs behind. Hidden among the graves of settlers, soldiers and aristocrats is a mound of rock with a simple iron cross, said to contain the headless corpse of a Mr Zett, a bandit and rapist, who terrorised the area in the early 1900s. To ensure he would not rise again he was decapitated and his head despatched to St-Denis (see page 196). Glasses of rum and cigarettes are sometimes placed around the grave to appease what's left of him.

If you'd rather hook a trout than a lost soul, follow the signs to **Parc Piscicole d'Hell-Bourg** (tel: 0692 82 29 19; Tue–Sun 9.30am–5.30pm), near the Relais des Cîmes Hotel. This freshwater trout farm provides bait and line, and you can have your catch cooked to order in the restaurant. For more active pursuits head for the waterfalls at **Les Trois Cascades**, about 1km (half a mile) south of Hell-Bourg, which provide ideal conditions for canyoning. And if hanging on a rope in a wetsuit in the thundering crash of a waterfall doesn't set your pulse racing, have a go at white-water rafting and career at breakneck speed to a calm inlet.

For the best views of Salazie cirque, head northwest out of town along the D48 towards **Îlet à Vidot**. Rising to 1,352 metres (4,436ft) from the centre of the cirque is the flat-topped **Piton d'Enchaing ❻**. You can follow a very challenging section of the GR1 to the peak either from Hell-Bourg or Îlet à Vidot, but take plenty of supplies. You'll

need to allow at least five hours to go there and back from Hell-Bourg. A longer but more popular trek is south to the top of **Piton des Neiges ❼**. The best option is to stay overnight at the Gîte de la Caverne Dufour, and then head on up to the summit first thing, before the clouds have descended (see page 183).

CIRQUE DE CILAOS

Cilaos is named after a runaway slave called Tsilaos, from the Malagasy *tsy laosana*, meaning 'the place one never leaves' – and you probably won't want to after you've negotiated the 400 hairpin bends along the RN5, the only access road from St-Louis on the south coast. Following the course of the Rivière Bras de Cilaos, the RN5 climbs steadily to the entrance to the cirque at **Le Pavillon**. Early travellers were confined to sedan chairs as the only means of transport to continue their journey beyond Le Pavillon, along narrow roads which at each twist and turn open up new vistas of cloud-capped mountains and isolated villages dotted along the deep ravines.

A traditional house at Hell-Bourg.

The town of **Cilaos** , at 1,220 metres (4,000ft), is similar in some respects to the French alpine resort of Chamonix, its twin town. It's an excellent starting point for hikes and walks, with a few things to entertain you in the town itself.

Cilaos's 6,000 inhabitants are mainly the descendants of 19th-century settlers from Normandy and Brittany, who dreamed up evocative names for the peaks that surrounded them, including Les Trois Salazes or Le Bonnet de Prêtre (The Priest's Bonnet). These days, the local people make a living through tourism and farming, though the area is also known for its embroidery, wine and lentils.

In **Rue Père Boiteau** in the town centre there are some beautifully restored bijou Creole houses: notable examples include a pink and grey house called Soledad, across the road from the Stamm pharmacy; the 80-year-old restaurant called Chez Noé (which serves good goat masala); and Cilaos's oldest house, painted in blue and white.

Ever since **thermal springs** *(thermes)* were discovered in 1819 by a goathunter, Cilaos has been a health resort attracting the sick and infirm, who would make the long journey up from the coast. In 1948, a cyclone destroyed the springs but the **Etablissement Thermal d'Irenée-Accot** (Route de Bras Sec; tel: 0262 31 72 27; www.thermescilaos.re; Mon–Fri 8am–12pm, 1–5pm, Sat–Sun 9am–5pm; closed Wed afternoon) is still active. Whether you've got digestive problems, rheumatism or arthritis, the waters from the same thermal springs can help put it right. If you're after sheer indulgence, or a restorative after a long trek, treat yourself to a sauna or massage, have a work-out in the gym and then flake out in the Jacuzzi.

The best places to buy the local wine are Cilaos and nearby Bras Sec. Locals sell cheap bottles of Cilaos wine along the roadside, but it is often of inferior quality. Good-quality wine can be bought at the **Domaine du Petit Vignoble** (3a chemin de la Ravine; tel: 0692 35 81 50; call before visiting) in Bras

Alpine Cilaos.

⊘ SECOND CHANCE

Every April new moon hundreds of young Barau's petrels fly across Cilaos to the sea for the first time. Many of them won't make it. The birds, whose breeding colonies are high in the cliffs above the cirque, are confused by the town lights below and become stranded. Since 2009 Nights Without Light have been implemented, and during the critical period locals ceaselessly walk Cilaos's streets to recover the petrels. On a typical night they might find 20 young birds. Many others will collide with a cable, streetlight or vehicle – that's if they don't meet a stray dog or cat – and will never be found. After placing them in a cardboard box, volunteers take the birds to St-Pierre, where, together with schoolchildren, they set them free off the coast.

Sec, where you can also learn about local wine-making methods and enjoy a wine-tasting session. Modern methods using stainless steel vats are used, but the process of pressing, fermenting and bottling in makeshift cellars has not changed in years.

Many of the area's skilled embroiderers work from home and are concentrated in **Palmiste Rouge**, south of Cilaos on the RD240, but a handful come to work at the **Maison de la Broderie** (tel: 0262 31 77 48; Mon–Sat 9.30am–noon, 2–5pm, Sun 9.30am–noon) in Rue des Ecoles, which was founded in 1953 by the sisters of Notre-Dame-des-Neiges. A large number of the designs originated in Brittany, but today workers struggle to keep up traditional procedures and patterns.

STRETCHING YOUR LEGS

The tourist office (2 rue Mac-Auliffe; www.sudreuniontourisme.fr, email: accueil.cilaos@gmail.com; Mon–Sat 8.30am–12.30pm, 1.30–5pm, Sun and public hols 9am–noon) is where occasional evening slide shows are held, followed by wine tasting. Here you'll find every map and walking plan imaginable and details of accommodation and adventure sports available in the cirques, as well as a huge relief map of the whole island. And if you have ever wondered what a sedan chair looks like, there's an original one on display, dating from 1922.

For one of the most straightforward walks from Cilaos, requiring four hours for the return trip, turn left at Route de Bras Sec and follow the signs north to **Roche Merveilleuse**. (It is also possible to drive along the RF11.) No real effort is needed to climb the rock and the views from the summit are great. From left to right you will see the village of Bras Sec, perched on a plateau overlooking the cirque, followed by Palmiste Rouge and Îlet à Cordes, where the best lentils are grown. Access to the Roche Merveilleuse is

through the **Forêt du Grand Matarum**, noted for the local *tamarins-des-hauts*, Japanese cryptomerias and Réunion's only oak trees. Marked paths weave through the forest.

For a more ambitious hike (three to four hours one way), head to the Col du Taïbit and then on to Marla in the cirque of Mafate (see page 221), which is more easily reached from Cilaos than anywhere else. Cilaos is also the start of the shortest but steepest route to the Piton des Neiges. It takes around three hours to the Caverne Dufour *gîte* from the start of the path at Le Bloc (signposted on the road between Cilaos and Bras Sec). Other possible walks from the town are along the GR2 to Bras Sec and beyond to Palmiste Rouge.

The area around the hamlets of **Îlet Fleurs Jaunes** and **Îlets du Bois Rouge** is very popular for canyoning. The sport is enough to scare the pants off you as you abseil off cliffs into water-filled gorges, but at least a guide goes with you, and life-jackets, harnesses, helmets and jump suits are provided.

Canyoning at the Gobert Waterfall, Cilaos.

Anse Source d'Argent beach.

Bushwalking from Grand Anse to Petit Anse Beach, La Digue.

Snorkelling in the sea,
Cousine Island.

SEYCHELLES

The islands' reputation as a tropical paradise is well earned and preserving the environment continues to be a crucial concern.

Tropical birds of the Seychelles.

The Seychelles are the oldest ocean islands on earth – once part of the ancient super-continent Pangaea, the archipelago became isolated some 65 million years ago, evolving its own flora and fauna, from which man, and indeed all land mammals, were absent. Seychelles' human history is much more recent, beginning just a few hundred years ago. In 1609 a small party of English sailors made the first recorded landing in Seychelles. They had left England in March the year before, and sailed past the Cape, through the Mozambique Channel, calling in at the Comoros and Pemba, north of Zanzibar. They stumbled upon Seychelles by accident, but were glad they did. The boatswain, one Mr Jones (see page 239), declared the islands 'an earthly Paradise'.

Seychellois are proud of their spectacular country, and happy to share it with visitors. They have a certain reserve on first acquaintance, but when relaxed are incredibly warm and generous. They love to talk, make music and create delicious Creole dishes, and throw open their homes and the bounty of their table to those they come to know.

This is a young nation, dealing with the inevitable problems a small and isolated island population faces when struggling to keep up with the outside world. The characteristic 'mañana' syndrome is in some conflict with the need to modernise and perform to the standards of a faster, busier world beyond the coral beaches.

A group of performers at the Carnaval International de Victoria.

But it's precisely this relaxed attitude to life that appeals to visitors who come here in search of a stress-free environment and unrivalled natural beauty. If all you want out of your holiday is sun, sea and sand, there are other, cheaper tropical destinations. But if you are prepared to pay extra to enjoy unique flora and fauna, witness spectacular marine life and loll on some of the best beaches in the world, look no further. Many changes to the landscape have occurred since 1609, but there are so many beauty spots that still fit Bo's'n Jones' definition of 'an earthly Paradise'.

THE ORIGIN OF SEYCHELLES

An Indian Ocean Atlantis, the ancient Seychelles archipelago has the oldest and only granitic ocean islands in the world.

The Seychelles islands can be divided into five main groups: the granitic islands, the Amirantes, the Alphonse Group, the Farquhar Group and the Aldabra Group. The 40 islands that make up the granitic group are the world's only ocean islands built from the stuff of continents. All other isolated ocean islands are made up of coralline or volcanic rocks, both of which have grown out of the ocean. The main islands of Seychelles are different. Their rocks have never been completely submerged. They were formed from material ejected from deep within the fabric of the earth some 750 million years ago, perhaps in a frozen, lifeless wasteland close to the South Pole.

For millennia, the rocks of Seychelles were a part of Pangaea, the ancient super-continent that once encompassed all the world's land masses. Some 200 million years ago, the forces of continental drift tore Pangaea apart. It split into Laurasia (modern Europe, Asia and North America) to the north and Gondwanaland (South America, Africa, Antarctica, Australasia and the Indian subcontinent) to the south. Seychelles at this time lay near the point where Madagascar, India and Africa were linked.

As the process of continental drift continued, about 125 million years ago, Madagascar, Seychelles and India broke away as one land mass. Madagascar became an island around 90 million years ago, drifting away with its own unique assemblage of wildlife. Then 65 million years ago, Seychelles drifted from the western coast of India.

THE DEATH OF THE DINOSAURS

It may not be pure coincidence that the birth of the world's only oceanic fragments of continental rock coincided with the death of the dinosaurs. There are many dinosaur extinction theories.

Corals on Aldabra Atoll's beach.

Many scientists believe that their disappearance was caused by the earth's collision with a comet that struck the Yucatán Peninsula in Mexico, sending shock waves through the globe and triggering volcanic activity at the opposite side of the earth. A second theory suggests that a vast comet broke up on entering the earth's atmosphere, major fragments of which hit the Yucatán, and 12 hours later, as the earth turned, struck the Indian Ocean. Other scientists believe that extinction was not instantaneous, but the result of an extensive period of volcanic activity in western India, close to the point where Seychelles was once attached to the subcontinent.

Isolated in mid-ocean, this new micro-continent was one land mass, covering an area of around

300,000 sq km (116,000 sq miles) – roughly the size of Britain and Ireland combined. Today, all that remains are the peaks of the highest mountains. The combined forces of erosion, sea level change and the sheer weight of coral growth (forming what geologists term a carbonate platform) have submerged all but 250 sq km (100 sq miles) of granite, less than one thousandth of its original extent, creating the archipelago we see today.

Though superficially similar to the other granitic islands, Silhouette and North Island are younger and made up largely of a type of volcanic rock called syenite. Silhouette was born rapidly and dramatically, the result of an eruption that probably occurred on land. Limited outcrops above the surface today make it difficult to determine with certainty, but it is probable that the volcano's crater lies southeast of La Passe, now almost entirely eroded away and submerged. This volcano erupted many times and Silhouette may have towered 3,000 metres (10,000ft) or more at one time. At Pointe Zeng Zeng, you can see the only volcanic ash above sea level in Seychelles, while fingers of basalt reach out from the island to Mahé and can be seen at Glacis and elsewhere.

VOLCANIC AND YOUNGER ISLANDS

On the edge of the Seychelles Bank lie the much younger islands of Bird and Denis, thought to have emerged about 4,000 years ago when the sea level dropped as a result of a change in ocean currents. These currents stirred the waters, causing a shift in the average local sea levels. Mahé's sea level, for example, is now 5 metres (16ft) below the level in southern India. It is thought that the sea level change that revealed Bird and Denis exposed the Amirantes Group at the same time.

The Amirantes is a linear chain of coral islands and atolls that rises no more than 3 metres (10ft) above sea level. Volcanoes once rose out of the ocean, but as they died and were reclaimed by the sea, coral growth maintained contact with the surface. Farquhar Atoll, in the south of the Seychelles, must also have witnessed volcanic activity at one time. It is believed that while the granitic group was a micro-continent, Farquhar may have been a nano-continent (a tiny fragment of continent). Aldabra, Assumption, Cosmoledo and Astove in the southwestern corner of Seychelles are different again. These islands of the Aldabra Group are raised coral islands. In fact Aldabra is the largest raised atoll in the world. Unlike the usual low-lying coral atolls, they rise to up to 8 metres (27ft) above sea level. This appears to go against the conventional wisdom that the volcanic basement of coral atolls is contracting and sinking.

The cycle continues today. The biggest fear is that global warming and the rise in sea levels may spell disaster for low-lying coral islands. Signs of beach erosion can be seen throughout Seychelles and nowhere more than in the coral islands, which could disappear if present trends continue.

L'Union Estate Monolith.

⊘ ON SOLID GROUND

Granite islands are what differentiate Seychelles from other tropical idylls and make them so instantly recognisable. The best example of ancient granite rock that can be seen today lies at L'Union Estate, covering half a hectare (an acre) of land at Anse L'Union on the west coast of the island of La Digue. This impressive monolith, which was formed during the Precambrian period (around 750 million years ago) by the slow cooling of molten rocks (magma) deep within the earth's crust, is a National Monument. The estate is also home to the cemetery of the original settlers of La Digue.

DECISIVE DATES

EARLY DISCOVERERS

851
Arab traders probably visit Seychelles. An Arab manuscript of this date refers to the 'high island' beyond the Maldives.

961
Seychelles is referred to as Zarin (Sisters) on Arab charts.

1502
On its way to India via Mozambique, Vasco da Gama's expedition sights the outer islands, which later became known as the Amirantes.

1609
A ship from the English East India Company makes the first recorded landing on Mahé.

FRENCH POSSESSION

1742
Lazare Picault leads an expedition to chart the islands, reporting to Mahé de Labourdonnais, the French governor of nearby Mauritius.

1756
Nicholas Morphey claims Mahé for France.

1778
A 15-man garrison is established at L'Etablissement du Roi (later Victoria).

1786
The colony now comprises 24 military personnel, five civilians and 122 slaves. Its income is derived from provisioning ships. A legal system is introduced.

Africa and the Indian Ocean in 1663.

1790
In the wake of the French Revolution, the Seychelles settlers create a Colonial Assembly to run the colony.

THE WAR YEARS

1794
First capitulation to the British is signed by Quincy. It is renewed seven times.

1801
French political deportees arrive.

BRITISH CONTROL

1815–1901
Britain assumes control of Seychelles.

1818
The population of 7,500 prospers from the cultivation of cotton.

1822
Price of cotton falls. Many planters return to Mauritius.

1835
Slavery is abolished.

1860s
Coconut oil is almost the sole export.

1861
Arrival of the first of around 2,400 liberated Africans.

1891
Vanilla becomes an important cash crop.

INDEPENDENCE

1903
Seychelles becomes a separate Crown Colony under its first governor, Sir Ernest Bickham Sweet-Escott.

1906
A fall in the price of vanilla rocks the economy.

1914–18
World War I causes hardship in Seychelles due to isolation from shipping. Seychelles Pioneer Corps serves in East Africa.

1921
The population reaches 24,500.

1926
Electricity and telephone services are installed.

1937
Creation of the League of Coloured Peoples to lobby for plantation workers.

1939–45
World War II. Seychelles is used as a refuelling base for flying boats and warships. Seychelles Pioneer Corps again serves with British forces.

1963
America begins the construction of a satellite tracking station on Mahé.

1964
Creation of two new political parties, the Seychelles People's United Party (led by Albert René, demanding independence) and the Seychelles Democratic Party (led by James Mancham, wanting closer links with Britain).

1965
Creation of a new British colony, called British Indian Ocean Territory, including several islands from the Seychelles group.

1967
Universal adult suffrage is introduced.

1970
First Constitutional Conference discusses the future of Seychelles. A legislative assembly is created.

1971
Completion of the International Airport. Tourism is now key to the economy.

The flag of the Seychelles.

THE MODERN AGE

1976
Seychelles becomes an independent republic. A coalition government is formed, with James Mancham as president and Albert René as prime minister.

1977
Mancham is overthrown in a coup that establishes René as president of a socialist government.

1979
A new constitution makes Seychelles a single-party system, led by the Seychelles People's Progressive Front.

1981
A mercenary force led by Colonel 'Mad Mike' Hoare attempts to seize control of the country, and fails. The following year a mutiny in the Seychelles army is put down by Tanzanian troops.

1984–9
René is re-elected twice.

1992
Return to a multi-party system.

James Michel.

1993
A new constitution is adopted. René and his SPPF party are elected back into power.

1998
René is re-elected. Mancham's Democratic Party is forced into third place by the United Opposition (later renamed the Seychelles National Party or SNP).

2001
René wins snap presidential elections.

2003
René retires and James Michel succeeds him as president.

2006–2011
James Michel is re-elected twice as president.

2016
Michel retires and Danny Faure, former vice president, is sworn in.

2018
Seychelles signs a world-first landmark debt-for-conservation agreement, creating two huge marine parks the size of the UK in return for US$22 million wiped off its national debt.

BIRTH OF AN ISLAND NATION

Quincy and René, the historic heavyweights of Seychelles, were key to its transformation from deserted paradise to modern independent state.

We can only speculate as to early human history in Seychelles. Polynesians, who eventually settled on Madagascar, may have lingered here around the 3rd and 2nd centuries BC. It is likely that Arab traders plying the Indian Ocean in around the 9th century knew of the islands' existence. A manuscript dated AD 851, written by an Arab merchant, refers to the Maldives and higher islands beyond them, possibly Seychelles. Evidence also suggests that long before European discovery of the islands, Arabs were trading the legendary coco de mer nuts, found only in Seychelles (see page 314). Because of the mystery surrounding their origin, the nuts were highly sought after. No shrewd trader would reveal the source of supply of such a rare and valuable commodity. To keep the myth alive the Arabs claimed they found them washed ashore in the Maldives, but as the nuts are not buoyant in saltwater, this is unlikely.

THE FIRST EUROPEANS

The early history of Seychelles is a story of people passing through. In 1502, Vasco da Gama, on his way to India via East Africa, sighted the outer islands, which became known as the Amirantes, but the Portuguese made no attempt to colonise them. Later in the 16th century, the inner granitic islands began to appear on Portuguese charts as the 'Seven Sisters'.

The British were next on the scene. In 1609 the *Ascension*, one of the ships from a trading fleet of the English East India Company on its way to India, got lost in a storm. Its crew sighted 'high land' and headed for it, anchoring 'as in a pond'. They found plentiful fresh water, fish, coconuts, birds, turtles and giant tortoises with which to replenish their stores.

Vasco da Gama.

⊘ EARTHLY PARADISE

On 19 January 1609, the *Ascension*, a merchant vessel under the command of the English captain Alexander Sharpeigh, was separated from the fleet by a storm and anchored off Mahé. On board was one John Jourdain, an agent sent by the East India Company to trade and negotiate in India. He wrote an enthusiastic account of the 'earthly Paradise' they had happened upon. His is the first known written description of Seychelles:

'It is very good refreshing place for wood, water, coker nutts, fish and fowle, without any feare or danger, except the allagartes: for you cannot discerne that ever any people had bene there before us.'

The ship's captain reported the bounty they had found, but the British took no action and Seychelles was to remain unoccupied for more than a hundred years.

By the end of the 17th century, piracy in the Indian Ocean was rife. Pirates fleeing from the Caribbean, whose waters were by this time heavily policed, based themselves in Madagascar. From here they preyed upon vessels plying the Red Sea and the Gulf, probably using the islands as a hiding place and refreshment stop.

FRENCH OCCUPATION

It wasn't until 1710 that the French occupied Île de France (as Mauritius was then known), but the colony quickly grew in importance. In 1735 an energetic administrator, Bertrand François Mahé de Labourdonnais, was appointed. His brief was to protect the French sea route to India. Labourdonnais, himself a sailor, turned his attention to making a speedier passage from Île de France to India and in 1742 he commissioned Lazare Picault to lead an expedition to chart the islands northeast of Madagascar. On 21 November 1742

'A Fleet of East Indiamen at Sea', by Nicholas Pocock (1741–1821).

⊘ LAYING THE HERCULEAN TRAIL

Olivier Le Vasseur, also known as La Buse (the Buzzard), was a notorious French pirate operating in the early 18th century. For a number of years, he teamed up with fellow brigands from Britain, Edward England and Charles Taylor. Together they cruised the Indian Ocean and terrorised European merchant ships. Their most lucrative haul came from a royal Portuguese ship, which they plundered as she lay helpless in the harbour of Réunion. The booty taken included the 'Fiery Cross of Goa'. Encrusted with diamonds, rubies and emeralds, it took three men to lift it. Le Vasseur kept this magnificent piece of treasure for himself. He was finally captured by the French authorities and on 7 July

1730 was taken to Réunion and hanged. The story goes that just before they put the noose around his neck, he threw a sheaf of documents into the crowd crying, 'Find my treasure, who can!' The search for this priceless cross has continued ever since.

Most famous of the treasure hunters was Reginald Cruise-Wilkins, who dedicated his life to the quest. He was convinced the treasure was buried on Mahé and that Le Vasseur had laid a series of traps and clues based on the labours of Hercules. He died in 1977 without finding the treasure, but his son has continued the diggings, some of which may still be seen by the shore at Bel Ombre.

the *Elisabeth* and the *Charles* anchored off Mahé at Anse Boileau (not Baie Lazare, later mistakenly named as Picault's landing place). They found a land of plenty. In fact, Picault's first name for the island was Île d'Abondonce.

Picault's mapping was poor, so in 1744 he was sent back on a second mission, this time anchoring off the northeast coast near present-day Victoria. He renamed the main island Mahé, and the archipelago the Îles de la Bourdonnais. He had high hopes for the islands, but his plans for settlement were thwarted. The colonial war between England and France had reached India. Labourdonnais was called away to fight a campaign and the islands were once more forgotten. It wasn't until 1756 that the authorities on Île de France decided to take possession of the islands before the British did. Two ships were sent to claim them, commanded by Corneille Nicholas Morphey.

After a thorough investigation of Mahé and the surrounding islands, Morphey raised the French flag and took possession for his king and the French East India Company on 1 November 1756, to hearty cries of 'long live the king' and nine shots from the ships' cannon. He renamed the largest island Île de Séchelles (the name later used for the island group, when the largest granitic island reverted to the name of Mahé).

The end of the Seven Years' War, France's loss of Canada and its reduced status in India accelerated the decline of the French East India Company. The settlements of Île de France and Seychelles, formerly controlled by the company, now came under direct royal authority and in 1768, during a commercial expedition for the collection of timber and tortoises, French sovereignty was extended to cover all the islands of the granitic group. But the French were in no hurry to settle Seychelles. A colony there could not pay for itself, and would be costly to maintain. Then, in 1769, the navigators Rochon and Grenier proved that a faster route to India could safely be taken via Seychelles and the importance of its strategic position began to be realised.

Frenchman Brayer du Barré (died 1777) was given royal permission to run a settlement in Seychelles at his own expense. He decided that the best place to begin a colony was the little island of Ste Anne, off the northeast coast of Mahé. On 12 August 1770, with 15 white colonists, seven slaves, five Indians and one African woman on board, Du Barré's ship, the *Télémaque*, set sail from Île de France and arrived on the island 14 days later.

Du Barré himself did not join the expedition, but stayed in Île de France seeking funds, though his appeals for help to Île de France and Versailles fell on deaf ears. In desperation, he went to Seychelles to try to rescue the situation, but to no avail. A ruined man, he left for India and died there shortly afterwards. By August 1772, Du Barré's people had abandoned Ste Anne and moved to Mahé or returned home.

Mahé de Labourdonnais.

⊙ IN THE NAME OF THE KING

On 1 November 1756, a Stone of Possession was laid on Mahé by Company Officer Corneille Nicholas Morphey, who claimed the islands for the French king Louis XV and christened them the Seychelles. It is generally thought that the islands were named after Louis XV's finance minister, the Viscount Jean Moreau de Séchelles. However, the name may also be a reference to the relationship through marriage of a female member of the Hérault de Séchelles family (themselves related to Moreau de Séchelles) and the man who sent Morphey on his voyage, Magon de la Villebague, governor of Île de France.

CINNAMON, NUTMEG AND CLOVES

The intendant of Île de France at this time was Pierre Poivre (1719–86), a man of ideas. Determined to break the Dutch monopoly of the lucrative spice trade, he thought Mahé would be perfect for spice cultivation. He had obtained seedlings of nutmeg and clove, and 10,000 nutmeg seeds, but his attempts to propagate them on Île de France and Bourbon (later Réunion) met with little success. So, in 1771, Poivre sent former soldier Antoine Gillot to Mahé to supervise the creation of a spice garden. Gillot chose Anse Royale, on the

Pierre Poivre (Peter Pepper), brought spices to the Seychelles.

southeast coast, as the site, and set about establishing the 'Jardin du Roi', which was planted with nutmeg, clove, cinnamon and pepper.

When British ships were sighted around Seychelles, the French authorities were spurred into action and despatched a garrison from Île de France under the command of Lieutenant de Romainville. They built the Etablissement du Roi (Royal Settlement) on the site of modern Victoria. Gillot was nominally in charge of the civilian colonists, but had no real authority over them. So Île de France sent as replacement a man of stronger mettle, Jean-Baptiste Philogène de Malavois. He drew up 30 decrees which protected the timber and tortoises. In future, only

sound farming techniques and careful husbanding of resources would be tolerated. He assumed command of the settlement in 1788.

In 1790, as a result of the French Revolution, the settlers declared independence from the other French colonies and formed a Colonial Assembly. They drew up their own constitution and decided that land in Seychelles should only go to the children of existing colonists, who should be able to dispose of the colony's produce as they chose, not as Île de France dictated. But independence did not last long. Enthusiasm for the Revolution began to wane, not least because revolutionary theory supported the abolition of slavery, which the colonists wholeheartedly opposed, believing that without slave labour, they could not survive. Eventually they agreed to hand over control to a commandant.

THE WAR YEARS

In 1794, Jean-Baptiste Queau de Quinssy (1748–1827), whose name was later anglicised to Quincy, took command of the colony. A wily man, he used skill and expediency to steer Seychelles through the years of war ahead.

Seychelles became a haven for French corsairs (pirates carrying *lettres de marque* from the French authorities entitling them to prey on British enemy ships). Quincy hoped this might go unnoticed, but in 1794 a squadron of three English ships arrived. They were well armed and in no mood for resistance. The British commodore, Henry Newcome, asked for help with his wounded, many of whom were French prisoners, but Quincy refused.

This resistance meant little in practical terms and was but a gesture. Quincy knew he was powerless and Newcome gave him an hour in which to surrender. There were only 20 colonists on the French side 'capable of carrying arms'. Newcome had almost 13,000 men. Quincy had eight cannons, Newcome had 166. In all, Quincy made seven capitulations to the English. While they were in port, he flew the English flag, but as soon as their ships were out of sight he raised the tricolour. The strategy worked. In effect, Seychelles remained neutral, supplying both British and French ships. The islanders avoided conflict and the colony flourished.

This was not an end to Quincy's problems, however. To his dismay, on 11 July 1801 the French frigate *Chiffonne* arrived with a cargo of notorious French prisoners sent into exile by Napoleon and Quincy was warned that there were more on the way. Together, these deportees would outnumber the local population. Were this not enough, the British ship HMS *Sybille* arrived soon after. Quincy had no choice but to try to defend the *Chiffonne*, but after a brief battle, she was taken. Captain Adam of the *Sybille* demanded to know why Quincy had interfered,

in contravention of his capitulation terms. With characteristic guile and charm, the commandant managed to talk his way out of the difficulty, and even persuaded Adam to let Seychelles vessels fly a flag bearing the words "Seychelles Capitulation", allowing them to pass through the British blockade of Mauritius unmolested.

Although confrontation with the British may have been avoided, the problem of deportees, whom the Seychellois feared, still remained. As political prisoners they refused to work and talked of liberty and equality within hearing of

'View of Mahe' by Sigismond Himely (1801-1872).

☉ THE LOST KING OF FRANCE

An intriguing anecdote concerns the mysterious figure of Pierre-Louis Poiret. Late in 1804, a boy of 19 years old came to Poivre Island, having been brought from France by a Monsieur Aimé, who treated him with great respect. Aimé continued to Mahé, where he presented secret letters to Quincy, the commandant. After working the cotton gin on Poivre, Poiret came to Mahé. He was given land at Cap Ternay and Grand Anse and slaves to help him farm it.

An aloof man, respected by his fellow planters, he led a largely unremarkable life. Then he suddenly declared he was actually Louis XVII, heir to the French throne. He said that, after the execution of his parents, he had been

placed in the care of a cobbler, Simon Poiret. Later, Royalists smuggled him out of Paris in a box of hay, and brought him out to Seychelles. In his later years, he wrote repeatedly to Charles X of France, whom he said was his uncle. Interestingly, the names he gave all his four sons began with Louis, and the names of his five daughters with Marie.

Official history records that the crown prince Louis died of tuberculosis in 1795. His heart was removed and preserved in a crystal urn. This was opened in 1999, DNA extracted and compared to that of Marie-Antoinette and living relatives. Tests confirmed a relationship, though not necessarily that the heart was that of Louis.

the slaves. Quincy was afraid that the slaves and deportees might join forces and revolt. So he transported a number of them to the small island of Frégate and wrote to the Île de France authorities pleading for assistance with the rest. In the long run, however, his fears proved unfounded as very few of the deportees ended up staying: 33 were redeported to the Comoros, six stowed away aboard visiting ships, and a number of others were taken to Île de France. Only a few of the most peaceable settled down in Seychelles.

Victoria clock tower in 1856.

☉ A GILDED CAGE

The British saw Seychelles as a useful place to exile political prisoners. Over the years, it became home to prisoners from Zanzibar, Egypt, Cyprus and Palestine. The first was the Sultan of Perak, who arrived in 1875 after his implication in the murder of the British Resident there. Like many exiles who followed, he settled well into Seychelles life and became fond of the islands. Perhaps the most famous exile was Archbishop Makarios, who arrived in 1956. He too fell in love with his prison. 'When our ship leaves harbour,' he wrote, 'we shall take with us many good and kindly memories of the Seychelles... may God bless them all.'

BRITISH CONTROL

The colony entered the 19th century with a population of 215 whites, 86 free blacks and 1,820 slaves. The war raged on, but the British were fast gaining the upper hand. They tightened the blockade on the French Indian Ocean colonies. Réunion surrendered, followed in December 1810 by Île de France, which they renamed Mauritius. In April 1811, Captain Beaver arrived in Seychelles on the *Nisus* to announce that while the preferential terms of Quincy's capitulation could stand, Seychelles must recognise the terms of the Mauritian surrender. Beaver left behind a royal marine, Lieutenant Sullivan, to monitor the Seychelles situation, but there was little Sullivan could do to stop the settlers continuing to provision French frigates and slavers. The British had outlawed the slave trade and Sullivan, later given the title of Civil Agent, played cat and mouse with the pro-slaver colonists. Once, acting on a tip-off, Sullivan was rowed over to Praslin and confiscated a cargo of newly landed slaves. It was but a small triumph among many frustrations, and Sullivan, complaining that the Seychellois had 'no sense of honour, shame or honesty', resigned. In 1814, the first civilian administrator of the British regime, Edward Madge, arrived. Quincy was kept on as Justice of the Peace and remained a respected figure in the colony until his death in 1827.

The British allowed customary French practices to remain in place. The administrator may have been British, reporting to London, but he governed according to French rules.

The colonists had two main grievances with their new masters. One was their dependence on Mauritius. The other was the abolition of slavery in 1835. The plantations were already in decline, their soil exhausted by years of cultivation and a lack of investment. The plantocracy believed they could not farm without slave labour. Some planters took their slaves and left. The liberated slaves had no land, and most squatted on the estates they had tended in bondage, working sporadically to keep themselves from starvation. It was a poor sort of freedom, and the colony entered a period of stagnation. There were no exports, and no money to pay for new infrastructure. The situation was only improved when planters realised they could grow coconuts with less labour and more profit than the traditional crops of cotton, sugar, rice and maize.

The British took their anti-slavery stance seriously, and operated patrols along the East African coast, raiding Arab dhows transporting slaves to the Middle East. Slaves liberated south of the Equator were brought to Seychelles and apprenticed to plantation owners. It was these ex-slaves who saved the economy as they were a source of cheap labour. They worked the land in return for rations and low wages. Over a period of 13 years, from 1861, around 2,400 men, women and children were brought to Seychelles.

> On 12 October 1862, Mahé was hit by a storm. Torrential rain and strong winds caused an avalanche of mud and rocks to fall on Victoria, killing more than 70 people and devastating the town.

The main settlement on Mahé (named Victoria in 1841, to mark the marriage of Queen Victoria and Prince Albert) began to grow and prosper. Licences granted in 1879 give us some idea of the range of businesses in the town: there was a druggist, two auctioneers, five retailers, four liquor stores, a notary, an attorney, a jeweller and a watchmaker.

CROWN COLONY

Seychelles yearned to be a colony in its own right, not an appendage of Mauritius, and the authorities in the mother colony supported this desire. Sir Arthur Gordon, the Mauritian governor, sent a petition on their behalf to London. Concessions were made, but Seychelles did not become a separate Crown Colony until 1903, when its first governor, Sir Ernest Bickham Sweet-Escott, took office. Befitting its new status, the colony acquired botanical gardens, and a clock tower in the heart of Victoria.

World War I brought great hardship to the islands. Ships could not bring in essential goods, nor take away exports. Wages fell and prices soared. Many turned to crime and the prisons were bursting. Joining the Seychelles Labour Contingent formed during the war seemed to offer an escape, but it was no easy option. The 800-strong force was sent to East Africa. After just five months, so many had died from dysentery, malaria and beriberi that the depleted corps was sent home. In all, 335 men died.

By the end of World War I, the population of Seychelles, which was around 24,000, was feeling neglected by Whitehall. There was agitation from the newly formed Planters' Association for greater representation in the governance of Seychelles affairs. After 1929 a more liberal flow of funds was ensured by the Colonial

A Seychelles Governor troops inspection in 1972.

Development Act, but it was a time of economic depression; the price of copra was falling and so were wages. Workers petitioned the government about their poor working conditions and the burden of tax they had to bear. Governor Sir Arthur Grimble instigated some reforms, exempting lower income groups from taxation. He was keen to create model housing and distribute smallholdings for the landless. Sadly, many of his reforms were not approved before World War II had broken out, and everything was put on hold.

The Planters' Association lobbied for the rich white land owners, but those who worked for them had no voice. In 1937, the League of Coloured Peoples was formed to demand a minimum wage, a wage tribunal and free health care for all.

World War II caused more distress in the colony and led to political change. In 1939, the Seychelles' first political party, the Taxpayers' Association, was formed, but it was entirely concerned with protecting the interests of the plantocracy. A British governor described it as 'the embodiment of every reactionary force in Seychelles'. After the war, literate property owners were granted the vote; just 2,000 in a population of 36,000. At the first elections in 1948,

the support of an independent. Subsequent elections in 1970 and 1974 gave Mancham a small majority in votes, but a large one in seats, through the 'first past the post' voting system.

Meanwhile, Britain's lack of enthusiasm for integration convinced Mancham to join René in calling for independence. In 1975, a coalition was forged between the two rivals.

INDEPENDENCE

Independence was declared on 29 June 1976. James Mancham became the first president

Fishermen landing their catch in the early 1970s.

most of those elected to the Legislative Council were predictably members of the Planters' and Taxpayers' associations.

It was not until 1964 that any new political movements were created. In that year, the socialist Seychelles People's United Party (SPUP) was formed. Led by Albert René, it campaigned for autonomy. By contrast, James Mancham's Seychelles Democratic Party (SDP), created the same year, wanted to retain its close links with Britain.

Britain was cool on the idea of integration, while opinion in Seychelles appeared to be split. In 1967, universal adult suffrage was introduced and at the first election each party gained three seats, with Mancham claiming victory through

of the Republic of Seychelles and René his prime minister. Less than one year later, on 5 June 1977, while Mancham was in London to attend the Commonwealth Conference, René's supporters staged a coup. New elections were called in 1979 with René as the sole candidate. A one-party socialist state was established and the SPUP changed its name to the Seychelles People's Progressive Front (SPPF).

René used Seychelles' strategic importance to play America and Russia off against each other, while remaining non-aligned, obtaining substantial help from both superpowers without having to commit himself to either.

There were several attempts to oust René by force. The most dramatic of these took place in

November 1981, when 50 mercenaries arrived on a Royal Air Swazi flight posing as a charitable organisation bringing toys for local orphaned children. Beneath the toys, however, hidden in secret compartments of their luggage, were guns and ammunition. The mercenaries were led by 'Mad Mike' Hoare, whose previous exploits had included installing Mobutu as president of Zaire. They passed undetected through customs, until an official discovered a bunch of bananas in the case of a French tourist, the only non-mercenary on the plane. The importation of fresh fruit into Seychelles is illegal and the customs officers decided to give the luggage of the last two passengers a more thorough check. On discovery of a gun, all hell broke out. The mercenaries took over the airport and after a shoot-out escaped to South Africa in a hijacked plane, where they were promptly arrested. Mancham maintained that the plot had nothing to do with him, and commented wryly that the coup 'had been foiled by a bunch of bananas'.

Mancham remained in exile in London for 15 years. In 1992, with the resumption of multiparty democracy, he returned and rivalry between the DP, as it was now known, and the SPPF, resumed. In 1993 the first multi-party presidential election since independence in 1976 was held. But it was René who triumphed with 59 percent of the votes cast.

Meanwhile, a third force was emerging. At the 1998 elections, the Seychelles National Party (SNP) gained more votes than the DP, but still fell short of the number of votes cast for the SPPF. Once again René was elected president of the Seychelles Republic. René managed to get re-elected for a third time at snap presidential elections held in August 2001. Mancham and his DP party declined to stand at this election but Wavel Ramkalawan of the SNP doubled his share of the vote. At the next National Assembly elections in December 2002, SPPF took 22 seats, while SNP took 11. Mancham's DP, however, received just 3 percent of the vote and was wiped out. In 2003, René announced his retirement and James Michel his successor as president of Seychelles.

Just as Quincy had done centuries earlier, Albert René used craft and guile to steer a course through the changes taking place in the world. Both have left their indelible marks as they led their small country through times of great change.

SEYCHELLES TODAY

Seychelles today has a focus. The tiny population of around 95,300 has largely rejected the traditional agricultural and fishing way of life, as a new generation embraces tourism, which now dominates the economy. It's a strategy that's paying off, with The World Travel & Tourism Council's 2018 annual report revealing tourism and travel contributions are forecast to rise by 2.9 percent per annum from 2018–2028 in the Seychelles, amounting to 63 percent of GDP. This healthy outlook

James Michel at the White House.

has helped to trigger further investment, such as British Airways launching a direct service to Mahé from Heathrow in 2018, the only airline offering a non-stop service from the UK and a real boost for tourism. Best of all, its self-promotion as one of the planet's last sanctuaries for unique nature ensures that the environment will be preserved for generations to come. And now the future of its marine life is looking more secure too, thanks to the Seychelles government signing a world-first landmark debt-for-conservation agreement in 2018, which will see the creation of two huge marine parks the size of the UK in return for US$22 million beng wiped off its national debt.

A young Creole man.

THE SEYCHELLOIS

Descended from African slaves, French settlers, British colonists and Asian immigrants, the Seychellois are an intriguing mix of people.

The Seychellois could be called a 'new' people. They have a short history, having existed as a separate entity only since 1903, fused more closely since independence in 1976, while facing the difficulties of a small island state embarking upon nationhood. They are heartening proof that people of differing ethnic backgrounds can live together in peace.

ORIGINS

From the time the first settlers arrived in the 18th century, the Seychelles have been a melting pot. French colonists, who sought their fortunes in Mauritius and Réunion before arriving in Seychelles, brought with them slaves of both African and Indian origin and the process of racial intermingling began almost immediately. Pierre Hangard, probably the colony's first permanent settler, was an emigrant from Mauritius, who came to Seychelles with five slaves. He does not appear to have married, but did have a daughter by Annette, one of his slaves. He freed Annette and gave her a property at Bel Ombre. His daughter later married a Frenchman who owned one of the finest properties on Mahé. It was a scenario that was to be repeated again and again in the history of Seychelles; and there in a nutshell is the origin of the Seychellois. The colonial government census grouped people by ethnic origin until 1911, when it was decided that this was no longer possible. This bureaucratic decision can perhaps be seen as the date of birth of the Seychellois people.

Although slaves came, in the main, from eastern Africa, some were from Madagascar, but only a few came from India. The largest influx of Indians came much later, along with the Chinese. They arrived during the 19th century,

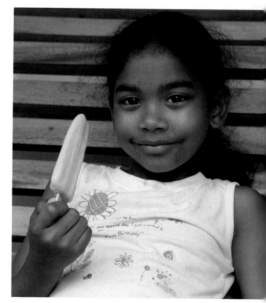

Local girl on La Digue.

working as road labourers or setting themselves up as traders. They brought with them their religions and customs, which they have retained. But the largest cultural influences are African and French. Despite the British takeover in the 19th century, few Britons settled in Seychelles, and the colonial government was slow to change French laws and institutions or the use of French in public life. Indeed, the British were reluctant rulers, initially attempting without success to persuade France to retain the islands in exchange for French possessions in India. French social customs were already well entrenched. Britain retained the same French governor and did very little to change the existing way of life. The British did contest the influence of the Roman Catholic Church as opposed to Anglicanism, but Catholicism was the faith that won the heart of the Seychellois.

SEYCHELLOIS TODAY

The modern Seychellois, particularly the young, look more to American and European culture than African or Asian, such as following the fortunes of a US basketball team or football team like Manchester United (both sports are popular), and wearing Western clothes. This is not the third world, but a middle-income country where few go hungry. Prices in the shops may be high, but the ocean is full of fish and fruit is plentiful. There is no apparent tension between tourist and local. The Seychellois may display a certain reserve, which sometimes comes across as indifference, but when barriers are broken down, visitors soon learn that the Seychellois can be among the most kind and friendly people you could ever hope to meet. Top of the list given by many visitors of reasons to return to Seychelles, apart from the obvious natural beauty of the country, is the friendliness of its people.

Beach football at Beau Vallon Beach.

⊘ A MULTILINGUAL SOCIETY

Seychelles has three official languages: Kreol, English and French. The Seychellois seem to have an innate ability to pick up languages quickly, not surprising perhaps in view of the nation's history. Unlike Mauritius and Réunion islands, Kreol has official language status and is spoken by the majority (95 percent) of the population who can also switch easily to English when in conversation. Some of the islands' longer-established families do make a point of speaking French in the home and among themselves.

Seychelles Kreol evolved from a mixture of influences. Though largely based on French, it has many African, Malagasy and Arab words, as well as an increasing number of English words. Terms used at football matches, a popular sport, are English, not French. A good goal kick, for example, becomes a *zoli goal kick*. The most noticeable features of Kreol are a very simple grammar, the extensive use of the letter 'z' (for example, *les oiseaux*, French for birds, becomes *zwazo*), and the use of 'k' instead of 'c'.

While English is spoken in hotels, shops and offices, a few words of Kreol are useful away from tourist sites and Victoria, particularly when talking to older Seychellois. If you can speak a bit of French, you should have no trouble understanding basic Kreol.

LANGUAGE

When the early French planters were trying to communicate with slaves, who often spoke only their own tribal languages, they used a simplified form of French, interspersed with words they picked up from their slaves' conversations. In this way, Kreol evolved. Since it is based on a form of French spoken in the 18th century, it retains many archaic and dialect words rarely heard in modern French. Over time, Mauritius, Réunion and Seychelles developed their own accents and patterns of speech. Today, despite the inevitable local differences, all the islanders can generally understand each other's forms of Kreol. (For more information on language, see page 23. A list of useful Kreol words and phrases appears on page 360.)

see processions of little girls in frothy white lace dresses and formally attired little boys arriving at the cathedral in Victoria.

Anglicans, Seventh Day Adventists, Pentecostals and Jehovah's Witnesses are also represented in Seychelles. In Victoria, there is a Hindu temple and an Islamic mosque, while in recent years, the Bahá'í faith has become quite popular.

FAMILY RELATIONSHIPS

The Seychellois have a relaxed approach to marriage. Polygamy isn't practised, but it

Palm Sunday Procession, Victoria.

RELIGION

Most Seychellois (around 76 percent) are Roman Catholics. Going to church is a social event, as well as a spiritual occasion, and an opportunity to get dressed up. Women compete in their colourful outfits, while older men wear long-sleeved white shirts as a mark of respect. You won't see anyone in shorts or skimpy beachwear, which are considered disrespectful. First holy communion is a major landmark in the life of a young Seychellois, and it is not unusual to

⊘ GHOSTS AND SUPERSTITIONS

The Seychellois revel in a good ghost story. Certain islands are said to be haunted: Ste Anne by a cruel French woman who had a slave girl beaten to death; Long Island by a Creole girl who drowned her child; Moyenne by an eccentric Englishwoman who lived there with her dogs. They are also renowned for their superstitions linked with good and bad luck, death and evil. It is said, for example, that bad luck will follow if you sweep the house after sunset; that a kestrel found roosting in the eaves of your house is a portent of death in the family; and that an unfamiliar voice in the dark should go unanswered – it could be a zombie.

is common for couples to *kantmenm zot an menage*, in other words live together informally, often producing large families. It is not unusual for a man to drift away (a practice known as *marse marse*), set up a new relationship and father other children (although Seychelles' law requires fathers to provide financial support for all their offspring). Sometimes, in later years, the wanderer returns to an earlier partner, to end his days in a more committed relationship. The reunited couple may even go so far as to have an

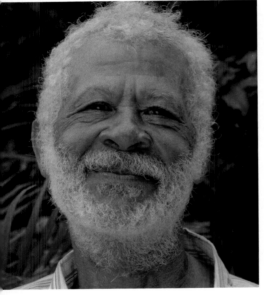

A Creole elder.

elaborate and expensive wedding, with their children as pageboys and bridesmaids.

The family unit is female-dominated, with extended families often consisting of a mother and her children, some of whom will be adults with offspring of their own. Consequently children in such households tend to grow up with a great respect for their mothers, but less for their errant fathers, perhaps reflected in the traditional mourning period for parents: 18 to 24 months for a mother, nine to 12 months for a father.

EXORCISING GHOSTS

Like the Malagasy people of Madagascar, the Seychellois have a healthy respect for ghosts and departed spirits, and death is treated very seriously. Modern Seychellois are perhaps no more superstitious than other peoples, but old traditions from Africa and Madagascar are still, to some extent, followed alongside Catholic rites. People still hold vigils at home for deceased loved ones, laying the body out in the best room of the house, with the head pointing towards the mountains and the feet towards the sea. In flickering candlelight, a solemn procession of visitors, family, acquaintances and the idly curious pass by the open coffin and sprinkle the body with holy water. The closest family and friends spend the whole night beside the body, but they certainly don't sit in silence. They play cards or dominoes, and make as much noise as possible to scare evil spirits away from their loved one and prevent them from stealing the body and turning it into a *dandosya* or zombie.

Funerals have always had a huge turnout, though sleek black hearses have now replaced the traditional handcarts that once conveyed the dead to church. A long trail of mourners follows the coffin and buses are often hired to bring the many guests to church.

GRIS-GRIS

For generations, this blend of folklore, black magic and traditional medicine played an important part in people's day-to-day lives. Black magicians were once quite influential people and the power of gris-gris was greatly feared by the Roman Catholic Church and colonial administrators, who tried to stamp it out. It certainly still goes on, but like so many traditions, it is losing the hold on people's lives it once had.

The traditional theory is that *gris-gris* came with the slaves from Africa or Madagascar, but some experts claim that European beliefs in witchcraft also found their way into its practices. Two books on magic written in 1800 that came here from Europe were particularly influential. The spells and potions described in them became absorbed in local magic customs.

A *gris-gris* 'practitioner', known as a *bonnonm* or *bonnfanm dibwa* (man or woman of the woods), supposedly has the power to protect you from the evil eye, help you in your career or love life, or get revenge on your enemies. He or she might provide a love potion, a protective talisman or small package with bits of cooked food, iron, even urine and hair; or they might foretell your future using playing cards, tea leaves or by casting pebbles on a table.

A sound knowledge of herbal medicine is often combined with these more spurious talents, and the Seychelles flora is a veritable medicine chest. Seychellois were using the Madagascar periwinkle medicinally long before Western scientists used it in the treatment of childhood leukaemia, with spectacular results. Tea made from lemon grass to settle the stomach, *tokmarya* for sore throats, *montosyel* for hernias and bred mouroung leaves for liver complaints are just a few items from the herbalist's store cupboard.

Gris-gris is taken most seriously by older people, but younger people will certainly resort to a bonnonm, especially for the love potions. It is still a sensitive and secretive subject. Unless you were inquisitive and went out of your way to seek it out, it's unlikely that you would see any evidence of its existence.

MUSICAL RHYTHMS

Seychellois love to dance. Nowadays, it is most likely to be in a club to modern music, but traditional music is far from dead. The most commonly seen dance is the sega. In Seychelles, the sega is a flirtatious, light-hearted dance, less smoulderingly sexy than its Mauritian counterpart, the *sega typic* (see page 73). In fact, it is often performed by school children in dance competitions. It's not as easy as it looks. There is a definite knack to it and you need flexible

hips. Men wear a long-sleeved white shirt, long black trousers and a colourful cummerbund, with perhaps a straw hat. Women dress in long, full, swirling skirts and bare feet are de rigueur. Although the movements are swaying and lascivious, dancers do not touch.

The *moutya* is more erotic and is unique to Seychelles. Invented by the slaves as a secret escape from the drudgery of plantation life, it was performed late at night in the forest. Colonial governors and bishops were outraged by its sexiness and tried to ban it (as they had tried

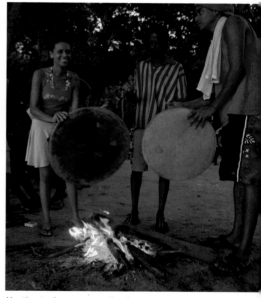

Heating tanbour moutya fire drums.

⊘ TRADITIONAL INSTRUMENTS

Sadly, the traditional instruments that once plucked out the rhythms and tunes for the sega and *moutya* dancers are no longer commonplace. These simply constructed instruments were introduced to Seychelles by the African and Malagasy slaves, who made them with whatever raw materials they could find. There are several stringed instruments, or zithers. The *zez* has one string and its sound box is a hollow dried out gourd. The string is plucked to produce music. The *bonm* is similar, but the string is attached to a wooden bow with a gourd on the end and played with a thin stick. The *mouloumpa* is a cross between a wind and a string instrument. It is

made of a piece of bamboo with strings on the outside that the player plucks and blows down at the same time.

The most unusual of all these instruments is the *makalapo*. It is made of a string attached at one end to a sheet of tin half buried in the ground, and to a flexible stick a few feet away at the other. Notes are produced by plucking the string and their tone is varied by manipulating the stick to tighten or slacken the string. For percussion there are the skin drums, the *tam tam* and tambour, and the *kaskavel*, which is a small container filled with seeds or grit and shaken.

to ban *gris-gris*). A description of a *moutya* from the 1930s reveals the attitude of the authorities: 'As soon as these drums are beaten with rhythmic measure the men and women dance back to back, occasionally turning round and facing each other while making suggestive signs. Compared to the *moutya*, the notorious *danse du ventre* [belly dance] is as innocent of offence as... a children's Christmas party.'

The dance begins with the men chanting, either a known song or an improvised one – usually a bawdy tale or a taunt aimed at a

Scottish reel), *berlin* and *pas-dikat*. No doubt the transition to Seychelles livened many of them up. A kanmtole band must have at least a fiddle and a triangle, but can also include banjos, accordions and a drum. The most important band member is the komandan, who shouts instructions to the dancers in time with the music, in much the same way as a caller in a barn dance.

The dance shows laid on by the bigger hotels tend to revolve around sega. Only the more 'serious' cultural shows will include *moutya*, a more

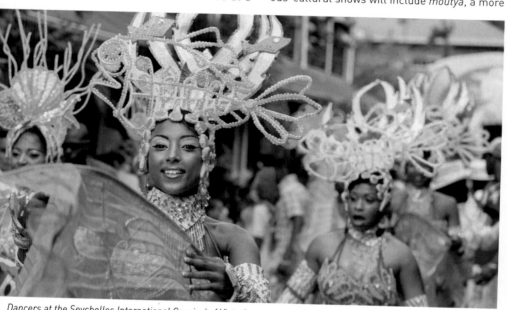

Dancers at the Seychelles International Carnival of Victoria.

rival in love. In the old days, this would also have been an opportunity for slaves to vent their anger against the plantation owners. In due course, the drums begin the beat and the men approach the women of their choice, arms outstretched. The partners dance back-to-back with sensuous, shuffling movements, but again, never touch.

Both the sega and the *moutya* were of African origin, but from their European forebears, the Seychellois took the *kanmtole*, a dance tradition still very much alive. *Kanmtole* refers to a whole set of dances modified from their formal origins in the courts of France: the *lavals* (waltz), *ekosez* (Scottish jig), *mazok* (mazurka), polka, *kontredans* (similar to a

sombre dance that doesn't lend itself so well to the glitz of a tourist spectacle. *Kanmtole* nights are often advertised. They are usually held at smaller hotels, local social centres or restaurants, and anyone going along would certainly be made welcome.

In recent years *seggae*, a hybrid of sega and reggae, has caught on in Seychelles, and further afield in Europe. Groups such as Mersener and its lead singer Lyrical Sniper bring a whole new feel to sega with rap-like lyrics and electronic instruments. And listen out for the music of Seychelles' artist Sonny Morgan, who blends sega with different sounds such as pop and blues, and whose music is regularly played on the radio and in hotels.

AN ARTS TOUR

Seychelles has an active arts scene, particularly nature-inspired batik, watercolours and craft, with numerous galleries and local artist studios to browse in.

In the short time since the arrival of tourism, there has been an explosion in the arts and crafts output of Seychelles. Though the roots of the industry are not deep, they are uniquely Seychellois, drawing their inspiration from the dazzling colours and pristine nature of the environment. A tour of the numerous small art studios is a pleasant diversion from the beach and an opportunity to view paintings, prints, batiks and ornaments with little pressure to buy and, frequently, an opportunity to meet the artists themselves.

A good place to begin an arts tour of Mahé is the capital, Victoria, where there is no shortage of craft shops (see page 284). On the Bel Air road, north of Victoria, Thoughts Stained Glass Studio sells beautiful and colourful glass souvenirs of Seychelles.

CRAFT VILLAGE

South of the capital on the east coast, the Craft Village is an essential port of call. At the entrance is Maison de Coco, a shop dedicated to the coconut palm, housed in a building made of palm products. The range of goods includes leaves woven into bags and baskets, while the fibre that swathes the shoots, known as tami, is used to make various items including decorative stuffed fish, or wrappings for soaps perfumed with vanilla. The nut itself is used for napkin rings, candleholders, cups and trinket pots. Coconut oil is used to perfume soaps and bath oils. Inside the village there are 12 craft huts, some featuring works by local painters, such as Serge Rouillon (who specialises in detailed watercolours of plants), etchings and vivid watercolours by George Camille, and prints by Christine Harter of local scenes. Nearby is the studio of Colbert Nourrice, one of the most innovative of Seychellois artists. His abstract works are a narrative on canvas, telling small anecdotes from his life and experiences almost in comic-strip form. One of his favourite themes is the local folklore character Soungoula, a tricky customer, always full of mischief.

GALLERIES AND STUDIOS

Gerard Devoud has two art galleries, one on the east coast at Les Mamelles and one on the west opposite the entrance to Plantation Club. He uses light and colour broken into 'bits', creating mosaic-like landscapes and village scenes predominantly using watercolours.

The west coast of Mahé is the location for the studios of two of Seychelles' most famous creative geniuses, artist Michael Adams and sculptor Tom Bowers

One of George Camille's vivid creations.

(see page 289). Donald Adelaide is another artist based on the west coast. He produces bright, piecemeal images of the island and island life, mostly in watercolour. He has a studio near Harvey's Café where he sells prints and originals. Almost opposite Harvey's Café is the turning to Anse Gouvernement. It's worth a detour to see the distinctive wood sculptures on display at Studio Antonio, shortly before the beach on the right (see page 289).

On Praslin, there are several small galleries, including Cap Samy Art Gallery at Baie Ste Anne, and George Camille Art Gallery at Côte d'Or.

Silhouette Island is the home of Ron Gerlach, who produces authentic stylised batiks celebrating the natural history of Seychelles, on sale at La Passe.

Hawksbill turtles are an endangered species.

PRESERVING NATURE

The natural history of Seychelles echoes the ancient land link between Africa and Asia; much of the environment is still in relatively pristine condition.

Islands are laboratories of evolution. Nature's experiments have been going on for a longer period in Seychelles than in any other group of ocean islands, so it is no surprise that such a unique assemblage of flora and fauna should have evolved here. The roots of some species can be traced back to Africa, Madagascar, Asia and even to Australasia, originating from a time when all these land masses were linked in the supercontinent of Gondwanaland, before continental drift cast them apart.

BATS, TORTOISES AND TURTLES

Seychelles was isolated in mid-ocean long before mammals appeared on earth. No mammals ever reached here by natural means except for those with the power of flight, namely the bat. Of the two endemic species, the sheath-tailed bat and the Seychelles fruit bat, the latter is by far the most common. It is one of the few creatures to have benefited from the arrival of humans and the consequent proliferation of fruit trees. Not so beneficial from the bats' point of view is the culinary speciality, curried fruit bat, a local favourite which often pops up on restaurant menus. Despite the Seychellois' taste for them, however, bats remain very common and their noisy squabbling in the trees at night is one of the islands' characteristic sounds.

With no mammals for competition, Seychelles became the last Kingdom of Reptiles. The estuarine crocodile was an early casualty of human settlement, but the giant tortoise still thrives. Aldabra atoll has the world's largest population, with more than 100,000. Giant tortoises occupied islands across the Indo-Pacific for millions of years, safe from the mammals that came to dominate the continents. Their waterproof exoskeletons, ability to survive for weeks without food and the female's

A brown noddy on Bird Island.

⊘ PROTECTED AREAS

Literally 1,000 miles (1,600km) from anywhere – India to the north, Africa to the west, Sri Lanka to the east and Madagascar to the south – the Seychelles islands were uninhabited until the late 18th century. While the natural beauty of other Indian Ocean islands was gradually destroyed, that of the Seychelles has been carefully preserved. There are many protected areas where nature lovers can marvel at unspoilt flora, fauna and marine life: the Morne Seychellois National Park, Mahé; the Vallée de Mai, Praslin; the Veuve Reserve, La Digue; and special reserves on the islands of Cousin, Aride and Aldabra.

inbuilt mechanism for storing sperm made them ideal candidates for ocean transport. The luckier ones that had been swept away by the tide from the shores of the mainland were washed up on remote tropical islands. This happened rarely enough for unique island races to evolve. Sadly, most of these are now extinct, victims of human exploitation. It was thought the granitic island form had suffered the same fate until the discovery of some unusual tortoises. These were brought to Silhouette by the Nature Protection Trust of Seychelles for captive breeding. It is possible that they retain some char-

Likewise, the future of turtles is slowly brightening. In the past they were slaughtered mainly for their 'tortoiseshell', which was converted into jewellery and other trinkets for sale to tourists. Thankfully, the authorities recognised that live turtles have a higher value, enhancing the reputation of the country while encouraging ecotourism. The sale of all tortoiseshell products is now banned.

Two species breed here – the hawksbill turtle and the green turtle. Remarkably, the granitic islands are the only place in the world where hawksbill turtles come up to breed in the day-

Mealtime for a giant tortoise on Curieuse Island.

acteristics of two granite island forms of tortoise, the Seychelles giant tortoise and Arnold's tortoise. However, most scientists believe there was only one species throughout Seychelles, the Aldabra Giant Tortoise, which survives in the granitics (Curieuse, Frégate, Cousin and Cousine) in several introduced wild populations. Many are also kept in pens in hotel gardens, at the Botanical Gardens and elsewhere, so there are plenty of opportunities to see this lovable Seychelles symbol.

Once it was traditional to present a baby tortoise to a newborn girl and raise the animal as a family pet until the girl grew up and married. The tortoise would then be slaughtered at the wedding feast. This tradition has died out, though many Seychellois still keep a few lumbering giants as pets.

The call of the male Aldabra tortoise is said to be the loudest noise in the reptile kingdom. It is, in fact, a seduction technique – the actual mating is a silent affair.

time. Green turtles occasionally nest in the granitic islands but their stronghold is Aldabra where around 4,000 females haul themselves ashore each year to breed. In the past, they were heavily exploited for their meat and, although poaching still poses a threat, they have escaped the near total extermination suffered elsewhere. Aldabra is one of the few places on earth where turtles, classed as among the most endangered of creatures under the Convention on International Trade in Endangered Species (CITES), are increasing in number.

UNIQUE REPTILES

For sheer quantity of reptiles, there is nowhere quite like the seabird islands of Seychelles, particularly Cousin, Cousine and Aride, which have a greater concentration of these beasts than anywhere else on earth. It is partly thanks to the seabirds that the lizards survive in such

Amazingly, the only other places frogs do this are New Zealand and tropical South America – opposite ends of the former super-continent.

LAND AND SEA BIRDS

The lure of birdwatching in Seychelles is not the number of species. You may see more varieties in a single day in East Africa than in a lifetime in Seychelles. Also, island birds tend to be less colourful than their continental cousins. However, what they lack in variety and spectacular plumage they more than make up for in their rarity value.

A green gecko lizard on La Digue.

large numbers. They feed on eggs or chicks left unguarded or a catch that has been dropped. Most reptiles found here are unique to Seychelles, including the Seychelles skink, Wright's skink and several species of green gecko.

One of the characteristics of ocean islands is the absence of amphibians. Once again, Seychelles is an exception to the rule. The islands support 13 amphibian species in all, 12 of which are unique to Seychelles; one of these was described for the first time in 2002. Among the frog species is the minuscule pygmy piping frog. Though difficult to spot, its high pitched squeak is often the only sound to be heard in the higher hills. Another species, the croaking carrycot frog, has evolved the surprising habit of carrying its tadpoles on its back.

Successful programmes have been implemented to restore the fortunes of two of the rarest birds in the world, the Seychelles warbler and Seychelles magpie-robin. Programmes are also underway to study, protect and reverse the historical decline of other species. This includes probably the most beautiful of the endemic birds of Seychelles, the Seychelles black paradise flycatcher. It is the symbol of La Digue, where a special nature reserve has been established for it. The male is staggeringly beautiful with its shiny black plumage and long tail feathers. Though less spectacular, the female is also an attractive bird, chestnut above, white below, with a black head.

The enigmatic Seychelles scops owl occurs only on Mahé, its population concentrated in the Morne Seychellois National Park, while the white eye survives on five islands. Both are among the rarest birds in the world. Praslin, too, has its own special bird, the Seychelles black parrot. Its piercing whistle is often the only sound echoing around the Vallée de Mai. One of the world's smallest birds of prey, and the only bird of prey in the granitics, is the Seychelles kestrel. It is found mainly on Mahé with smaller numbers on Praslin and elsewhere, often announcing its presence with its far-reaching 'ti-ti-ti-ti' cry (its name in Kreol is *katiti*). The

Seychelles fody (*toktok* in Kreol) survives on five islands, including Aride and Cousin, the easiest places to spot it.

More common, but also unique to the granitic islands, are the Seychelles blue pigeon, Seychelles cave swiftlet, Seychelles bulbul and Seychelles sunbird. Even the laziest of birdwatchers can spot them, possibly in their hotel grounds, but certainly in Victoria's Botanical Gardens in the early morning or late afternoon.

Aldabra Atoll is particularly rich in avifauna (see page 344). This World Heritage Site is home to the

Birds on the beach at Praslin.

⊘ SAVED FROM EXTINCTION

Conservation success stories are few and far between but Seychelles has more than its fair share. Take the humble Seychelles warbler. By 1960, it stood on the threshold of annihilation. An international appeal was launched and in 1968 Cousin was placed under the protection of the Royal Society for Nature Conservation and BirdLife International. The warblers thrived. By the 1980s numbers reached around 350. However, it was too early to take the species off the critical list so long as they remained confined to one island, where a local disaster might threaten their survival. In 1988, 29 birds were transferred to Aride. It was hoped they might settle to breed around the usual time in January. The birds had

other ideas. With virtually unlimited space and food supply they bred year-round and by 1999 there were almost 2,000 birds. With smaller colonies also established on Cousine and Denis, the species is now one of the few to be taken off the Red Data list of endangered species.

The Seychelles magpie-robin is now receiving similar treatment. Once widespread in the granitic islands, its tame and trusting behaviour meant it fell victim to man and introduced predators. Down to fewer than 20 birds on Frégate, a BirdLife recovery programme was launched. Cousin, Aride, Cousine and Denis now host breeding populations and numbers have increased to more than 250 birds.

last surviving flightless bird of the Indian Ocean, the Aldabra rail. Aldabra is also famous for its sea-bird colonies, including the world's second largest colony of frigate birds. Closer to the main islands, Bird Island, is named in honour of its million-plus sooty terns that return to breed annually between April and October. The attraction here is the sheer number of birds competing for every inch of space.

Yet the Seychelles species list contains far more visiting birds than breeding ones, most of which turn up between October and December.

PLANT LIFE

The large-scale deforestation that laid bare almost every tropical island during the age of exploration did not pass Seychelles by altogether but, unlike most islands, the scars have healed. Although virgin forest is now confined to the higher areas of Mahé and Silhouette, and the Vallée de Mai on Praslin, there are no large expanses of wasteland, no vast areas of cultivation or big sugar cane plantations. Seychelles is like one gigantic botanical garden.

Today, there are well over 1,000 species of plants in the granitic Seychelles. About 250 occur naturally, of which around 75 are unique to the islands. Symbols of the tropics such as bougainvillaea, frangipani and hibiscus appear in almost every garden. The colourful flame tree and fruit trees such as breadfruit and jackfruit are common. Coconuts, once confined to the beach crest, have been planted in huge numbers further inland. In the coral islands, as with the birds, there is a much smaller variety of species, but again Aldabra is an exception. Here, a remarkably diverse flora includes about 40 endemics.

Some of the endemic plants of Seychelles are so rare they are only found in a few remote locations, such as the bwa-d-fer and bwa-d-nat trees, once prized for shipbuilding. The jellyfish tree has apparently always been rare, but still clings to survival on a few Mahé hilltops. The insect-eating Seychelles pitcher plant, though not so rare, can be elusive until you know where to search. Other unique plants are more common, including the beautiful wild vanilla, its leafless stems climbing over bushes.

No one can fail to notice the majestic palms of Seychelles. There are six species unique to the granitics, including the fabled coco de mer, confined to Praslin and Curieuse. The female

tree has the largest, heaviest seed in the world, a double nut with an uncanny resemblance to the female pelvic region. The enormous catkin of the male tree also has to be seen to be believed! Certainly, some male and female toilets in Seychelles bearing the nut and the catkin as symbols to tell them apart, leave no visitor in any doubt as to which is which.

For those able to drag themselves away from the beaches, there are several well-marked trails where many of the plants of Seychelles can be seen. More sedentary visitors may take a trip

Pitcher Plants at Mount Copolia in Mahé.

to Victoria's Botanical Gardens, while a visit to Vallée de Mai is virtually mandatory for any visitor to Praslin. However, such is the profusion of life in the hot and humid tropical climate of Seychelles, that even a stroll round a hotel garden can be very rewarding.

It is fortuitous that so many of the flora and fauna of Seychelles have survived to a more enlightened age in which their intrinsic value is appreciated. This is partly due to the fact that when compared to most other places in the world, Seychelles was settled comparatively recently. Thankfully, the government was quick to recognise how essential it was to protect its country's natural assets. Today, more than 40 percent of its land mass is given some form of legal protection.

Big eye and striped grunts.

UNDERWATER WORLD

Exploring the waters of the Indian Ocean, where coral reefs support spectacular fish, is like swimming in a giant aquarium.

The islands of the Seychelles provide visitors with access to some of the best protected ocean areas in the world, thanks to a long history of conservation which began with the establishment of the Ste Anne Marine National Park in the 1970s.

This enlightened and far-sighted approach has paid dividends in terms of the range and abundance of marine life found. Because spear-fishing and other destructive fishing techniques commonly used in other island states have long been banned, tourists are often impressed to find that fish species that are normally shy and elusive are easy to find and apparently visitor friendly.

An exciting new development in 2018 saw the Seychelles' government sign an agreement to create two enormous marine reserves the size of the UK in exchange for wiping US$21million off the country's national debt; this should further cement the archipelago's future as an international leader in marine conservation.

Scissortail sergeant and diver, Ste Anne Marine National Park.

EXPLORING THE DEEP

Most hotels and resorts rent out snorkelling equipment (though the quality varies) or you can buy your own from one of the dive centres selling masks, snorkels and fins at very reasonable prices. A number of tour operators and some private companies offer snorkelling excursions by boat to favourite spots such as Ste Anne Marine National Park, Baie Ternay Marine Reserve and St Pierre in Curieuse Marine Park. These trips may be for a half or full day and many include lunch at one of the renowned Creole restaurants to be found on the smaller islands.

For scuba divers, Seychelles is a well-established world-class diving destination both in terms of diving conditions and professionally run diving operations. Most diving centres belong to the Association of Professional Divers, Seychelles

☑ GENTLE GIANTS

The largest fish in all the oceans is the whale shark, found around the coastal waters of Seychelles. This harmless plankton feeder can grow to a length of 18 metres (59 ft) and weigh over 25 tonnes. Until recently, these sharks were not regularly hunted; now, however, there is a big demand from the Far Eastern restaurant trade, particularly for their fins. Little is known of this impressive fish except that, like many sharks, it is extremely slow growing. Several treaties recognise the need to protect sharks, but international cooperation is lacking. The whale shark has been listed on Appendix II of two treaties, the Convention of Migratory Species in 1999 and CITES in 2002.

(APDS), which sets additional standards for the operation and provision of diving services. Their members also support marine-related environmental and conservation projects, such as the Whale Shark Monitoring Programme run locally by the Marine Conservation Society of Seychelles, which tracks the numbers and migration of whale sharks. For those who have never tried diving, the shallow waters and rich coral reefs around Seychelles islands provide the perfect opportunity to learn, combining safe and enjoyable diving conditions with world-class diving instruction.

A scuba diver sees a school of fish.

If you tread on a sea urchin, rub papaya onto the wound: the juice of the fruit contains an enzyme that helps dissolve the spines.

LEARNERS AND PROS

APDS centres offering the PADI programme introduce complete beginners to scuba diving, starting with a tutorial and confined water skill session prior to the first shallow open water dive. They all offer four-day courses culminating in the internationally recognised PADI Open Water Diver certificate. For already qualified divers they also offer a number of advanced

and supervisory courses right through to those aspiring to become Dive Instructors. There are dive centres on Mahé, Praslin and La Digue, as well as on the outer island of Desroches.

Diving is possible all year round, with the calmest sea conditions and best visibility being in March, April and May and then in October and November. Visitors hoping for the thrill of diving with a whale shark should consider July and August or November and December. December is when the APDS hosts the annual SUBIOS Seychelles' Festival Of The Sea, where some of the world's top underwater photographers, film-makers and conservationists present a programme of films and lectures.

SEYCHELLES SEASCAPE

Whether you're an experienced or first-time diver, Seychelles has so much to offer. The unique granite rock formation of the northerly island group, known as the Inner Islands, creates underwater conditions that are much more varied than might be expected, supporting a prodigious variety of marine life. The diversity is further broadened by the coral atolls to the south, which include Aldabra, the world's largest raised coral atoll and a designated Unesco World Heritage Site.

The water temperature, which is somewhere between 26 and 30°C (79–86°F), traditionally promoted the prolific growth of sponges, corals and invertebrates, which painted the granite walls and canyons in a kaleidoscope of colours. Unfortunately huge chunks of reefs were decimated by coral bleaching in 1998, when El Niño caused sea temperatures to rise dramatically. It took years to recover, and tragically was hit again during a particularly hot summer in 2016 when water temperatures rose by 2°C for weeks. Groups such as Nature Seychelles are monitoring reefs and growing coral in underwater nurseries, which is then transplanted to degraded sites. The underwater terrain of the Inner Islands is a mirror image of the landscape above the surface, characterised by dramatic granite formations. The rocks and boulders form natural gullies and crevices that are prime real estate for many marine creatures such as the moray eel, a species with an undeserved notoriety. Its reputation stems mainly from the habit of greeting visitors with its toothy jaws gaping in an apparently threatening manner. But appearances are deceptive; these eels live quiet lives. There is little water flow and so they have to gulp water over their gills in order to breathe, hence the gaping jaws. Morays are successful hunters of fish, crabs and snails, but have little interest in bigger fare.

Another crevice inhabitant occasionally found around the reef during the day is the octopus. This, the most highly developed of all the molluscs, is a most active predator, feeding mainly at night on other molluscs, crabs and small fish. The octopus is also a master of disguise, especially the marbled octopus commonly found on the granitic reefs. Its skin has special cells which allow it to change colour and alter its texture.

DISTINCTIVE FISH

Visitors to Seychelles are always impressed by the sheer volume of fish encountered. The brightly coloured butterfly and angelfish are often the most apparent but with a little practice you can become familiar with the extreme body shapes of some species. The elongated cylindrical forms of the trumpet fish and flutemouths are an easy first step; however, discerning between the two is tricky – the trumpet has a fan-like tail and is generally seen in several colour forms on the coral reef, while the flutemouth is normally seen just below the water's surface and has a whip-like tail.

Another easy to distinguish group are box fish and pufferfish, the former having angular cube-like bodies with apparently undersized fins while the puffers resemble deflated tropical fruit swimming over the reef – they only 'puff' up if harassed or cornered. Both these groups have teeth sharp enough to cut through coral and can deliver a deep and painful bite if tormented.

Lionfish and their cousins the scorpionfish are also fairly easy to identify; lionfish by their dramatic array of long feather- or whip-like spines on their back and side fins; scorpionfish by their camouflaged and bottom-dwelling habit. The problem with scorpionfish is actually finding them to begin with.

Once the odd-shaped fish species have been identified you're still left with a bewildering array of 'fish-shaped' fish. Of the reef dwellers, the majority belong to the parrotfish or wrasse families. Parrotfish come in a huge range of sizes and colours but all exhibit the characteristic

Yellowmouth sweetlips, Aldabra Atoll.

⊘ CLEANING SERVICES

Apart from moray eels and octopuses, the gaps and crevices in the granite rocks house creatures that would happily feature on the moray's diet sheet, especially crabs, shrimps and lobsters, but one group most closely associated with the moray is the brightly coloured cleaner shrimp. This little creature performs a valuable service not just for morays but for many fish species, cleaning parasites off skin, scales and even from between their teeth. The shrimp's bright red and white banding and long white antennae act as an advertisement for their cleaning services and seem to guarantee that they will not be eaten by their larger clients.

Another creature offering cleaning services to reef inhabitants is the little striped cleaner wrasse, whose vertical black and blue stripes are easily identified. Wrasse are very territorial and set up shop by particular rocks or coral heads where they bob and weave in a characteristic display to attract business. The careful observer will be able to see these little fish working away deep inside the mouths or gills of larger reef fish in apparent security.

Closer to the shore, meanwhile, the long sausage-shaped sea cucumbers scattered across the shallow sands keep the sea bed clean, as they feed on detritus and algae in the sand's surface layer.

horny coral-cutting beak, like that of a real parrot. Wrasse, an equally large group, have no such distinguishing characteristics. Keen divers and snorkellers should invest in a fish spotter's guide to identify fish beyond this level.

Some fish have the ability to change sex: parrotfish, anthias and wrasse start as females and can become males as needed.

Blacktip reef shark, Aldabra Atoll.

OUTER ISLAND TERRAIN

Visitors to the Outer Islands will notice a distinct difference in the underwater terrain to that of the Inner Islands. These islands and atolls are either large sandbanks, such as Bird Island and African Banks, or coral atolls such as Aldabra. The coralline islands often have dramatic walls, which plunge from the surface into deep water and thus have a very different range of inhabitants. The deeper sections of these walls are characterised by intricate gorgonian fan corals supported by a springy backbone of horn-like material. They grow at right angles to the current so that they can filter out food particles from the water as it runs along the reef's perimeter. Keen underwater photographers home in on these fans as they support their

own array of co-inhabitants, ranging from small cowry shells and spider crabs to their own specialised, if somewhat small, predator. The long-nosed hawkfish uses the fan corals as a lookout point from which to capture small crustaceans.

BIG FISH

The other attraction of these remote island spots is the chance to spot larger fish and pelagic species such as barracuda and tuna. Diving and snorkelling along the vertical walls of some islands almost guarantees the sighting of the dog tooth tuna, a real warrior of the deep. These large powerful fish swim with a slightly open mouth proudly displaying a set of canine-like teeth. Shark sightings are another highlight, most commonly blacktip reef sharks. Larger species, such as bull and tiger sharks, patrol the Indian Ocean but snorkellers and divers rarely encounter them. Sadly, two fatal shark attacks did occur in Seychelles at Anse Lazio in the north of Praslin in 2011; however these were the first in 50 years and numerous measures have been taken since, including underwater nets. If in doubt, it's recommended to stick to water-based activities off beaches protected by a coral reef (Anse Lazio isn't).

As there is comparatively little fishing here, the marine ecosystems in the outer regions are under less pressure and should have more abundant marine life. The food chain supports a larger number of predators and on many reefs the various species of grouper, such as the rare potato cod, are typically abundant. These large fish can grow to well over 1 metre (3ft) in length and are characterised by large, black potato-like blotches on their grey bodies. They have a reputation for being aggressive, which may or may not be deserved; however, any fish of this size should be treated with respect.

TURTLE SPOTTING

Turtles are another common sight on the Outer Islands. While hawksbill turtles are the predominant species of the Inner Islands, as you travel south the green turtle becomes more common. Green turtles are generally larger than their sharp-billed cousins and have a broader head and less pronounced bill. A third species, the loggerhead turtle, is rarely seen; while it seems to have a blend of characteristics from the other two species, it can normally be recognised by its massive head, large eyes and immensely thick and powerful beak, which is much more heavy-duty than that of either of the common species.

TOP DIVE SITES

Seychelles offers a wealth of world-class underwater experiences, from wreck and drift dives to encounters with reef sharks, stingrays and even whale sharks.

There are many world-class dive sites in Seychelles. The following are the top Inner Island sites as rated by resident divers. Apart from Ave Maria on Praslin, most of these are only suitable for seasoned divers. The list is by no means comprehensive and the dive centres on Mahé, Praslin and La Digue offer other sites in their programme, suitable for all levels.

SHARK BANK

A granite plateau with large boulders and a depth of between 20 and 35 metres (65–115ft), this outcrop between northwest Mahé and Silhouette island is a focal point for schooling fish and predators. The rocks are especially renowned for sightings of large marbled stingrays and whale sharks. A deep site which can have strong currents, it is suitable for experienced divers.

L'ÎLOT

This classic granite island off the northwestern tip of Mahé lies at the confluence of the east and west coast currents, so its waters support a plethora of marine life. As one of the few Inner Island sites with good soft coral formations, there's a chance of spotting schooling fish and whale sharks (October to December). Although the maximum depth is only 23 metres (75ft), currents and patchy visibility mean that in adverse conditions divers need to have suitable experience.

BRISSARE ROCKS

A granite massif 5km (3 miles) off the northeast coast of Mahé, this site attracts many schools of fish including snappers and Napoleon wrasse, plus Hawksbill turtles, moray eels and reef sharks. With depths of down to 20 metres (65ft) this site isn't for novices.

THE WRECK OF THE ENNERDALE

The remains of this stricken tanker lie 8km (5 miles) off the northeast coast of Mahé at a depth of 30 metres (98ft). Due to the distance from shore and its exposed position, the wreck is not often visited and so hosts good marine life. The structures are encrusted with corals and invertebrates but over time metal fatigue and corrosion have begun to compact some sections. When conditions are good, this is an excellent dive for experienced divers, with schooling fish, shark and ray prospects.

MARIANNE

The southern tip of Marianne Island is rarely visited. The terrain of jagged granite rocks and giant boulders

There are some excellent sites to see schooling fish.

hosts many large fish and is the seasonal home for a group of grey reef sharks that, for some unknown reason, are all female. An exciting dive to 27 metres (88ft), with or without the sharks, will suit experienced divers.

AVE MARIA

Praslin's version of L'Îlot; this granite group is renowned for a broad range of fish species as well as regular shark and stingray sightings. With a maximum depth of 26 metres (85ft), in good conditions this site is suitable for all divers.

THE OUTER ISLANDS

Outer Island sites have not been included here as this area would need a whole chapter to do it justice. The Desroches Drop is one of the best-known sites, but anyone diving off Alphonse, Astove, Cosmoledo and Aldabra will find the richness of marine life incomparable.

FISHING

Fish and fishing are dear to the souls of Seychellois, hardly surprising when they're ringed by waters so rich with marine life.

Fish is the staple diet of the Seychelles and, indeed, quite a few tourists. The fisheries sector is the second top contributor to the economy after tourism. The bounty of the Indian Ocean includes a tremendous variety of fish, excellent for both sport fishing and the dinner table. There are many game fishing boats to serve the tourist industry, equipped with the finest fishing gear. Fly-fishing is a relatively new sport in Seychelles, following the discovery of unexploited grounds described by experts as among the best in the world. Indeed, Seychelles holds world records for both fly-fishing and game fishing.

BIG GAME FISHING

Most game fishing boats operate out of Mahé. However, with the growth of tourism on Praslin and La Digue, these islands also have a number of good boats available. Each of the resorts on Silhouette, Frégate, Bird, Denis (a popular venue for serious big game fishermen), Desroches and Alphonse also have boats. Most charter boats fish exclusively by trolling (drawing bait through the water with rod and line), as this is the best way to catch the finest game fish. Tag and release is favoured by some operators and, if you believe in promoting this technique, it is as well to discuss it in advance.

The quality of fishing will depend partly on weather conditions, but the best fishing grounds are at the drop-off at the edge of the Seychelles Plateau (up to 32km/20 miles offshore), within easy reach of all the granitic islands: bigeye tuna, dogfish tuna and yellow fin tuna all inhabit the edge of the Seychelles Bank; sailfish are commonly caught in waters between Mahé and Silhouette; dorado can be caught over the Bank in season; and barracuda, jobfish (zob), even sharks are sometimes caught on trolling lures.

Big game fishing is a popular activity in Seychelles.

Though some fish – tuna and bonito, for example – can be caught all year round, others come and go seasonally. The best time of year for catching sailfish is during the southeast monsoon, from June onwards. Though dorado can be caught all year round, it is most commonly seen between January and September. Kingfish, also known as wahoo, are most plentiful from January to March, and trevally (karang) from November to December. Huge marlin weighing in at 150kg (330 lb) or more can be caught year round, including blue, striped and black marlin, but they are encountered far less often than sailfish.

Sea conditions can be rough during the southeast monsoon (June to September). Larger boats afford a more stable platform but, unless you are sharing the cost with other people, this can be expensive.

For the real enthusiast, live-aboard charters are available and may be customised to take into account the needs both of the fisherman and family members who may want to explore the islands.

FLY-FISHING IN ST FRANÇOIS

Seychelles offers world-class fly-fishing, primarily for bonefish and trevally. A few may be caught at Denis Island, but the best place by far is in the St François lagoon, reached via the nearby Alphonse Island Resort (see page 341). St François is a natural reservoir that remains virtually unexploited. The resort is trying to keep it that way by restricting numbers to 10 anglers per week. Hooks are barbless and all fish caught are released. Anglers are transported to the lagoon on two mother boats then transferred to flat boats (two fishermen per boat), which, depending on the state of tide, can travel throughout the lagoon, even in shallow water.

A reasonably good fly-fisherman can hope to catch over 50 fish in a day, while beginners as many as 20. The average bonefish caught here weighs 2–3kg (5–7 lb) though they can weigh up to 7kg (15 lb). Unsurprisingly, St François boasts several world records. Other fish caught here in the traditional way include small hammerhead shark, lemon shark, bigeye and barracuda. In 2002, fly-fishing operators at Alphonse pioneered a technique for catching milkfish, a fearsome fish despite its innocuous name.

BOTTOM FISHING

Bottom fishing may lack the excitement of game and fly-fishing, but if it's dinner you're after, fishing with lines, lead weight and natural bait is a great way to get it. Local fishermen traditionally fish this way, baiting lines with crabs, shellfish, squid, mackerel or other fresh fish, and using two or three hooks. The most sought-after of the 200 or so species of fish that can be caught on lines are red snapper (bourzwa) and grouper (vye). They feature on most menus and are among the tastiest fish you can eat here.

Apart from in the Marine National Parks, where fishing is prohibited, you can fish almost anywhere. Enquire locally about renting a little boat and if you don't have your own equipment, you should be able to pick up what you need in Victoria.

A fly fisherman with bluefin trevally, off Alphonse Island.

⦿ LUCRATIVE WATERS

In 1977, the Seychelles Exclusive Economic Zone was established, giving the country control of 370km (200 nautical miles) of ocean around its shores. Commercial exploitation of these waters, which are rich in tuna fish, has proved lucrative, and Victoria port, which has its own tuna processing plants, throbs with activity. About 40,000 tonnes of fish (including 36,000 tonnes of canned tuna) make a huge contribution to the Seychelles economy each year.

In November and December, the waters of Beau Vallon on Mahé are like a pond, and huge schools of mackerel come close inshore. They are harvested daily, but because they are so plentiful the market price of fresh fish drops dramatically at this time of year.

Local fishermen still favour traditional methods, and use hand lines, nets and their own special basket traps. The traditional Seychelles fishing boat is a long canoe-like vessel called a *pirogue* that is designed to be easy to manoeuvre in shallow waters and over reefs, and is usually painted in black and white. The *katyolo*, a smaller version, is painted in bright colours. The popularity of both these boats is diminishing as they are slowly being replaced by more modern motorised vessels. Thankfully, traditional boat-building is still a thriving skill, particularly on La Digue.

A Creole fish barbecue on the beach at sunset.

CREOLE CUISINE

Seychelles cuisine is rooted in its history and geography, from the riches of the sea to the tasty tropical spices.

With the exception of the family pig, a clutter of chickens kept behind the house and a few cattle, there has never been a tradition of rearing livestock in Seychelles because of the limited land available. Meat was only served on special occasions. The ocean has always been the main food supplier, and little has changed. Today, the Seychellois are among the biggest per capita consumers of fish in the world.

FISH AND SHELLFISH

Seychellois love fish; but not just any old fish. They have such a bounty of marine life around their islands that they can afford to be choosy. For example, the meaty tuna known locally as bonito can make a delicious curry, but most Seychellois look down on it as inferior and feed it to their dogs. They love the firm, white, flaky flesh of the *bourzwa* or red snapper, which is left whole but scored with long slits on both sides that are stuffed with ginger, garlic, chilli, onions and other spices. It is then wrapped in banana leaf (for purists) or tin foil and cooked over charcoal. Many Seychellois consider the finest meat from a red snapper is to be found in the head, and make good use of it in fish soup. Mackerel is also grilled in a parcel over hot coals, or on bamboo skewers, and drizzled with freshly squeezed lime to keep the flesh moist. *Zob* (another type of snapper) and *karang* (trevally) are served as steaks.

Parrotfish is put into fish stews, or battered for a Seychelles slant on the British favourite, fish and chips. Steaks of tuna, kingfish and swordfish are marinated in oil and spices then grilled on the barbecue. Shark meat is grated with garlic, ginger, *bilimbi* (a sour fruit), lime, onions and turmeric, then stir fried until it looks like yellow desiccated coconut. This dish is known as shark chutney. Sailfish

Roadside display of tropical fruit near Grand Anse.

is cut wafer thin and smoked, to produce a delicacy every bit as good as smoked salmon, delicious on crusty bread with salad.

Shellfish are also popular in Seychellois cuisine. The favourites are *tektek* and *palourdes*. *Tekteks* are winkle-like shells collected fresh from the sandy beaches and put into soup. It is not uncommon, even on busy Beau Vallon beach, to see a Seychellois woman, often assisted by a couple of her young children, stooped over the sand at the point where the waves lap the shore. As the water recedes it uncovers the *tektek*, which quickly burrow out of sight, pursued by a darting hand.

By contrast, *palourdes* are found on muddy shores such as in the estuarine area north of

Victoria's Inter-Island Quay. They are similar to cockles and delicious when cooked in herbs and garlic butter. The superb local prawns offered in most restaurants are a relatively new addition to the local diet. Prawns do not occur naturally in sufficient numbers around Seychelles to be worth harvesting. However, there is now a farm on Coetivy Island producing both for the local and export markets. The prawns are excellent, particularly the large ones, grilled in garlic butter, in a traditional Seychellois curry or in sweet and sour sauce.

HOT AND SPICY

Indian and Chinese cuisines have not influenced Seychellois cooking as much as in the Mascarenes. Most restaurants specialise in Creole cooking and seafood. However, one Indian dish Seychelles has taken and made very much its own is curry. A Seychelles curry (usually fish, but also, commonly, chicken, pork, goat or beef) is simply crammed with flavours, and is hot! An exception to this rule is the *kari koko zourit*, a mild octopus curry with creamy coconut milk. How they get the octopus so tender is kept a closely guarded secret by some;

Grilled goatfish at Lanbousir Restaurant.

⊘ CONSIGNED TO HISTORY

Seabird eggs were once of great importance to the Seychellois, simply because the annual bounty of eggs was a welcome variation in an otherwise monotonous diet. Egg exploitation is now controlled, in an attempt to ensure the survival of the sooty tern colonies, but a seabird egg omelette is still considered a delicacy. Turtles and tortoises were also eaten on special occasions. Traditionally, a baby tortoise was bought on the birth of a daughter and kept until the girl's wedding day, when it would be eaten at the wedding breakfast. This practice is now illegal. Both the giant tortoise and the turtle are protected species.

others will happily confess the secret is to cook your octopus in a pressure cooker. Whatever the truth, when cooked properly, it comes out more tender than chicken, melting in the mouth.

Spicy local sausages figure in a local speciality, sausage and lentil stew. Although there are tenrecs on the islands (small mammals similar to hedgehogs in appearance), originally introduced from Madagascar as food, Seychellois no longer eat them. They occasionally eat fruit bat, caught by hanging nets close to the fruit trees where the animals feed.

As for accompaniments, be warned, Seychellois love their chillies hot. The tiny ones are the hottest. To the average Western palate a single seed can set the mouth on fire, yet Seychellois think nothing of eating them whole or ladling copious amounts of the minced chilli in vinegar that comes separately in a little dish onto their meal.

VEGETABLES AND SALADS

Rice (plain, white, boiled) is the staple, but you will occasionally be offered breadfruit, a versatile potato-like 'fruit' served up as crispy chips, boiled and mashed, or stewed in coconut milk and sugar to make a gooey dessert. Best of all is baked breadfruit, the perfect complement to any beach barbecue. It is put whole among the burning coals until black on the outside and tender on the inside, then cut into piping hot slices and served with melted butter. Local legend has it that if you eat breadfruit, you'll be sure to return to Seychelles.

There is not a great deal of variety in the vegetable department. It is not easy to grow them in Seychelles due to the limited amount of flat land and the relatively poor soil. Exceptions include aubergines (usually served as deep-fried fritters), watercress and the tasty spinach-like *bred*. Avocados are abundant in season and salads are more than just the token lettuce leaf. Any true Creole spread will come with a range of so-called chutneys – finely grated pawpaw, mango or *fisiter* (golden apple) with onion, lime juice and pepper. They make a refreshing and cooling addition to a spicy meal.

Starters on a Creole menu usually include octopus salad, raw fish marinated in lime juice, and *palmis* salad. This became known as millionaire's salad because the whole tree had to be sacrificed to obtain the shoot. Conservation legislation now protects this unique majestic palm and today the salad is made with the living shoot of the coconut palm, which grows all over Seychelles, chopped into thin slices.

BANANA FEAST

More often than not the dessert choice is limited to local ice creams or fruit salad. Occasionally the fruit salad will come with coconut nougat (caramelised coconut) or coconut milk. There are 25 species of banana in Seychelles, ranging from the foot-long *sen zak*, used to make crisps, to the stubby *mil*, which is extremely sweet.

DRINKS

There are plenty of fruit juices, soft drinks, locally brewed beers and imported (expensive) wines available. At restaurants, it pays to ask if fresh juice is available. Try passion fruit juice or lime with a pinch of salt and sugar to taste. *Sitronel*, a kind of tea made from lemongrass, is also refreshing.

You are unlikely to be offered any of the local alcoholic brews with your meal. *Kalou* (or toddy) is made from coconut sap, which ferments quickly and naturally, and makes the ideal lazy man's tipple. *Baka* is a rum-like drink made from fermented sugar cane juice (a far cry from Bacardi and incredibly strong). The most lethal of the local firewaters is *lapire*, made from almost anything that will ferment when mixed with sugar.

Preparing tropical fruit juice along La Retraite road.

⊘ CRACKING COCONUTS

Many a tourist works up a sweat trying to crack a coconut found at the roadside by hurling it against a rock or attacking it with a small penknife. It doesn't work. To remove the thick fibrous husk that protects the nut, most Seychellois have a sharpened spike stuck in the ground. The husk of the coconut is impaled on this and worked loose. It takes an islander a few seconds, but for the novice a little practice is required.

On some excursions you may be offered *koko tann*, a green coconut with the top lopped off so you can drink the milk (refreshing, but an acquired taste). The thin jelly-like flesh of the unformed nut is delicious.

Villa on La Digue.

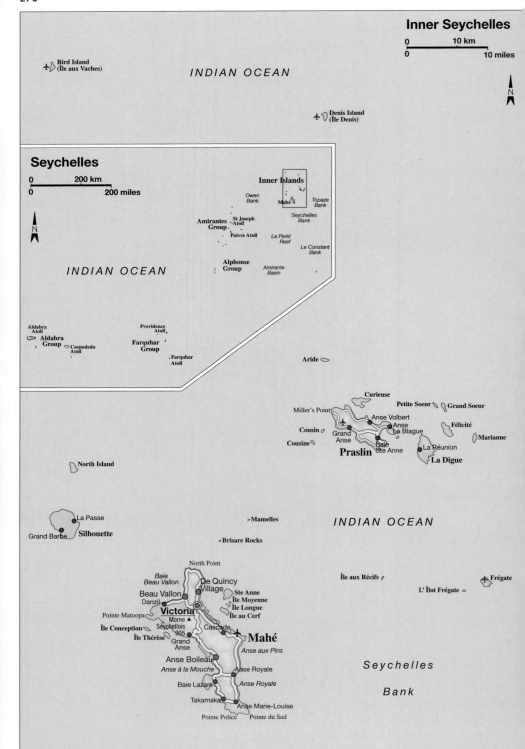

SEYCHELLES: PLACES

A detailed guide to Seychelles, with principal sites clearly cross-referenced by number to the maps.

A boat on Praslin.

To plan the perfect Seychelles holiday, you have to get three things right: the time of year (make sure you know beforehand when and where the monsoons hit); the quality of hotel (Seychelles is renowned for its five-star escapes but there are plenty of budget-friendly bed-and-breakfasts too); and, last but not least, the choice of island.

Each of the many Seychelles islands that now welcome overseas tourists has its own special draw. Most tourists flying into Mahé head straight for their final destination, without taking time to explore the main island. It may be more commercial and developed, but beyond the tiny capital of Victoria, Mahé has some superb beaches and forests of its own, with the added advantage of art and cultural attractions.

However, if you only have time to visit one island, Praslin is the one. Apart from its beaches, bordered with granite boulders, the other main attraction is the Vallée de Mai, a magnificent dense palm forest home of the coco de mer, its notorious love nut. Praslin also makes a perfect island-hopping base: Cousin, Curieuse, St Pierre, La Digue and Aride are all just a short boat ride away.

Laid-back La Digue can be visited on a day trip from Praslin, but to take in the spectacular coastline – a favourite location for commercial shoots – and explore the inland trails by bike or on an ox-cart, a couple of days here would be well spent.

Coco de Mer Hotel.

Even quieter than La Digue, Silhouette and North Island are the least known of the Inner Islands. Seemingly stuck in a time warp, Silhouette is a paradise for walkers. There are no roads but plenty of paths – not all well-trodden – that cut through the tangled and mountainous interior. North Island is home to a world-famous luxury eco-resort that draws environmentally conscious (and wealthy) tourists.

Frégate, another remote and exclusive granitic island, is privately owned. At five-star prices, for most of us it remains the stuff of dreams.

The coral islands of Bird, Denis, Desroches and Alphonse are perfect for getting away from it all. Each island has its own luxury resort, but has been developed to carefully preserve the environment. With facilities for sailing, diving, snorkelling, deep-sea fishing and birdwatching among other activities, there's plenty on offer for those who want to do more than just dream the days away lounging by crystal waters.

Mahé

0 1 km
0 1 mile

INDIAN OCEAN

North Point
L'îlot
Vista Bay
Glacis
Sunset Beach Hotel
Hilton Seychelles
Northolme Resort
Beau Vallon
Coral Strand Hotel
Le Méridien
Fisherman's Cove
Bel Ombre
Bel Ombre Treasure Dig
Anse Major Trail
Anse Major
(Anse Jasmin)
Cap Ternay
Baie Ternay
Baie Ternay National Park
Cap Matoopa
Pointe Matoopa
Baie Ternay Marine National Park
Le Passe Ternay
Île Conception

Carana Beach
Machabée
Mont du Nord
Mt Howard 458
La Gogue Village
La Gogue Reservoir
St-Antoine
La Retraite
Mon Plaisir
Glacis
Baie Beau Vallon
Mare Anglaise
Beau Vallon
Barclay Beau Vallon Bay Resort
Savoy Resort & SPA
Le Niol
Mt Le Niol 681
Mare aux Cochons
Mte Jasmin 643
Danzil
Sixpenny Hill
Anse Jasmin Estate
Du Riz
Pointe L'Escalier

Anse Nord d'Est
Kreol Fleurage
North East Point
North East Point Estate
Pointe Cèdre
Maldive Village
Hangard 374
Mt Signal 417
Crève-Coeur
St-Louis Minor 588 232
Pascal Village
Dens Cedres
Mont Coton
Morne Seychellois National Park
Mont d'Or
L'Islette
Port Glaud
Petite Île
L'Islette
La Plaine
Port Launay
Constance Ephelia Resort
Port Launay Marine National Park
Anse l'Islette
Thérèse 160
Port Glaud

De Quincy Village
Île Aurore
Île Cèdre
Anse Étoile
Pointe Conan
Mon Plaisir
Bel Air Cemetery
Pied du Morne
Trois Frères
Morne Seychellois 905
Morne Blanc 667
Trois Frères Trail
Congo Rouge
Dugand
Tea Factory
La Brûlotte

La Préservance
La Bastille
Seypot Factory
Pointe au Sel
Victoria
Victoria Lighthouse
National Stadium
Romainville
Mont Fleuri
Sans Souci
Chemin Sans Souci
Morne Seychellois 699
Mission Historical Ruins and Viewpoint
Val Riche
Grand Bois
Audibert
Rochon Dam
Sans Souci 500
Chemin La Misère
La Misère
Fairview
Rosebelle
Dans Letchis
Grand Anse

Eden Island
Isle of Farquhar
Wreck
La Rochée 335
Ma Joséphine
Providence
Solitude Mission
Belliant
Cap Ma Georgine
Cascade
Petit Paris
La Misère
New Savy 587
Whensides
Seychelles International Airport
Anse Talbot

INDIAN OCEAN

Frégate

0 500 m
0 500 yds

INDIAN OCEAN

Anse Victorin
Anse Bambous
Frégate Island Private Hotel
Glacis Cafoule
Plaine Magnan
Mont Signale
Signal Rock 125
Frégate Island 121
Pointe Fouquë
Grand Anse
Petite Grand Anse
Au Salon
Bambous
Anse Felix
Anse Coup de Poing
Airstrip
Settlement
Plantation House
Anse Parc
Pointe Sud

Praslin, La Digue

Ste Anne Marine National Park

Anse Cabot
Grand Anse
Albert Rock
Anse Manon
Ste Anne 250
Ste-Anne Resort
Anse Cimetière
Anse Mare Jupe
Ste Anne Channel
Jolly Roger Bar and Restaurant
Île Moyenne
Île Ronde
Île Longue
Kapok-Tree Restaurant
Cerf Island 108
Île au Cerf
Île Cachée
Île Seche
Grand Rocher
Cerf Passage
INDIAN OCEAN
Île Anonyme
Île aux Rats
Roche Tortue

Waterfall near Port Glaud.

MAHÉ AND SATELLITES

Away from the spread of the capital, Victoria, there is breathtaking beauty around the scenic coast and rainforest-clad mountains.

Mahé is the largest and most densely populated island in Seychelles, home to 90 percent of Seychellois. The instinct of many visitors soon after touching down at the International Airport is to rush away to Praslin, La Digue or even further afield to discover the real Seychelles. This is a mistake.

Of course the capital, Victoria, has its fair share of traffic jams and building works, but it's still the sort of place where everyone knows everyone else and where a game of dominoes outside the local shop is a social highlight. Beyond the town, there are plenty of opportunities to leave the paraphernalia of modern life behind, with escape routes down to the beach or up into the mountains.

Mahé covers an area of 158 sq km (61 sq miles) and rises to 905 metres (2,970ft) above sea level. It is 27km (17 miles) long and, at its widest, 8km (5 miles) across, so it can easily be covered by car in a day. There is a good network of roads, both coastal and inland, and a day spent driving round the island in an open jeep or Mini Moke is a great way to start your holiday.

Most of Seychelles' present population of 95,300 lives on Mahé, concentrated on the north and east coasts. Land reclamation along the east coast created valuable stretches of flat new terrain for development, and allowed

Market Street in Victoria.

for the building of a straight route from the airport to Victoria, cutting out the many twists and turns of the old coast road. The creation of this 'new' land has meant that the vital development of the island's infrastructure has been largely concentrated in the area around the capital, thus limiting its impact on the rest of the island.

Being the largest and highest island, there is an element of grandeur in Mahé's beauty the other islands don't have. The coastal scenery goes from wild granite cliffs where waves crash

 Main attractions

Sir Selwyn Selwyn-Clarke
  Market, Victoria
Botanical Gardens,
  Victoria
Michael Adams' Studio,
  Mahé
Ste Anne Marine National
  Park
Île au Cerf
Île Moyenne

Map on page 278

⊙ Tip

Parking is restricted in Victoria and police are keen. If you have come to town by car, the best place to park is the Stadium Car Park on Francis Rachel Street, which is free. Otherwise, you have to buy parking coupons (available from many shops).

The clock tower of Victoria is also known as Little Big Ben.

against massive boulders tumbling into the ocean, to tranquil palm-fringed coves. If you feel jaded by turquoise waters and silver sands, you can escape into the high hills and experience the eerie silence of the remote rainforest. The atmosphere is unforgettable, and one which many tropical islands have long since lost.

VICTORIA

Victoria ❶ is still a tiny capital by modern standards. It lies on the east coast, 8km (5 miles) north of the airport, bounded by mountains on one side and sea on the other. The town grew up around the natural harbour formed by the sheltering satellite islands of Ste Anne, Moyenne, Ronde, Longue and Cerf. The original settlement was founded in 1778 by the French, who built a military base here. In the early days of colonisation the islands, considered remote by the colonial powers, remained sparsely populated and expansion of the settlement was slow. It was known quite simply as L'Etablissement (The Settlement) until

1841, when it was named after Queen Victoria. Today, Victoria is the commercial centre of Seychelles and during business hours the streets throng with people and traffic. 'Old' Victoria, the area that lies at the foot of the mountains, is built around narrow streets with eccentric pavements that rise over great storm drains one minute, and drop into a gutter the next. Elegant if dilapidated French colonial-style buildings are huddled around them. The modern avenues of 'new' Victoria, laid out on the reclaimed land, are more stately, their pavements broad and flat, and lined here and there with attractive garden areas, bright with canna lilies and bougainvillaea.

If you're interested in Seychelles culture and the day-to-day life of its capital, it's worth spending a bit of time here. However, if your top priority is to experience the forests and coasts, half a day in Victoria should be enough.

THE HEART OF TOWN

The centre of Victoria is easy to explore and its hub, standing at a central crossroads, is the **Clock Tower Ⓐ**. It was built in 1903 both as a memorial to Queen Victoria and to commemorate the establishment of Seychelles as a Crown Colony in its own right. Next to the Clock Tower stands the **Court House Ⓑ**, a typical colonial-style building with a fancy ironwork balustrade on the upper storey. The nearby fountain is topped with the replica of a very small bust of Queen Victoria. The original, now in the History Museum (see page 284), was unveiled in 1900 to mark Queen Victoria's 60th year on the throne.

On the corner of Albert Street and Revolution Avenue is the Anglican Cathedral of **St Paul**, Seychelles' oldest church, consecrated in 1859. A new cathedral, preserving the original tower, was completed here in 2003.

THE CATHEDRAL OF THE IMMACULATE CONCEPTION AND CAPUCHIN HOUSE

The Roman Catholic **Cathedral of the Immaculate Conception Ⓒ**, built in the French colonial style, was finished in 1874, but has had many additions since. On weekdays the church is quiet, but on Sunday mornings the strains of the organ and choir ring out from the open doorways, and the congregation, dressed in their best, spill out onto the steps. Sunday Mass is as much a social occasion as a religious one.

Just down the street from the cathedral is Victoria's most impressive building, **Capuchin House Ⓓ**. Built in 1933 with funds from the Swiss Capuchin order, and designed by one of the monks, it is used as a seminary for priests and brothers, some of whom still teach in the schools.

MORNING MARKET

Heading back south towards the town centre, you'll pass the pedestrianised Market Street and the **Sir Selwyn-Clarke Market Ⓔ**, also known as Victoria Market. Saturday morning is the

best time to visit. The fish stalls are the commercial heart of the market, piled with freshly caught barracuda, parrotfish, cordonnier, bonito and kingfish. Produce stalls are stacked with neat pyramids of exotic fruits and seasonal vegetables. Others are laid out with trays of mixed spices, neatly rolled quills of fresh cinnamon bark, packets of turmeric and old jars crammed with small but deadly red and green chillies.

For a bird's-eye view of the goings-on, climb the stairs to the upper floor. There are a few craft shops open here, selling the more usual lines in souvenirs.

Cutting through the market, leaving by the side entrance, you come out into a little alley called Benezet Street. Turning left, past the bakery (which does excellent bread), you'll come back on to Revolution Avenue. If the heat and noise have made you weary, turn right and keep walking until you reach **Kaz Zanana Ⓕ** (Pineapple House), a quiet spot to pause for a bite to eat. The restaurant is on a terrace at the back, overlooking the garden. They serve light meals

Capuchin House.

throughout the day and the best cappuccino and chocolate cake in Seychelles. The rest of the house is made up of small galleries which exhibit paintings and drawings by local artist George Camille.

STROLLING SOUTH ALONG FIENNES ESPLANADE

The shady **Fiennes Esplanade**, which runs alongside Francis Rachel Street, was laid out by a British governor with the splendid name of Sir Eustace Edward Twisleton-Wykeham Fiennes (1918–21), father of explorer Sir Ranuph Fiennes. At the start of the esplanade is a **bust of Pierre Poivre**, the governor of Mauritius who arranged for the first spice plants to be brought to Seychelles for propagation (see page 242).

Towards the end of the Esplanade is a large modern building, the National Library. The National **History Museum** (Mon–Tue, Thu–Fri 8.30am–4.30pm, Sat 9am–1pm) is housed on the ground floor. In the entrance is the Stone of Possession,

An artist at Creole Craft Village, Anse aux Pins.

a stone placed by the French in 1756 to claim the islands. Displays are fairly basic, but they give an excellent introduction to the history of the islands, from pirates and explorers through wars and colonial times to the modern day. The tranquillity of the hall is a pleasant contrast to the hustle and bustle of Victoria, while the cool air-conditioned atmosphere is welcome after a hot walk.

There is a small commercial art gallery on the opposite side of the museum car park to the library, Carrefour des Arts (Mon–Fri 9am–5pm) with original paintings on sale. Across the road is Kenwyn House (Mon–Fri 8am–4pm, Sat 9am–noon). Built in the 1860s and renovated in 2005, it is probably the best preserved 19th-century building in Victoria. It also contains an excellent art gallery featuring a range of local artists.

EAST TO THE QUAYS

East of the Clock Tower, on Independence Avenue, is the **Natural History Museum** (Tue–Fri 9am–5pm, Sat

⊘ SOUVENIR SHOPPING

Codevar is an artisans' association set up by the government to promote local craftsmanship. One of the best places to pick up gifts and souvenirs is the **Codevar Craft Centre** at **Camion Hall** in Albert Street (named after the old open lorries, or *camyons*, used as buses, which used to set out on their routes from this spot). There is a shop on the street front selling pottery, woodcarvings, textiles and various objects made from coconuts and shells. In the arcade **Kreol Or** has a wide range of jewellery made out of green snail shell, tiger cowrie and coconut shell in combination with gold, and crafts made from local woods, coconut shell, coconut wood and polished palm seeds. Round the corner in Revolution Avenue, **Memorabilia** sells a wide range of crafts and books. **Sunstroke Gallery** on Market Street has a range of locally made beachwear, jewellery, hand-printed tablecloths and bed linen. Upstairs there is a gallery of local artwork. **Antigone**, the town's best bookshop, is in Passage des Palmes. **Antik Colony**, in the Pirates Arms building, sells quality souvenirs on colonial themes. On either side of the entrance to the Stadium Car Park are craft kiosks that sell beachwear, T-shirts, coconut crafts and spices.

9am–2pm, Mon 9am-12pm), with displays of endemic birds, reef life, tortoises, geology and the skulls of estuarine crocodiles that once lived in the mangrove swamps around Mahé's coast and terrorised the colonists.

A little further down the street is the **tourist office**, a good place for advice and literature on accommodation, excursions and museum opening times. It also has leaflets on walks and trails in Mahé, Praslin and La Digue.

Continuing straight on, past the Trwa Zwazo (Three Birds) roundabout (named after the sculpture erected in 1978 to celebrate 200 years of human occupation), the road swings left. This is Flamboyant Avenue, leading to **Inter-Island Quay** ❶, the departure point for ferries and boats to the islands, and for fast catamarans to Praslin. The traditional island schooners also ply between Mahé, Praslin and La Digue from this point, and the fleets of the largest charter boat operators are based here.

While waiting for your ferry, **Fish Tail** restaurant on the quayside offers a ringside seat to watch the comings and goings, or take a break in the Seychelles Port Authority's new passenger shelter, which has seating for 500 passengers, toilets, luggage storage and boat ticket and car hire booths. The charter boat marina is at the north end of the jetty, where catamarans and schooners line the pontoons. Just south of the Trwa Zwazo roundabout, on 5th June Avenue, is the **Marine Charter Association**, the departure point for glass-bottom boat and subsea viewer trips, and for some charter yachts.

THE BOTANICAL GARDENS

The walk from the Clock Tower to the **Botanical Gardens** ❶ (daily 7.30am–5pm) at the foot of Mont Fleuri takes about 20 minutes. They were laid out in 1901 by a Frenchman, Rivaltz Dupont, who collected many of the plant specimens on his travels. The site he chose was not ideal – the soil was poor and the land scattered with huge boulders – but it was the only affordable piece of land near town. Wandering through this green oasis today, it is hard to

Shopping for fresh seafood at Victoria Market.

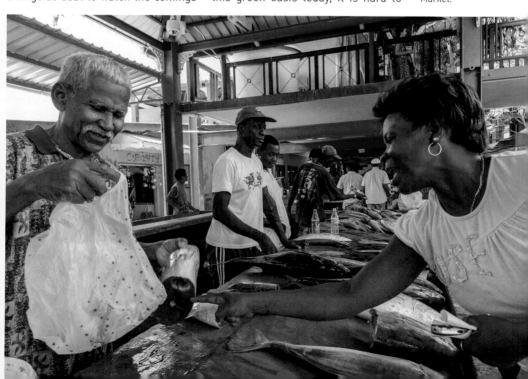

imagine the unprepossessing site Dupont was confronted with. The boulders are now an attractive feature, and the bubbling streams that run down either side of the park create a cool, soothing atmosphere.

At the top of the hill the gardens open out onto broad lawns dotted with specimen trees and shrubs. One of the most noticeable is the elephant apple, with fruits like huge, heavy apples that smell of rubber. There are attractive ponds with water lilies and darting dragonflies. The path leading from the ponds takes you past a mighty banyan tree and several drumstick trees that shed remarkable, long, thin fruits. One tree you can't miss, if it is in flower, is the cannonball tree, which sheds its leaves when flowering to reveal bizarre, fleshy coral pink flowers. A number of Aldabra giant tortoises are kept here in a large pen shaded by a coco de mer palm.

The gardens are shady enough to explore at any time of day, but it's best to avoid the heat of the midday sun.

Ask at the entrance kiosk for the leaflet which maps out the gardens and names all the plants. There are no refreshment facilities inside the gardens, so it's a good idea to pick up a drink on the way.

BEL AIR CEMETERY

On the outskirts of Victoria, at the beginning of the Sans Souci Road, is **Bel Air Cemetery** , Seychelles' oldest cemetery. Tombstones lie strewn haphazardly, there are no signposts and no guide, but it is an atmospheric place, nonetheless. Settlers and their slaves were buried here from the earliest times. The more splendid tombs bear the names of illustrious Seychelles families. According to legend, a young giant was killed by local people and buried here in the 1870s. The grave of the French corsair Hodoul is also rumoured to be here.

THE EAST COAST

There are two roads leading out of Victoria that head south towards the airport. For speed and convenience, Bois de Rose Avenue is the one to take. But if you're in no hurry, a journey along the narrow, winding, rather chaotic old Mont Fleuri Road (which becomes East Coast Road further along) will tell you far more about Mahé. The buildings that line it are a fascinating jumble of the modern (such as the Pentecostal Assembly on the junction of Mont Fleuri Road and Liberation Road) and the charmingly dilapidated. You can catch glimpses of elegant old planters' homes peeping over high stone walls, identifiable by their steep-pitched roofs, shuttered windows, wide verandas and high, stone foundations.

The two coast roads recombine at Providence, leading to **Cascade**, a traditional fishing village now dominated not by the fishing industry, but the nearby airport built on reclaimed land. The blessing of the fishing boats here

Victoria's streets back on to stunning scenery.

on the feast of St André (November) used to be an important celebration in Seychelles, attracting spectators from all over Mahé. The number of boats is far fewer nowadays, but about half a dozen pirogues, decorated with flags and flowers, still gather here for the annual blessing.

CRAFT VILLAGE

Another 6km (4 miles) down the coast road, past Anse aux Pins, on the site of a former plantation, is the **Craft Village** ② (Le Village Artisanal), where you can while away a bit of time looking at the workshops and shopping for souvenirs.

In the middle of the village the old plantation house, dating from 1870, has been furnished in typical colonial style. The cool, dark rooms smell of wax polish and cinnamon, and conjure a picture of the genteel existence once enjoyed by the privileged few. It's easy to imagine a candlelit social gathering, the ladies in their long dresses frantically fanning themselves and the gentlemen in full evening dress savouring the fine wines imported at great expense from France. **Vye Marmit Restaurant** is a good place to sample local specialities such as fruit bat, octopus, crab and fish.

ANSE ROYALE

Beyond the Pointe au Sel promontory, **Anse Royale** ③ is the main east coast beach. The sheltered, sandy bay is scattered with giant boulders, dividing the beach into a series of mini-coves, pretty much deserted on most weekdays. The snorkelling is reasonably good around the offshore islet of Île Souris. The currents between the mainland and the island can be strong, but run parallel to the beach, and it is fairly easy for a confident swimmer to cross them.

Kaz Kreol, at the southern end of Anse Royale, is an informal restaurant right on the sand, where you can turn up in your swimming costume for lunch.

THE KING'S GARDEN

Continuing south, the next turning off the main road is Les Cannelles. Sweet Escott Road is a left turning off this road. It was around here, in 1772, that Antoine Gillot, under instruction from the French government, planted a Royal Spice Garden (see page 242), but this is long since overgrown. In its memory, the **Jardin du Roi** ④ (King's Garden; daily 10am–5.30pm) has been established on the hillside above Sweet Escott Road. This renovated spice plantation, based on the former L'Enfoncement Estate, gives you a chance to see many aromatic plants growing (including nutmeg, pepper, cinnamon, vanilla and cloves). There is a walk laid out which you can follow using the printed guide. The small museum in the plantation house has some interesting exhibits, including old prints, maps and photos of Seychelles, and information on growing and using spices. On Sunday the restaurant serves a popular curry buffet.

Fishermen bringing in the catch on Anse Royale.

THE WEST COAST

The East Coast Road continues to Anse Marie-Louise, where it turns sharply inland and cuts across the southern end of Mahé. At Quatre Bornes, a road leads down to a spectacular bay, **Anse Intendance** ❺, where there is a very exclusive hotel, **The Banyan Tree Resort**. The long, pristine beach is pounded by crashing breakers, exhilarating to watch as they sweep in with a tremendous roar and a haze of spray. A strong swimmer might enjoy body surfing in the waves, but it's easy to get caught in the rollers and dumped hard on the beach or rocks. As with many of Seychelles' beaches, conditions vary according to the monsoon season. Seas are at their roughest during the southeast monsoon (May to October) and there can be a strong undertow. During the northwest monsoon (October to April) the waves here are still big, but the water is calm enough to swim in. Intendance is a popular picnic spot for Seychellois at weekends and can get quite busy, but the beach is so long there is room for all.

Rock formations in the surf, Baie Lazare.

Rejoining the main road at Quatre Bornes and heading west, you'll reach **Anse Takamaka** ❻, the first beach on the west coast road, whose large shady takamaka trees and golden sands entice many tourists and surfers. However, currents are strong around here and swimming is dangerous.

BAIE LAZARE

The road swings northward, staying fairly close to the shore, offering dramatic views at Pointe Maravi of the rocks below before it descends again to **Baie Lazare** ❼. Here, beside the coast, there is a **monument** (an anchor on a stone pedestal) commemorating the 250th anniversary of the first recorded French landing on Mahé by Lazare Picault in 1742 (in fact, Picault landed at Anse Boileau). Baie Lazare has a long expanse of beach, though swimming here during the southeast monsoon is not recommended. The best way to explore it is to park near the monument and stroll along the beach towards the luxurious Kempinski Seychelles Resort.

ATTRACTIVE BAYS

Just north of Quatre Bornes takeaway a road leads on to a western promontory which has three bays. The best of these is **Anse Soleil** ❽, an enchanting small sandy beach, rated the second best 'hidden secret' in the world by the German magazine *Reise & Preise*, with good swimming and excellent views. It is rarely busy, except on Sundays, when the simple but very good restaurant is popular with locals. Neighbouring **Petite Anse** is another attractive sandy cove, about 10 minutes' walk along a shaded track. Reaching **Anse Gouvernement** from here requires backtracking to the junction and following the signpost pointing to the right. The narrow concrete track leads downhill, passing on the right Studio Antonio – where unusual wooden sculptures are on display – before emerging at the beach. This sandy bay, dotted with massive granite boulders, is wild and windswept during the southeast monsoon, so not good for swimming at this time of year. Weekends apart, it is very quiet and romantic.

ARTISTS' STUDIOS

Continuing northward on the coast road, the next place you come to is **Anse aux Poules Bleues** ❾ where you'll find **Michael Adams' Studio** (Mon–Fri 10am–4pm, Sat 10am–noon). The best-known artist in Seychelles, his jungle landscapes are a riot of leaves, stalks and stems, crisscrossing and clashing in every shade. He also takes a wry look at village life. Excellent prints of his work are on sale at the plantation-style studio, but they are expensive so the postcards and calendars may be more appealing.

The wide vistas of **Anse à la Mouche** open up as the road curves around the bay. The beach has the usual pristine white sand and plenty of shade, and the shallow waters are calm all year round, which makes it ideal for children. It's also a good place for beach parties, and groups of Seychellois often get together here at weekends, although on weekdays it is usually very quiet. The **Anchor Café** serves drinks, snacks and simple meals at reasonable prices.

Les Cannelles Road at the end of Anse à la Mouche leads inland to Santa Maria and **Tom Bowers' Studio** (Mon–Sat 10am–4pm), which is signposted on the right as you climb Les Cannelles from the coast. Like so many artists before him, the London-born sculptor visited Seychelles, fell in love with it and settled. He uses resin for his sculptures of local people, which are then cast in bronze.

COASTAL VIEWS

Back on the west coast, the next right turn is Chemin Montagne Posée, not worth the diversion unless you intend to walk the mountain trail near the summit. For a less strenuous introduction to the lower slopes of Mahé there is an attractive palm forest at the Seychelles National Biodiversity Centre at Barbarons, including the rare coco

The Banyan Tree Resort.

NATURE WALKS

Discover unique indigenous plants, secluded beaches and vantage points with stunning ocean and island views during a hike on one of Mahé's many trails.

The best season for walking is during the cooler, less humid months from June to September. The worst time is at the height of the rains from mid-December to January, when paths are muddy and slippery. Avoid the middle of the day for your trek; early morning and late afternoon are best, remembering that it gets dark around 6.30pm. Do not attempt any walk (except Danzilles to Anse Major) after rain as the path will be dangerous. You will need a solid pair of shoes (trainers with a good grip are fine), a hat, sunglasses, a bottle of water and a snack to enjoy when you reach the top or the end.

COASTAL WALKS

Danzilles–Anse Major Walk: An easy one-and-a-half hour walk (this one can be done in flip flops), most of which is within Morne Seychellois National Park. The peaceful walk follows the coast (one of the few coastal

The trail to Mount Copolia.

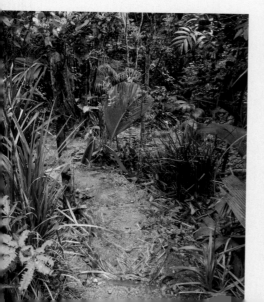

stretches in Mahé with no road access) and leads to a small, secluded beach. It starts at the end of the road from Beau Vallon to Bel Ombre, which turns into a well-marked path crossing the Danzilles River. Highlights include wonderful views of Beau Vallon and Silhouette Island, and spectacular areas of granitic rock slopes.

La Réserve and Brûlée Walk: This is Mahé's answer to Praslin's Vallée de Mai; it's the island's best area of palm forest, with five of Seychelles' six unique palm species – only the coco de mer is missing. This walk should take about an hour and a half up and another hour back down. The trail begins by the Cable and Wireless station, with a steep climb under mahogany trees. It is signposted but there are a couple of points where you may go wrong, so go with the trail brochure, available at the tourist office, or, better still, take a guide. There are three main vantage points along the way, which offer fabulous views over the west coast and the islands of Île aux Vaches, Thérèse and Conception.

MOUNTAIN HIKES

Tea Factory–Morne Blanc Walk: This is a short, sharp climb up to Morne Blanc in the Morne Seychellois National Park. The views from here are breathtaking and the rainforest very spooky. The walk starts at the Tea Company off the Sans Souci Road and should take about two hours altogether. The trail is marked with dabs of yellow paint on trees. Along the way you will see many of Seychelles' unique plants, but surprisingly few birds. Take care at the summit – the cliff you are standing on is almost vertical and it's a long way down. Return via the same route.

The Congo Rouge Trail: The best mist forest is on this trail, which circles the summit of Morne Seychellois. It's a Grade 3 walk, taking three to six hours, which should never be attempted without a guide as it is easy to get lost. You may get more enjoyment from your exploration of the mountains with a knowledgeable guide. Basil Beaudouin knows all the trails and can identify most of the 250 indigenous species of plants you may see. He leads walks of varying difficulty, lasting from as little as one to two hours to as much as six to eight hours. Excursions with him can be organised through your hotel or the tourist office.

de mer, and at the opposite end of the bay just after the hotel, an excellent well-marked walk, the **Sentier Vacoa Trail** ⑩. The shaded trail leads uphill alongside a clear stream bordered by endemic palms and trees.

The following turn-off, just after the unmistakable giant masts of the BBC World Service Relay Station, is La Misère Pass, which rejoins the east coast at Mont Fleuri close to Victoria. Cutting across the west side of the mountains, this pass is quiet, with few houses, and views over the coast. The road falls steeply from here and the views over the east coast and the Inner Islands are spectacular. There is an off-road **viewing point** about 2km (1 mile) after the summit.

The west coast road continues past Grand Anse Agricultural Station to the bay of **Grand Anse** ⑪. This is a majestic, tree-lined beach with fine white sand and granite rocks, but the treacherous offshore currents make it unsuitable for swimming (a governor of Seychelles drowned here in 1962). Over the brow of the hill, the road descends to tiny picturesque Petite Île.

The last 5km (3-mile) section of the west coast road is a narrow stretch that comes to a dead end just before **Baie Ternay**. There is no access beyond this point. The drive is spectacular, passing over a causeway and through a mangrove swamp and, as it climbs, giving marvellous views over the **Port Launay Marine National Park** ⑫ (formed in 1979 to protect the reef). To reach the beaches of **Port Launay Bay**, pull over in a convenient spot and stroll down to the shore. The snorkelling here is good and reaching the reef is easy over calm waters.

NORTHERN MAHÉ

If you only have a day on Mahé, the first place you should drive to is the Sans Souci Road, most of which runs through the Morne Seychellois National Park. The circuitous drive from coast to coast takes about an hour and is an ideal way to experience the mood of the mountains; the eerie silence is broken only by the distant croaking of frogs and the

Port Launay village.

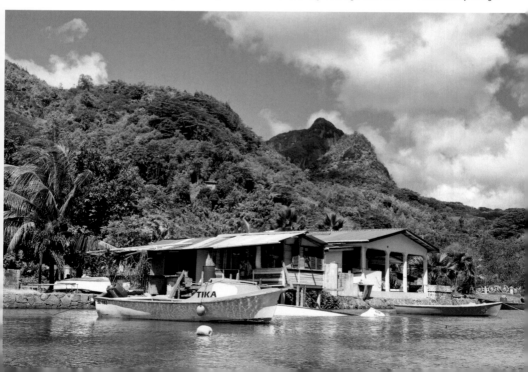

mighty trees rustling in the cool winds. Even on a clear day, clouds can suddenly settle on the heights or roll up from the sea enfolding you in a damp chill and a complete silence. There are breathtaking views at almost every turn and many places to pull over and enjoy them. Some of the highest slopes are planted with tea or mahogany trees, but much of the vegetation is a wild tangle of forest. On the Sans Souci Road, around 20 minutes from Victoria, you will pass **The Station Seychelles**, a small hotel and wellness spa that has an excellent café, with rainforest and sea views. Stop off for breakfast before a day's sightseeing, or linger over the bargain 'meal of the day' three-course lunch, made from fresh, local dishes.

MOUNTAIN PASSES AND NATURE TRAILS

The **Morne Seychellois National Park ⓭** was established as a protected area in the 1970s. If you want to explore the area on foot, there are a number of well-marked nature trails and mountain walks varying in length and degree of difficulty (see page 290). Trail guide booklets are available from the Seychelles tourist office in Victoria.

Two places are worth a detour on this route. The **Tea Factory ⓮** (Mon–Fri 8am–4pm, guided tours only) makes a pleasant refreshment stop. Locally grown tea is served here, but the coffee is imported and not of high quality. Just after the summit of Morne Blanc the **Mission Historical Ruins and Viewpoint ⓯** offers one of the most stunning panoramas in Seychelles.

BEAU VALLON AND AROUND

Mahé's main tourism centre is the bay of **Beau Vallon ⓰**. It might well be Seychelles' busiest beach, but most visitors would not call it crowded. The water is excellent for bathing, the sand is white and seaweed free, and there is plenty of shade. It is one of the best places in Seychelles for water sports, with facilities for windsurfing, diving, sailing and water-skiing, even parascending and 'sausage' riding – where you, and whoever else is along for the ride, sit astride an inflatable tube

Sunday Evening jam session, Beau Vallon.

towed through the water by a speed-boat. The Coral Strand, Berjaya Beau Vallon Bay Resort, Le Meridien Fisherman's Cove and luxurious Savoy Seychelles are the main hotels on the bay, but there are plenty of guesthouses and apartments to rent too. The poolside bistros of the Berjaya and Coral Strand are accessible from the beach.

BEAU VALLON BY NIGHT

Beau Vallon is the only beach on Mahé that stays lively in the evenings. The stretch of pedestrianised road between the Coral Strand Hotel and the pizzeria is particularly busy. Apart from the hotels, there are three main eateries to choose from. During the day the **Boat House** runs game fishing trips to Silhouette Island. The day's catch is barbecued the same evening and served with a Creole buffet. It's a popular event and good value for money, so it's best to book and arrive about half an hour early so you can choose a good table and enjoy a drink before dinner. On the beach itself, tucked in the northern corner, is the

ever-popular **Baobab Pizzeria**, which is simple, cheap and quick. **Perle Noire** restaurant, a short distance inland from Coral Strand, offers more substantial up-market fare.

On Wednesday evenings the road between Coral Strand Hotel and the Boat House is lined with craft stalls. Drinks are also offered at very reasonable prices.

There is no road around the north-west coast, but there is a beautiful and easy walk from Danzilles to **Anse Major** ⑰, a charming little beach; sheltered, secluded and good for bathing (see page 290).

TO NORTH EAST POINT

North of Beau Vallon is Victoria's 'commuter belt', with occasional stunning views to the west of Silhouette and North islands. As the road climbs it passes several spectacular villas clinging to the granite cliffs. It also passes the **Hilton Seychelles Northolme Resort & Spa**, where you could stop for lunch or afternoon tea. This was the site of Seychelles' oldest

Explaining the view from Mission Lodge Lookout over the coastline and Mahé's rainforest.

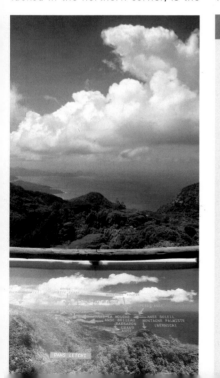

⊘ MISSION RUINS

The area known in colonial times as Venn's Town is now called Mission. The ruins, dating from 1875, are those of a school built by Anglican missionaries for the children of rescued slaves and were declared a National Monument in 1984. Following the abolition of slavery in the colonies, the British ran an anti-slavery patrol in the Indian Ocean. Their main purpose was to intercept Arab dhows transporting captive Africans to the Middle East. Those they managed to save from slavery were not taken back to Africa for fear they would be rounded up again, so they were brought to Seychelles and freed. Their children were given a basic education by the missionaries prior to being apprenticed or sent into service. Unesco speculates that this was probably the only place in the world at that time that educated freed slave children, and the school gave birth to formal education in Seychelles.

Marianne North, an intrepid Victorian traveller and botanical artist, made a trip to Venn's Town in 1883 by mule, and later commented in her diary 'The situation...is one of the most magnificent in the world, and the silence of the forest around was only broken by the children's happy voices.' Nowadays the only sound here is the rustling of the trees.

You can see this view. An avenue leads to the viewing platform, called Mission Lodge, which was built for the visit of Queen Elizabeth II in 1972.

hotel, now completely rebuilt. In its heyday, it attracted several famous literary guests including Noel Coward, Somerset Maugham and Ian Fleming – you can stay in the Fleming Suite, the inspiration behind the author's book and Bond film *For Your Eyes Only*.

Just beyond the Hilton Hotel and Vacoa Village is **Glacis** , surrounded by some beautiful scenery. There are a number of hotels and guesthouses here, the most exclusive of which is the **Sunset Beach Hotel**, built on a promontory, whose beach is open to non-residents. The road carries on around the northern tip of the island, passing **Machabeé** and **Carana Beach**, a good spot for bathing, though there are no facilities.

The road between **North East Point** and **Pointe Cèdre** runs very close to the beach; sand and waves often blow onto the tarmac. It is a very attractive beach, but not ideal for swimming as it's rocky underfoot and a bit too close to the road for comfort. Just before the road curves around Pointe Cèdre to Anse Etoile, look out for **Kreol**

The tombstone of famous pirate Olivier Le Vasseur (nicknamed 'La Buse', the buzzard) in Saint-Paul cemetery.

Fleurage (Mon-Sat 9am–5pm) across the road from the beach on North East Point. This perfumery, founded by a German microbiologist, manufactures a range of natural perfumes made from 102 local plants.

The Chemin la Gogue from Anse Etoile to Northolme is a pleasant two-hour walk (or a 20-minute drive) across the northernmost peninsula, which takes you past **La Gogue Reservoir**, an attractive lake and ideal picnic spot.

Once around Pointe Cèdre, the hillsides to the right and cliffs to the left become more thickly dotted with houses as you approach Victoria's environs. The most notable building before you reach town is **La Bastille**, just after Pointe Conan. This sombre, impressive house was built in the 1930s as a family home. Today it is occupied by the National Heritage division of the Ministry of Arts, Culture and Information. The gardens are open to the public (Mon–Fri 8am–4pm). There is a collection of traditional medicinal plants, a sugar cane press and a dilapidated model of a traditional Creole house.

⊘ BEL OMBRE TREASURE DIG

In 1949, Reginald Cruise-Wilkins, a Grenadier Guard recuperating from malaria on Mahé, got hold of some documents that he believed belonged to the notorious pirate Olivier Le Vasseur (see page 240). He was convinced that Le Vasseur had laid a trail for would-be treasure seekers involving riddles and puzzles based on astrology, astronomy and mythology. He devoted his life to the quest for the fantastic treasure – gold coins, silver bars, diamonds, silks and the jewel-encrusted regalia of the archbishop of Goa, which included a huge cross studded with rubies, emeralds and diamonds – seized in 1721 from the Portuguese merchant ship *Virgen de Cabo*, en route from India.

Cruise-Wilkins concluded that the clues were based on the twelve labours of Hercules and he was spurred on by a series of proofs that he was on the right track – a pig's jawbone, bits of china, a bull's horn – but found no treasure. One unsolved riddle led him to Bel Ombre, where he believed the end of the trail lay in an underwater cavern. He brought in pumps, but to no avail. The treasure was undiscovered when he died in 1977. His son, Seychellois John Cruise-Wilkins, has since taken up the challenge and continues to explore caves and invest in expensive radar equipment and machines to find the elusive hoard.

Nothing is labelled, but the staff are friendly and willing to help.

THE SATELLITE ISLANDS

The Portuguese called Seychelles the Seven Sisters on their charts because Mahé stands like a grand elder sister surrounded by her lesser siblings, of which six lie just off the east coast, encircling Victoria's magnificent natural harbour. These islands lie within the **Ste Anne Marine National Park**, created in 1973, the first such park in the Indian Ocean. Unfortunately, the coral has been harmed by siltation from land reclamation around Victoria, the effects of the El Niño weather system and perhaps global warming. To protect this fragile environment, motorised sports, fishing and the collection of coral, shells and live shellfish are banned. The marine life is still prolific (with more than 200 species of fish) and the short journey to the marine park, combined with lunch on one of the charming and peaceful islands that have restaurants, is still a very pleasant way to spend a day. Tour operators offer full-day trips by glass-bottom boat or subsea viewer starting from Marine Charter in Victoria (see page 285). The subsea viewer gives a superior view, but is completely enclosed and some people might feel claustrophobic. Either way, you'll have plenty of time to swim or snorkel.

Ste Anne ⑲ is the largest of the islands off Victoria. The first Seychelles settlers lived here rather than on Mahé, perhaps because of the crocodiles then inhabiting Mahé's extensive coastal mangrove swamps. Once people began to settle on Mahé, Ste Anne was largely left in peace as a coconut plantation, and since then has been put to various uses. In 1832 a whaling station was established here and in World War II the British had a fuel store here. In the 1980s, Ste Anne was briefly a centre for the National Youth Service, a political experiment that was eventually abandoned. Then it became the headquarters of the Marine Parks Authority (now moved to Baie Ternay on Mahé). In more recent years it's been home to a luxury five-star hotel, the Ste Anne Resort & Spa, which will be transformed into Club Med's first resort in the Seychelles, due to open in 2020.

Île au Cerf ⑳ is a small, low-lying island, mostly covered in coconut palms and scrub, and it is easy to find trails up the hill if you want to explore inland. You can either come here as part of an excursion organised by a tour operator, or hire a boat from the Marine Charter Association. Tourist boats land on the sheltered northern coast near **Kapok Tree Restaurant**, where lunch is provided. After an excellent Creole meal, you can take a walk along the shore, past the homes of some of the 80 or so residents, a number of whom commute to Victoria by speedboat. One of Seychelles' most famous residents, South African writer Wilbur Smith, used to have a house here.

Île au Cerf and Île Cachée.

The best hotel is **Cerf Island Resort**, with 24 villas dotted among trees on a hillside and the excellent 1756 Restaurant, open for lunch and dinner. To stay on Cerf is a wonderful way to experience the tranquillity of life on an island with no roads or shops and just two small resorts, secure in the knowledge that all the conveniences of modern life are just a 10-minute boat ride away. The beach is always sheltered, good for swimming and snorkelling. Guests often hire pedalos to visit the beaches around Cerf, and even get as far as Moyenne, Ronde or Ste Anne.

Île Cachée is a tiny dot off the southeast coast of Cerf. It's possible to wade over to the islet at low tide.

Île Moyenne National Park ㉑ was declared a national park in 2008 (the smallest in the world) and is open to visitors daily (some hotels arrange excursions). It was previously owned by Englishman Brendon Grimshaw, a former newspaper editor who spent decades reintroducing native flora and fauna. He died in 2012. The island covers just 9 hectares (4 acres) and is easy to explore. Around 16,000 trees were planted here, including rare endemics such as coco de mer and Wright's gardenia, and there are giant tortoises and two supposed pirate graves (rumours abound that pirate treasure is buried on the island). A circular trail, which takes no more than an hour at a leisurely pace, goes past the house Miss Best built for her dogs, along the beach at Coral Cove and past the graveyard (where Grimshaw is buried) and the chapel, through Coco de Mer Vale, past the tiny, shambolic museum and back to the former Jolly Roger bar (no longer in operation). While the island's buildings are, sadly, looking run down, Moyenne is still a magical place to visit. Snorkellers should head for the northwest coast and the waters between Moyenne and Ste Anne.

You can walk around the tiny **Île Ronde** ㉒ (Round Island) in less than 10 minutes. The island is now the exclusive domain of the residents of the small, up-market hotel JA Enchanted Island Resort Seychelles.

Île Ronde is best known for its excellent restaurant, **Chez Gaby**, housed in old buildings once part of an isolation camp for women suffering from leprosy. The menu features Creole cuisine and its barbecued tuna steak is a Seychelles legend. After lunch, most people are happy just to relax in the shade of the flame trees by the restaurant.

Île Longue (Long Island) was once a prison and has been earmarked for a five-star resort. Longue was a quarantine station in the days when the dreaded smallpox might arrive aboard a ship and spell disaster for the isolated Seychelles' population.

Île Thérèse ㉓ on the west coast is a beautiful island for a day trip. There is no longer a regular boat service to the island but it's possible to paddleboard or kayak across the channel from the mainland. A beautiful beach faces Mahé, and the shelter of the mainland makes swimming here easy.

Snorkelling at Cerf Island Resort.

The pristine beach and crystal-clear waters at Cerf Island Resort.

Frégate Island, Anse Victorin.

FRÉGATE

Once home to pirates, Frégate Island Private is now an exclusive destination with seven beaches, 3,000 giant tortoises and one luxury resort.

The most isolated of the granitic islands, Frégate lies 55km (34 miles) east of Mahé. Covering 3 sq km (1 sq mile) and surrounded by coral reefs, this privately owned island is the kind of place most of us can only dream of staying in. Frégate is very exclusive; most of the guests (limited to 40 at a time) are super rich and come here to hide away in one of the resort's 16 luxury villas.

PIRATES' LAIR

Frégate was christened by the French explorer Lazare Picault during his 1744 expedition. He probably named it 'Île aux Frégates' after the frigate birds once present here. Among the mysterious ruins found on the island were the walls of a large enclosure, thought to be the remains of a pirate settlement, a lead-lined water conduit and three tombs built of coral. Early residents found a teak mast set in a stone platform at Anse Lesange and in 1812 a gold cross-belt and shoulder strap were discovered. In 1838, a visitor from Mauritius reported that golden Spanish coins were frequently found on the beaches. He also described the wreck of a large ship lying offshore. There is no direct evidence that these artefacts were left by pirates; they could just as easily be

traces of an Arab trading post. Whatever their origin, these various finds make Frégate one of the few sites of archaeological interest in Seychelles.

In 1802 Frégate became a place of exile. A shipload of Jacobin terrorists, accused of having plotted to assassinate Napoleon, had been sent from France to Seychelles. Quincy, the commandant of Seychelles, suspected several of these deportees of joining forces with the slaves and inciting them to rebellion, and so he sent the ringleader, Louis

Main attractions

Plantation House restaurant
Wildlife walks to see the magpie-robin
Grand Anse

Map on page 278

Guiding privileged guests on their way.

Sepholet, together with three slaves, to Frégate. They were among the first inhabitants of the island, though they didn't stay long. Later the same year, Sepholet was transported to Anjouan in the Comoros with 35 of the other deportees. They all died there; it is said they were poisoned on the orders of the sultan.

LUXURY RESORT

The only way you can stay on Frégate is as a guest of the hotel **Frégate Island 'Private'** ㉔. Opened in 1998, this resort is a celebrity haunt: Bill Gates, Pierce Brosnan and Brad Pitt and Angelina Jolie have all checked in. The design of the spacious villas, strung along the beautiful **Anse Bambous**, was influenced by the architecture of Bali and Thailand. Each one has a living room, large bedroom and two bathrooms with showers inside and out, all linked by a terrace, plus a private garden, secluded outdoor jacuzzi with amazing views, and a sundeck with a king-size sunbed. The resort is centred around

Frégate Island 'Private'.

Frégate House, where the main dining room, gymnasium and library are located, with a freshwater swimming pool and bar nearby. There's also a chapel, one of the island's oldest buildings, which can be used for weddings, and the Rock Spa, where you can enjoy anything from a yoga lesson to a hot stone massage while gazing at the Indian Ocean. Facilities for every water sport you can think of are available and the German multimillionaire owner has also built a marina here for his own private yacht and other boats, which can be chartered. In short, Frégate is completely kitted out for the ultimate paradise island experience.

PLANTATION HOUSE

As a result of intense farming, most of the island is now covered with introduced vegetation. The higher hills are dominated by indigenous trees, among which coffee, breadfruit, banyan, cashew and ylang, ylang all grow. Plantations were laid out on the flat land and have been

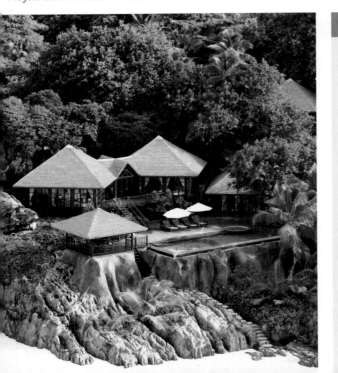

regenerated to provide fresh food for the new resort, including pawpaw, banana, cabbage, lettuce and sweet potato. Cattle, pigs and chickens are also reared to provision the hotel. The original **Plantation House ㉕**, not far from the airstrip, has been restored and houses a restaurant specialising in Creole cuisine, and a small museum with displays of antique furniture and information about the island's flora and fauna.

WILDLIFE WALKS

Apart from four other islands, Frégate is the only place where the Seychelles magpie-robin now survives. This pretty black and white bird had become extinct on the other granitic islands where it was once common. It was perilously close to disappearing from Frégate too but was rescued from extinction by the intervention of BirdLife International. It is now thriving again and new populations have been reintroduced to the other islands. Other birds that hotel guests can spot here include the Seychelles fody – a sparrow-like endemic species – and the Seychelles blue pigeon, which has a striking red, white and blue plumage. There is a resident conservationist available for guided nature walks.

Frégate is also the only home of the giant tenebrionid beetle. When this strange-looking creature was first shown to European entomologists, it was thought to be a hoax specimen made up of bits of different insects. It is a large, flightless beetle, which spends much of its life clinging to the bark of woodland trees. Gardiner's gecko, a species of green gecko, is also found only on Frégate.

Each guest is given the use of an electric golf cart to get around, but the best way to experience the diversity of Frégate's flora and fauna is to follow on foot one of the shady tracks that criss-cross the island.

Apart from the path that runs around the main plantation, there are three trails worth exploring that radiate from the Plantation House. For the best snorkelling, take the path to the southeast of the island to **Anse Parc**. The walk takes only about 10 minutes. Close to the beach a sign points to the **Pirate's Wall**.

To reach the superb **Anse Victorin ㉖**, considered by some to be one of the finest beaches in the world, start from the Plantation House and take the path that runs inland at an angle from the airstrip. Cross the Bambous River and continue to the coast. At a leisurely pace, the walk takes about 30 minutes.

A third walk along a well-marked track heading inland from the plantation heads due west to **Grand Anse**, another beautiful beach. The hill to your left as you approach the bay is called Au Salon, where sangdragon trees flourish. To your right is **Signal Rock**, at 125 metres (410ft) the highest point on the island. The walk to Grand Anse takes about 20 minutes.

Anse Victorin, Frégate Island.

Sunset over Silhouette Island.

SILHOUETTE AND NORTH

Despite their close proximity to Mahé, Silhouette and North have a separate geology and an atmosphere akin to the Outer Islands.

Silhouette, the third largest island of the granitic group and the fifth largest in Seychelles, lies 20km (12.5 miles) northwest of Mahé. The island's topography and limited development mean an exceptional diversity of plants and animals has been preserved. Indeed, conservationists regard Silhouette as one of the most important biodiversity hotspots in the Indian Ocean. The highest of its three main peaks, Mont Dauban, rises to 740 metres (2,430ft) and is the second highest summit in Seychelles. Although it is bigger than La Digue, Silhouette is much quieter.

Silhouette has no roads, so its thick virgin forests remain largely untrodden. However, there is plenty to recommend it, not least the fact that it is one of the least known Inner Islands. The beaches on the east coast are sheltered by a coral reef and are perfect for swimming and snorkelling, and the forest trails, while not always easy going, take you through beautiful, dense vegetation. In 1987, the surrounding waters were declared a Marine National Park.

North Island is similar to Silhouette though less mountainous and it suffered more from forest clearance. However, the current owners developed the island with ecotourism in

mind and reintroduced much of the endemic flora and fauna.

THE DAUBAN FAMILY ISLAND

The first recorded sighting of Silhouette was made in 1609 by the crew of the *Ascension*, an English East India Company vessel, yet the island was not settled by Europeans until the early 19th century. It was named after the French minister Etienne de Silhouette, Controller of Finances in 1759. It's a perfect name for the island, which appears as a mysterious shadow on

> **Main attractions**
> Snorkelling, Silhouette
> Aldabra tortoises, Silhouette
> Dauban Mausoleum, Silhouette
> Mont Pot à Eau hike, Silhouette

Map on page 304

An aerial view of the coast.

the horizon when viewed from Beau Vallon on Mahé.

In the mid-19th century, Silhouette was gradually bought up by a French naval officer, Auguste Dauban, and it remained in the family for over a hundred years. They built a plantation house, cleared several paths across the island and introduced vanilla, cloves and other plants. Many coconuts were planted, often in seemingly inaccessible locations, because land had to be 'under coconuts' before it was deemed of any value. Today, most of these paths and crops lie abandoned and much of the forest has recovered. The Dauban era came to an end in the 1970s when the island was sold to a French hotel group that handed it over to the Seychelles government in 1983.

LA PASSE TO POINTE ZENG ZENG

The majority of the island's 200 inhabitants live in and around the main settlement of **La Passe ❶**. Standing close to the harbour is

The Dauban Mausoleum.

The Dauban Plantation House (La Grande Case), the former Dauban family residence. Made up of four wooden buildings – the main house, toilets and bathroom, kitchen and dining room – the layout is typical of an island plantation house. The kitchen was usually built away from the house because of the risk of fire, with the dining room nearby so that the food could be served hot. In the days before air-conditioning was invented, the wide veranda provided the main living space. Today you can dine there on Creole dishes for lunch or dinner.

A little south of La Grande Case, along the same track, is a gated enclosure containing the island's small population of captive Aldabra tortoises. Immediately behind the pens is the **Dauban Mausoleum ❷**, a grand, rather incongruous construction surrounded by tall palms, modelled on the Madeleine in Paris. Adjacent to this is a marsh, where grey heron and black-crowned night heron (a recent coloniser) can be seen.

Silhouette

0   1 km
0   1 mile

N

INDIAN OCEAN

Anse Mondon
Pte la Varangue
Grebau
Pte Machabée
Camp Bloc
Anse Mondon
Grebau 166
Casse Tonnère
Belle Vue
Baie Cipailles
Dans l'Inde
Roche Marcelline
Grand Congoman
Anse La Passe
Glacis Roundé
Dans Giroffe
Silhouette Island ▲621
Hilton Seychelles Labriz Resort & Spa
Pte Cocos
Mont Dauban 740
Mont Pot à Eau 630
La Passe
La Passe
Pointe Étienne
Pte Varreur
Pte Étienne
Silhouette Marine National Park
La Grande Case
Dauban Mausoleum
Grand Machabée
Gratté Fesse 516
Anse Cimetière
Pte Jardin
Rende d'Avance
Anse Lascars
Anse Lascars
Anse Grand Barbe
Grand Barbe
Sème
Pte Zeng Zeng
Grand Passe Petite Passe
Anse Patates
Trevor 88
Mont Cocos Marrons
Coco dans Trou
Glacis Platte
Pte Grand Barbe
Pte Civine
Glacis Cocos Marrons
INDIAN OCEAN
Grande
Machabée
Gratte Cent

Continuing uphill from the mausoleum, the path leads to **Anse Lascars** ❸. Legend has it that Arabs settled here prior to European settlement and for a long time it was thought that the graves found at Anse Lascars were those of Arab tradesmen who plied the Indian Ocean around the 9th century. However, bones from these graves have since been carbon-dated to around 1800 and are more likely to be the remains of the slaves who were the first occupants of Silhouette, having fled from Mahé in the late 18th century. From here, the path winds uphill to a viewing point at the headland of **Pointe Zeng Zeng**. It then descends to the secluded bay of **Anse Patates**, with its mature mangrove swamp and beach crest of windswept sea hibiscus. The walk to Pointe Zeng Zeng from La Passe takes about 20 minutes at a leisurely pace.

BEST OF THE BEACHES

Hilton Seychelles Labriz Resort & Spa ❹ lies north of the La Passe jetty on **Anse La Passe**, a beautiful sandy beach that stretches northwest of the hotel. Beyond it lies an equally lovely, palm-fringed and deserted beach, **Baie Cipailles** ❺. The path running along the coast between the bays winds through an abandoned coconut plantation and a line of takamaka trees.

At the northern end of Baie Cipailles, there are two paths leading to **Anse Mondon** ❻, a one-house settlement that offers the best snorkelling on Silhouette. The lower path is overgrown and best avoided. The upper path, which runs over Belle Vue through thick forest, is easier and more scenic. Just before the descent back to the coast, the forest opens up to reveal a spectacular view of Anse Mondon. If landing at Anse Mondon, this walk may be done in reverse. Either way, it takes about two hours.

The old path from Anse Mondon to Grande Barbe has all but disappeared so this walk is no longer possible. However, the path connecting La Passe and **Grande Barbe** is well worn. It's about a three-and-a-half-hour walk from one side of the island to the other, but you

Take a sunset cruise from the Hilton Seychelles Labriz Resort & Spa.

can arrange for your boat to drop you at one side and collect at the other. Once home to many families, Grande Barbe is now a virtual ghost town. A short way inland from the beach, on the coastal plateau, is a marsh.

MOUNTAIN WALK

The trek from La Passe to the summit of the magnificent **Mont Pot à Eau** 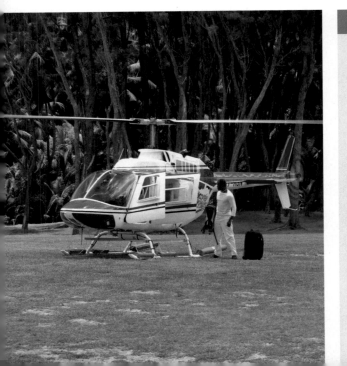 (630 metres/2,067ft) takes the best part of a day. It is not for the faint-hearted, and should not be attempted without a guide (obtainable from Silhouette Island Lodge): as it is infrequently used, the path is sometimes unclear and is often muddy and slippery due to high rainfall on the mountain side. However, if you enjoy a challenge, it's a wonderful walk that takes you through a fascinating mist forest, rich in exotic flora including the insectivorous pitcher plant that grows on its exposed summit.

NORTH ISLAND

Travel by helicopter to see North Island.

North Island lies 7km (4.5 miles) north of Silhouette and is considerably smaller and less mountainous. Most of the original forest was cut down, but a restoration programme has successfully reintroduced indigenous trees and a conservation team has worked to save nesting sea turtles, Aldabra giant tortoises (of which there are now more than 100) and the Seychelles white-eye. The white-eye was once one of the world's rarest birds, with just 25 left, but the 2014 census revealed more than 120. There is a beautiful beach on each side of the island, separated by a plateau across the middle and rocky promontories either end. Day visits from Mahé by helicopter (15 minutes) can be arranged, and there is a five-star resort comprising 11 large villas, made famous in 2011 as the honeymoon destination of the Duke and Duchess of Cambridge. Their villa came with a chef, butler, open-air bathroom with sunken bath, four-poster bed made of driftwood and a freshwater rock pool in its private garden.

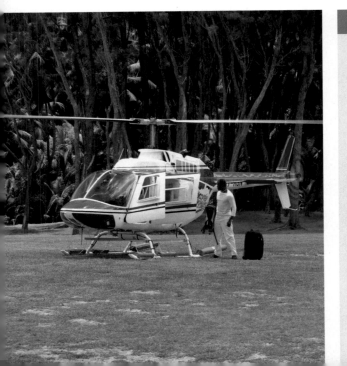

⊘ NATIONAL PARKS

In 1987 the waters surrounding Silhouette Island were declared a Marine National Park. Silhouette Island itself was declared a National Park in 2010, with around 93 percent of the landmass included in the conservation area. The island is considered one of the most important biological spots in the Indian Ocean (most of the 75 endemic plant species of Seychelles are found on Silhouette) and the move to create a National Park has secured its virgin rainforest and helped to ensure the future of the critically endangered sheath-tailed bat, of which there was a population of less than 40. The creation of the park also means that Seychelles' largest area of freshwater marsh (Grande Barbe) is now protected.

Volcanic outcrops rise above the sandy beaches on Silhouette Island.

A particularly striking tree on Praslin.

PRASLIN

A slower pace of life, glorious beaches and the Vallée de Mai – a designated World Heritage Site – set Praslin apart.

Praslin is the second largest granitic island of Seychelles and lies 45km (28 miles) northeast of Mahé. It is much less mountainous, reaching a height of just 367 metres (1,204ft), and less populated, with about 5,500 inhabitants. The hills look rather threadbare after the green profusion of Mahé's mountains, but the sheltered valleys harbour primeval palm forest. Away from the shadows of the trees, there are many superb beaches and hotels. The island's popularity stems from these dreamy stretches of soft white sand and crystal waters, which have been declared the best in the world by many travel writers.

The pace of life is much more leisurely here than on Mahé. There are no towns and very little traffic. Taxis are available, but there is no taxi rank other than at the airport and Baie Ste Anne jetty. Buses are cheap, but it may involve a long wait at the roadside for one to appear and timetables are flexible. Ask any local when the next bus is due and they will tell you 'very soon'. This is more a hope than a statement of fact. The best way to explore the island is by car, though getting around by bicycle is a pleasant alternative and there are plenty of trails for those who prefer to explore on foot.

Praslin is connected with Mahé by air and by sea. The flight takes just 15 minutes and Air Seychelles operates

services between the two islands throughout the day. Two fast catamaran ferries depart from the Inter-Island Quay, Victoria, and take one hour to reach Baie Ste Anne. They are popular with locals, making booking essential at weekends and advisable during the week. The same trip by schooner is cheaper, but takes three hours.

BAIE STE ANNE TO ANSE LA BLAGUE

If you are arriving by boat, your first sight of the island will be the pretty **Baie Ste**

○ **Main attractions**
Anse Lazio
Black Pearl (Seychelles) tour
Vallée de Mai

Map on page 310

A smiling face at Praslin Airport.

Praslin

INDIAN OCEAN

INDIAN OCEAN

Anne **❶**. It is one of the two 'capitals' of Praslin (the other being Grand Anse) and there is some rivalry between them. The village has a couple of supermarkets, a hospital, church, bank and petrol station, but apart from a couple of self-catering establishments, a boat rental company and a handful of takeaways (Coco Rouge is excellent), tourist facilities here are minimal. Baie Ste Anne is a short drive from the Côte d'Or and the Vallée de Mai, and you can arrange a hire car as soon as you step off the ferry. If you are flying in, it would be best to collect your hire car at the airport.

The coast road running north from the pier forks at the northern end of the bay. The right-hand branch cuts across the headland to the eastern shore at **Anse La Blague ❷**, a beautiful and secluded bay, which is great for snorkelling. There is a snack bar on the beach or for something more substantial dine at the boutique hotel **Villa Anse La Blague**, on a terrace overlooking the sea. Diving, windsurfing and jet surfing can be arranged by **Bleu Marine**, based at the small hotel. A pleasant walk from the bay takes you along the shore, past Petite Anse and up a hill towards Anse La Farine. From the top of the hill you can see Île Ronde and La Digue.

THE CÔTE D'OR

The inland road that links Baie Ste Anne to Anse Volbert and the northeast coast passes through casuarina woodland. **Anse Volbert ❸**, also known as Côte d'Or, is the island's main tourism centre. Its long beach is sheltered by Curieuse Island so swimming is safe all year and there are no large breakers, making it ideal for children. The beach shelves very gradually so you need to walk out a long way to find water deep enough for swimming. The best snorkelling is around the boulders at the northern end of the beach and out towards **Chauve Souris Island**.

While it is by no means overdeveloped, Anse Volbert is relatively crowded by Seychelles standards. Beside the beach there are several hotels, guesthouses, restaurants and souvenir shops, with more restaurants, boat operators and water-sports centres strung along the coast road. Several of these organise snorkelling trips to **St Pierre Islet**, as well as trips further afield to the islands of Curieuse, Cousin and Aride.

Next stop on the east coast road is **Anse Possession ❹**, a lovely bay with a view of Curieuse Island. It was around here, in 1768, that the first French explorers erected a plaque, claiming possession of the island. A cairn of stones and a flagstaff marked the spot. However, the location was lost. The French accused the English, who visited the island soon after, of deliberately obliterating the spot. The coast north of here, facing Curieuse island, is picturesque, quiet and good for swimming. The road runs through takamaka and casuarina groves and passes the pretty bays of **Anse Takamaka**, overlooked by five-star Raffles Praslin resort, and **Anse Boudin**. The short excursion from here to the top of Grand Fond (340 metres/1,115ft) is

Ferry docks at Praslin port.

worthwhile for the view across Praslin and the surrounding islands.

THE BEST BEACH IN THE WORLD

After Anse Boudin the road turns inland over the hill to **Anse Lazio ❺**, often hailed as 'the best beach in the world'. The sand here is as fine and soft as caster sugar and is scattered with granite boulders. The swimming is excellent except when the northwesterly winds are at their strongest, mainly around January and February. Snorkelling is best around the rocks and at the two small coves at the northeastern end of the bay. To enjoy the beach at its finest it is best to come early in the morning before the crowds. There are two restaurants, **BonBon Plume**, with thatched umbrellas dotted across a lawn by the sea; and at the opposite end of the beach, **Le Chevalier Restaurant**, set back from the shoreline. Both offer mainly seafood and Creole cuisine.

EXPLORING THE WEST COAST

Clear turquoise waters at Anse Lazio.

If you are flying in, you will land on the west side of the island, 3km (nearly 2 miles) from Grand Anse – the other place to pick up a hire car (see Travel Tips, Transport). The coast road leading north of the airstrip from Amitié goes through a coconut plantation and farmland, past **Anse Kerlan ❻** to **Petite Anse Kerlan**, both beautiful sandy beaches framed by granite rocks. The sea can be wild in rough weather but on calmer days the area is excellent for swimming and snorkelling, though you should always beware of strong currents.

Petite Anse Kerlan is home to the **Constance Lemuria Resort**, an exclusive hotel complex in a spectacular location spread over 36 hectares (90 acres) with three beaches and Seychelles' only 18-hole golf course. Birdwatching in the grounds is excellent but it is necessary to call in advance to arrange access. Further north, lying within the grounds of the golf course, is **Anse Georgette**, a wild and remote beach worth exploring.

Back at Amitié, opposite the airstrip by the sea, is **Black Pearl (Seychelles) Ltd** (Mon–Fri 9am–4pm, Sat 9am–noon), where black pearls are cultured in the first and only pearl farm in the Indian Ocean region. A series of open concrete aquarium tanks have also been set up; here you can see giant clams and corals, reef fish and invertebrates. The guide is helpful and informative. Within the same complex is a jewellery boutique.

AROUND GRAND ANSE

The first settlement south of the airport is **Grand Anse ❼**. It's the largest village on Praslin, but it is far from commercialised and retains a sleepy character. The beach here is good, though often covered in seaweed. There are several small hotels, as well as shops, banks, takeaways and restaurants. The travel agents all have their Praslin offices here.

From Grand Anse the coast road continues southward past a series of picturesque bays. The 5km (3-mile) walk from Fond de l'Anse to Anse Marie-Louise is pleasant and easy with beautiful views. There are a couple of hotels and restaurants en route. This is the best stretch of coastline for deserted beaches, though not all are good for swimming as the water is shallow except at high tide. The first bay along this road is **Anse Citron**, followed by **Anse Bateau**, which has Les Rochers Restaurant, one of the best on Praslin, at its far end. **Anse Bois de Rose** is noteworthy for the Hibiscus Restaurant and **Coco de Mer Hotel and Black Parrot Suites**. Rounding Pointe Cocos, Anse Consolation is less ideal for swimming due to the beach rock barrier, but neighbouring **Anse Marie-Louise** ❽ is the best bathing beach of all the above and a particularly quiet and picturesque spot. From this bay, the road winds steeply and passes the exclusive **Château de Feuilles Hotel and Restaurant** before descending to **Baie Ste Anne**.

A JOURNEY BACK IN TIME AT THE VALLÉE DE MAI

One of Seychelles' greatest natural treasures is the **Vallée de Mai** ❾ (www. sif.sc; daily 8am–5.30pm), a primeval forest claimed by General Gordon in 1881 to be the Garden of Eden. The valley,

designated a Unesco World Heritage Site, occupies the heart of Praslin, midway between Grand Anse and Baie Ste Anne. Several well-marked nature trails run through it; the brochure maps these out quite clearly. It also lists the plants and wildlife you are likely to come across en route. You can choose between a short tour (about an hour) taking in most of the botanical sites, or a longer circular route, which includes a spectacular viewpoint (allow two to three hours). There are free guided tours by park staff at 9am and 2pm; tipping is discretionary. Or you can download the Vallée de Mai app for your smartphone before you visit, which is full of helpful information.

A visit to the Vallée de Mai is a journey back in time. Dinosaurs would have ambled through prehistoric valleys just like this. It is thought that the coco de mer palm evolved the world's longest leaf stems to keep its leaves out of the reach of herbivorous dinosaurs. Likewise, young palms probably developed spines to protect them from being eaten by the giant tortoises that dominated the ecosystem at one time. The enormous

The Pagoda and beach at Coco de Mer Hotel.

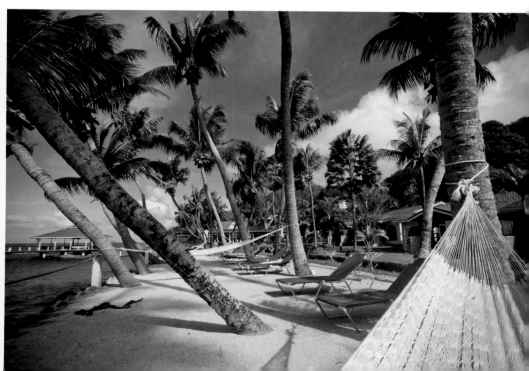

COCO DE MER

The world's largest, heaviest seed is a much-prized symbol of the Seychelles and grows wild only on Praslin and Curieuse islands.

When he visited the Vallée de Mai in 1881, the British general Charles Gordon (of Khartoum fame) was so struck by its natural beauty that he truly believed he had discovered the original Garden of Eden. He concluded that the coco de mer tree (*lodoicea maldivica*) must be the Tree of Knowledge and its nut the forbidden fruit. His reasoning was that 'The heart is said by the scriptures to be the seat of desires and...the fruit [of the coco de mer] externally represents the heart, while the interior represents the thighs and belly...which I consider to be the true seat of carnal desires.' While some might disagree with his biblical conclusions, few people could argue that the coco de mer nut that grows on the female tree does resemble the thighs and belly of a woman, complete with a strategically placed tuft of hair. The enormous catkin of the male tree is equally suggestive.

Some people believe the voluptuous coco de mer nut has aphrodisiac properties.

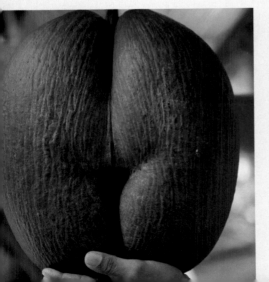

HEIGHT AND WEIGHT

The average male coco de mer grows to 15 metres (50ft) and the average female to 9 metres (30ft). Each nut weighs somewhere between 18 and 22kg (40–49 lb), which makes it the heaviest seed in the world. The male tree, which can reach up to 32 metres (105ft), grows taller because it lives longer, but its height is also thought to facilitate wind pollination. The female tree, on the other hand, which can be heavily laden with more than a dozen nuts, is more susceptible to being felled by high winds. This may be nature's way of ensuring that the trees spread up the steep slopes as well as down the valley.

SPREADING THE SEED

The pollination of the coco de mer is still a mystery. The wind probably acts as one agent, but the large white slugs often seen feeding on the male flowers and the green geckos common among the trees may also act as pollen carriers. Legend has it that on stormy nights the male trees uproot themselves and engage in passionate love-making with the female palms. Some say that witnesses to this orgy are certain to die. It is estimated that the coco de mer palm can live for between 200 and 400 years. Though now confined to Praslin and Curieuse, coco de mer trees may once have been much more common worldwide. During excavations for a new airport in Brussels in the 1980s, skeletons of large tortoises and fossils of nuts similar to the coco de mer were unearthed and dated to about 50 million years ago. 'Love nuts' have been highly prized since their discovery. They fetched such a high price in Europe that they became like gold dust.

RICH PICKINGS

Today, they are carefully protected. Nuts gathered by the Ministry of Environment are hollowed out to reduce the weight and polished to be sold as souvenirs. Official collection is controlled and each nut is numbered and stamped, and sold with a permit. The fact that they fetch a high price (a good one costs around 4–5,000 rupees, around €300) has encouraged poaching, which has had a detrimental effect on the rare palm forests. If you are offered a nut without a licence you can be sure it has been acquired illegally and is liable to be confiscated at the airport.

leaves of the coco de mer palms tower far above you like green vaulting and the dry leaf-litter that lies like a thick carpet on the forest floor rustles as geckos scuttle by. Streams can be heard tinkling and the giant leaves clatter in the breeze.

PRIMEVAL PALMS

About a quarter of the trees in the valley are coco de mer palms and almost half the remainder are endemic palms found only in Seychelles. These include the thief palm *(latannyen fey)*, with its broad, undivided leaves, so called because the first specimen sent to Europe was stolen from Kew Gardens; the millipede palm *(latannyen milpat)*, whose divided leaves are reminiscent of the legs of a millipede; and the Cinderella palm *(latannyen oban)*, a comparatively short tree with a slender trunk. The palmiste *(palmis)* is a splendid, tall palm that was once the source of the main ingredient for millionaires' salad, so called because an entire tree had to be sacrificed to obtain the edible shoot near its tip. (The *palmiste* salad you now see on restaurant menus is made from the shoots of coconut trees, so you can tuck in with a clear conscience.)

BLACK PARROTS

You will see few birds inside the valley; they tend to stay above the tree tops. Only the piercing whistle of the black parrot reminds you that they are out there, somewhere. Of all the forest birds, the black parrot is the star attraction. It breeds only on Praslin, nesting in the hollows of rotten coco de mer palms and screwpines (artificial nest boxes have been erected in the valley). Because the vegetation is so dense, black parrots are, in fact, easier to spot outside the valley. In the early morning and late afternoon, they can be seen from the car park, flying in and out of the tall trees. They are also commonly seen at sea level where there are suitable feeding trees (such as at Villa Flamboyant and Britannia Restaurant at Grand Anse, and Coco de Mer Hotel at Anse Bois de Rose).

There is an Information Centre at the entrance which also sells souvenirs, snacks and drinks. It's a good idea to arrive early to beat the crowds. Take

Vallée de Mai.

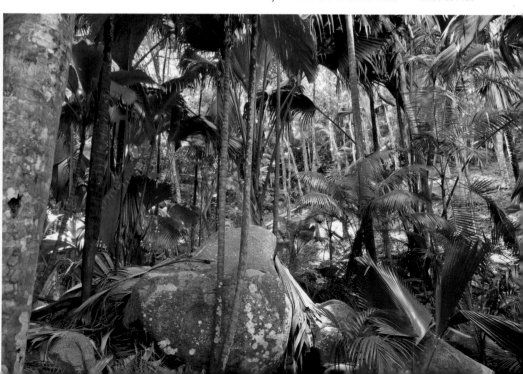

drinks with you, but don't forget to dispose of the rubbish properly. Visitors are requested to stick to the paths, avoid the temptation of touching the plants, and smoking is strictly forbidden.

A short drive, or a 10-minute walk, from the entrance in the direction of Grand Anse will take you to a spectacular **waterfall**.

THE RED ISLAND

Just off the north coast of Praslin, **Curieuse Island** ❿ lies at the centre of a Marine National Park. From the sea, Curieuse is noticeably red, which explains why the island was first known as Île Rouge. The sparseness of the forest and redness of the soil is due to the many fires that have swept the island. The first recorded fire was in 1771, when the French suspected the English of arson. However, it seems more likely that fire is part of the natural cycle in the palm forest, helping new, vigorous plants to establish themselves and clearing out the old and dead vegetation.

A leper colony was established in 1833 at **Anse St José** on the south coast of the island. The old Creole-style **Doctor's House** (daily 9am–5pm) has been renovated as a Visitors' Centre and museum, though most of the leprosarium buildings lie in ruins. A footpath leads from here to **Baie Laraie**. (The causeway across the bay, which used to enclose a pond where turtles were kept prior to export, was destroyed in the tsunami of December 2004 so it is no longer possible to take a shortcut across.)

A boardwalk follows the margins of the bay through mangroves where large *Cardisoma* crabs and colourful fiddler crabs are dominant. The path emerges at Baie Laraie, where there is a Tortoise Conservation Project. The young tortoises are kept in pens, while the adults over five years old are allowed to roam wild. These animals have been transferred from Aldabra, which has the world's largest giant tortoise population.

There aren't any hotels or villas on the island, but day trips can be arranged through most Praslin hotels and tour operators, and are often combined with a visit to Cousin Island nature reserve (see page 319).

Taking a snorkelling excursion to St Pierre.

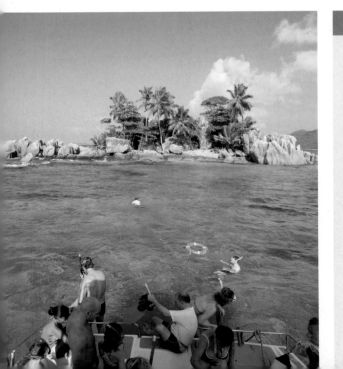

⊘ SNORKELLING

The tiny uninhabited island of St Pierre, 15 minutes' boat ride from Curieuse, is a Robinson Crusoe-esque granite pile dotted with coconut palms. It has appeared in numerous adverts and glossy travel brochures and the sea surrounding it is a hotspot for snorkelling and diving. It's safe, the water is crystal-clear and an abundance of underwater boulders ensure an active marine world teeming with large bumphead parrotfish, Moorish idols, surgeonfish and emperor angelfish. If you wade ashore, there's the chance to see Wright's skinks and native sea birds. The coco de mer once grew on St Pierre, but can no longer be found there. The best way to visit is to book an island-hop day trip from Praslin to Curieuse, Cousin and St Pierre through a resort or local tour operator.

Walking through mangroves at Curieuse Marine National Park.

A catamaran at the northeastern edge of Cousin.

COUSIN, COUSINE AND ARIDE

A refuge for rare land birds and breeding ground for thousands of sea birds, these islands are key to conservation efforts in the Seychelles.

These islands belong to the birds. Cousin and Cousine are the breeding ground for hundreds of thousands of sea birds; Aride is home to over a million. All three provide a habitat for rare land birds, most notably the Seychelles warbler and Seychelles magpie-robin. Thanks to the efforts of conservationists, particularly the Royal Society for Nature Conservation (RSNC), Government of Seychelles, and BirdLife International, both species have been saved from extinction.

COUSIN

In the mid-1960s, **Cousin Island** ❶ came on the market. As a 34-acre coconut plantation of insignificant proportions with no other source of income it was not deemed to be a particularly desirable investment. However, it emerged that Cousin was the final refuge of the Seychelles brush warbler, which was down to the last couple of dozen specimens. An international appeal was launched by conservationists and interest in the island grew, as did the owner's price. It was finally purchased by the RSNC on behalf of BirdLife International for £15,500 ($25,000), a small price for saving one of the rarest birds in the world. Today it is managed locally by Nature Seychelles.

Cousin is now a nature reserve for many other bird and animal species and attracts around 10,000 visitors a

year. It is easily visited from Praslin, being just 2km (1.25 miles) from Amitié on the west coast, and is accessible all year round (Mon–Thu, mornings only), though landing is generally easier during the southeast monsoon (May to October), when Praslin provides shelter from the strong trade winds. This is also the best time to see the greatest numbers of nesting seabirds.

Most Praslin hotels and many independent boat owners arrange trips, which are often combined with afternoon visits to Curieuse and St Pierre

⊘ **Main attractions**
Seychelles brush warbler and magpie-robin
Hawksbill turtle, Cousin and Cousine
Sooty tern, Aride

Map on page 320

Pair of fairy terns on Cousin.

⊙ Tip

The landing on Cousin is a wet one, so put on beachwear or cotton shorts and a T-shirt – they'll soon dry off in the sun – and pack camera equipment in plastic splash-proof bags. A pair of solid walking shoes for the nature trail is also a good idea.

islands to make a full-day excursion. There is a resident Nature Seychelles warden and several knowledgeable rangers who provide guided tours that last about 75 minutes. Tours are given in French, English and Kreol. Visitors are not permitted to explore the island unaccompanied and there is no overnight accommodation available.

BIRDLIFE

To minimise the risk of rats or other pests getting ashore no boats are allowed to land directly; instead, visitors transfer to the island's own boat to reach the sandy shore. As the noise of the engine is cut, the noise of the sea birds takes over. Seven species thrive on the island: four species of tern (lesser noddy, brown noddy, bridled tern and fairy tern), two shearwaters (Audubon's and wedge-tailed) and the white-tailed tropicbird.

However, it is the land birds for which Cousin is most famous, the Seychelles warbler in particular. The cessation of plantation activity and the regeneration of the native vegetation led to a rapid recovery in its numbers. The future of

this tiny wren-like bird has been deemed secure enough to remove it from the current world Red Data list of critically endangered species. It is a remarkable bird in that the sex of its offspring is determined by food availability. When food is plentiful, 80 percent of chicks are males, which leave soon after fledging to seek territories of their own. When food is scarce, nearly 90 percent will be female, which remain to help parents with future broods.

The Seychelles magpie-robin, a distinctive black and white bird, was once found on most of the granitic islands, but was wiped out by a combination of direct persecution and introduced predators, which had confined the bird to Frégate island; there were only 23 left in 1990, making it one of the most critically endangered birds in the world. Attempts to establish a breeding population on Cousin, begun in 1994, then on Cousine the following year, met with success. Today, this charming, tame endemic is often spotted hopping along the tourist paths. Nevertheless, it remains one of the rarest birds on earth. A third rare

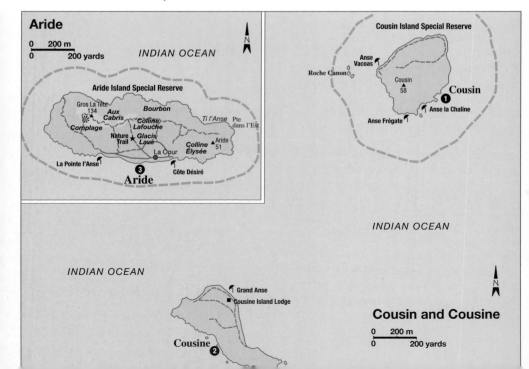

endemic, the Seychelles fody, breeds here and on just five other islands (Cousine, Frégate, Aride, Denis and D'Arros).

OTHER FAUNA AND FLORA

Of the 11 reptile varieties on Cousin, skinks are the most common. These bronze-coloured lizards feed on dead chicks and eggs. Hermit crabs are also common in the undergrowth and you'll probably spot one of the few giant tortoises that roam the island. Cousin is also one of the few places where a visitor stands a reasonable chance of seeing a **hawksbill turtle**, as Seychelles is the only place on earth where these animals come out by day.

The vegetation is dominated by indigenous species. These include the *bwa torti* (tortoise tree), so called because its fruits look like the carapace of a tortoise. They are also eaten by Cousin's resident tortoises, not put off by their unpleasant smell. Also common here is the remarkable pisonia that flowers to coincide with the peaks of activity in the lesser noddy nesting colony; its sticky seeds attach themselves to the birds' feathers, the

soft, malleable leaves make good nesting material and the horizontal branches are ideal nest sites.

COUSINE

Cousin's sister island is a more exclusive destination. It is a privately owned nature reserve with four colonial-style luxury villas that can accommodate up to 10 guests at a time. It is a rare opportunity to experience living on an island teeming with wildlife. Attractions on **Cousine** ❷ include hawksbill turtles that come ashore to lay their eggs, mainly between September and January, along the sandy beach that fringes the eastern coast. Endemic birds include the Seychelles magpie-robin and Seychelles warbler, while many thousands of sea birds also breed here, including the largest population of wedge-tailed shearwaters in Seychelles. Day-trippers are allowed by special arrangement made in advance (tel: 4321107).

ARIDE

Lying about 10km (6 miles) north of Praslin, **Aride** ❸ is the most northerly of the granitic isles and arguably the most

A scientist releasing hawksbill turtle hatchlings on Cousine.

⊙ HAWKSBILL TURTLES

Though famous for birds, Cousin is also one of the most important breeding sites for hawksbill turtles, with possibly the longest-running monitoring programme (more than 40 years) anywhere in the world. Elsewhere, the hawksbill turtle population has been greatly reduced following years of exploitation – not for the flesh, which is sometimes poisonous, but for the shell which, until the early 1990s, was made into trinkets to be sold to tourists. It will take decades for populations to recover as hawksbills do not breed until 25 to 40 years of age.

In Seychelles, the turtles nest in daylight hours from September to March. A single female may emerge up to six times per season to lay her eggs at intervals of 14 days. Each nest may contain up to 180 eggs. Older turtles lay even more eggs, more frequently. They hatch after about 60 days. The young turtles that emerge scurry straight to the sea, but not all of them make it. On the way, some fall victim to crabs, others to sea birds. Those that reach the sea are still not safe, as many will be eaten by large fish. As a result, very few survive to adulthood. Recent research includes attaching transmitters to adult turtles linked to satellites in order to discover the mystery of where they spend their time outside the breeding season.

unspoilt island in the Indian Ocean. The name Aride (so called because there are no streams or other sources of fresh water) first appeared on French charts drawn up after exploratory voyages in 1770 and 1771, but the island had no settlers until 1861. Thereafter, it was run as a plantation until 1973, when it was purchased by Christopher Cadbury of chocolate fame (1908–95), a keen conservationist and at the forefront of campaigns to set up nature reserves on Cousin, La Digue and Aride. But it was his purchase of Aride island, which he gave to the Royal Society for Nature Conservation, and its establishment as a nature reserve in 1979 for which he is most remembered. An engraved granite plaque on La Pointe l'Anse is dedicated to his memory. Today, Aride is owned by Island Conservation Society.

The island is covered in a rich flora and fauna and all species can be seen from the set nature trail. This begins at the settlement of **La Cour**, crosses the flat coastal plateau and winds uphill to a **viewing point** at the peak of Gros La Tête, 134 metres (435ft), where the cliffs drop dramatically to the sea. From here you can see hundreds of frigatebirds, noted for their huge wingspan, which can stretch to 2 metres (6.5ft), soaring over the sea. On clear days, the coral island of Denis is just visible on the horizon, but where the waves crash against the foot of Aride's cliffs are the last granite rocks before India and Sri Lanka. Once on the hill, visitors are not allowed to deviate from the path as the ground either side is riddled with the burrows of nesting shearwaters, which are easily inadvertently destroyed. You return to the Visitors' Shelter at the beach in time for lunch, with the afternoon free to swim, snorkel or explore the plateau.

The reserve is open Mon–Fri, and weekend visits are possible by prior arrangement with the island's manager (tel: 2719778); however days and times can vary according to weather conditions. The island warden and local rangers, the only inhabitants, give guided tours lasting about two hours. Most of the larger hotels organise day trips (the crossing from Praslin takes about 45 minutes), and lunch and the entrance fee to the reserve are included in the price.

A MILLION SEA BIRDS

Like Cousin and Cousine, Aride is a rat-free zone and consequently has remained a haven for vast numbers of sea birds. Eighteen species (including five found only in Seychelles) breed on Aride, more than the rest of the granitic islands combined. Chief among these is the sooty tern. Aride also has the world's largest colony of the lesser noddy, sheltering almost 200,000 pairs, as well as the largest surviving colony of the rare roseate tern in the Indian Ocean. The breeding season of terns and noddies coincides with the southeast monsoon, which lasts from May to October. All in all, there are over a million breeding birds milling about the island, making Aride an extremely noisy place at this time of year.

The elegant fairy tern, symbol of Air Seychelles, nests throughout the year, as does the white-tailed tropicbird, one of

Cousine's shore.

the most beautiful of all sea birds. They can be seen all over the island but you need to walk to the top of the hill to find the few pairs of red-tailed tropicbirds breeding in the only site outside the Aldabra group. Completing the sea bird scene are the wedge-tailed shearwater and Audubon's shearwater. Shearwaters leave their burrows before dawn, returning after nightfall and are more likely to be encountered at sea en route to Aride.

UNDER THE CANOPY

Indigenous vegetation was reintroduced to replace the monoculture of coconut palms. With the reappearance of a forest canopy, two species of land bird, the Seychelles sunbird and Seychelles blue pigeon, have now returned. The Seychelles warbler needed more of a helping hand. Since the transfer of 29 birds from Cousin in 1988 numbers have rocketed to around 2,000 so that Aride now holds more than 80 percent of the world population. In January 2002, two more rare endemic birds, the Seychelles magpie-robin and the Seychelles fody, were transferred to Aride and, within a short time, both began to breed. This means Aride can now boast more breeding native species than any other island.

The prolific sea bird life supports one of the highest densities of lizards in the world, including three species of skink and three of gecko. The wolf snake can also be found. Large millipedes may be seen on the hillside; do no touch them as they emit an obnoxious spray.

Among the most beautiful of Seychelles' endemic plants is Wright's gardenia, and Aride is the only place in the world where it occurs naturally. Its large white flowers, spotted with magenta, have a delicate fragrance and appear precisely 10 days after heavy rain.

REEF FISH

The naturalist Sir Peter Scott, visiting Aride in 1986, recorded 88 species of reef fish in little more than 1.5 hours in the water. Since then, other visitors and successive wardens have added to the list, which now records over 450 species – more than on any other granite island. Dolphins, whale sharks and flying fish have also been seen around the island.

Frigate surveying the landscape.

⊘ GIANTS OF THE SKY

After a long, hot walk to the viewing point near the summit at Gro Latet, it is refreshing to emerge from the woodland onto the bare granite cliffs and feel the cooling breeze. Here, the enormous frigatebirds soar on outstretched wings, occasionally harrying other sea birds as they return to feed their young, forcing them to relinquish their catches. Though notorious as pirates, frigatebirds are quite capable of catching their own fish. Using their long tails as rudders they steer with amazing agility. Yet they are primitive birds, unable to land on the surface of the sea as they lack webbed feet to swim. Their feathers also lack waterproofing and quickly become waterlogged. These sea birds spend much of their lives flying several thousand kilometres from breeding colonies across open ocean. They cannot even walk on their tiny stunted legs and once they land on a branch are rooted to the spot. Once aloft, they cruise with barely a flicker of their enormous 2-metre (6.5ft) wingspan. Their bones are incredibly light, only around 5 percent of their total weight, and they weigh little more than a kilogram (just over 2 lb), about the same as a small chicken. This gives them the lowest wing loading (weight per wing area) of any bird in the world.

The famous, beautiful beach of Anse Source d'Argent.

LA DIGUE

Life proceeds at an agreeably slow pace on what is generally considered to be one of Seychelles' most beautiful islands.

In the early days of tourism in Seychelles, La Digue was billed as the island that time forgot, where life went along at a pace little faster than that of its ox carts, then the only form of public transport. Today, La Digue's ox carts are more of a tourist diversion than a necessity – bicycles and pick-up trucks and one or two cars now share the tracks beneath the palms. Tourism rubs shoulders with the traditional way of life and has combined with it to raise living standards. Nevertheless, having no airstrip and a tiny population, the island retains its 'out of the rat race' atmosphere and friendliness. The fourth largest island of the granitic group, La Digue is generally considered to be one of the most beautiful of the Seychelles islands and should not be missed. The spectacular coast, with its huge boulders towering over perfect beaches, has been used as a backdrop for many a film and fashion shoot. It is less than half the size of Praslin, just 4km (2.5 miles) to the west, but rises almost as high, to 333 metres (1,093ft) at Nid d'Aigles. The island population is also less than half that of Praslin, with around 2,000 inhabitants concentrated mainly on the west coast between La Passe and La Réunion. Most tourist accommodation is here too.

Tourists can enjoy rides in traditional ox carts.

EXPLORING LA DIGUE

There is no airstrip on the island, but it's no more than a 30-minute sail away from Praslin by schooner or 15 minutes by fast catamaran (see Travel Tips, Transport). A day trip is feasible, but to experience the island fully and soak up the atmosphere it is worth staying for at least two nights. Ferries from Baie Ste Anne arrive at the tranquil harbour of **La Passe** ❶, a haven for yachts and schooners that shelter close to the palm-fringed shore. There are a number of grand plantation-style houses at

Map on page 326

Main attractions

Veuve Reserve
Belle Vue
L'Union Estate
Anse Source d'Argent
Snorkelling off Île Cocos

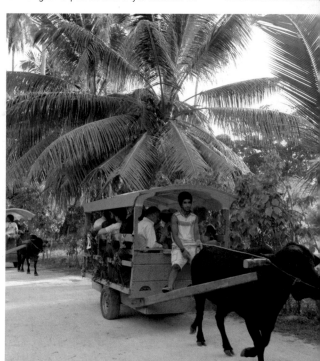

⊙ Tip

When cycling round La Digue, take care on the mountain tracks, particularly after the rains, when they can become slippery with mud. Wind-blown sand on the east coast road can also be hazardous.

La Passe, gracefully growing old and, on the whole, well maintained. The quiet fish market by the jetty turns into a hive of activity when the fishermen bring in their catches. Nearby is a small **café** next to a **Tourist Information Centre**.

You'll see very few cars here – there are only a handful of taxis and no hire cars – but La Digue is small enough (10 sq km/6 sq miles) to do without them. *Camions*, or open-sided lorries with fitted seats – four of them in all – pass for buses. There are no set timetables and they meander around the island according to the requirements of drivers and passengers. The flat coastal plateau and its beaches as far as L'Union Estate (see page 327) are easily explored on foot. Cycling is quicker, of course, and will enable you to travel further afield; south to Grand Anse or around the northern rim and south again to Anse Fourmis. To pedal at top speed from La Passe to L'Union Estate takes less than 10 minutes, but the whole point of La Digue is that no one does anything at top speed. There are plenty of bikes for hire at the jetty, including children's models, but these are of varying quality and it's a good idea to examine a few, the brakes in particular, before settling on one.

INLAND LOOP

Whether you're walking or cycling, the southbound road from La Passe is a good place to begin your exploration of the island (turn right on leaving the

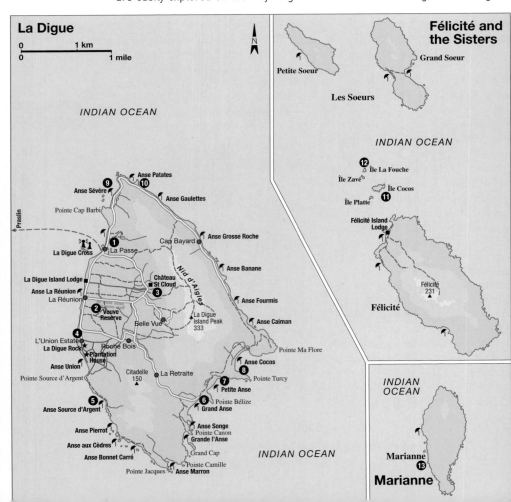

jetty). Looking out to sea as you head towards Réunion, the other main settlement, there is a view of **La Digue Cross**, a monument erected on top of granite rocks in the bay in memory of people who drowned while attempting to land on La Digue.

The road swings inland to round the chalets of **La Digue Island Lodge**, an up-market resort. It then runs parallel to the coast to a T-junction at Pont Bill. A left turning takes you to the **Veuve Reserve ❷**. Named after the beautiful Seychelles paradise flycatcher, the symbol of La Digue, the reserve was set up to preserve some of the last remaining takamaka and Indian almond *(badan-myen)* trees in which it feeds and nests. This habitat is under tremendous pressure from the island's growing population and boat-building industry. *Veuve* (*vev* in Kreol) means 'widow', a reference to the magnificent, long black tail feathers of the male, reminiscent of a widow's black veil. The female, by contrast, lacks the elongated tail feathers and is chestnut and white with a black hood. Once widespread in the Praslin group, the paradise flycatcher has survived as a breeding bird on La Digue, where there are less than 300 birds, and on Denis Island, where there are around 30 after a successful translocation project from La Digue. A few sightings have also been reported on neighbouring Félicité. They can be seen almost anywhere on the coastal plateau in the early morning, but chances of a sighting in the reserve are more or less guaranteed in the early morning and late afternoon. A Visitors' Centre at the reserve entrance provides information on the birds and the warden gives useful pointers on where they can be spotted. Entry is free and the path that begins at the roadside Visitors' Centre is navigable both on foot and by bike.

Continuing inland from the reserve, the road bends northwards to run parallel with the coast road leading to **Château St Cloud ❸**, a grand and enchanting

building that now houses a small hotel. It was built at the height of the Napoleonic wars as the plantation house of a vanilla farm. Vanilla was introduced to La Digue in 1866 and quickly overtook coconuts as the most lucrative commodity. The further development of synthetic vanillin in the early 20th century caused the industry to crash, bringing hardship to the islanders. Ruins of the slaves' quarters and remnants of the vanilla factory can still be seen.

A road near the chateau heads up the steep hillside to **Belle Vue**, just below the summit of Nid d'Aigles. It is too steep to ride a bicycle and a tough walk, except in the cool of early morning or late afternoon. The easiest way to tackle this road is by taxi. It is worth the fare for the fabulous view over the coastal plateau and out towards Praslin.

South of the Flycatcher Reserve the road leads back to the coast and turns southward once more past two art galleries, and the pretty Catholic church of **Notre-Dame-de-l'Assomption**. Beyond these, the track leads to **L'Union Estate ❹** (daily 7am–5pm), an

Early morning is the best time to catch a glimpse of the paradise flycatcher.

old plantation. Here, there is a working *kalorifer* where *copra* (dried coconut) is heated and dried, and a coconut oil press pulled by an ox. Other features include **La Digue Rock**, a towering granite boulder appearing like a natural sculpture, giant tortoises, horse riding (strictly within the plantation grounds) and a picturesque **plantation house**, for which there are currently plans to create a museum. The old colonial **cemetery** nearby, where the early settlers are buried, is also worth a look.

ANSE SOURCE D'ARGENT

On the far side of the plantation reserve is one of Seychelles' most celebrated beaches, **Anse Source d'Argent** ❺ (Bay of the Silver Spring). It is reached by following the palm-shaded trail that runs past La Digue Rock and the plantation house. There are no facilities here at all, but that is part of its beauty. The silver white sands are framed by giant granite boulders and perfectly positioned palms – the ultimate in exotic backdrops and a popular spot for weddings and fashion shoots.

Looking out over Anse Source d'Argent.

Be warned, its reputation means it attracts tourists, and low tide can prohibit swimming. A coastal path, easy to follow on foot, continues southward past a series of equally beautiful coves.

EAST TO GRAND AND PETITE ANSE

Near the entrance to L'Union Estate, the road turns inland and cuts through an area of marshland known as **La Mare Soupape** (*soupap* is the Kreol name for the terrapins, or mud turtles, that inhabit the area). Beyond the marsh, the road climbs steeply and it is quite an effort to cycle or walk to the crest of the hill. Perseverance is rewarded with stunning views as the road descends through thick vegetation to the velvety sands, granite outcrops and turquoise waters of **Grand Anse** ❻, the island's largest beach. It's a perfect place to relax and picnic, but the sea can be wild and dangerous, particularly between June and September, when the waves create a powerful undertow.

A footpath leads northeast of Grand Anse towards two more magical bays.

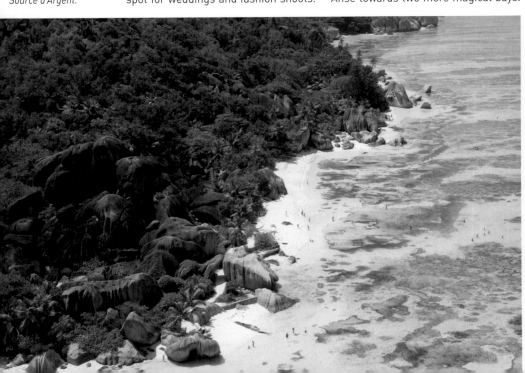

Often deserted, the white sands of **Petite Anse ❼** and **Anse Cocos ❽** are also surrounded by spectacular rock formations. Like Grand Anse, however, currents are strong and swimming can be dangerous. Unless you are particularly adventurous it is not worth exploring further than Anse Cocos, where the track turns inland crossing **Pointe Ma Flore** – which offers a lovely view over Anse Cocos and the northeast coast – to Anse Caiman, then peters out before you reach the road at Anse Fourmis.

LA PASSE TO ANSE FOURMIS

The easiest way to reach Anse Fourmis is by cycling the 4km (2.5 miles) around the northern coast from La Passe. Though walking is also easy, the route has not much in the way of shelter from the hot sun. The wild, unspoilt scenery is the main attraction. The beaches en route are all beautiful, though not all of them are good for swimming. The first of these is **Anse Sévère ❾**, which lies beyond the promontory of Pointe Cap Barbi, followed a little further on by the rockier bay of **Anse Patates ❿**.

Both beaches are good for swimming and snorkelling (snorkelling can be difficult at low tide due to the swell over the shallow reef but is relatively easy a couple of hours either side of high tide). The corals are not fantastic but fish life is prolific, particularly around the rocks where the waters teem with butterflyfish, angelfish, parrotfish, squirrel fish, Moorish idols, batfish and hawkfish.

Continuing south, you'll pass a succession of small, rocky bays, washed by rougher seas – **Anse Gaulettes**, **Anse Grosse Roche** and **Anse Banane**. The road comes to a dead end at **Anse Fourmis**. Here, in calm weather, snorkelling is good around the rocks.

ISLANDS NORTH OF LA DIGUE

The waters around the neighbouring islands of Félicité, Marianne, Petite Soeur, Grande Soeur, Île Cocos, Île La Fouche and Île Zavé are rich in bird and marine life. All are within close proximity to La Digue and make ideal day-trip destinations, offering a choice of activities: swimming, diving, snorkelling, birdwatching, fishing, or just

Time for surfing at Anse Sévère.

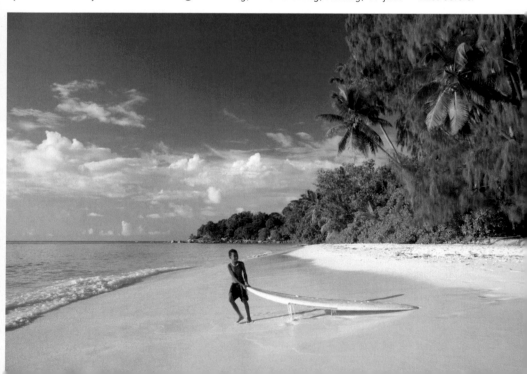

relaxing and eating. (All the islands, except Félicité, can also be reached by boat from Praslin.) Excursions to these largely uninhabited islands can be arranged through your hotel, the tourist information office at La Passe jetty or at one of the roadside stalls offering trips. Itineraries can be flexible if you discuss priorities in advance with the boat owner, and lunch and soft drinks are usually included. Most operators require a minimum of four people per trip.

For snorkelling, the best site is the tiny **Île Cocos** ⓫. Access to the waters of this Marine National Park was forbidden to visitors during the 1980s because of the damage to its coral reefs caused by tourists. The corals are now slowly recovering and it is still a beautiful site. Sea birds are the main attraction on **Île La Fouche** ⓬, a rocky islet off the north coast of Île Cocos, and **Île Zavé**; the latter, lying south of Île La Fouche, is little more than a jumble of rocks but holds five breeding species of sea bird: the wedge-tailed shearwater, bridled tern, lesser noddy,

Splitting coconuts at Historical L'Union Estate Mill.

brown noddy and fairy tern. This is also an excellent snorkelling site, weather permitting. There are large numbers of parrotfish, sweetlips and groupers. Whale sharks are commonly seen around November.

Just north of Cocos, **Marianne** ⓭ could have been Robinson Crusoe's very island. Uninhabited and blanketed with coconut palms, it has a single beach on the western coast where small boats can land. **Grande Soeur** and **Petite Soeur** (known collectively as The Sisters) are owned by the Praslin hotel Château de Feuilles, which reserves them exclusively for guests at weekends. During the week, other boat owners are allowed to offer trips.

Tourists can now stay on **Félicité Island**, 3km (1.5 miles) northeast of La Digue, following the opening of the luxurious (and expensive) Zil Payson (Isle of Passion) by Six Senses Hotels, Resorts and Spas. It occupies the north side of the island and takes up one-third of the total landmass, with 28 one- and two-bedroom villas, two restaurants, a bar and a Six Senses Spa.

⦿ DEPORTED TO PARADISE

In 1798 there was a rebellion in the French colony of Réunion. The insurrection, led by a former sergeant, Etienne Belleville, and a priest, Jean Lafosse, marched on the capital, St-Denis, protesting against taxation levels and rumours that the island was to be given to the English. The revolt was easily quashed, and the decision taken to exile the dozen or so ringleaders to a suitable location somewhere on the coast of India. They were put aboard the *Laurette* under the command of Captain Loiseau, but were never to reach India. Loiseau later claimed that they had to seek shelter from bad weather at Mahé. Holding the crew at knifepoint, the deportees mutinied and forced them to sail the ship to La Digue, where they went ashore, letting the *Laurette* sail on to Praslin. This story is probably a cover-up. As the deportees told it, they thought La Digue made as good a place of exile as any, and Loiseau did little to dissuade them. In fact, more than half of the newcomers did settle peacefully on La Digue, with their families joining them later. Among those who stayed was Célestin Payet, and to this day the Payets are one of the leading families of the island. Belleville and Lafosse, the rebellion leaders, both returned to Réunion in the early 1800s.

Landing on Denis Island.

BIRD AND DENIS ISLANDS

Similar in appearance, these privately owned coral islands, each boasting a luxury island lodge, have developed in radically different ways.

Although very similar on first appearance, Bird and Denis islands have developed along different lines in recent times. Both have been in private ownership for many years, having once been plantations. Denis is now a luxury island playground for tourists keen on water sports and game fishing. Bird, once a major source of sea birds' eggs for local cuisine, is now managed for ecotourism. Whichever approach you prefer, these dream islands are just a 30-minute flight from Mahé.

BIRD ISLAND

Bird Island is also known as Île aux Vaches (Island of Cows) after the dugongs or 'sea cows' that once thrived in its waters. Because it was an excellent source of oil, this marine mammal was soon exterminated. The island was named Bird Island by the British, after the millions of sea birds that flock here to breed. The secret of Bird Island is its simplicity. Lying 96km (60 miles) north of Mahé, it is relatively remote. There is only one flight a day, so the minimum stay is two nights here, though often visitors opt to spend longer than they originally planned. For many, it becomes addictive: 35 percent of guests are return visitors, who come back periodically to wash away the strains of modern life. The ethos of the island resort is firmly based on the ideal that a balance is possible between man and nature. Visitors are free to wander wherever they wish, providing they do not harm or disturb the wildlife. Organised sports and activities are deliberately kept to a minimum. You can walk, go birdwatching, swim, snorkel, go game fishing, play table tennis or billiards, or just laze in the sun and do nothing. The more energetic might wish to go in search of Esmeralda, the famous giant tortoise. He (the name is deceptive) once held the record as the heaviest land tortoise in the world.

Map on page 334

Main attractions

Hawksbill turtle, Bird Island
Sooty tern, Bird Island
Tortoises, Denis Island
Diving, Denis Island

Conservationist working on Bird Island.

TURTLES AND TERNS

Guests are also encouraged to help with the island's turtle conservation projects. **Hawksbill turtles** come ashore to lay eggs between October and February (see page 321), and green turtles from April to October. There is a tagging programme, and 'turtle-spotting' (hawksbill turtles lay their eggs in daylight) or nest-watching gives an exciting dimension to an island walk. Since nests are closely monitored, some visitors are treated to the unforgettable sight of hatchlings struggling down to the sea.

Birds, appropriately, are the chief attraction and the best time to see them is in the breeding season between April and October. The island's most famous attraction is the enormous (around 700,000) **sooty tern colony** ❶, which occupies one sixth of the island during these months. The colony was once harvested for sea bird eggs, considered a great delicacy by the Seychellois. In more recent years the birds have come to be appreciated more for the spectacle they provide than for their culinary value.

Bird Island is also a good place for birdwatchers outside the breeding season. Being on the edge of the Seychelles Bank, it is often a first landfall for migrants, and many rare species have been seen here. Regulars include turnstones, which are tame enough to peck about your feet, and there is a chance to glimpse rollers, bee-eaters, cuckoos and other species from far across the ocean.

RELAXING AT THE LODGE

The only place to stay here is **Bird Island Lodge** ❷ (www.birdislandseychelles.com), made up of 24 simple wooden chalets strung along the idyllic beach on the west side of the island. From here you can watch columns of spiralling birds in their thousands, circling over the colony. There are no televisions or in-room phones, so it's a great place for a break from modern life. There is a delightful bar at the main building of the Lodge in which to relax, and the cuisine, with strong Creole influences, is superb. Most of the dishes on the menu are prepared with produce of the island. Imagine the delights of chicken soup with coconut

A sooty tern colony.

milk, lemongrass and ginger, or fresh sailfish steaks grilled on a barbecue under the stars. The chef can cater to any special requirements and vegetarians claim Bird offers the best special dishes in Seychelles.

DENIS ISLAND

Similar in size to its sister island, Denis lies 80km (50 miles) north of Mahé. As with Bird Island, there is only one place to stay, but it's much more luxurious. **Denis Private Island Resort ❸** (http:// denisisland.com) is one of the best places you can stay in Seychelles; the 25 villas have private pools or gardens, and the delicious cuisine is based around home-grown produce and fresh fish. Close to the hotel is a large enclosure sheltering **tortoises**. After just a few hours in this quiet and stunningly beautiful refuge, the world outside seems to lose all importance.

When early navigators wanted to stake a claim to an island for their country, they could lay down a 'possession stone' if they had one handy; if not, they popped a deed of possession into a bottle and buried it. Somewhere on Denis Island such a bottle may still lie hidden, dating from 1773 and the visit of Denis de Trobriand, who claimed the island for France and blessed it with his name.

The lighthouse, dating from 1910, is still operational. It is open to the public and the view from the top is magnificent.

The local NGO Green Islands Foundation runs conservation programmes on Denis. Rats have been eradicated and three rare endemic birds introduced: the Seychelles warbler, Seychelles fody and Seychelles magpie-robin.

ON AND IN THE WATER

Situated on the edge of the Seychelles Bank, where the sea bottom plunges away to a depth of 2,000 metres (6,600ft), Denis Island has become a top game fishing destination: several records have been broken for dogtooth tuna and bonito. Other catches-of-the-day might include barracuda or sailfish. **Diving** has also become big here in recent years, and there are two resident divemasters.

Denis Island Resort's white sands.

A romantic moment on Desroches.

THE OUTER ISLANDS

Remote and visited by just a handful of people each year, these island groups have an unsurpassed beauty and timelessness.

Even in our shrinking world, Seychelles' so-called 'Outer Islands' are, for the most part, remote, uninhabited and possessed of an unspoilt beauty which those fortunate enough to have experienced find compelling. There are few who come away unmoved by these serene, isolated worlds; their encircling pristine beaches, vivid blue lagoons, kaleidoscopic reef life and the stillness beneath the palms, which is only disturbed by the sigh of the waves.

The Outer Islands are divided into four main groups. From east to west they are the Amirantes Group, the Alphonse Group, the Farquhar Group and the Aldabra Group. In the early 20th century, these distant outposts were important elements in the economy of the Inner Islands. Schooners plied slowly from isle to isle collecting exotic produce for home consumption or export, returning with holds filled with coconuts, dried sea cucumber, green sea snail, guano and tortoiseshell. All that remains of the former trading posts and settlements are a few crumbling buildings and scattered ruins, which offer nothing more than a hint of what the way of life was like here. Today only a handful of the Outer Islands are inhabited, their tiny settlements peopled by hardy Seychellois *îlois* (island workers) on contract, fishing or collecting and processing copra.

Although tourism is playing an increasingly important role, the Outer Islands remain largely unexplored. Shops and nightlife are non-existent, and the beaches and sea are consistently breathtaking and pristine. There is excellent game fishing, particularly around Poivre, and fly-fishing, especially in the St François lagoon. The diving is spectacular off Desroches and Alphonse, and around Assumption Island. Aldabra Atoll is a major wildlife attraction, being home to thousands of giant tortoises, while the whole area is rich in birdlife.

⊘ Main attractions

Diving, Desroches and Alphonse
Sooty tern, Desnoeufs
Giant tortoises, Aldabra

◉ Maps on pages 338, 342, 344

At anchor in calm waters.

SAIL AWAY

There are two ways to visit the Outer Islands: either on a charter boat or by basing yourself at one of the hotels. Desroches and Alphonse are currently the only two islands with hotels. It is also possible to stay at the Research Station on Aldabra and, if money is no object, you can book the entire islands of D'Arros and St Joseph Atoll for yourself. There is an increasing number of habitable boats visiting the area and these have the flexibility to go to all but D'Arros and Rémire, which are private. All the islands are within a short distance of each other and, depending on how long you want to spend in each, they can be visited in a few days. Chartering is fairly expensive due to logistics and the small scale of things, but not over the top (see Travel Tips, Activities). Whether you plan to base yourself on land or charter a boat, you should plan your trip to the Outer Islands in advance of going to Seychelles. It is difficult, though not entirely impossible, to turn up and book an Outer Island excursion.

THE AMIRANTES GROUP

Of all the island groups, this is the closest to Mahé, stretching from African Banks to the north, 235km (146 miles) from Mahé, down to Desnoeufs Island, 325km (200 miles) southwest of Mahé. The islands were discovered during Vasco da Gama's second great voyage in 1502, by which time he had been promoted to admiral, hence the name Ilhas do Amirante (Islands of the Admiral). Now largely uninhabited, the islands were once important components in the economy of Seychelles, producing copra, tortoiseshell, turtle meat, sea bird eggs and guano for local use and export. Life on these remote scraps of land was tough and lonely. As world markets changed, their relatively small harvests of goods became uneconomic to gather, and one by one they were abandoned to nature.

DESROCHES

The biggest island in the group is Desroches, a long thin strip of land with a fabulous sheltered lagoon and miles of sand, which make it the perfect get-away-from-it-all island. The flight from Mahé takes 40 minutes and lands at the grassy airstrip at the western end of the island by the **Desroches Island Resort ❶** (www.desroches-island.com), the only hotel in the Amirantes. There could hardly be a greater contrast between the arduous life of an *îlois* in the 19th century and the luxury of a holiday at this exclusive island lodge, nestling under the palms of an old coconut plantation. The 17 suites skirting the beach provide accommodation for no more than 40 guests.

Most of the 50 or so inhabitants of Desroches are contract workers, mainly from Mahé, engaged in agriculture. They live at **Settlement**, 2km (1 mile) northeast of the resort. Hotel guests and visitors on charter boats are free to visit this area, which is a good place to get a feel for island life in colonial times. Look out for the old copra drier and the circle where an oil press once stood. The little lock-up, with its barred doors, was the destination for anyone falling foul of island justice. Not surprisingly, the most common offence on these remote islands was drunkenness. The old hospital, if you can call it that, was little more than a room with a bed and a few basic medicines. In the early days, these would simply be medicinal plants that could be grown around the village, such as castor oil and datura.

Diving off Desroches is excellent, especially between November and April, and the island is famous among the diving fraternity for the amazing **Desroches Drop** – the edge of a coral plateau that forms the southern rim of the island, pitted with gulleys and deep caves (these can only be explored under the supervision of a qualified divemaster). The dive centre here runs courses for beginners and caters for other water sports (canoeing, windsurfing, sailing, snorkelling). A boat can also be chartered for game fishing trips or visits to nearby islands. The big game fishing is sensational, the waters rich in tuna, bonito, kingfish and sailfish. The hotel also has its own floodlit tennis court and hires out bicycles, perfect for exploring this flat island. A

Palm-fringed Desroches.

map with basically two routes – coastal and inland – is produced by the lodge.

SOUTHERN ISLANDS AND ATOLLS

Only a day's sail from Desroches, **Poivre Atoll** is the largest atoll in the Amirantes group. It is made up of three islands – Poivre, South Island (joined together at low tide by a man-made causeway) and Florentin – all with first-class beaches. Although it was a coconut plantation before it was abandoned, in its early days its major production was cotton. Plans for the building of an island resort have been in the pipeline for years, but at present, there is nothing here except a small settlement on Poivre. One of the most beautiful of the Amirantes islands, Poivre is named after the former governor of Mauritius (1763–72), Pierre Poivre, who was responsible for introducing spices to Seychelles (see page 242). It is famous for its deep sea fishing and diving and, although it is privately owned, a limited number of visitors are allowed access, provided

they have been given permission in advance: permission from IDC (Islands Development Company), New Port, Victoria; tel: 224640.

Étoile and **Boudeuse** are tiny uninhabited islands with nothing but breeding terns, notably the sooty tern and roseate tern, and Boudeuse has a huge colony of masked booby. The islands have the same uncanny beauty, enhanced by a sense of real isolation, as African Banks. You can only visit by charter boat, and landing is only possible in very calm conditions.

Marie Louise ❷ is in some ways the prettiest of the Amirantes, a coral island version of the granitic islands of Aride and Cousin, with large populations of sea birds. It has an airstrip to serve the small settlement, but there are no regular flights and no facilities for visitors. It is simply a beautiful place to include on your charter itinerary.

The southernmost island of the Amirantes group is **Desnoeufs**, famous in Seychelles for the vast numbers of sooty terns that breed here, the eggs of which are considered a delicacy in

The view from above of St Joseph Atoll and lagoon.

the granitics. Egg-collecting is carried out between June and August by the few Islands Development Company (IDC) staff who manage the island. Outside the egg-collecting season, the island is largely deserted. Again, visiting is only possible on a charter boat; even then it's difficult to get ashore. Landing should not be attempted by any but an experienced boatman or strong swimmer.

NORTHERN ISLANDS AND ATOLLS

African Banks is a tiny island with nothing but a lighthouse. The landscape of sweeping white sand hovers like a mirage on the brightest turquoise and ultramarine waters you have ever seen. Sea birds breed here in considerable numbers. The sands are criss-crossed by turtle tracks as if a safari rally had been held during the night. The urge to go ashore and explore makes landing irresistible.

Rémire, a small circular island, was originally named Eagle Island after a ship sent there in 1771 by the British in Bombay to find out what the French were up to in Seychelles. Not considered one of the most beautiful islands in Seychelles, it is however renowned for its fishing and the IDC operates a few basic bungalows to accommodate fishing enthusiasts (and other tourists) who venture so far.

D'Arros and neighbouring **St Joseph Atoll** were important coconut-producing islands during the early years of the 20th century, often yielding over 40,000 nuts a month. D'Arros has an oval-shaped platform reef, an airstrip and a research centre for conservation and student volunteer projects. St Joseph Atoll, separated from D'Arros by a deep channel, is made up of 13 small islets, which together make up less than 1 sq km of land. They are all deserted, but some have old colonial ruins, which are interesting to visit and speculate upon. Diving here is excellent, with scores of sharks, manta rays,

turtles and stingrays in the lagoon and surrounding reef.

THE ALPHONSE GROUP

The Alphonse Group consists of two neighbouring atolls, **Alphonse Atoll** and **St François Atoll**.

ALPHONSE ATOLL

Alphonse was a productive plantation in its heyday, generating 100,000 coconuts a month on a regular basis during the 1930s. The plantation was abandoned in recent times, and the island is now leased to **Alphonse Island Resort ❸** (www.alphonse-island. com), whose villas skirt the tranquil lagoon and silky white sand beaches. There is an **airstrip** for transfers from Mahé, an hour's flight away. (Visitors on charter boats need advance permission from IDC on Mahé, see page 340.)

The resort's Dive Centre offers facilities for diving the wall of Alphonse, where forests of gorgonian fan corals, sharks, rays and huge schools of predatory fish such

> **Tip**
>
> When tides are low, a good pair of plastic shoes or similar footwear is essential for wading ashore across reef flats with sharp coral fragments and possibly poisonous cone shells.

An aldabra giant tortoise.

⊙ Fact

The name Aldabra may originate from the Arabic al-khadra, 'the green', due to the reflection cast by the shallow lagoon waters on clouds above the atoll, a sight probably familiar to Arab traders between Comoros and the Middle East.

as barracuda, as well as a host of colourful reef fish, may be seen. The best snorkelling is at the pass into the lagoon, but this is a long way out and can only be reached by boat. Island Conservation Society runs programmes from its centre such as guided walks for visitors, daily turtle patrols, beach cleans and weekly talks. The Alphonse Island Resort arranges day trips to nearby Bijoutier and St François, the uninhabited islands of St François Atoll.

ST FRANÇOIS ATOLL

To reach the other islands from Alphonse you must cross the **Canal la Mort** – Death Channel! The water here is deep, cold and treacherous with powerful currents. The 5km (3-mile) journey is worth it, however, to reach the near-perfection of **Bijoutier**. The name means 'little jewel' and that is just what this island is. Perfectly round, capped with bright green vegetation, fringed with the whitest of coral beaches and encircled by purple reefs and turquoise

sea, this is the closest any island comes to the paradise ideal.

St François is surrounded by a fearsome reef, girdled by shipwrecks. At least six are still visible on the horizon, a grim reminder that the waters in these parts should be treated with respect. It is possible to enter the huge lagoon of St François in safety through **La Passe Traversé**. Over the coral crest, the tranquil lagoon waters are fairly shallow and a world away from the ferocity of the waters beyond the reef. The enormous plain of sand, left dry at low tide, is a feeding ground for hundreds of wading birds. Apart from its beauty and birdlife, the biggest attraction of St François is fly-fishing in the lagoon.

THE FARQUHAR GROUP

The Farquhar Group, which comprises Providence Atoll, St Pierre island and Farquhar Atoll, is about 700km (435 miles) from Mahé. The islands are only accessible by sea, but with the growth of habitable cruising they are no longer entirely out of reach. The

Bijoutier, a jewel in Seychelles' crown

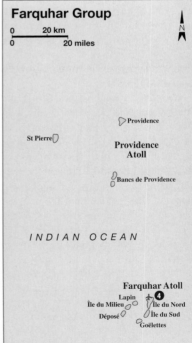

Farquhar Group

0   20 km
0   20 miles

N

St Pierre

Providence

Providence Atoll

Bancs de Providence

INDIAN OCEAN

Farquhar Atoll
Lapin
Île du Milieu   Île du Nord
Déposé   Île du Sud
Goëlettes

Islands Development Company (IDC) operates a small eight-room guesthouse on Farquhar, which gets fully booked during fly-fishing season from October to May.

PROVIDENCE ATOLL

This is a long, thin atoll oriented roughly north–south. **Providence**, the main island, lies at its northern tip, while across 40km (25 miles) of shallow water **Bancs de** Providence lies at its southern extreme. Most of the reef is out of sight of land and, consequently, many a ship has foundered here. The huge shallow lagoon attracts hundreds of grey herons and this is the only place in Seychelles where herons outnumber all other bird species. Providence has a small transient human population employed by IDC in copra production, but Bancs de Providence is strictly for the birds and turtles.

ST PIERRE

Due west of Providence is the extremely strange raised coral platform of **St Pierre**, rising to about 10 metres (33ft) above sea level. There is no beach at high tide and landing is only safe when the tide recedes to reveal a tiny sandy corner in the northeast. This island, now abandoned, was once mined for guano and you can still see the walls of the rotting stores and the twisted metal of what was once a quay.

FARQUHAR ATOLL

South of Providence are the 10 islands of **Farquhar Atoll** ❹. The lagoon is a popular anchorage for yachts and schooners. On the main island, Île du Nord, there is a small settlement where a little copra is still produced. The island also has an airstrip. Many of the trees on neighbouring Île du Sud have been turned white by the droppings of hundreds of red-footed boobies that nest here. The southern tip of the atoll, Goëlettes, is also the most southerly island of Seychelles. It is swept almost bare of vegetation by the strong southeasterly winds, but is a haven for sea birds, with up to 300,000 pairs of sooty terns and a healthy

Burning coconut husks on Farquhar.

number of black-naped terns, a species that breeds only on coral atolls.

THE ALDABRA GROUP

Aldabra is the most remote and most interesting of all the Outer Island groups. Geographically a part of Seychelles, these islands lie closer to Madagascar than they do to Mahé, more than 1,000km (625 miles) away. The archipelago is made up of **Astove** and **Cosmoledo Atoll**, lying due west of Farquhar Atoll, and **Assumption** and the **Aldabra Atoll** beyond. There are no hotels on the Aldabra Group, which, apart from visiting scientists and the occasional small cruise ship or charter boat from Mahé, sees few visitors. For the most part the only footprints in the sand belong to the birds and turtles.

ALDABRA ATOLL

Aldabra is the world's largest raised coral atoll; the exposed coral cap of a volcanic seamount rising more than 4km (2 miles) from the ocean floor. Geologically, it is part of a chain that

includes the Comoros. It is made up of four main islands – Picard, Polymnie, Malabar and Grand Terre – and a number of other small islets, stretching 32km (20 miles) from east to west. This ring of coral islands encloses a vast lagoon, which is fed by several channels that carry in new life with each tide.

Virtually untouched by the modern world, Aldabra Atoll is now listed as a Unesco World Heritage Site and is considered the Galapagos of the Indian Ocean. It does not possess the tranquil beauty of the archetypal tropical idyll as seen elsewhere in Seychelles, but has the atmosphere of an untamed wilderness lost in time. Its survival owes less to design than to its inhospitable terrain. Much of the interior is covered with sharp, jagged rocks and impenetrable scrub.

The atoll is home to nearly 95 percent of the world's **giant tortoise** population, with an estimated 150,000 animals. In addition, around 4,000 green turtles come ashore to breed each year, as do smaller numbers of hawksbill turtles. The atoll is now part of the Indian

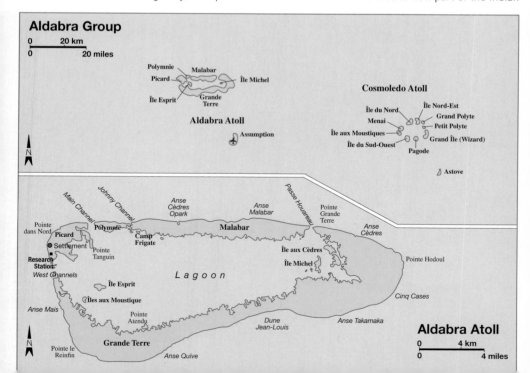

Ocean South-East Asian Network of Sites of Importance for Marine Turtles, after it was recognised as a critical site needed to be preserved to secure the future of marine turtles. Living along-side them is the Aldabra rail, the last surviving flightless bird of the Indian Ocean. Most of the other land birds are subspecies unique to Aldabra. It has the world's second largest colony of frigatebirds, with 10,000 breeding pairs, and the world's only oceanic colony of Caspian tern.

About 22 of the plant species are endemic, including the beautiful Aldabra lily. However, the vegetation is dominated by salt-resistant pemphis scrub, capable of surviving in the harsh conditions, and throwing a dense prickly blanket over much of the land surface. Around the inner rim of the lagoon is a dense thicket of mangroves.

Marine life is concentrated around the channels. Snorkelling or diving can be exhilarating here on the incoming tides that run at 10km (6 knots) per hour or more, taking swimmers on a roller coaster ride that sweeps them past sharks, rays, groupers and other exotic fish. This is not for the inexperienced and should never be attempted without a small boat to accompany your group.

There is a small **Research Station** on Picard with a warden and a staff of around 10 employed by the SIF (Seychelles Islands Foundation). There is also an accommodation block of six twin rooms for visiting scientists. When no scientists are in residence (which is most of the time) these rooms are available for visitors, but you need to apply in advance for permission from SIF on Mahé. Otherwise the atoll, one third of the land mass of Seychelles, is uninhabited. Except for Picard, Polymnie, Western Malabar and Camp Frigate, access to the atoll, even for resident visitors, is prohibited.

COSMOLEDO, ASTOVE AND ASSUMPTION

Cosmoledo Atoll has Seychelles' largest populations of red-footed booby, masked booby and sooty tern. It is also the last breeding site for the brown booby, exterminated elsewhere in the islands. The marine life around Cosmoledo and **Astove** is very rich, making for excellent diving territory. West of Cosmoledo is the island of **Assumption**. Guano mining wiped out most of the birdlife here, though there are three indigenous species of lizard, and the Mauritian tomb bat and turtles are successfully breeding. A small human population remains, focused on small-scale fishing and farming, but although Assumption is connected by air to Mahé, flights are few and far between except when officials are flown out to clear a cruise ship, or passengers arrive to join a dive boat based in the area from November to April. Nevertheless, the reefs here are largely intact and, as elsewhere in the group, diving is excellent. Advance permission to visit is required from IDC (Islands Development Company) on Mahé (see page 340).

Humpback snapper around the Aldabra Atoll.

Looking out over the turquoise lagoon off Rodrigues.

MAURITIUS, RÉUNION AND SEYCHELLES

TRAVEL TIPS

MAURITIUS – TRANSPORT

GETTING THERE

By air

Air Mauritius (airline code MK), the national carrier, flies from destinations in Europe (London, Paris, Amsterdam, Geneva), Africa (Johannesburg, Durban, Cape Town, Nairobi, Antananarivo, Dar-es-Salaam), Asia (Hong Kong, Singapore, Kuala Lumpur, Mumbai, Delhi, Bangalore, Chennai, Chengdu, Wuhan, Shanghai, Singapore, Kuala Lumpur, Bangkok), The Middle East (Dubai) and Australia (Perth), and has frequent daily flights from Réunion (St Denis and St Pierre). Flights to Rodrigues are only available from Mauritius.

Other international carriers are: Air Austral (UU), British Airways (BA), Air France (AF), Lufthansa (LH), South African Airways (SA), Qantas (QF) and Virgin Atlantic (VS). Emirates (EK) flies to Mauritius twice daily from Dubai, Kenya Airways flies via Nairobi and Alitalia via Rome.

Air Austral (tel: 020 7644 6124; www.air-austral.com), based in France, routes include Mayotte, South Africa (Jo'burg), the Comoros, Madagascar, Seychelles, Réunion and Mauritius and a Vanilla Islands Pass for discounted Indian Ocean island hopping.

TUI (tel: 0203 451 2688; www.tui.co.uk) is the only charter airline to serve Mauritius from the UK; Corsair flies from France (tel: (33) 17039 22109; www.corsair.fr) and Condor (tel: (49) 6171 6988920; www.condor.com) from Germany. Several planes a day fly between Réunion and Mauritius with Air Mauritius and Air Austral. It is important you have a recognised address to go to on arrival in Mauritius, or you will be denied entry to the country.

Airport tax is included in the price of all major airline tickets and many package deals.

Airline contacts

Air Mauritius: tel: 207 7575 (reservations); www.airmauritius.com
Air Mauritius (Rodrigues): tel: 832 7700; www.airmauritius.com
Air Austral: tel: 202 8050; www.air-austral.com
Air France: tel: 468 8425; www.airfrance.com
Austrian Airlines: www.austrian.com
British Airways: tel: 405 2929; www.ba.com
Condor: www.condor.com
Corsair: www.corsair.fr
Emirates: tel: 204 7700; www.emirates.com
Lufthansa: www.lufthansa.com
Qantas: www.qantas.com
TUI: www.tuifly.com

Tour operators

The following UK-based operators specialise in Mauritius:
Audley Travel: tel: 01993 838000; www.audleytravel.com
Beachcomber Tours: tel: 01483 445621; www.beachcombertours.uk
Carrier Indian Ocean: tel: 0161 826 1380; www.carrier.co.uk
Emirates Holidays: tel: 020 8972 8951; www.emiratesholidays.co.uk
If Only: tel: 0141 955 4000; https://ifonly.net
ITC Travel Group: tel: 01244 435137; www.inspiringtravelcompany.co.uk
Just2Mauritius: tel: 01342 547002; www.just2mauritius.com
Kuoni: tel: 0800 140 4777; www.kuoni.co.uk
Luxury Holidays Direct: tel: 020 8774 7298; www.luxuryholidaysdirect.com
Susie Freeman Travel: tel: 01488 668821; www.susiefreemantravel.com
Virgin Holidays: tel: 0344 739 1877; www.virginholidays.co.uk

From the airport

Sir Seewoosagur Ramgoolam (SSR) International Airport occupies the area of Plaisance, 48km (30 miles) south of Port Louis, and is often referred to simply as Plaisance. The international code for the airport is MRU (tel: 603 8000; https://mauritius-airport.atol.aero). Following a recent renovation, it has emerged shiny and new, and now features the slick Yu Lounge (www.yulounge.com) for those who want to start their trip in style.

Bus service: An hourly express bus service, often crowded with locals, links with Mahébourg and Port Louis 6.30am–6.30pm but is only convenient if you have no luggage.

Taxis: If a taxi is not equipped with a meter, which they should be, agree a price before starting any journey. A metered taxi ride to Grand Baie, for example, with two items of luggage, should work out at around R1,700, and to nearby Blue Bay, Rs1,200. An unmetered ride for the same journey, depending on your bargaining skills, may work out slightly less.

Sir Gaëtan Duval Airport, Rodrigues: Tour operators usually collect their own visitors from Rodrigues' airport, a modern building south of the island (tel: 832 7888; www.airportofrodrigues.com). Independent travellers can take the Supercopter bus to Port Mathurin for around R150. To return to the airport, call Ibrahim Nalla on 831 1859 for pick-ups from any guesthouse or hotel location in and around Port Mathurin.

By sea

There are no international passenger shipping services to Mauritius although cruise ships occasionally call at Port Louis, either as part of a round-the-world trip or on a cruise from South Africa. Nor can you travel by sea between the Mascarenes and Seychelles, unless, of course, you are chartering a yacht.

Mauritius Shipping Corporation Ltd (MSCL; tel: 217 2284; www.

☉ Driving times

Airport–Belle Mare: 1.25 hours
Belle Mare–Pamplemousses: 55 mins
Belle Mare–Trou d'Eau Douce: 30 mins
Belle Mare–Grand Baie (via the coast): 1 hour
Port Louis–Curepipe (without hold-ups): 40 mins
Le Morne–east coast (via interior): 2 hours

mauritiusshipping.net) operates the passenger/cargo vessel MS *Mauritius Trochetia* between Mauritius and Réunion. The journey takes about 12 hours and children travel half price. The ship also travels to Rodrigues three or four times per month (see page 350). Few travellers opt for the gruelling 36-hour crossing from Mauritius to Rodrigues.

Long-haul ocean trips are not generally made during the cyclone season.

GETTING AROUND

Driving

The British legacy of Mauritius and the Seychelles is most evident on the roads, where driving is on the left and the roundabouts operate as in Britain with priority on the right. Not every local driver seems to be aware of this rule, however, and in practice he who hesitates least goes first. Beware of poultry, goats and dogs on the roads, hawkers and foragers with heavily overloaded bicycles. Scooters carrying entire families need to be given a wide berth! Public buses often drive dangerously fast on small, winding roads – make plenty of room as they will often cross the central line on sharp bends. If driving through the sugar cane areas, watch out for deep gulleys on either side of the road, especially at night.

Mauritians tend to sound their horns when overtaking or approaching a junction. It is meant as a friendly warning, not as a reprimand.

Rules of the road: 100kmh (60mph) on 'motorways' and 50 kmh (30mph) elsewhere. The wearing of seatbelts, and rear seatbelts where fitted, is compulsory. Always carry your driving licence.

The police should attend any accidents resulting in personal injury. Where damage only is involved, exchange names and addresses on the prescribed form supplied by the car hire agency and notify them. In cases of doubt or difficulty, call the police.

There is a strong presence of traffic police, particularly on the Mahébourg–Grand Baie road, where speeding is common and driving habits verge on the dangerous.

Main routes

Mauritians refer to the road linking Mahébourg and Grand Baie as the 'motorway' but it is really only a well-surfaced trunk road which crosses the island from south to north linking the plateau towns. Most of the 2,149km (1,335 miles) of roads are surfaced, but many of the highways and minor roads are badly potholed. The best roads are the 'motorway' (M1), the new link road from Verdun to Terre Rouge and Trianon, which bypasses Port Louis, and the road through Black River Gorges National Park; the worst are in towns and villages. The south is by far the quietest when it comes to vehicles, and the city and the Central Plateau the most congested.

Names of towns and villages may appear in French and/or English and can be poorly positioned or concealed by sugar cane. Roads are adequately signed (with UK-style signposts) but navigating through towns can be a challenge. Make sure you have a good map (see page 355). Distances and speed limits are shown in kilometres and, more rarely, miles.

Parking

Parking can be a nightmare at all times in Port Louis so head for the car park behind Caudan Waterfront. Short-term parking up to two hours is also available at the Port Louis Waterfront.

Parking restrictions apply in towns and to avoid being fined, display a parking coupon on your windscreen. These can be bought in booklets at petrol stations.

Car hire

To hire a car you must be aged over 23 (or 18 to rent a scooter) and have a full valid driving licence, which must be carried with you when driving. Car hire rates usually include comprehensive insurance and collision damage waiver but always check first. Tyre punctures can be repaired cheaply at any garage. If you hire a motorcycle you should be provided with a crash helmet. If you only want a car for a short while to see round the island, consider hiring one with a driver-guide, who will know the best places to go and will save you the bother (and stress) of driving.

Major credit cards are increasingly becoming accepted by smaller companies.

Car hire companies

Avis/Budget Rent a Car: 116 Avenue Sir Guy Forget, Quatre Bornes; tel: 427 6312; https://avismauritius.com; www.budget.com.mu
Europcar: Near Mauricia Beachcomber Hotel, Grand Baie; tel: 286 0140; www.europcar.mu
Hertz: 84 Gustave Colin Street, Forest Side, Curepipe; tel: 604 3021; www.hertz.mu
Maki Car Rental: Royal Road, Triolet, tel: 5250 1260; maki-car-rental.com

By bus

Buses are plentiful, inexpensive and generally reliable although the service is less frequent in the evening. There are two bus stations in Port Louis, one linking it with the north and the other with the plateau towns in the south. Fares range from R12 up to R70 for travel by express service.

Some of the older buses do not inspire confidence; they chug along belching out heavy black exhaust, but get to their destination eventually. If you're in a hurry take one of the express buses but always check the destination with the conductor. Queues are orderly and tickets are bought on board. Stop bells are located at each seat. Avoid travelling between 8am and 9am and 4pm and 5pm during the week, when buses are very crowded; carry small change for the fare.

Buses operate in urban regions from 5.30am to 8pm and in rural regions from 6.30am to 6.30pm. In the country buses will normally stop on request. Night owls should note that the last bus from Port Louis to Curepipe via Rose Hill, Quatre Bornes and Vacoas leaves at 11pm.

The National Transport Authority (NTC; tel: 427 5000; www.ntcmauritius.com) provides bus information, but buses are so frequent during the day that a timetable is not really necessary.

In Rodrigues bus services grind to a halt at around 4pm.

By taxi

Taxis are equipped with meters but they are rarely switched on so always agree a price before starting a journey. Try to use them only for short journeys as the fare depends on the whims of the driver and includes the taxi's return fare to base. The official tariff should be displayed inside the vehicle, with waiting time chargeable for the first 15 minutes and every additional 15 minutes. Drivers do not expect to be tipped.

In practice drivers do not adhere to these rates. For longer journeys it may be cheaper to hire a taxi for the day and fix a price, which should be less than a day's car hire. If you find a knowledgeable taxi driver who can act as a guide, try to keep his custom by using him regularly.

Licensed 'taxi trains', or shared taxis, operate near bus stops in some towns and villages. They cover a prescribed route and the fare is divided between the number of passengers. The taxis are dilapidated and overloaded but travelling this way can be cheap and fast, with rates working out at not much more than the official bus fare.

Taxis are recognisable by black registration numbers on white plates. Unlicensed taxis or *taxis marrons* are instantly recognisable because they are nothing more than private cars – they have white numbers on black plates and lurk near taxi stands, bus stations and the airport. They often incur the wrath of their licensed competitors; their rates are low because they're uninsured to carry passengers.

Taxis can be hired from licensed taxi stands. Taxis are labelled with the name of the hotel or province they belong to on a yellow panel on the driver's door. Most hotels have a special arrangement with taxi drivers who are expected to charge reasonable fares. If you feel you are about to be ripped off, warn the driver that you will report him to the hotel. It usually works.

In Rodrigues there are only around a dozen taxis servicing the island. There is a taxi stand at the airport and beside Port Mathurin bus station.

By metro

By 2021, visitors will be able to use the Mauritius Metro Express, a 26km (16-mile) light rail transit (LRT) system connecting Curepipe to Port Louis in 40 minutes.

By helicopter

Modern Corail helicopters, which carry up to six people, undertake transfers and regular sightseeing tours with prices depending on flying time and route. Current tariffs start at R8,400 per passenger for 20 minutes. A transfer from the airport to hotels starts from R33,600 per trip.

Reservations can be made in your home country through Corail Helicopters (tel: 261 2266), travel agents or through www.corailhelico.com.

Sightseeing tours

There are numerous local tour companies but the following provide a wide range of sightseeing tours and other services and have hospitality desks at major hotels:

On Mauritius
Mauritours: 5 Venkatasananda Street, Rose Hill; tel: 467 9700; www.mauritours.net
Mautourco: 84 Gustav Colin Street, Forest Side; tel: 604 3000; www.mautourco.com
Summertimes: 5 Avenue Bernadin de St Pierre, Quatre Bornes; tel: 427 1111; www.summer-times.com

---

⊘ On your bike

Many visitors hire bicycles in Grand Baie. Several villages and resorts are only a few miles away and can easily be reached by bike. Most good hotels and island tour operators can organise bike hire and specialist Yemaya Adventures (tel: 5752 0046; www.yemayaadventures.com) hires mountain bikes and offers guided cycling trips. It is also becoming popular to cycle out on quieter roads from hotels in the south.

Emotions: 33 Stanley Avenue, Quatre Bornes; tel: 427 5845; www.emotionsdmc.com

On Rodrigues
Discovery Rodrigues: Rue de la Solidarité, Port Mathurin; tel: 832 1062; email: discoveryrodrigues@intnet.mu
Rotourco: Place François Leguat, Port Mathurin; tel: 831 0747; www.rotourco.com

Island hopping

Tour operators organise excursions to both Rodrigues and Réunion depending on sailings. The MS *Mauritius Trochetia* takes up to 108 cabin passengers, and has a bar and dining room, as well as leisure facilities including karaoke, a dance floor, cable TV, a library and a children's corner. It is advisable to book directly, as soon as you arrive in Mauritius, through island tour operators, with desks in major hotels. Better still, make arrangements through your own travel agent before you leave your home country, as you are unlikely to get a first-class cabin at short notice and the airline-style seats in economy class sell fast. Sailings between Mauritius and Rodrigues are between three and four times a month. At the time of writing, sailings between Mauritius and Réunion had stopped, but they are likely to be resumed.

In Mauritius, details of sailings can be obtained from **MSCL Coraline Ship Agency**, Nova Building, I Military Road, Port Louis (tel: 217 2284; www.mauritiusshipping.net) or through your tour operator/travel agent.

In Rodrigues, contact MSCL, François Leguat Street, Port Mathurin, R5126 (tel: 831 0640; email: msclrod@intnet.mu).

In Réunion contact SCOAM, 4 Avenue du 14 Juillet 1789, 97420, Le Port (tel: 262 42 19 45; email: passagers@scoam.re).

Boat trips from Rodrigues to the nature islands of Île aux Cocos, Île aux Chats and Île Hermitage can be organised through your hotel or tour companies such as **Discovery Rodrigues** in Port Mathurin. Bookings must be made in advance as there are restrictions on the number of visitors at a time.

MAURITIUS – A – Z

A

Accommodation

There are over a hundred hotels on the island, catering for every budget. Most are luxury beachfront hotels in the four- or five-star category, with gourmet restaurants, top-notch spas and world-class golf courses. They offer exceptionally high standards of service and facilities, including water sports, which are free except for scuba diving and game fishing, and the best have helicopter transfers, private plunge pools and 24-hour butler service. Leading local hotel groups **Beachcomber** (www.beach-comber-hotels.com), **Sun Resorts** (www.sunresortshotels.com), **LUX* Resorts** (www.luxresorts.com), **Attitude Hotels** (http://hotels-attitude.com), **Constance Hotels** (www.constancehotels.com), Veranda Resorts (www.veranda-resorts.com) and **Heritage Resorts** (www.heritageresorts.mu) rub shoulders with leading international brands.

Many of the top hotels, such as Royal Palm Beachcomber Luxury, Constance Le Prince Maurice and Oberoi Mauritius, offer a

⊙ Animal welfare

The sight of many stray cats and dogs, often in appalling conditions, may be upsetting for some visitors. If you want to do something about it contact PAWS (tel: 637 3025; www.pawsmauritius.org), a local animal welfare charity affiliated to World Animal Protection, at Mahébourg. Their activities include mass sterilisation campaigns, an adoption scheme and a humane animal welfare philosophy. The local MSPCA is not affiliated to the RSPCA International Section.

personalised service where they will make a point of knowing your name and will use it in the bar or reception, and even three-star hotels provide high standards of service. Most Mauritian hotels have a 'mini club' for children's activities and increasingly teen clubs. Many also offer all-inclusive packages, with premium all-inclusive packages including everything from champagne and gourmet picnic baskets to golf or spa treatments and excursions. All hotels have their own security guards.

Tour operators are adding a growing number of self-catering establishments to their brochures, and private guesthouses and bed-and-breakfasts are independent accommodation options, often chosen by repeat visitors to Mauritius. Many comfortable beach-side bungalows, villas and apartments are available for short- or long-term rental and the deal may include maid service, a chef and even excursions.

While the majority of independent accommodation options are in main tourist centres, such as Grand Baie and Flic en Flac, they are found island-wide, with some of the best in Tamarin, Blue Bay and Pointe D'Esny, La Gaulette and even Le Morne. Local rental agencies in Grand Baie, such as Horizon (tel: 403 5308, www.horizon.mu), **Ocean Villas** (tel: 263 1000; www.ocean-villas.com) or **Grand Baie Travel & Tours** (tel: 454 4038; www.gbtt.com) can help you find reasonably priced accommodation.

There are many bungalows to rent in Flic en Flac, where you can pay around R6,000 a week for two people, or a whole bungalow for five people for around R9,000 a week. Self-catering apartments, studios and beach-front properties are also available. Contact Flic en Flac Tourist Agency, Royal Road, Flic en Flac; tel: 453 9389; www.fftourist.com or try the

following: **Jet 7 Group** (tel: 453 9600; www.jet-7.com) or **Mauritours** (tel: 467 9700; www.mauritours.net).

Specialist agencies, such as UK tour operator **Elegant Destinations** (tel: 01296 334138; www.elegantdestinations.com), have a wide selection of self-catering properties for all budgets. The Association of Hoteliers and Restaurants in Mauritius (AHRIM; tel: 208 8181; www.mauritiustourism.org) is also a useful source of information. The Authentic Hotels and Guesthouses of Mauritius leaflet, available from the MTPA (Mauritius Tourism Promotion Authority) in your home country, features a handpicked selection of small hotels, bed-and-breakfasts and guesthouses. Independent accommodation options are also featured at Housetrip (www.housetrip.com), Homeaway (www.homeaway.co.uk), Vacation Rentals by Owner (www.vrbo.com), Airbnb (www.airbnb.co.uk) and Booking.com (www.booking.com).

Admission charges

Government-run museums are free but always check to make sure they are open before setting out. There is an entrance fee for all private museums and tourist attractions. Discos and nightclubs may charge admission for men (although they shouldn't) but women often get in for nothing. Sometimes free cultural and dance shows take place at the Caudan Waterfront, so ask around for what's happening or check out www.caudan.com.

B

Budgeting for your trip

Allow at least R1,000 per day per person to cover meals and snacks, soft

☉ Cyclone warnings

In the southwestern region of the Indian Ocean the following terms describe the intensity of different cyclonic disturbances:

Tropical depression: speed of gusts is less than 90km (56 miles) per hour.

Moderate tropical depression: speed of gusts is 90–134km (56–83 miles) per hour.

Strong tropical depression: speed of gusts is 135–179km (84–111 miles) per hour.

Tropical cyclone: speed of gusts is 180–250km (112–155 miles) per hour.

Tropical cyclone of strong intensity: speed of gusts is 251–335km (156–208 miles) per hour.

Tropical cyclone of very strong intensity: speed of gusts is more than 335km (208 miles) per hour.

When a cyclone approaches the islands, the Meteorological Office regularly broadcasts cyclone bulletins and red flags are raised on public buildings to denote their intensity:

One red flag: Warning Class I – low risk of gust up to 120km (75 miles) per hour.

Two red flags: Warning Class II – increased risk of gusts up to 120km (75 miles) per hour.

Three red flags: Warning Class III – great danger of gusts up to 120km (75 miles) per hour.

Four red flags: Warning Class IV – gusts of 120km (75 miles) per hour have been registered.

Weather information: http://metservice.intnet.mu has a forecast and cyclone warning bulletin in English.

---

drinks and entrance fees. Avoid your hotel room's minibar if you're on a budget. Bottled water, wines, spirits, cigarettes and food are much cheaper at the local supermarket. Eating and drinking outside your hotel is also much cheaper but remember when ordering food that not all menu prices include 15 percent VAT. Portions tend to be generous so unless you're famished it can be quite hard getting through a full three-course meal.

C

Children

Kids are welcome at restaurants, festivals and all places of worship throughout the Mascarene Islands. Luxury hotels in Mauritius cater specially for youngsters and offer supervised activities in free kids' and teens' clubs, special meals, babysitting services, family rooms and child discounts on excursions.

If you're travelling with very young children avoid December and January, which may be too hot for them. Leading hotels provide everything from sterilisers to wet wipes for babies, which saves the need to bring a lot of heavy equipment with you. Supermarkets also stock a wide range of baby food and nappies but you should bring your own from home if you have a favourite brand.

Climate

Mauritius and Rodrigues enjoy a tropical climate with two seasons: summer and winter.

Summer (November to April)

The weather is hot and humid with prolonged sunshine and temperatures of up to 35°C (95°F) on the coasts, broken by short heavy bursts of rainfall, especially during December and January. Humidity is high even at night. The north coast, where temperatures are highest, can get unbearably hot in summer, whereas the southeast trade winds freshen the south and east coasts with welcome cooling breezes. Average annual rainfall is around 2,000mm (79 ins), and most falls in summer.

Cyclones can occur between November and April. They are born hundreds of miles to the northeast of Mauritius and take days to meander westwards. Various weather stations track their route and warnings that a cyclone may develop are broadcast days in advance. Most pass by harmlessly, bringing only heavy rain and winds which clear the air after a spell of very hot humid weather. Others may have more devastating effects and you should listen to all cyclone warnings and comply with any directions or advice. Cyclones can cause serious disruption to telephone and power

lines, and transport, but hotels are generally equipped with generators so that tourists will experience minimum discomfort.

Winter (May to October)

The weather is pleasant, warm and dry, with little rain, cool nights and less humidity than in summer. Temperatures can climb up to 25°C (77°F), with the highest temperatures found on the north coast. The west is the most sheltered coast in winter. It can get uncomfortably windy on the south and east coasts in winter as the southeast trade winds pick up.

When to go

Although Mauritius can be visited year round, as the hot season coincides with the European winter, it's mostly known as a winter-sun destination, with peak tourist season in Mauritius' summer (November to April). This is also the season with the best conditions for diving and deep sea fishing. For visitors who like to walk, tour and explore, the best time to go is October and November, when it is early in the summer, and therefore hot but not stifling. The weather is still good on the coast from June to September, the low season, with fewer mosquitoes and discounted fares – prices can be up to a third cheaper than in high season. This is the time for both participation and spectator sports, with cooler, drier weather for outdoor adventures. For surfers, the waves are best from June to August.

The differences in Mauritius' altitude, topography and wind direction produce varied microclimates; the towns on the central plateau can be cloud-capped, damp and cooler,

CLIMATE CHART

Port Louis

Maximum temperature
Minimum temperature
Rainfall

while the coast is clear and sunny at any time of year.

Rodrigues' peak tourist seasons are November to February, Easter, and June to August. With a relatively small number of tourists visiting the island, many restaurants are only open during peak times.

What to wear

The emphasis is on smart casual wear such as loose cotton shorts, shirts, T-shirts and dresses around town and in the evenings. For the feet, light sandals are appropriate and comfortable. Take long-sleeved shirts and trousers for summer nights, when mosquitoes are at large. You should also bring insect repellent and a pair of plastic water shoes for protection against injury from sharp coral and stone fish (see Health and Medical care).

Women are expected to cover up when venturing from beach to hotel, and swimsuits should not be worn around town or in hotel dining rooms. Male visitors need not bring a jacket and tie unless they plan to attend formal functions or dine in the smartest hotels and restaurants.

Most hotels used by tour operators have a dress code for dinner which specifies smart casual wear, but no shorts or T-shirts. You might need a light jumper or pashmina for the evening breeze.

Take sturdy shoes for outdoor activities such as walking in the Black River Gorges National Park.

Crime and safety

Generally, Mauritians are a law-abiding people. However, you should take basic precautions as you would at home. Don't flaunt jewellery and money in public; never leave property on view in your car; always lock doors and windows when you go out, particularly in self-catering accommodation; and after dark don't give a lift to a stranger or go out walking alone.

English is spoken at all police stations in Mauritius and specially trained Tourist Police are based at Grand Baie (tel: 210 3894). The police number for emergencies is 999. If you are a victim of crime, try to get names and addresses of witnesses and report the matter to the police. In cases of theft ensure you have documentation for insurance purposes.

Be extra wary of over-friendly characters hanging around isolated locations during the day. Instances have been reported at Rochester Falls and Black River Gorges where tourists have been forced to part with money and valuables.

Serious incidents, such as rape and knife attacks on tourists, have been reported in recent years in Grand Baie, so walking alone at night is not recommended. And however friendly a situation appears, never accept a lift from a stranger.

Customs regulations

Travellers are allowed to bring in the following duty-free items: 250 grams of tobacco (including cigars and cigarettes); 1 litre of spirits; 2 litres of wine, ale or beer. There are stiff penalties for the importation of illegal drugs.

D

Disabled travellers

Top-class hotels provide good facilities for disabled travellers but check with your travel agent before leaving home. Beyond the hotels, facilities are generally dire but disabled people joining an organised tour will find that islanders are willing to lend a helping hand.

E

Eating out

Most visitors to Mauritius eat in their hotels in the evening, but eating out at local restaurants and street stalls around the island is a highlight of a visit. It gives an opportunity to savour the colour and tradition of Mauritian cuisine – a fascinating and mouth-watering fusion of the island's French, Indian, African and Chinese heritage. This produces everything from fiery hot curries with rice and home-made pickles to hearty casseroles with potatoes and delicate desserts flavoured with island produce such as mango and vanilla. The service, quality of cooking and reasonable prices all add to the enjoyment. Dress is informal, the atmosphere is relaxed and there

are scores of restaurants to choose from; some are included in island excursions.

Mauritians typically eat out at lunchtime. Bear in mind if you do venture out at night that it's wise to choose a restaurant in the region where you're staying, as distances can be deceptive and many roads are narrow and poorly lit, so driving is inevitably slow. Restaurants generally close by 11pm and booking is not usually required.

Street stalls abound in towns and markets, and by the beach. These sell *gadjacks* – snacks such as fresh fruit cut into pieces and in bags for a few rupees. The mix could include cucumber and mango spiced up with some chilli, if you choose. Stalls also fry up everything from *gateaux piments* (chilli cakes made of yellow split peas), *mine frite* (similar to chow mein) and *boulettes* (fish and potato croquettes), or *dhol puri* (Indian flatbread stuffed with curried lentils). Some still sell snacks from a glass case off the back of a bicycle or motorbike as they did in past times. Hygiene standards are generally good on the island, and for the price of a few rupees, these delicious snacks are worth trying. The food hall at Port Louis Central Market is one of the best places to find typical food, from street snacks to lunches, all under one roof. Other good spots to try street food is Mahébourg market, Curepipe town centre, and Grand Baie or Flic en Flac beaches at weekends.

Fish tends to dominate **menus**, with octopus curry and smoked blue marlin (usually served with palm heart salad) local specialities. There's a wide choice of meats as well, with game such as wild boar and venison from island estates a seasonal speciality. Typical Mauritian dishes to try in island restaurants include *biriyani* (a spiced meat dish from the Muslim Indian community), *vindaye* (fish or meat coated with a mix of chilli, ginger, turmeric and mustard seeds), Creole *rougaille* (fish or meat in a spicy tomato sauce with thyme and chilli) and French-style stew or *daube* with beef or chicken. More rarely, you can find dry beef curry with raisins and chicken and prawn curry.

Fast food restaurants are inevitably on the increase, with KFC being the most popular, as well as McDonald's in Port Louis. Pizzas are

⊘ Electricity

220 volts throughout the Mascarene Islands. In Mauritius and Rodrigues square three-pin plugs are used as in the UK, as well as Continental two-round-pin plugs.

available at Caudan Waterfront, Port Louis, and in shopping centres with food courts, popular with Mauritians at weekends.

Many of the chefs at hotels are European and so there is often an international flavour to meals, with everything from Italian to sushi on offer. Most **hotels** have weekly Mauritian nights or Indian evenings, and some, such as LUX* Resorts, have introduced Island Kitchen to give guests a taste of street food. With some of the world's leading hotels, the island has plenty of gourmet restaurants. It regularly attracts Michelin-starred celebrity chefs, whether to create restaurants such as Amari by Vineet at LUX* Belle Mare, or for gourmet weeks or cooking schools, or to participate in Constance Hotels' annual Bernard Loiseau Culinary Festival each March.

What to drink

Rum is the national drink, the most popular being Green Island rum. Other brands are Old Mill and Spiced Gold (more like a liqueur). Mauritius now appears on the international gourmet rum map, with artisanal rums produced at sugar estates or 'domaines'. Traditional restaurants also typically offer home-made rum arrangé as a digestive – flavoured with everything from coconut to chilli.

Imported alcohol is very expensive as it carries a 300 percent tax. Some hotels don't have very good wine lists, although they are improving, and many people tend to drink beer. Phoenix beer, a Mauritian lager that is very palatable, and island craft beers are now making it onto menus. Most of the wine is from South Africa, although some is made in Mauritius with imported grapes and is cheaper.

Citronelle – hot water spiced with lemon grass and ginger – is often offered after dinner to cleanse the palate. Port Louis is one of the few places where you can taste *alooda*, a Persian import made from coconut milk, basil seeds, rosewater and gelatine.

Embassies and consulates

If you are arrested or need legal representation contact your embassy or consulate. However, it should be stressed that officials can't advise on legal matters but may help you find an interpreter or arrange to contact friends or relatives. The main addresses are:

British High Commission: 7th floor, Les Cascades Building, Edith Cavell Street, Port Louis; tel: 202 9400; email: bhc@intnet.mu

British Honorary Consul: Paul Draper, Careco Centre, Camp du Roi, Port Mathurin; tel: 831 1766; email: pdraper@intnet.mu

Consulate of Canada: 18 Jules Koenig Street, Port Louis; tel: 212 5500; email: canada@intnet.mu

South African High Commission: 4th floor, BAI Building, 25 Pope Hennessy Street, Port Louis; tel: 212 6925; email saecon@intnet.mu

US Embassy: 4th floor, Rogers House, John Kennedy Avenue, Port Louis; tel: 202 4400; email: usembass@intnet.mu

Entry requirements

Nationals of the EU, US and all Commonwealth countries do not require visas, and entry as a tourist is for a maximum of six months. On entry, you will be asked to produce a passport valid for more than six months, your return or onward ticket and details of your address in Mauritius. Always check entry requirements before you travel as they can change.

Applications for longer stays should be made at the Passport and Immigration Office at Sterling House, 9–11 Lislet Geoffroy Street, Port Louis; tel: 210 9312; email: piomain@mail.gov.mu. Take two passport-size photographs, a valid return ticket, evidence of funds to meet the cost of your stay and a letter from your host explaining why you want to extend your stay. Applications can be

⊘ Emergency Numbers

Police: tel: 999
Fire: tel: 115
Ambulance: tel: 114

made Mon–Fri 8.45am–2.30pm, Sat 8.45am–noon. There is no charge for a visa extension, but allow five working days to process it.

Etiquette

Social etiquette in Mauritius stems from the French *savoir-faire*, the British aplomb and the Asian desire to please, and throughout the Mascarene Islands, *bonjour*, thank you and *salam* (goodbye) are all frequently heard in everyday life.

Handshaking is expected when meeting someone for the first time but kissing on each cheek, in the French tradition, is also perfectly normal.

Local political scandals can be discussed quite freely and often get a good airing in the press. You're more likely to witness laughter, infectious smiles and giggling than outright aggression, but use your own common sense when choosing with whom to bring up touchy subjects such as slavery, colonialism and race issues. The people of the Mascarenes accept Western whims, however strange some might appear to be, and will gladly pose for photographs, show you the way if you get lost, and rescue you from trouble. However, they do tend to exaggerate and their laid-back attitude to life means that they are not often very good time-keepers. But if you show tolerance, respect and good humour you'll take home fond memories of a warm and welcoming people.

H

Health and medical care

Malaria has been eradicated in the Mascarenes and no vaccinations are necessary unless you are coming from an infected area, but check the latest advice before you travel.

Travellers should be aware of **chikungunya**, a mosquito-borne virus that in 2005–6 affected the Indian Ocean islands, including Mauritius, Rodrigues and Réunion, although outbreaks are now extremely rare. The virus causes severe debilitating illness with muscle and joint pain often accompanied by fever and a rash (conjunctivitis, headaches and minor bleeding are also possible symptoms), and can result in sufferers being left with chronic joint pain or, more rarely, in death. It is spread by the *Aedes aegypti* (yellow fever mosquito), an aggressive daytime biter. There is no vaccine or preventative drug for chikungunya and if contracted you should rest and take plenty of fluids. Paracetamol may help relieve the symptoms of aching and fever but the best way to avoid infection is to prevent mosquito bites. Although hotels regularly fumigate their grounds, it's wise to use insect repellent containing deet, cover up, and close windows and doors against mosquitoes.

The cost of private treatment in Mauritius is substantially lower than in Europe. Shop around for an insurance policy that suits your circumstances and in the event of a medical claim ensure that you keep all receipts and documentation.

Remember that many insurance companies exclude extreme sports, such as rock climbing and mountaineering. If you plan to take part in any land or sea sports, confirm that the activity is within your capabilities, that your guide is a qualified first-aider and that drinks and first-aid equipment are carried at all times. But most important of all – and this cannot be stressed enough – ask what emergency backup security measures are in place in case of accident or sudden illness. If there is any doubt at all, don't book.

Health hazards
In Mauritius avoid wading in unclear waters without wearing protective shoes. This is the habitat of the laff, or stone fish, which if trodden upon emits a poisonous venom from its spines. Local fishermen resort to a poultice remedy but immediate removal to hospital is necessary as the wound, if untreated, can be fatal. In Rodrigues the only nasties you may encounter are large centipedes. They frequent dark corners in old buildings and can emit a painful sting.

Medical treatment
Emergency hospital treatment is free at public hospitals. They tend to be very crowded and most visitors go to a private clinic. Your hotel can provide a doctor in cases of sudden illness and help locate out-of-hours pharmacists. Western medicines or their equivalent and antibiotics are also available over the counter.

If you fall ill in Rodrigues, where facilities are very basic, you should return to Mauritius as soon as possible for treatment.

Dental facilities in Mauritius are very good and most practitioners speak English. Contact lens and spectacles are good value, of a high standard and prescriptions can be made up in a few days.

Private clinics
Centre Médical du Nord, Royal Road, Pointe aux Canonniers; tel: 263 1010; www.cliniquedunord.mu
Grand Bay Medical and Diagnostic Centre, Sottise Road; tel: 263 1212
Clinique du Nord, Coastal Road, Tombeau Bay; tel: 247 2532; www.cliniquedunord.mu
Clinique de L'Occident, next to Villas Caroline Hotel, Flic en Flac; tel 247 1056, www.cliniquedunord.mu
Fortis Clinique Darné, G. Guibert Street, Floreal 9, and a branch at La Croisette shopping complex, Grand Baie; tel: 601 2500; www.fortiscliniquedarne.com

I

Internet
Almost all accommodation has Wi-fi and/or internet access, which you may or may not have to pay for.

L

LGBTQ travellers
Homosexuality, while tolerated, is illegal, so forced underground in Mauritius. It's not blatantly obvious in public places, and although gay couples are free to behave as at home within the confines of hotels, any open displays of full blown affection in public may offend, or attract stares. Attitudes have improved in recent years with an openly gay British High Commissioner in function until 2017; he attended functions with his husband, despite causing quite a stir at the time.

Lost property
There is no central lost property facility but if you have lost something report the matter to the police

and obtain a copy of the report form for insurance purposes. Loss of passport or other travel documents should be reported to your consulate or embassy. For enquiries regarding lost property in the terminal building of the airport, check with the Information Desk at the Arrivals exit.

M

Maps
You can pick up pocket-size maps from most bookshops in Port Louis and most good hotels should have a stock of tourist maps produced by the MTPA (Mauritius Tourism Promotion Authority) at reception. These will only highlight tourist spots, however. French IGN produces a more detailed and accurate map (1:100,000) which is available from Stanfords in the UK, 12–14 Long Acre, Covent Garden, London WC2E 9LP; tel: 020 7836 1321; www.stanfords.co.uk.

Media

TV and radio
The Mauritius Broadcasting Corporation (MBC) transmits television news in English at 7am, 5.40pm and 9pm and radio news at 8am, 3pm and 9pm daily. French TV comes from Réunion. BBC World Service can be received on various frequencies mainly in the morning and late evening. BBC World, CNN and Sky are now available in many hotels.

Publications
English-language newspapers and magazines are available in tourist areas. *The Independent* is the leading local English-language daily. The *Côte Nord* magazine is distributed free in hotels and shops in the Grand Baie area, and many hotels produce their own magazines now, with interesting articles in both French and English. All are ideal for news, reviews and tourist information. *Kozé* (www.koze.mu/events) magazine, published monthly, is the most useful for listings and is available online.

There are plenty of local French-language newspapers, including the morning *L'Express* (www.lexpress.mu) and the evening *Le Mauricien* (www.lemauricien.com). *Le Matinal* (www.

lematinal.com) is excellent value and contains a daily English features and news section; *L'Express* carries a Tuesday supplement in English. *News on Sunday* (www.defimedia.info), published on Friday, provides rather poorly written news in English but is useful for finding out what's on.

The Mauritian Wildlife Foundation (tel: 697 6097; www.mauritian-wildlife. org) publishes its latest news on its website. Set up in 1984, the foundation aims to protect and manage the rare flora and fauna of Mauritius and to inform, educate and involve locals in all aspects of its work.

Money

The Mauritius rupee (R or MUR) is divided into 100 cents ©. There are 1, 5, 10 and 20 rupee coins and 20 and 50 cent coins. Notes come in the following values: R25, 50, 100, 200, 500, 1,000 and 2,000.

Major currencies, major credit cards and traveller's cheques are accepted in banks, bureaux de change, most hotels and some shops. There is no restriction on the amount of foreign currency you can bring into the country. Banks offer a better rate of exchange than hotels. If you have a surplus of rupees on departure you can change them back into your own currency but keep any bank receipts as you can only export a maximum of R350.

Banks

Banks are open 9.15am–3.15pm Monday to Thursday and 9.15am–5pm on Friday. In tourist areas and Port Louis they are also open on Saturday 9.15–11.15am.

Bank of Mauritius has small branches everywhere and branches of **Barclays** and **HSBC** can be found in Grand Baie and other tourist areas. The only bank in Le Morne is a branch of **MCB** (Mauritius Commercial Bank). Banks at the airport open to coincide with arrivals and departures of international flights.

Change facilities are widely available at bureau de change offices in tourist areas such as Flic en Flac and Grand Baie and opening times are 3.15–5pm Monday to Friday, 9am–5pm on Saturday, 9am–noon on Sunday and public holidays.

You can use your credit card to withdraw cash from ATMS (automatic teller machines) in large towns and shopping centres.

Tax

Value Added Tax (TVA) of 15 percent is added to goods and services, including hotel and restaurant bills, but there is no VAT on foodstuffs and books. Duty-free goods are available everywhere but you can't take them with you at the time of purchase; they are sent to the airport for you to collect on departure.

O

Opening hours

Non-government offices: Mon–Fri 8am–4.30pm, Sat 9am–noon.
Government offices: Mon–Fri 9am–4pm, Sat 9am–noon.
Shops in Port Louis: Mon–Fri 9.30am–5pm, Sat 9am–noon.
Shops in plateau towns: Mon–Wed 10am–6pm, Thu–Sun 10am–noon.
Municipal markets: Mon–Sat 6am–6pm.

P

Photography

White sand, turquoise seas and blue skies contrasting with the colourful dress of the islanders provide stunning pictures but these are the very ingredients which may play havoc with auto-exposure programmes on single lens reflex and compact cameras. The dense dark green foliage against sunlit sky can induce similar problems resulting in over- or under-exposure and care in metering is required to provide the perfect shots one expects from such a photogenic location.

What to take: With high temperatures and humidity, all equipment should be adequately protected with silicon crystals and kept in an insulated bag. Great effects can be produced by shooting straight into the sun, so consider purchasing a graduated grey filter which allows this without over exposure.

Some accessories are available in the main towns but be prepared for high prices.

Keen photographers may want to consider a half- to full-day tour with Mauritian Photographic Safari (tel: 250 6990; www.cliquemauritius. com) in select island locations or tailor-made.

Postal services

Post offices open Mon–Fri 8.15am–4pm, Sat 8.15–11.45am. After 3pm they are open only for the sale of postage stamps. **Post Office Headquarters:** 3 Dumas Street, Port Louis; tel: 208 2851; www.mau ritiuspost.mu.

R

Religious services

Mosques, temples and churches, often within close proximity to each other, reflect the religious tolerance of the Mascarenes' multicultural society and respect should be shown by removing your shoes before entering a mosque or temple. English services are held as follows: **Church of England:** St Paul's Church, La Caverne, Vacoas; tel: 686 4819. 9.30am every Sunday (except the second Sunday of each month).
Presbyterian: St Columba's Church, Phoenix; tel: 696 4404.
Roman Catholic Mass: St Joseph's Chapel, Celicourt Antelme Street, Rose Hill, every Saturday (tel: 464 2944 for times).

In Rodrigues, there is one Hindu temple and one mosque. Most of the churches are in Port Mathurin. St Barnabas Church in Rue de la Solidarité holds an English service once a month on Sunday at 8.30am.

S

Shopping

What to buy

You could be spoilt for choice in your wanderings round the new shopping malls in Mauritius, where local products and handicrafts stand alongside luxury imported goods. Haggling in markets is perfectly acceptable. Shops tend to have fixed prices but may offer you a small discount for bulk or major purchases.

Model ships and **wooden handcarvings** make good buys. Replicas of wooden Creole houses and handcarved salad bowls, miniature tropical fruits and the inevitable dodo can be bought everywhere. Raw materials such as straw, wood and fabrics turn up as appealing patchwork

☉ Public holidays and festivals

All public services are closed on public holidays. Many of these are religious festivals celebrated by various ethnic groups in Mauritius and some, but not all, shops and businesses are closed. In Rodrigues, Chinese-run shops (which are most shops) shut for a week during the Chinese Spring Festival. (See page 74 for more about Hindu festivals.)
1–2 January New Year's Day
Mid-January/February Cavadee (varies)
1 February Abolition of Slavery
February/March Chinese Spring

Festival (varies)
February/March Maha Shivaratree (varies)
12 March Republic Day
March/April Ougadi (varies)
1 May Labour Day
15 August Assumption Day
September Ganesh Chaturthi (varies)
September/October Id El Fitr (varies)
October/November Divali (varies)
1 November All Saints' Day
2 November Arrival of Indentured Labourers
25 December Christmas Day

Creole dolls representing people from the various ethnic groups.
Textiles and **clothing** are good quality but not necessarily cheap – good buys to look for are woollens, T-shirts, saris, silk and cotton shirts and casual wear. In up-market shops you'll find rich tapestries, murals, rugs and cushions, embroidered tablecloths and napkins, quilted wall hangings and colourful pottery depicting scenes from Mauritian life.
Markets sell *tentes* or baskets made from the vacoas or pandanus leaf, coconut leaf, raffia, aloe, bamboo and banana fibre, which serve as useful shopping bags as they are very strong and hardwearing.
Jewellery Unusual buys include pieces made from mother-of-pearl, coconut or local dried seeds; also gold jewellery, mounted with precious stones.
Flowers Long-lasting cut andreanums and anthuriums, in small, medium or large blooms, travel well and can be bought at the airport in convenient

pre-packaged boxes, just prior to your flight. Alternatively, you can visit the plantations and order flowers from there.
Glass-blowing demonstrations from recycled glass can be seen at the Mauritius Glass Gallery, next to Phoenix Beverages at Phoenix. Slender vases and ornaments can be bought from the adjacent shop (tel: 696 3360; email: mgg@pbg.mu; Mon–Fri 9am–5pm, Sat 9am–noon).
Chinese goods such as kimonos, silks and *objets* made from brass, jade and porcelain can be found in specialised shops, particularly in Curepipe.
Objets d'art can be bought at Diane, Royal Road, Trou aux Biches, tel: 265 5156.
Mauritian food specialities such as spices, sugar, salt, tea and smoked marlin don't cost the earth and make nice gifts.
There are **art galleries** dotted all over the island, although they are concentrated in Grand Baie, where you can pick up paintings and handicrafts by local artists and artisans.

Shopping centres
Bagatelle, Moka. The island's most popular shopping centre, with local and international clothing brands, a food court, bars and restaurants and a cinema.
Cascavelle, Flic en Flac. A mix of local and international clothing brands, and a bar/nightclub, on the road to Tamarin.
Caudan Waterfront, Port Louis. Some of the best shops on the island. Several clothes shops and duty free, plus a food court and crafts market.

☉ Model ships
Making intricate model boats and ships – including replicas of famous galleys – is an art in Mauritius and they can be bought from workshops dotted around the island, ranging from the affordable to the very expensive. The **Historic Marine** factory, at Zone Industrielle de St Antoine, Goodlands (tel; 283 9404; www.historic-marine.com), where nautical furniture in teak and mahogany is made, also gives tours of the workshop.

La Croisette, Grand Baie. Large shopping complex on the edge of town with mainly international clothing brands.
Currimjee Arcades, Royal Road, Curepipe. Small centre with a few clothes and duty-free shops.
Garden Village, Sir Winston Churchill Street, Curepipe. This small shopping complex on the outskirts of Curepipe is a shopping stop on tours of the island.
Jumbo, Phoenix. Large American-style shopping centre with an enormous supermarket and a street of other shops, but not many clothes outlets.
Jumbo, Riche Terre, a modern complex with attractive boutiques stocking clothes and handicrafts, a fast food court and a pleasant supermarket for shopping in air-conditioned comfort.
Orchard Centre, Quatre Bornes. More glitzy inside than out. Lots of local clothes stores and possible bargains.
Port Louis Waterfront, Port Louis. Boutiques selling everything from bonsai to arts and crafts.
Ruisseau Créole, Black River. A few trendy shops selling everything from designer wear to health foods.
Sunset Boulevard, Grand Baie. A shopping village with some good clothes stores and some of the island's most interesting shops, including designer clothing.
Super U, Grand Baie. Combines internet facilities with European-style shopping in a supermarket that stocks just about everything and is flanked with inexpensive eateries.
Trianon Shopping Complex, Quatre Bornes. Popular complex comprising supermarkets, fast food, shops and boutiques. Huge parking area.

Duty free
Remember to take your passport and airline ticket when shopping for duty-free goods outside the airport, and that your purchases must be paid for in foreign currency or by credit card. Duty-free shops will arrange for your purchases to be delivered to the airport before your departure, but you must allow at least one day for the formalities to be completed.
Mauritius Duty Free Paradise (MDFP) has duty-free outlets in Port Louis, Grand Baie and the airport, but other names to look for are Sashena Trading, Etoile d'Argent, Linea Azzura Shop, Parure and Bijouterie Bienvenue for perfumes,

photographic equipment, cosmetics, sportswear, shoes and jewellery.

Some Duty-Free Shops

Adamas Diamond Duty Free Boutique, Floreal Square; tel: 686 1248; www.adamasltd.com

Caudan Waterfront, Marina Quay, Port Louis; tel: 211 9500. Has Poncini, Shiv Jewels and Adamas outlets among its 120 shops.

Tara Cashmere, Espace Ocean, Grand Baie, tel: 263 6688

Bookshops

Publications in both French and English are widely available in the island's bookshops.

Bookcourt Ltd, Caudan Waterfront, Port Louis; tel: 211 9262; www.bookcourt.mu

Le Cygne, Magic Lantern Complex, 307 Royal Road, Beau Bassin-Rose Hill; tel 464 2444. Browse all day in this well-stocked bookshop tucked in the arcades at Rose Hill. Choose your books over a cup of tea or coffee at the back of the shop.

Papyrus, Richmond Hill Complex, La Salette Road; Grand Baie; tel 263 0012

Trèfles, Currimjee Arcade, Royal Road, Curepipe; tel: 676 3025

Textiles and Clothes

Floreal Square shopping complex (Floreal; tel: 698 8016) sells quality garments made from raw imported materials such as cashmere, cotton and silk.

Men fare rather better than women in **made-to-measure outfits** and you can select from a wide range of imported or local cloth to make top-quality trousers and shirts. A wool worsted three-piece suit can be made for less than £200. **Caustat Apparel** (Padaruth Lane, La Caverne, Vacoas; tel: 686 6818) is considered the best men's tailor in Mauritius, with a client list that includes guests of the Royal Palm Hotel. Suits can be made up in 24–48 hours at **Karl Kaiser** (Europe's Hugo Boss), Le Caudan Waterfont (tel: 211 7262) or Sunset Boulevard (tel: 263 4890; www.karlkaisergroup.com) but your tailor will expect you to have one or two fittings before the final stitches are put in place. They will keep measurements on file, if asked, so that new or repeat orders can be made in advance.

Bargain designer clothing

Mauritians make the clothes for many European designers and often have stock left over that is sold at a third of the normal price, such as at Floreal Knitwear, Shibani and Tara Cashmere.

Rodrigues

In **Rodrigues**, a **Saturday market** selling everything under the sun, from souvenirs to home-made chutneys and fresh produce, operates on Fishermen Lane, Port Mathurin, from 6–10am. You can buy baskets made from vacoas leaves at the **Women's Handicraft Centre** in Mont Lubin, and other handicrafts at **Careco** in Port Mathurin and at **Sir Gaetan Duval airport** at Plaine Corail.

Student travellers

There are no concessions for visiting student travellers. There are no youth hostels and while budget accommodation is available don't expect any great deals. The University of Mauritius at Le Réduit (tel: 403 7400; www.uom.ac.mu) has quite a large student population and dozens of clubs affiliated to the Students' Union. The move to set up UK University campuses in Mauritius has sadly failed to generate enough interest.

T

Telecommunications

Information technology has taken off in leaps and bounds in recent years and internet access is available from just about anywhere on the island. All hotels have **email** and **internet** access and most have Wi-fi. Making overseas calls from public telephone boxes in tourist areas, using a prepaid phone card, rather than from the hotels, will avoid hefty surcharges.

Phonecards can be bought in shops and supermarkets in various denominations.

Alternatively you can make calls at **Mauritius Telecom Tower** at Edith Cavell Street, Port Louis (tel: 203 7000; www.mauritiustelecom.com; Mon–Fri 8.30am–5pm) or **Mauritius**

⏱ Time zone

GMT+4, with no daylight saving.

Telecom, Mont Venus, Rodrigues (tel: 831 1532).

In Mauritius mobile numbers begin with the prefix 5. Mauritius has two mobile phone networks, Emtel (Air Mauritius Building, President John Kennedy Street, Port Louis; tel: 572 95400; www.emtel.com) and MyT (9th floor, Telecom Tower, Edith Cavell Street, Port Louis; tel: 203 7000; www.myt.mu/mobile). If you intend to make a lot of local calls it may be cheaper to buy a SIM card in Mauritius, although you will be asked to show your original passport and provide a photocopy.

If your own mobile/cell phone does not function, you can rent a phone through either provider.

International dialling codes: 230 for both Mauritius and Rodrigues. To make international calls from Mauritius and Rodrigues dial 020.

Tipping

The Islands are not tip-conscious societies, although any tip for good service is always appreciated. In Mauritius tipping is not necessary if the 15 percent TVA tax has already been added to bills, but ask if unsure. Airport porters do not expect a tip but it's not a bad idea to give them at least R20 to steer you through the airport and into a taxi; hotel porters are happy with R20; taxi drivers do not expect tips.

Toilets

Toilets are free and are generally clean and well maintained. Those in supermarkets and shopping malls are normally attended and you are not expected to tip. Most public beaches have a toilet and/or shower facility but avoid those in markets, which should be reserved for dire emergencies.

Tourist information offices

Mauritius Tourism Promotion Authority offices (MTPA):
UK: Hills Balfour, 58 Southwalk Bridge Road, London SE1 0AS; tel: 020 7593 1700; email: info@hillsbalfour.com
South Africa: Meropa Communications (Pty) Limited, Building 9, Inanda Greens Office Park, 54 Wierda Road West, Wierda

⊘ Weights and measures

The metric system is used in the Mascarenes, though in Mauritius and Rodrigues you may come across road signs in miles and the occasional shop still weighing in pounds.

Valley, Sandton; tel: (27) 11 506 7305; email: alanrab@meropa.co.za

Information can also be obtained from high commissions and embassies and www.tourism-mauritius.mu.

Local tourist offices

Mauritius Tourism Promotion Authority (MTPA) Head Office: 5th floor, Victoria House, St Louis Street, Port Louis; tel: 203 1900; www.tourism-mauritius.mu

Sir Seewoosagur Ramgoolam Airport; tel: 637 3635

Rodrigues Tourist Office – Port Mathurin; tel: 832 0866; www.tourism-rodrigues.mu

U

Useful addresses

Corona, part of Corona Worldwide (tel: 0207 793 4020; www.corona-worldwide.org), based in the UK, is an invaluable organisation for anyone planning to live or work overseas. There are three branches in Mauritius and meetings are held monthly. Membership includes a monthly newsletter, talks by guest speakers and a round-up of social and sporting activities aimed mainly, but not exclusively, at women. In Mauritius visit https://coronanorth.webs.com or www.corona-plateau.org for information.

Economic Development Board Mauritius: Level 10, 1 Cathedral Square Building, 16 Jules Koenig Street, Port Louis; tel: 203 3800; www.edbmauritius.org. Useful resource for people thinking of living, working or investing in Mauritius.

Mauritius Chamber of Commerce and Industry: 2nd Floor, Anglo-Mauritius House, 6, Adolphe de Plevitz Street, Port Louis; tel: 203 4830; www.mcci.org. Represents the interests of the Mauritian business community and produces economic indicators for investors and members.

W

Websites

http://metservice.intnet.mu – official meteorological site for Mauritius.
www.gov.mu – official government website.
https://koze.mu – useful online guide for whats on.
www.mscl.mu – MS *Mauritius Trochetia* sailing schedule from Mauritius to Rodrigues and Réunion.
www.pawsmauritius.org – animal welfare charity set up to reduce stray dog population.

Weddings

Planning your wedding: There are a number of specialised tour operators (see page 348) who can arrange everything for you, but they should be approached at least six months before your wedding date. Places get booked up well in advance and there's a certain amount of paperwork to deal with. UK residents can find ideas and offers through the wedding specialist Marry Abroad (www.marryabroad.co.uk).

When shopping around for a tour operator, ask if there are any special deals. Discounts or extras range from complimentary champagne, dinners and spa treatments to a room upgrade or even the wedding package thrown in for free.

Things you will need: Photocopies of the following documents must be sent to your destination around 10 weeks before the big day (and remember to take the originals with you): birth certificates; passports; if divorced, the relevant divorce papers; in the case of a widow/widower, a death certificate and any previous marriage certificates; proof of any change of name by deed poll, if relevant (this must be stamped and signed by a solicitor or relevant official, according to your country); if either the bride or groom is adopted, an adoption certificate. Always check the latest requirements before booking your wedding.

For a religious wedding, christening certificates and a certificate of 'good morality' from respective parish priests may be required. Church weddings may have to be backed up by a civil ceremony to be recognised by the law of the country in which you reside.
When to travel: In Mauritius, couples must be on the island three days before a civil wedding and 15 days before a religious wedding. (Always check the latest requirements well in advance of your wedding.)

On arrival: Once at your hotel, you will meet with the wedding co-ordinator to decide on final details such as flowers and any extras. Then you will visit the local Civil Status Office to check you have the correct documents, and the Supreme Court where certificates are issued. In Mauritius you must visit the Civil Office that oversees the district your hotel is in. Reputable hotels will arrange taxis for these trips.

Going it alone

If you want to arrange your wedding abroad independently, contact:
Mauritius: Registrar of Civil Status, 7th Level, Emmanuel Anquetil Building, Sir S. Ramgoolam Street, Port Louis, Mauritius; tel: 230 201 1727; http://csd.pmo.govmu.org

What to Bring

To protect yourself from the sun and rain, bring a hat, sunglasses, suncream and a light mac. Bring insect repellent if you have a preferred brand. Sturdy shoes are needed if you plan to do any walking in the countryside, and a multipurpose sarong is useful for when you need to cover up in temples or in town.

Women travellers

To find a woman travelling alone in these islands is unusual since most visitors are couples or families. At most you'll be regarded as strange when you explain why you're not with a friend, relation or husband but you're unlikely to be harassed, except perhaps by youths in questionable nightspots in Mauritius' Grand Baie area; elsewhere, opportunistic groping, unwanted attention or blatant propositioning is rare.

If you find yourself in an awkward situation, deal with it immediately in a positive way. Don't get involved in inane chatter, avoid eye contact – being polite but firm usually works. It's not a good idea to fend off advances with a few choice Kreol expletives as this tends to encourage more attention.

In Mauritius and Rodrigues it's not the done thing to sunbathe topless on any beach.

MAURITIUS – LANGUAGE

Over a dozen languages are spoken by the various ethnic groups living in Mauritius, Réunion and Seychelles but Kreol is spoken by most of the islanders (see feature Lingua Franca on page 23). This colourful language, which has evolved from French to have its own grammar and a vocabulary enriched by several languages, is so popular that it is threatening to render obsolete other widely spoken tongues such as Bhojpuri and Hakka, the ancestral languages of north Indians, and most of the Chinese.

Other minority languages you may hear on the streets of Mauritius include Marathi, Tamil (Madras), Telegu and Hindi. A small number of Muslims speak Gujerati.

In Mauritius, which was a British colony until 1968, French dominates at the expense of English. Newspapers, shop signs and street names are mostly in French. English-speaking films are also dubbed in French. Government forms and road signs, however, are in English. People in tourism and commerce speak English out of necessity but the standard is variable.

Unlike Seychelles, which has elevated Kreol to the status of an official language used in schools and the media, in Mauritius it has been merely a means of verbal communication and until recently has been undervalued. But times are changing, with the first Kreol–French dictionary published in 2009, and Kreol introduced as an optional language in schools in 2012. However, it will take time to shake off the perception of Kreol being inferior to French. The grammar of Mauritian Kreol was traditionally never taught in schools and until recently there has been no universally accepted way of writing it, so many Mauritians assumed that Kreol had no rules. In fact, it is a sophisticated language, with its own tenses and grammatical forms and a simplified pronunciation of French terms that gives Kreol a unique means of making double-entendres. This is exploited to the full in sega lyrics and in island humour.

In Seychelles, English is widely spoken, especially in hotels, shops and offices. Many Seychellois speaking to each other drift effortlessly between English and Kreol, often within the same sentence. A few words of Kreol are useful away from tourist sites and Victoria, particularly when talking to older Seychellois.

PRONUNCIATION TIPS

Do not try to imitate a French accent. Indeed, the best approach is not to try speaking with an accent. Do not worry too much about the frills of the French language, such as tenses, declining verbs and the gender of objects, as they have no place in Kreol. If you run into difficulty do not worry about using English for most nouns, as these are likely to be well understood.

Common features of Indian Ocean Kreol include the use of the word *ban* as a marker of plurality: thus *ban zenfants* means children and *ban zil* is islands. The word *zot* means you in the plural form.

COMMON WORDS AND PHRASES

Airport *Erport*
Bank *Labank*
Bed *Lili*
Breakfast *Ti dezennen*
Bus stop *Bestop*
Excuse me *Eskiz*
Good morning *Bonzour*
Good afternoon/evening *Bonswar*
Goodbye *Orevwar*
Key *Lakle*
Later *Plitar*
Meal *Manze*
No *Non*
Now *Konmela*
Please *Silvouple*
Room *Lasanm*
Swimming pool *Pisin*
Thank you *Mersi*
Today *Ozordi*
Tomorrow *Demen*
Towel *Servyet*
Yes *Wi*
Yesterday *Yer*
Do you speak English? *Ou kapab koz angle?*
How are you? *Konman sava?*
I'm fine, thank you *Mon byen mersi*
I'm staying at a hotel *Mon reste lotel.*
I don't know *Mon pa konnen.*
I don't understand *Mon pa konpran.*
Please speak more slowly *Koze pli lantman silvouple.*
Where can I get a taxi? *Kote mon kapab ganny en taksi?*

⊙ Kreol Institute

The Seychellois take their Kreol seriously and have set up an institute devoted to the preservation of the language and the promotion of Creole culture. The Kreol Institute (Lenstiti Kreol), near the Craft Village at Anse aux Pins on Mahé, has just over 20 staff members who run several departments, namely literature, research, promotion, graphics, documentation, and education and training.

The premises are used for Creole functions throughout the year, from plays and poetry workshops to masked balls and karaoke nights. The institute is also the central venue for the Creole Festival, held every year in October.

EMERGENCIES

Call an ambulance *Apel lanbilans*
Call the police *Apel lapolis!*
Fire! *Dife!*
Help! *Sekour!*
I am not well *Mon pa byen*
They've had an accident *Zot in ganny en aksidan*
We need a doctor *Nou bezwen en dokter*
Where can I find a telephone? *Kote mon pou ganny en telefonn?*
Where is the nearest clinic? *Kote klinik pli pre silvouple?*

SHOPPING

chemist *farmasi*
Do you accept credit cards? *Eski ou pran kart kredi?*
Have you got...? *Eski ou annan...?*
How much is it? *Konbyen sa?*
I'm just looking *Mon pe rode selman.*
I'll take this one *Mon pran sa enn.*
It is too expensive *I tro ser.*
market *bazar*
money *larzan*
newspaper *gazet*
post office *lapos*
shop *laboutik*
Where can I find a bank? *Kote labank?*

SIGHTSEEING

church *legliz*
closed *fermen*
garden *zarden*
lake *lak*
mountain *montanny*
open *ouver*
river *larivyer*
town *lavil*
village *vilaz*
waterfall *kaskad*

AT THE RESTAURANT

bill *kont*
dinner *dinen*
fork *forset*
glass *ver*
knife *kouto*
lunch *dezenen*
menu *meni*
plate *lasyet*
spoon *kwiyer*

What to order

bef **beef**
labyer **beer**
dipen **bread**
diber **butter**
gato **cake**
fromaz **cheese**
poul **chicken**
lasos piman **chilli sauce**
kafe **coffee**
kari/cari/carri **curry**
deser **dessert**
kannar **duck**
dizef **eggs**
pwason **fish**
zifri **fruit juice**
ayskrim **ice cream**
dile **milk**
delo mineral **mineral water**
fri delapasyon **passion fruit juice**
dipwav **pepper**
lavyann koson **pork**
diri **rice**
disel **salt**
delo gaze **sparkling water**
stek **steak**
disik **sugar**
dite **tea**
diven **wine**

Fruit and vegetables

brenzel **aubergine/eggplant**
zavoka **avocado**
bannann **banana**
friyapen **breadfruit**
kokonm **cucumber**
fri **fruit**
lay **garlic**
mang **mango**
zananann **pineapple**
ponmdeter **potatoes**
tomat **tomatoes**
legim **vegetables**

Fish and seafood

palourd **clams**
vieille rouge **grouper**
oumar **lobster**
zourit **octopus**
cateaux **parrot fish**
kanmaron **prawn/shrimp**
bourgeois/bourzwa **red snapper**
ton **tuna**
karang/carangue **trevally**
cordonnier **surgeon fish**

Local specialities

Mauritius

bol renversée **spicy meat and rice**
bouyon bred **clear soup made of edible leaves**
brèdes **spinach-like vegetable**
carri de poulet aux grains **chicken curry with red beans and wheat**

Numbers

0	*zero*
1	*enn*
2	*de*
3	*trwa*
4	*kat*
5	*senk*
6	*sis*
7	*set*
8	*wit*
9	*nef*
10	*dis*
11	*onz*
12	*douz*
13	*trez*
14	*katorz*
15	*kenz*
16	*sez*
17	*diset*
18	*diswit*
19	*disnef*
20	*ven*
30	*trant*
35	*transenk*
40	*karant*
50	*senkant*
60	*swasant*
70	*swasandis*
80	*katreven*
90	*katrevendis*
100	*san*
1,000	*mil*

cochon marron **wild boar**
dite lavani **vanilla tea**
espadron fime **smoked sailfish**
fooyang **Chinese omelette**
gateaux piments **fried lentil and chilli balls**
gros pois **fat butter beans**
kari koko **curry with coconut milk**
meefoon **fine noodles**
mine frit **fried noodles**
pain frit **fried bread with sugar**
rougaille **Mediterranean-style meat or fish stew**

Réunion

achards **vegetable pickles**
bonbon piment **chilli cake**
cari de bichiques **young alevin fish curry**
cabri au massalé **kid goat masala**
gratin chouchou **christophene bake**
manioc frit **fried manioc**
tarte bredes chouchou **vegetable pie**
rougailles **spicy chutney**

Seychelles

kari koko zourit **mild octopus curry**
ladob **creamy banana and sweet potato dessert**
tectec **tiny white shellfish**

MAURITIUS – FURTHER READING

amazing dive sites in Mauritius, Rodrigues and the Seychelles.

Voyages and Adventures by François Leguat. Written by Rodrigues' first settler and acknowledged as Rodrigues' first guidebook, this book is a must for anyone going there. Ask your public library to order it for you.

MASCARENE ISLANDS

The Age of Kali: Indian Travels and Encounters by William Dalrymple. Contains an interesting chapter on Réunion and Creole beliefs in black magic.

Bourbon Journal by Walter Besant. Short and amusing diary of a British schoolteacher who holidayed in Réunion and climbed Piton de Neiges.

Culture Shock! Mauritius: A survival Guide to Customs and Etiquette by Roseline NgCheong-Lum. Cultural insights into Mauritius – good reading for anyone intending to work or stay long term.

The Dive Sites of Mauritius by Alan Mountain. A well-illustrated comprehensive guide to diving and snorkelling in Mauritius.

Dodo – the Bird behind the Legend by Alan Grihault. The most comprehensive and up-to-date examination of Mauritius' fated bird. Grihault is also the author of *Solitaire: the Dodo of Rodrigues Island*, the only book on the subject.

Golden Bats & Pink Pigeons by Gerald Durrell. A hilarious account of Durrell's travels to Mauritius and Rodrigues in search of specimens for his Jersey Zoo.

History of the Indian Ocean by August Toussaint. A general background

history of countries in and around the Indian Ocean, with a good reference to pirates, the Anglo–French conflict and British supremacy of the Mascarenes and Seychelles.

The Island of Rodrigues by Alfred North-Coombes. A most readable history and background to Rodrigues by the Mauritian-born author whose interest goes back to 1937, when he was posted there as a civil servant.

Islands in a Forgotten Sea by T.V. Bulpin. One of the finest books you'll come across for an overview of pirates and corsairs in the western Indian Ocean, including the history and development of the Mascarenes and Seychelles to the 1960s.

The Mauritian Shekel by Genevieve Pitot. The full story of Jewish detainees in Mauritius, 1940–45.

Six months in Réunion by P. Beaton. Life in Réunion as seen by a British clergyman.

Studies of Mascarene Island Birds edited by A.W. Diamond. Academic study of the dodo, solitaire and other extinct birds of Mauritius and Rodrigues.

Sub Tropical Rambles in the Land of the Aphanapteryx by Nicholas Pike. Highly readable and often amusing account of experiences in Mauritius by the US Consul to Mauritius.

Underwater Mauritius by Al. J. Venter. The author describes some

FICTION

The Book of Colour: A Family Memoir by Julia Blackburn. Set largely in Mauritius, this is the story of the author's meditation on the lives of her father and grandfather, which unfolds with surreal precision.

Bourbon Island 1730 by Lewis Trondheim and Olivier Appollodorus. A unique historical drama about Réunion in the form of a graphic novel.

The Mauritius Command by Patrick O'Brian. Naval adventures around Mauritius during the Napoleonic Wars.

Journey to Mauritius by Jacques-Henri Bernardin de Saint Pierre (translated by Jason Wilson). This romantic novel tells the story of the ill-fated St Géran which sank off the coast of Mauritius in August 1744.

The Prospector by J.M.G. Le Clézio (translated by Carol Marks). The Mauritian narrator, Alexis, of Nobel laureate J.M.G. Le Clézio's tale, embarks on a search for pirate gold in order to restore his family's fortunes. His quest is interrupted by World War I and service in the trenches of Ypres and the Somme.

Sens-Plastique is a surrealist collection of aphorisms and *pensées* by Malcolm de Chazal, the 20th-century Franco-Mauritian writer who extolled the natural beauty of Mauritius through poetry as well as paintings.

RÉUNION – TRANSPORT

GETTING THERE

By air

There are two airports in Réunion: **Roland Garros Airport** (tel: 0262 48 81 81; www.reunion.aeroport.fr), 10km (6 miles) from St-Denis; and **Pierrefonds** (tel: 0262 96 80 00; www.pierrefonds. aeroport.fr) on the south coast, 5km (3 miles) from St-Pierre. The national carrier is Air France (AF).

Regular daily flights operate between Mauritius and Réunion with Air Mauritius (MK) and Air Austral (UU). Based in Réunion, the latter operates direct flights from Réunion to Paris, Marseille, Mauritius and elsewhere (Johannesburg, Moroni, Mayotte, Seychelles, Chennai, Bangkok, Rodrigues (seasonal) and several destinations in Madagascar).
Air Austral: 10–18 place de Catalogne, 75014 Paris; tel: 08 25 01 30 12; www.air-austral.com

Other airlines

Corsair International: 2 Avenue Charles Lindbergh, 94636 Rungis; tel: 3917; www.corsair.fr
French Bee: a French low-cost, long-haul airline based at Paris Orly Airport; tel: 0825 205 205; www. frenchbee.com
XL Airways: a French company based in Paris; tel: 0892 692 123; www.xl.com

Airline offices in Réunion

Air Austral: 4 rue de Nice, St-Denis; 6 Boulevard Hubert Delisle, St-Pierre; and at Roland Garros airport; tel: 0825 01 30 12; www.air-austral.com
Air France: 7 Avenue de la Victoire, St-Denis; 73 rue Luc Lorion, St Pierre; tel: 0820 82 08 20; Roland Garros Airport (only open three hours before Air France flights depart) tel: 0262 40 38 38; www.air france.re

Air Madagascar: 31 rue Jules Auber, St-Denis, and at Roland Garros and Pierrefonds airports (depending on flight schedules); tel: 01 40 06 01 01; www.airmadagascar.com
Air Mauritius: 13 rue Charles Gounod, St-Denis; tel: 0262 94 83 83; Roland Garros Airport; tel: 0262 48 80 18; Pierrefonds Airport; tel: 0262 96 80 18; www.airmauritius.com
Corsairfly: 2 rue Maréchal Leclerc, St-Denis; 1 rue Désiré Barquisseau, St-Pierre; Roland Garros Airport; tel: 3917; www.corsair.fr
French Bee: travel shop at Roland Garros Airport; tel: 0825 205 205; re.frenchbee.com
XL Airways: has an office at the airport that opens for flights

From the airport

You can hire a car or take a taxi from the airport; expect to pay at least €25 plus €4.20 or more if travelling after 8pm or on public holidays. Cheaper at €5 is the *car jaune* (yellow bus) to St-Denis, with regular departures 6am–8.30pm.

By sea

The Mauritius Shipping Corporation (MSCL; www.mauritiusshipping.net) has operated passenger sailings

Road over volcanic lava in Sainte-Rose de La Réunion.

between Mauritius and Réunion, although at the time of writing these had temporarily stopped. If services resume, ships normally depart one island late afternoon and arrive at the other the next morning. See the website for more details, but unless you have a particular aversion to flying you're probably better off taking the plane.

GETTING AROUND

By car

Whether travelling by hire car or public bus, getting around Réunion is easy thanks to an excellent, well-signposted road system. Driving is on the right, as in France. The speed limit on dual carriageways is 110kmh (68mph), dropping to 50kmh (30mph) in towns and built-up areas. Avoid driving during the rush hours, particularly on the main roads, which can become a four-lane traffic jam; the winding roads in the Cirques can be quite busy during the peak holiday season.
Hazards: Pedestrians also use the roads, even the four-lane *routes nationales*, and it is not practical to drive fast on the winding mountain roads, so it is always advisable to respect speed limits. However, some locals tend to treat all roads as racetracks and also jump the traffic lights, so do beware! Look out for scooterists and cyclists at night riding without lights or helmet.
Road conditions: The main coastal route is well-maintained, but the surfaces of the high roads are not so good and they are often narrow and winding – the road to Cilaos has 400 bends.

After heavy rain the four lanes of the coast road between St-Denis and La Possession are reduced to two to avoid the risk of rock falls, although

⊘ Driving times

Depending on the time of day at which you are travelling and the weather conditions, here is an estimate of how long it will take you to drive between different parts of the island:
St-Denis–west coast:
40–80km/25–50 miles: 40–65 mins
St-Denis–Hell-Bourg: 55km/34 miles: 1 hour 10 mins
St-Denis–volcano: 150km/93 miles: 2 hours 15 mins
St-Denis–Cilaos (centre): 113km/70 miles: 2 hours
St-Gilles–Hell-Bourg: 100km/62 miles: 1.5–2 hours
St-Gilles–volcano: 100km/62 miles: 2 hours
St-Gilles–Cilaos (centre): 75km/47 miles: 1.5 hours
Hell-Bourg–west coast: 90–107km/58–68 miles: 1.5 hours
Hell-Bourg–volcano: 135km/84 miles: 2–2.5 hours
St-Pierre–Hell-Bourg: 96km/62 miles: 2 hours
St-Pierre–west coast: 40–54km/25–34 miles: 30–45 mins
To Roland Garros Airport from:
St-Denis: 14km/9 miles: 20 minutes
St-Gilles: 51km/32 miles: 45 minutes
Hell-Bourg: 41km/26 miles: 1 hour
St-Pierre: 91km/57 miles: 1.5 hours

this situation will be alleviated once the new coast road is opened.

Car hire

Most companies ask that you come equipped with a full driving licence from your home country as well as a credit card or cash deposit, and in some cases they will insist on full payment in advance. If your driving licence is not in French some hire companies may request it be accompanied by a certified translation or an international driving licence. Hirers should be at least 21 years old. For reliability, it's best to choose a company belonging to the French National Car Syndicate (CNPA). The companies below all have desks at the airport, but there are others that offer seasonal special deals.

Car hire companies

Ada: tel: 0262 21 59 01; email: info@ada-reunion.com; www.ada-reunion.com
Au Bas Prix (Car Go!): tel: 0262 48 81 89; email: aubasprix@wanadoo.fr; www.aubasprix.re
Avis: tel: 0262 31 20 00; email: contact@avisreunion.com; www.avisreunion.com
Budget: tel: 0262 28 92 00; email: contact@budget-reunion.com; www.budget-reunion.com
Entreprise-Citer: tel: 0262 48 83 77; email: citer.gillot@foucque.fr; www.enterprise-reunion.re
Europcar: tel: 0262 28 27 58; email: europcar-reunion@europcar-reunion.com; www.europcar-reunion.com
Hertz: tel: 0825 951 974; email: reservationshertz.remirex@gbh.fr; www.hertzreunion.com
ITC Tropicar: tel: 0262 240 101; email: contact@itctropicar.re; www.itctropicar.re
Jumbo Car/Dacia Easy Rent: tel: 0262 29 79 79; email: resa.runcar@gbh.fr; www.jumbocar-reunion.com or www.daciaeasyrent.com
MultiAuto: tel: 0262 48 83 82; email: aeroport.reunion@multiauto.fr; www.multiauto.re
RentACar: tel: 0825 959 974; www.rentacar-reunion.fr (no office at the airport, but has a free shuttle to and from).
Sixt: tel: 0262 47 44 74; email: reservation@sixt.re; www.sixt.re

By bus

Réunion's buses are a comfortable and cost effective means of travel. As there are no stop bells, be prepared to clap your hands to alert the driver when you want to get off or just shout *devant* (ahead). There are 16 lines or routes which interconnect with towns. Buses start running at around 5am with last departures being between 7pm and 8pm. For schedules and information visit www.cg974.fr/index.php/Horaires-des-Cars-jaunes.html; for bus timetables see www.carjaune.re or call 0262 81 82 83.

By taxi

Taxis in Réunion are an expensive alternative to buses and cars. The fare between St-Denis and Boucan-Canot (40km/25 miles), for example, can cost around €70. However, if you're a woman travelling alone after dark they are probably the safest way of getting around. Cheaper deals can be had if

you negotiate a fare for a whole day's hire and split the cost between several passengers. Tipping is not compulsory. Taxis can be hired either at taxi ranks in main towns, by telephone or through your hotel. Uber does not exist in Réunion.

Sightseeing tours

A range of sightseeing tours is available through the following travel agents based on the island:
21eme Parallèle: 11 avenue de la Grande Ourse, St-Gilles-Les-Bains, tel: 0262 22 72 27; email: info@21parallele.fr; www.21parallele.fr
Bourbon Tourisme: 14 rue Rontaunay, St-Denis; tel: 0262 33 08 70; email: contact@bourbontourisme.com; www.bourbonvoyages.fr
Connections: 53 Route de Domenjod, Ste Clotilde; tel: 0262 93 13 98; email: resa@connections-reunion.com; www.connections-reunion.com
Horizon Réunion: 93 allée de la Source, St-Pierre; tel: 0262 02 40 00; email: contact@horizon-reunion.com; www.horizon-reunion.com
Mille Tours: 9bis rue Sarda Garriga, St-Paul; tel: 0262 22 55 00; www.milletours.com
Nouvelles Frontières: Residence Claire 1, 31 Place Paul Julius Benard, St-Gilles-les-Bains; tel: 0262 33 11 99; email: receptive.run@nouvelles-frontieres.fr
Papangue Tours: Résidence La Tonnelle, 17 route de la Rivière des Pluies, Ste-Clotilde; tel: 0262 41 61 92; email: contact@papanguetours.com; www.papanguetours.com
Sentiers et Découvertes: 310 chemin Boissy, St-Pierre; tel: 0692 63 60 80; email: contact@sentiersetdecouvertes.com; www.sentiersetdecouvertes.com
Wel'come vacances: 2 boulevard Bonnier, St-Leu; tel: 0262 34 74 85; www.welcome-vacances.com

⊘ Helicopter tours

A wonderful way to see the grandeur of the island's volcanic landscape is to go on a helicopter trip (see page 217).
Helilagon: Gillot Airport or Eperon, St-Paul Base; tel: 0262 55 55 55; www.helilagon.com
Corail Helicopters: St-Gilles Base or Pierrefonds Airport; tel: 0262 22 22 66; www.corail-helicopteres.com

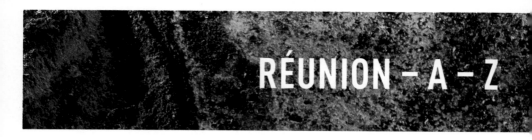

RÉUNION – A – Z

Accommodation

Whether you're looking for luxury or simplicity, Réunion has accommodation to suit a wide range of tastes, needs and budgets.

Choosing a hotel

All of Réunion's 80 classified hotels meet French standards, and are clean, comfortable and well run. There are few large internationally owned chain hotels, and only two five-star hotels. Book in advance as hotels fill quickly during the high season, and expect price hikes over the Christmas and New Year period. The largest choice of accommodation is on the island's west coast, in the St-Gilles area. If you are coming from Mauritius, don't expect the same kind of quality or service, although the staff are still professional and helpful.

Camping

There are municipal campsites at Etang-Salé (tel: 0262 91 75 86; www.camping-reunion.com) and St-Gilles (tel: 0262 96 36 70; campingermitage.re), otherwise book a place at one that's privately run (see www.reunion.fr for more details). You can also camp in the wild provided you have permission from the landowner.

Self-catering

See www.reunion.fr or contact a tourist office for details of self-catering accommodation, furnished flats, *gîtes ruraux* (rural *gîtes*), bed and breakfast in *chambres d'hôtes* and farm guesthouses *(ferme auberges)*.

Youth hostels

There's an **Auberge de Jeunesse** at Bernica, Rue de l'Auberge,
St-Gilles-les-Hauts (tel: 0262 22 89 75; mobile: 0692 59 34 11).

Family holiday villages (VVF)

There are two VVFs *(Villages Vacances Famille)* in Réunion geared to families or groups, who can choose from an inexpensive range of studio, bungalow or dormitory-style accommodation. A group joining fee of around €16 is payable before bookings can be made at the following:

St-Gilles-les-Bains
VVF St-Gilles 'Le Village de Corail', 80 Avenue de Bourbon; tel: 0262 24 29 29

Cilaos
VVF 'Le Village des Sources', Chemin Fleurs Jaunes; tel: 0262 31 71 39

In the mountains

On a hike that lasts for more than a day you can plan your overnight stays in an assortment of lodgings en route, from the very basic to the more comfortable. For information and reservations, contact local tourist offices or see www.reunion.fr.

Gîte d'étape: basic overnight *gîte* offering dormitory-style lodging and breakfast and makeshift kitchens where guests can cook up their own pot noodles.

Gîte de montagne: dormitory bunk-bed accommodation in an isolated location, sometimes without a shower or hot water and in dry periods no water at all. Basic self-catering facilities, although meals can be provided if booked.

Refuge: private, basic lodging with an evening meal and sometimes breakfast provided by the owner.

Chambre d'hôte: bed and breakfast in someone's home. Evening meals can also be provided as a *table d'hôte* (see page 374).

Gîte rural: self-catering cottage located in the countryside. They are normally well equipped and probably the best option for families or groups.

Admission charges

Admission charges for tourist attractions and most museums, whether private or government-owned, vary between €2 and €9 per person, with reductions for children under 16, students, disabled people and senior citizens. Entry to discos and nightclubs is normally free but expect to pay high charges for drinks.

Budgeting for your trip

Allow at least €40 per day per person to cover meals and snacks, soft drinks and entrance fees. It's always a good idea to keep some spare euros handy and carry your credit card with you as you may not find ATMs in more out of the way places.

Tips on how to save money

The cost of living is appreciably higher than in France so don't expect to find many bargains to take home. Eating in the most ordinary of restaurants can take a chunk out of your budget but many areas have small cafés, and mobile food wagons sell cheap, filling fast food.

Taxis are expensive so look for a deal on car hire or buy a *carnet* of six bus tickets for €6 if you intend to do a lot of travelling by bus.

See www.reunion.fr for a comprehensive list of good-value accommodation.

CLIMATE CHART

St Denis

- Maximum temperature
- Minimum temperature
— Rainfall

C

Children

Children are welcome everywhere. Many hotels cater specially for youngsters and offer supervised activities, special meals, babysitting services, family rooms and child discounts on excursions.

If you are travelling with very young children avoid Dec–Jan, which may be too hot.

Supermarkets stock European baby food and nappies.

Climate

Like Mauritius and Rodrigues, Réunion has two seasons: the hot rainy summer season from December to April and the cool dry winter season between May and November. On the coast daytime temperatures are similar to Mauritius, averaging around 23°C (73°F) in winter and 30°C (85°F) in summer, but on the high plains and mountains variations between 4°C (39°F) and 25°C (77°F), depending on altitude and season, are normal. At heights approaching 2,500 metres (8,200ft) temperatures can drop to below freezing at night during the cool season.

Cyclones in the Indian Ocean usually occur between December and April. On average between 10 and 12 cyclones develop in the southwestern Indian Ocean a year, causing devastation if they happen to pass over land. Réunion, which holds most of the world's rainfall records, tends to suffer more than Mauritius as the many rivers flood,

☉ Pint of 'dodo'

The name of the local beer is Bourbon, which has an emblem of the dodo, hence a bottle of beer is referred to as *une dodo*. For draught beer, ask for *une pression*. Wine is popular and as well as being produced in Cilaos, it is also imported from France. But rum in an assortment of concoctions is a speciality of Réunion – as *rhum arrangé*, rum flavoured with spices and fruit, or *punch créole*, rum blended with fruit, cane syrup and juice.

washing away anything in their path.

Crime and safety

In general, the Réunionnais are willing to help anyone in distress. However, as with everywhere, you should take the same basic precautions that you would at home. Don't flaunt expensive jewellery and money in public places; never leave property on view in your car; always be aware of your personal safety;

Even in this tropical climate, temperatures drop the higher you go.

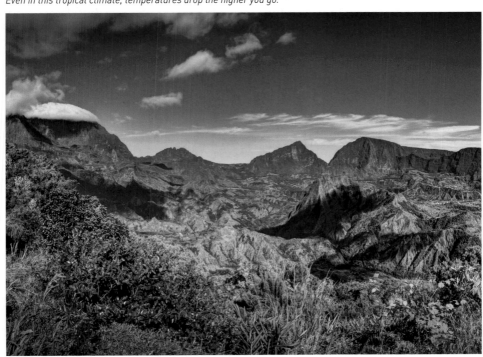

lock doors and windows when you go out, particularly in self-catering accommodation; and after dark don't give a lift to a stranger or go out walking alone.

If you become a victim of crime, try to remain calm, take stock of the situation and get names and addresses of witnesses. Report the matter to the police and in cases of theft ensure you have all the documentation for insurance purposes. However, English is not spoken by all police officers, so if you have a problem ask staff at your hotel or your holiday representative to find an interpreter for you.

D

Disabled travellers

Facilities for travellers with disabilities are on a par with mainland France. Roland Garros Airport has facilities for disabled travellers, including walkways, lifts and escalators, and offers assistance on request. Many hotels, especially the larger ones, also have specially equipped rooms but always check with your travel agent or direct with the hotel before making a booking.

E

Eating out

Where to eat

Réunion boasts a rich culinary tradition inspired by the various ethnic groups that make up its population, and the range of eating places is just as varied. Some of the island's best restaurants form part of the *Saveurs et Senteurs de la Réunion* (Flavours and Fragrances) group, which is affiliated to the Guild of French Provinces Restaurateurs. Some bear the label(s) *Restaurateur de France*, *Restaurant de Tourisme* or *Qualité Tourisme Île de La Réunion*. Such restaurants may be attached to hotels and mainly feature French cuisine and local Creole specialities, such as *carri* (curry), *chou chou* (christophine), *brèdes* (spinach-like leafy greens), and pork, chicken and seafood dishes. If locals eat out at a restaurant it

tends to be Creole, Chinese or Italian cuisine. There are some 'exotic' places to eat (Thai or Japanese), but they are generally concentrated in the larger towns.

Most restaurants keep to standard lunch times from noon to 2.30pm and offer a fixed-price *menu du jour* as well as à la carte options. Buying a meal in restaurants outside these times is virtually impossible and you will have to wait until the evening. Réunionnais tend to eat out from about 7.30pm onwards, and most restaurants will not accept orders after 10pm. Bear in mind that many restaurants are closed on Sundays and/ or Mondays (see page 172 for more about Réunion's cuisine). For cheaper fare don't overlook the many brasseries, bistros, crêperies, bars, cafés, food stalls and markets for mouth-watering morsels of freshly cooked snacks such as *samoussas* and *bouchons* (small Chinese-style meatballs served with soy sauce). An inexpensive option, found all over the island, is a *camion bar* (food truck) serving a variety of pre- or freshly made baguette sandwiches or *carris*. Hygiene standards for street food are normally reliable.

Country cooking

Many of the island's farmers and country dwellers offer lunches at good value for hungry visitors to their homes. Typically the food

is traditional Creole (so if you're vegetarian or looking for something daring head elsewhere) and in some establishments it is eaten with the hosts. Main courses, rather than being served individually on a plate, will be dished up on a single platter, making it a very convivial affair. Contact the local tourist office or visit www.reunion. fr for more details. It's advisable to book in advance, especially for Sunday lunch.

Table d'hôte: traditional Creole meals are served at the large family table of the host, seating up to 20 people. Popular with locals on Sundays. Many are also *chambre d'hôtes*.

Fermes auberges: farmhouse-inns where a traditional Creole meal is cooked with local produce. See www.bienvenue-a-la-ferme.com for a list of the island's *fermes auberges*.

⊘ Cyclone warnings

In Réunion, there are three levels of cyclone warning:
Vigilance cyclonique (cyclone watch): an early warning system advising people to stock up on basic goods (food, candles, bottled water, batteries) and to listen to broadcasts on TV and radio.
Alerte orange (orange alert): cyclone approaching within the next 24 hours. Schools close but some businesses remain open and everyone is advised to bring moveable objects and animals indoors and to batten down windows and doors.
Alerte rouge (red alert): imminent danger, given with three hours warning. Driving is banned and everyone must stay indoors or face a fine. You are strongly advised to listen to the radio or follow the situation online if you have electricity.

Once the red alert is over, find out about the state of the roads before setting off anywhere (tel: 0262 97 27 27 – in French only). Do not touch fallen electric cables, do not drink tap water unless you have boiled it for at least 5 minutes, and do not go into the mountains or cross fords or submerged roads.
Cyclone information: tel: 08 97 65 01 01. General weather information for the following 24 hours and hourly updates are available in French on 08 92 68 08 08 or on the website: www. meteofrance.re.

⊘ Emergency numbers

Ambulance: tel: 15
Police: tel: 17
Fire: tel: 18
Emergency services: 112 (from a mobile phone even if not connected to the GSM network).

In less urgent cases of difficulty, English-speaking visitors could go to the Air Mauritius office in St-Denis at 13 rue Gounod; tel: 0262 94 83 83.

Auberge de campagne: a country inn at which the farmer can cater for up to 80 people with traditionally cooked home-grown produce.

Self-catering

If you're renting a bungalow or trekking from *gîte* to *gîte* you might want to try self-catering. For breakfast head to a *boulangerie* where you'll find coffee, fruit juice and pastries. The cheapest places for groceries and drinks are supermarkets, but fruit and vegetables are generally better value at a market. Depending on the season and which part of the island you're in, you'll also see stalls by the side of the road selling mangoes and lychees (December–January), goyaviers (strawberry guavas; May–July), bananas, passion fruit and pineapples (all year round).

Hot drinks

Unless otherwise requested, coffee and tea will always be served black. Specify *au lait* if you would like milk.

Electricity

220V, but standard European round two-pin plugs are used – so visitors from the UK and outside Europe should take an adaptor.

Embassies and consulates

As Réunion isn't an independent country, only a few countries have diplomatic representation. There are Chinese, Indian and Malagasy consulates; countries such as Germany, Belgium, Italy, Norway and Switzerland have Honorary Consuls. The nearest consulates for other countries are in Mauritius. For the addresses of the UK, US, Canadian and South African representatives there, see page 354.

Entry requirements

French and European Union (EU) nationals must be in possession of a valid identity card or passport. Others need a valid passport and a return or onward ticket and may be asked for an address in Réunion. Citizens of the US, Canada, South Africa, New Zealand, Australia, China and India do not need visas for visits of up to three months. Other nationals should check

Church in Cayenne on Réunion.

with the French Embassy; note that Réunion is not part of the Schengen Area so a visa that is valid for France will not necessarily work for Réunion. Always check the latest entry requirements before you travel.

Applications for visa extensions can be made at the Service de l'État Civil et des Étrangers at La Préfecture, St-Denis; tel: 0262 40 75 42.

For **customs allowances** see page 353. The Customs Department (Direction Régionale des Douanes et Droits Directs) is at 7 Avenue de la Victoire, St-Denis (tel: 0262 90 81 00; www.douane.gouv. fr).

Etiquette

Réunion retains much of its Gallic tradition with a great emphasis on politeness, and were it not for the Réunion Creole language and the ethnic mix of the Creole people you might at times feel that you were

actually in mainland France. With the majority of tourists coming from France, the Réunionnais are perfectly aware of Western norms and you'll find that most subjects, including sex, race, religion and politics, can be discussed without causing offence.

Few people speak English so it really helps to learn some French to get by. Having said that, most Réunionnais are warm, helpful and friendly and often go that one step further to get visitors out of trouble. It's a good idea to greet people with a formal *bonjour*, and *merci* is always appreciated.

H

Health and medical care

Medical services in Réunion are excellent and with nearly 2,500 doctors, 247 pharmacies and an efficient emergency service you will find yourself in good hands should you happen to fall ill. The cost of treatment is on a par with mainland France. There is no need for vaccinations (unless you are coming from an infected area) and malaria has been eradicated from the island since 1948 (for information on the chikungunya virus see A–Z – Mauritius, see page 354). Always check the latest medical advice before you travel.

Make sure you are adequately insured before you leave home and in the event of a medical claim keep all receipts and documentation. EU visitors should bring their European Health Insurance Card (EHIC).

Drinking tap water is fine but you can also order bottled water, especially advisable if there's just been a period of heavy rain.

There are no dangerous animals in Réunion on land; in the lagoon watch you don't step on a sea urchin or stonefish.

There can be strong currents and sharks frequent the waters around the coast so only swim where there is a lifeguard, and never if there is a shark flag or warning sign on display. Be aware that Réunion has the highest per capita rate of shark attacks in the world. Avoid

☉ Public holidays

Most shops and businesses are closed on *jours fériés* (public holidays) which are the same as in France except for the extra day in December celebrating the abolition of slavery.
1 January New Year's Day *(Jour de l'An)*
March/April Easter Monday *(Pâques)*
1 May Labour Day *(Fête du Travail)*
8 May Victory Day *(Victoire 1945)*
Ascension Day *(Ascension)*
May Whit Monday *(Pentecôte)*
14 July Bastille Day *(Fête Nationale)*
15 August Assumption *(Assomption)*
1 November All Saints' Day *(Toussaint)*
11 November Armistice Day
20 December Abolition of Slavery Day *(Abolition de* l'Esclavage or Fèt Kaf)*
25 December Christmas Day *(Noël)*

swimming in the sea at dawn, dusk and after a period of heavy rainfall.

Mosquitoes can be a pest especially at night during the summer; wear long clothes, use repellent or keep them at bay with a plug-in diffuser *(un diffuseur électrique)*, which can be bought locally.

Medical treatment

Tourists are strongly advised to take out comprehensive travel and medical insurance. Most large towns have a hospital and/or private clinic and plenty of doctors.

General hospitals

Centre Hospitalier Universitaire (CHU) Félix Guyon, Bellepierre, 97400 St-Denis; tel: 0262 90 50 50; www.chu-reunion.fr
Hôpital des Enfants (Children's Hospital) Association Saint François d'Assise, 60 Rue Bertin, 97400 St-Denis; tel: 0262 90 87 00
Hôpital Gabriel Martin, 38 Rue Labourdonnais, St-Paul; tel: 0262 45 30 30; www.chgm.re
Groupe Hospitalier Est Réunion, 30 Route Nationale 3, St-Benoît; tel: 0262 98 80 00; www.gher-reunion.fr
Hôpital Sud Réunion, Avenue Président Mitterrand, St-Pierre; tel: 0262 35 90 00

Private clinics

Clinique de Sainte Clotilde, 127 Route Bois de Nèfles, 97400 St-Denis; tel: 0262 48 20 20; www.clinifutur.net
Clinique Avicenne (ophthalmology), 4 boulevard Verdun, Le Port; tel: 0262 42 17 97; www.ophtalmoleport.re

I

Internet

Almost all accommodation has Wi-fi and/or internet access, which you may or may not have to pay for. Free Wi-fi in restaurants and shopping centres is also widespread.

L

LGBTQ travellers

Réunion is a LGBTQ-friendly destination and even has an (unofficial)

gay beach: La Souris Chaude, just south of La Saline. LGBTQ-friendly establishments often display a multicoloured rainbow motif and since 2005 the tourist office has published a helpful booklet called *Charte d'Accueil – Gay-Friendly*, with listings of accommodation, eateries and activities. The main gay-friendly bars and clubs are listed below, but you can find plenty more at https://g2f.re/accueil:
Le Prince Club
108 Rue Pasteur, St-Denis; tel: 0692 66 25 53. Popular late-night haunt, dancing and fun.
Le Zanzibar
41 Rue Pasteur, St-Denis; tel: 0262 20 01 18. Convivial bar-cum-pub popular with gay and lesbian crowd.
Coco Beach
Plage de l'Hermitage, St-Gilles-les-Bains; tel: 0262 33 81 43. Lively restaurant and bar right on the beach.

Lost property

If you have lost any property at Roland Garros Airport contact the lost property office based there (tel: 0262 48 80 19 or email: parking@reunion.aeroport.fr). Otherwise report details of property lost elsewhere to the local police station, where you will be asked to fill out a form. You should ask for a copy of the form for insurance purposes.

M

Maps

You can buy good maps covering mountain walks and road routes from bookshops and tourist offices, including the French IGN 1:100 000 map, which covers the whole island on one sheet (also available from Stanfords, 12–14 Long Acre, Covent Garden, London WC2E 9LP; tel: 020 7836 1321; www.stanfords.co.uk). For more detailed coverage you'd need one of the six 1:25 000 maps numbered 4401RT to 4406RT.

Media

Most hotels are equipped with satellite TV showing French and English programmes, although

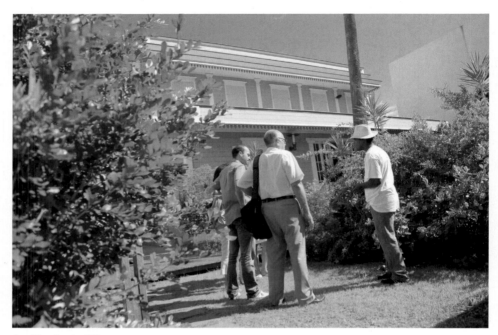

Outside a Tourist Office.

the latter is generally limited to CNN , Al Jazeera, or BBC World. French radio stations that can be listened to in Réunion include RTL, RMC, Europe 1, NRJ and Chérie FM, which broadcasts mainly British and American music. Apart from the odd newspaper or magazine you'll find very few English-language publications. The two locally produced daily papers are *Le Quotidien* (www.lequotidien.re) and *Journal de l'Île de la Réunion* (www.clicanoo.re).

Money

As with mainland France, the currency of Réunion is the euro. Visa and Mastercard credit cards are widely accepted in most hotels, shops and restaurants but it's wise to keep a surplus of euros, particularly if you're heading for the Cirques, where there are fewer ATMs and banks. You can use your credit card to withdraw cash from ATMs but memorise your PIN number before leaving home.

Few banks have exchange facilities and there are hefty charges for changing foreign currency and traveller's cheques. To save costs it may be better to buy euro traveller's cheques before leaving home.

You will need a 1 euro coin for a trolley at the airport or pick up one of the free tokens from the counter there.

Banks

Major banks are open Mon–Fri 8am–4pm. There is an ATM outside Roland Garros airport (but not Pierrefonds), which accepts major foreign credit cards, however there are no are change facilities on the island other than those found at banks.

Tax

Value Added Tax (TVA) of 8.5 percent is added to goods and services and 2.1 percent to foodstuffs and books. Duty-free goods are not available in Réunion except at the airport, and duty-free won't apply if you're flying between Réunion and mainland France. There is no hotel or restaurant tax, although service may be included in the bill.

O

Opening hours

Most shops open daily except Sunday, 9am–6pm; many close

for lunch noon–2.30pm. Shopping centres have longer opening hours, including Sunday mornings and some public holidays. Some museums also close for an hour or so at lunchtime. Places that have been open on Sunday are likely to be closed on Monday.

P

Postal services

Look for yellow La Poste signs indicating the post office where, as in France, a wide range of services is on offer. Most *tabacs* (tobacconists) also sell stamps if you want to avoid the post office queues.

All towns have a post office and poste restante service (Mon–Fri 8am–6pm, Sat 8am–noon). Most close for lunch between noon and 2pm. To send any last-minute mail There is a post box at Roland

☉ Time zone

Greenwich Mean Time + 4 hours. There is no Daylight Savings Time.

Garros Airport, and a shop where you can buy stamps.

The **main post office** in St-Denis is at the intersection between Rue Maréchal Leclerc and Rue Juliette Dodu.

R

Religious services

Réunion is 70 percent Roman Catholic, and church services are always in French. At mosques and Hindu temples the proceedings are likely to be in French and/or Kreol.

S

Shopping

You're unlikely to find the bargains in clothing that you can get in Mauritius but Réunion excels in producing original handicrafts. These items are the work of cottage industries throughout the island and end up for sale in many retail outlets. Things to look for are miniature replicas of **Creole houses** made from fragranced wood, toiletries and perfumes made from **essential oils** such as citronelle, vetyver and geranium, and *tentes* or baskets woven from pandanus leaves.

Gourmets may like to shop for a range of local **speciality foods** such as local jams, compôtes, confectionery, spices and **traditional drinks** such as rum, punch and liqueurs, and sweet wine from Cilaos. For typically Réunionnais chocolate, visit the Chocolaterie Mascarin factory for a guided tour and tasting at Le Port (tel: 0262 55 10 20; www.mascarin.fr).

Tourist offices *(Syndicats d'Initiative)* sell products from the region; look for **Gol chairs** at Etang-Salé-les-Bains, **vanilla** products at St-André and **fruity wines** and lentils at Cilaos.

For a full range of **island crafts** in St-Denis, visit the **Galerie Artisanale** at Carrefour Hypermarket, Espace Continent, Ste-Clotilde (http://lagalerieartisanale.re; near Roland Garros Airport).

No visit to Réunion would be complete without a souvenir of the volcano. There's a good range of postcards, decorative pieces of basalt, photographs and illustrated books on volcanology at the **Cité du Volcan** shop at Bourg-Murat.

Women in Cilaos have been embroidering for over a century. There is now an embroidery school in the cirque, and many skilled craftswomen embroider everything from lovely christening robes to tablecloths and napkins, all in natural white or beige. No two pieces are the same and each piece can take up to several months to produce – hence the hefty price. The best selection can be found at **Maison de la Broderie**, in Rue des Écoles, Cilaos.

Student travellers

Youth hostels, budget accommodation and a lively night scene, particularly around St-Denis and St-Pierre, will appeal to student travellers. Concessions are available at some tourist attractions on production of your student ID card. The concessions aren't always made that obvious so don't be afraid to ask. The University of La Réunion has an active student population and there is a students' portal via the university website, www.univ-reunion.fr.

T

Telecommunications

Agreements between mobile/cell phone companies overseas enable subscribers to use a mobile phone in Réunion. If coming from a European country check with your service provider before leaving home whether Réunion is included in 'European' roaming.

Réunion has three cell phone networks: SFR Réunion, Free and Orange Réunion. Cell phone numbers start with 0692 or 0693. If you intend to make a large number of local calls it may be more convenient to buy a SIM card in Réunion, although you will be asked to provide some form of identification at the time of purchase.

Numbers that start with 08 are generally premium rate services.
International Dialling Code: Dial the international code followed by the Réunion country code, 262.

Tipping

A service charge is normally added to restaurant bills. When service is not included *(service non compris)*, a 10 percent tip is perfectly acceptable. Taxi drivers do not expect to be tipped.

Toilets

Clean and well-maintained public toilets on a par with Western standards are found in St-Denis, the main tourist sites and large supermarkets. If you get caught short ask the owner of a bar or restaurant if you can use their facilities.

Tourist information offices

Tourist information for Réunion is centralised by the Comité Régional de Tourisme de la Réunion (IRT): email: contact@reunion.fr; www.reunion.fr. You can also contact the French tourist office of your home country via www.franceguide.com.

Local tourist offices

Most main towns have a tourist office that can book *gîte* accommodation and supply maps. The free tourist information publications *RUN* and *Welcome to Réunion* are published in English as well as French and are widely available.

North
OTI Nord; email: info@lebeaupays.com; www.lebeaupays.com
St-Denis:
Maison Carrère, 14 Rue de Paris, St-Denis; tel: 0262 41 83 00; Mon–Sat 9am–6pm
Ste-Suzanne:
18 Rue du Phare, Ste-Suzanne; tel: 0262 52 13 54; Mon–Thu & Sat 9am–12pm, 1.30–5pm

West
OTI Ouest; email: accueil@ouest-lareunion.com; www.ouest-lareunion.com
Le Port:
22 rue Léon Lepervanche, Le Port; tel: 0262 42 31 31; Mon 1:30–5pm, Tue–Sat 9:30am–12:30pm, 1:30–5pm
St-Gilles:
1 place Paul Julius Benard, Galerie Amandine, St-Gilles-les-Bains; tel: 0262 42 31 31; Mon–Fri 8:30am–12:30pm, 1:30–5:30pm, Sat 8am–12pm

St-Leu:
Bâtiment Espace Laleu, 1 rue Barrelier, St-Leu; tel: 0262 42 31 31; Mon–Sat 9am–noon and 1.30–5.30pm

East
OTI Est; email: info@reunionest.fr; www.reunionest.fr

St-André:
Maison Martin Valliamé, 1590 chemin du Centre, St-André; tel: 0262 46 16 16; Mon, Wed–Fri 8:30am–12.30pm, 1.30pm–4:30pm

St-Benoît:
Place de l'Église, Ste-Anne; tel: 0262 47 05 09; Tue–Sat 9am–12.30pm, 1.30–5pm

Plaine des Palmistes:
Maison du Parc National, 258 rue de la République, La Plaine des Palmistes; tel: 0262 41 17 10; Mon–Wed, Fri–Sat 8:30am–12.30pm, 1.30–5pm

Bras-Panon:
21 RN2, Bras-Panon; tel: 0262 23 98 36; daily 8.30am–noon, 1:30–5pm

Salazie:
Centre Artisanal d'Hell-Bourg, 47 rue du Général de Gaulle, Salazie; tel: 0262 47 89 89; Mon–Sat 9am–noon, 1–5pm

South
OTI Sud; tel: 0820 203 220; www.sudreuniontourisme.fr

Etang-Salé:
74 avenue Octave-Bénard, Etang-Salé; email: accueil.otetangsale@gmail.com; Mon–Sat 9am–noon, 1–4.30pm

Entre-Deux:
13 rue Fortuné-Horau, Entre-Deux; tel: 0262 39 69 80; email: ot.entre2@gmail.com; www.ot-entredeux.com; Mon–Sat 8am–noon, 1.30–5pm

St-Pierre:
Capitainerie du Port de Plaisance Lislet Geoffroy, Place Napoléon Hoareau, St-Pierre; email: saint-pierre.tourisme@gmail.com; Mon–Sat 8am–6pm, Sun 8–noon

St-Philippe:
41a rue Leconte-de-Lisle, St-Philippe; tel: 0262 97 75 84; email: otstphilippe@gmail.com; Mon–Sat 9am–5pm

St-Joseph:
Maison du Tourisme du Sud Sauvage, 15 allée du Four à Chaux, Manapany-les-Bains, St-Joseph; tel: 0262 37 37 11; email: accueil.sudsauvage@gmail.com; Mon–Fri 9.30am–noon, 1–5.30pm, Sat 10am–5pm

Tampon/Plaine des Cafres:
160 rue Maurice et Katia Kraft, RN3, La Plaine des Cafres; tel: 0262 27 40 00; email: officetourismetampon@gmail.com; www.tampontourisme.re; daily 9am–5pm

Cilaos:
2 bis rue Victor MacAuliffe, Cilaos; email: accueil.cilaos@gmail.com; Mon–Sat 8:30am–12.30pm, 1.30–5pm, Sun and public hols 9am–12pm

Tour operators

Many tour operators based throughout Europe, South Africa, Australia, Canada and the US offer package and specialist holidays, such as trekking or golfing, to Réunion. For details contact Maison de la France or your local travel agent.

The following UK-based operators specialise in Réunion:

Africa Collection: tel: 01403 256 655; email: web@africacollection.com; www.africacollection.co.uk

Black Tomato: tel: 0207 426 9888; email: enquiries@blacktomato.com; www.blacktomato.com

Rainbow Tours: tel: 0203 733 6894; email: info@rainbowtours.co.uk; www.rainbowtours.co.uk

W

Websites

www.cg974.fr – *car jaunes* bus timetables and information.

www.clicanoo.re – news and handy information put together by the daily *Journal de l'Île de la Réunion* publication online.

https://elitetourreunion.com – airport transfers, sightseeing tours and transport all over the island (with or without a driver).

www.gov.uk/foreign-travel-advice/reunion – UK Foreign Office travel advice for Réunion.

www.reunion.fr – the official Réunion Island tourism website (multilingual).

www.ipgp.fr/fr/ovpf/actualites-ovpf – webcams showing the Piton de la Fournaise volcano.

www.reunionisland.net – an online guide to Réunion in English.

www.transfert.re – private transfers to and from Roland Garros and Pierrefonds airports, and excursions.

www.travelssmart.blogspot.com – blog and practical information about Réunion, in English.

https://uk.france.fr/en/reunion-island – information in English about Réunion on the France.fr website.

What to bring

In the mountainous interior the climate is much cooler so take something warm; during the cool season the evenings can be fresh along the coast, so a light wrap, jacket or cardigan may be necessary. Réunion is quite laid-back about dress: casual wear such as loose cotton shorts, shirts, T-shirts and dresses are acceptable around town and in the evenings, but swimsuits are not. Men may need a tie for a smart occasion. In St-Gilles-les-Bains women are allowed to sunbathe topless on the beach.

For the feet, light sandals are advisable on the coast, and a pair of reef shoes will protect against injury from sharp coral. A pair of good walking boots is essential if you are planning on doing any hiking in the mountains or a pair of comfortable but sturdy shoes for short walks.

What to read

Most books written about Réunion are in French but there are several books in English that cover the Mascarenes and include Réunion (see page 362).

Women travellers

Réunion is a generally safe destination but, as in any country in the world, women should exercise caution if travelling alone, especially at night. Women are rarely hassled but if you encounter unwanted attention deal with it firmly. Avoid beachwear away from the beach, don't accept lifts from strangers and if you're travelling alone and plan to be away for the day let someone know where you are going and at what time you plan to return.

⊘ Weights and measures

The metric system is used in Réunion.

It is worth trying to master a few simple phrases in French before holidaying in Réunion. The fact that you have made an effort is likely to get you a better response. Pronunciation is the key; they really will not understand if you get it very wrong. Remember to **emphasise each syllable**, but not to pronounce the last consonant of a word as a rule (this includes the plural 's') and always to drop your 'h's. Whether to use '**vous**' or '**tu**' is a vexed question; increasingly the familiar form of 'tu' is used by many people. However, it is better to be too formal, and use 'vous' if in doubt. It is very important to be polite; always address people as **Madame** or **Monsieur**, and address them by their surnames until you are confident first names are acceptable. When entering a shop always say, 'Bonjour Monsieur/Madame,' and 'Merci, au revoir,' when leaving.

WORDS AND PHRASES

How much is it? *C'est combien?*
What is your name? *Comment vous appelez-vous?*
My name is... *Je m'appelle...*
Do you speak English? *Parlez-vous anglais?*
I am English/American *Je suis anglais/américain*

☉ The alphabet

Learning the pronunciation of the French alphabet is a good idea. In particular, learn how to spell out your name.
a = ah, **b** = bay, **c** = say, **d** = day **e** = er, **f** = ef, **g** = zhay, **h** = ash, **i** = ee, **j** = zhee, **k** = ka, **l** = el, **m** = em, **n** = en, **o** = oh, **p** = pay, **q** = kew, **r** = ehr, **s** = ess, **t** = tay, **u** = ew, **v** = vay, **w** = dooblah vay, **x** = eex, **y** = ee grek, **z** = zed

☉ Réunionese words

Below is a list of words you may come across on the island – some are Réunionese Kreol, and some are French words with a specific meaning in Réunion.
babouk large house spider
bibasse Japanese medlar fruit (loquat)
camaron large freshwater shrimp
kaz house
Cilaos if seen on a menu: a local brand of sparkling water
combava kaffir lime
faham rare endemic orchid (*jumellea fragrans*) used in *rhum arrangé*
fanjan tree fern root mass used as a natural plant pot
fénoir darkness, night
filao casuarina tree
gabier ATM
goyavier strawberry guava (*psidium cattleyanum*)
grains beans or lentils in sauce accompanying a *carri*
les hauts uplands or highlands of Réunion
ladilafé gossip
lontan in the past
marmay child(ren)
métropole mainland France
moring a combat sport similar to capoeira
péi anything that is local
safran turmeric
ti zak jackfruit (*artocarpus heterophyllus*)
zourit octopus

I don't understand *Je ne comprends pas*
Please speak more slowly *Parlez plus lentement, s'il vous plaît*
Can you help me? *Pouvez-vous m'aider?*
I'm looking for... *Je cherche*
Where is...? *Où est...?*
I'm sorry *Excusez-moi/Pardon*
I don't know *Je ne sais pas*
No problem *Pas de problème*
Have a good day! *Bonne journée!*
That's it *C'est ça*
Here it is *Voici*
There it is *Voilà*
Let's go *On y va. Allons-y*
See you tomorrow *À demain*
See you soon *À bientôt*
yes *oui*
no *non*
please *s'il vous plaît*
thank you (very much) *merci (beaucoup)*
you're welcome *de rien*
excuse me *excusez-moi*
hello *bonjour*
OK *d'accord*
goodbye *au revoir*

good evening *bonsoir*
here *ici*
there *là*
today *aujourd'hui*
yesterday *hier*
tomorrow *demain*
now *maintenant*
later *plus tard*
this morning *ce matin*
this afternoon *cet après-midi*
this evening *ce soir*

ON ARRIVAL

I want to get off at... *Je voudrais descendre à...*
Is there a bus to...? *Est-ce qu'il y a un bus...?*
How far is...? *À quelle distance se trouve...?*
airport *l'aéroport*
bus station *la gare routière*
bus *l'autobus, le car*
bus stop *l'arrêt*
ticket *le billet*
hitchhiking *l'autostop*
toilets *les toilettes*

This is the hotel address *C'est l'adresse de l'hôtel*
I'd like a (single/double) room... *Je voudrais une chambre (pour une/deux personnes)...*
...with shower *avec douche*
...with a bath *avec salle de bain*
...with a view *avec vue*
Does that include breakfast? *Le prix comprend-il le petit-déjeuner?*
May I see the room? *Je peux voir la chambre?*
washbasin *le lavabo*
bed *le lit*
key *la clé*
lift/elevator *l'ascenseur*
air conditioned *climatisé*

ON THE ROAD

Where is the nearest garage? *Où est le garage le plus proche?*
Our car has broken down *Notre voiture est en panne*
the road to... *la route pour...*
left *gauche*
right *droite*
straight on *tout droit*
far *loin*
near *près d'ici*
opposite *en face*
beside *à côté de*
car park *parking*
at the end *au bout*
on foot *à pied*
by car *en voiture*
town map *le plan*
road map *la carte*
street *la rue*
square *la place*
give way *céder le passage*
dead end *impasse*
no parking *stationnement interdit*
petrol *l'essence*
unleaded *sans plomb*
diesel *le gasoil*
water *l'eau*
oil *l'huile*
puncture *un pneu crevé*
bulb *l'ampoule*
wipers *les essuies-glace*

SHOPPING

Where is the nearest bank/post office? *Où est la banque/Poste la plus proche?*
I'd like to buy *Je voudrais acheter*
How much is it? *C'est combien?*
Do you take credit cards? *Est-ce que vous acceptez les cartes de crédit?*
I'm just looking *Je regarde seulement*

Have you got...? *Avez-vous...?*
I'll take it *Je le prends*
I'll take this one/that one *Je prends celui-ci/celui-là*
What size is it? *C'est de quelle taille?*
Anything else? *Avec ça?*
size (clothes) *la taille*
size (shoes) *la pointure*
cheap *bon marché*
expensive *cher*
enough *assez*
too much *trop*
each *la pièce (eg 15 la pièce)*
bill *la note*
chemist *la pharmacie*
bakery *la boulangerie*
bookshop *la librairie*
grocery *l'alimentation/l'épicerie*
tobacconist *tabac*
market *le marché*

SIGHTSEEING

town *la ville*
church *l'église*
town hall *l'hôtel de ville/la mairie*
colonial mansion *grand domaine*
sugar factory *l'usine sucrière*
museum *la musée*
exhibition *l'exposition*
tourist information office *l'office de tourisme/le syndicat d'initiative*
free *gratuit*
open *ouvert*
closed *fermé*
every day *tous les jours*
all year *toute l'année*
all *day toute la journée*

EMERGENCIES

Help! *Au secours!*
Stop! *Arrêtez!*
Call a doctor *Appelez un médecin*
Call an ambulance *Appelez une ambulance*
Call the police *Appelez la police*
Call the fire brigade *Appelez les pompiers*
Where is the nearest telephone? *Où est le téléphone le plus proche?*
Where is the nearest hospital? *Où est l'hôpital le plus proche?*
I am sick *Je suis malade*

⊘ Non, non, garçon

Garçon is a word for waiter but is never used directly; say *S'il vous plaît, Monsieur* or *Madame* to attract his or her attention.

I have lost my passport/purse *J'ai perdu mon passeport/porte-monnaie*

AT THE RESTAURANT

Table d'hôte (the 'host's table') is one set menu served at a set price. **Prix fixe** is a fixed-price menu. **À la carte** means dishes from the menu are chosen and charged separately.
breakfast *le petit-déjeuner*
lunch *le déjeuner*
dinner *le dîner*
meal *le repas*
first course *l'entrée/les hors d'oeuvre*
main course *le plat principal*
made to order *sur commande*
drink included *boisson comprise*
wine list *la carte des vins*
the bill *l'addition*
fork *la fourchette*
knife *le couteau*
spoon *la cuillère*
plate *l'assiette*
glass *le verre*
napkin *la serviette*
ashtray *le cendrier*

Breakfast and snacks

baguette **long thin loaf**
pain **bread**
petits pains **rolls**
beurre **butter**
poivre **pepper**
sel **salt**
sucre **sugar**
confiture **jam**
oeufs **eggs**
à la coque **boiled eggs**
au bacon **bacon and eggs**
au jambon **ham and eggs**
sur le plat **fried eggs**
brouillés **scrambled eggs**
tartine **bread with butter**
yaourt **yoghurt**
crêpe **pancake**
croque-monsieur **ham and cheese toasted sandwich**
croque-madame **...with a fried egg on top**

Meat and fish

la viande **meat**
saignant **rare**
à point **medium**
bien cuit **well done**
grillé **grilled**
agneau **lamb**
bifteck **steak**
canard **duck**
entrecôte **beef rib steak**
farci **stuffed**

faux-filet **sirloin**
feuilleté **puff pastry**
grillade **grilled meat**
jambon **ham**
lapin **rabbit**
lardons **small pieces of bacon, often added to salads**
magret de canard **breast of duck**
médaillon **rolled meat**
porc **pork**
poulet **chicken**
poussin **young chicken**
rognons **kidneys**
rôti **roast**
saucisse **fresh sausage**
saucisson **salami**
poissons **fish**
anchois **anchovies**
calmars **squid**
coquillage **shellfish**
crevette **prawn, shrimp**
fruits de mer **seafood**
homard **lobster**
langouste **crayfish**
langoustine **large prawn**
thon **tuna**

Fruit and vegetables

ananas **pineapple**
banane **banana**
citron **lemon**
citron vert **lime**
fruit **fruit**
fruit de la passion **passion fruit**
goyave **guava**
grenadille **type of passion fruit**
mangue **mango**
noix de coco **coconut**
pamplemousse **grapefruit**
pêche **peach**
poire **pear**
pomme **apple**
raisin **grape**
aïl **garlic**
avocat **avocado**
carotte **carrot**
cassava **manioc**
chips **potato crisps**
chou **cabbage**
chou chou **christophine**
concombre **cucumber**
cru **raw**
crudités **raw vegetables**
frites **chips, French fries**
haricots **beans (red or white)**

☉ Time

At what time? A quelle heure?
When? Quand?
What time is it? Quelle heure est-il?
  Note that the French generally use the 24-hour clock.

☉ Numbers, days and months

Numbers

0	zéro
1	un, une
2	deux
3	trois
4	quatre
5	cinq
6	six
7	sept
8	huit
9	neuf
10	dix
11	onze
12	douze
13	treize
14	quatorze
15	quinze
16	seize
17	dix-sept
18	dix-huit
19	dix-neuf
20	vingt

Days

Monday lundi
Tuesday mardi
Wednesday mercredi
Thursday jeudi
Friday vendredi
Saturday samedi
Sunday dimanche

Months

January janvier
February février
March mars
April avril
May mai
June juin
July juillet
August août
September septembre
October octobre
November novembre
December décembre

légumes **vegetables**
lentilles **lentils**
oignon **onion**
patate douce **sweet potato**
petit pois **peas**
piments **chillies**
pomme de terre **potato**
riz **rice**
salade verte **green salad**
tomate **tomato**

IN THE CAFÉ

If you sit at the bar, drinks will be cheaper than at a table. Settle the bill when you leave; the waiter may leave a slip of paper on the table to keep track of the bill.

drinks les boissons
coffee café
with milk or cream au lait ou crème
decaffeinated déca/décaféiné
black/espresso express/noir
tea thé
herb infusion tisane
hot chocolate chocolat chaud
milk lait
mineral water eau minérale
sparkling gazeux
still non-gazeux
fizzy lemonade limonade
fresh lemon juice served with sugar citron pressé
full (eg full cream milk) entier
fresh or cold frais, fraîche
beer bière
bottled en bouteille
on tap à la pression

orange juice jus d'orange
white wine with cassis (blackcurrant liqueur) kir
kir with champagne kir royale
with ice avec des glaçons
red rouge
white blanc
rose rosé
dry/sweet brut/doux
sparkling wine crémant
house wine vin maison
local wine vin de pays
pitcher carafe/pichet
...of water/wine d'eau/de vin
half litre demi-carafe
before dinner drink apéritif
after dinner drink digestif
cheers! santé!
hangover gueule de bois

TABLE TALK

I am a vegetarian/vegan Je suis végétarien/végétalien ('vegan' is also used)
I am on a diet Je suis au régime
What do you recommend? Qu'est-ce que vous recommandez?
Do you have local specialities? Avez-vous des spécialités locales?
I'd like to order Je voudrais commander
That is not what I ordered Ce n'est pas ce que j'ai commandé
Is service included? Est-ce que le service est compris?
May I have more wine? Encore du vin, s'il vous plaît
Enjoy your meal Bon appétit!

SEYCHELLES – TRANSPORT

GETTING THERE

By air

In 2018 British Airways launched the only direct flights from the UK to Seychelles, taking around ten hours and departing twice a week (Wed and Sat). The archipelago's national carrier, Air Seychelles, run by Etihad, flies from all over Europe to Mahé via a stop-off at Abu Dhabi, Hong Kong, Johannesburg or Mauritius. Air France flies from London to Mahé via Amsterdam or Paris and Abu Dhabi; Emirates flies via Dubai and Qatar Airways via Doha and Abu Dhabi.

All international flights arrive at **Seychelles International Airport**, Mahé. The **Domestic Terminal** north of the international departure terminal serves Air Seychelles' and IDC flights.

It is essential to reconfirm your return flight at least 72 hours prior to departure. **Airport tax** is included in the cost of air tickets.

Airline contacts

The following numbers are for calling from within Seychelles:
British Airways: tel: 225 307
Air France: tel: 297 180
Air Seychelles: tel: 439 1000
Emirates: tel: 292700
Qatar Airways: tel: 224519
Seychelles International Airport (SEZ): tel: 384 000

GETTING AROUND

Most of the granitic islands may be visited from bases on either Mahé or Praslin. Mahé is the base for trips to the islands of Ste Anne Marine National Park, Silhouette, North and Thérèse. Praslin is the base for trips to Aride, Cousin, St Pierre and Curieuse. Either Praslin or La Digue may be used as a base for visits to Grand Soeur, Marianne and Cocos. La Digue may be visited on a day trip from Praslin but a longer stay is preferable, to enjoy the atmosphere of the island. To visit Bird, Denis and any of the Outer Islands requires overnight accommodation.

By air

Air Seychelles (tel: 439 1000) offers internal flights to Praslin throughout the day and its charter service allows you to book flights to Frégate Island, Bird Island, D'Arros and Denis Island. **Islands Development Company** (IDC; tel: 4384640; www. idcseychelles.com) has four planes and operates a daily flight to Desroches and weekly flight to Farquhar during fly-fishing season (Oct–May). IDC planes may be chartered to other islands where airstrips exist, including Alphonse, Assumption, Coetivy, Marie-Louise, Platte and Remire. There are no facilities on planes and no in-flight services. It's important to be aware that Praslin is the only island where hotel confirmation isn't needed prior to landing.

Inter-island flights

The small Air Seychelles planes make regular trips throughout the day from the Domestic Terminal on Mahé to Praslin, and operate a single flight daily to Bird and Denis (chartered by the hotels on these islands, through which bookings must be made). IDC operates scheduled flights most days to Alphonse and Desroches plus charter flights to other outer islands:
Mahé – Praslin: 15 mins
Mahé – Bird: 35 mins
Mahé – Denis: 25 mins
Mahé – Frégate: 15 mins
Mahé – Alphonse: 1 hour 40 mins
Mahé – Desroches: 65 mins

By helicopter

ZilAir (tel: 375100; www.zilair.com) is the main provider of helicopter luxury transfers and scenic flights in the region. It operates three high-tech machines, which fly out of ZilAir's base next to the International Airport runway. There's a VIP lounge with Wi-fi, computers and refreshments. The company has access to 21 licensed helipads and seven landing strips in the archipelago, including Aride, Bird Island, Cap Lazare, Cerf Island, Frégate, La Digue, Félicité, Round Island, Lemuria, Cousine, North Island, Ephelia, Grand Barbe, Grand Soeur, Kempinski, Maia, Marie Anne, Alphonse and Rémire.

Up to four passengers are allowed aboard each helicopter; children over two must occupy their own seat (infants under two can be seated on a parent's lap). Passengers should avoid taking more than 20kg (22 lb) of baggage without prior consultation.

By sea

Ferries operate between Mahé (from **Inter-Island Quay**, Victoria), Praslin (Praslin Quay/Baie Ste Anne) and La Digue (La Passe jetty). A fast **catamaran, Cat Cocos** (tel: 4324843; www.catcocos.com) takes one hour to cross between Mahé and Praslin. A trip between Mahé and La Digue, via Praslin, takes one hour 30 minutes, and a direct trip from Mahé and La Digue is one hour 10 minutes. The first Mahé–Praslin catamaran leaves at 7.30am, the last at 6pm.

Inter Island Ferry Pty Ltd operates daily between Praslin and La Digue. It is essential to book seats in advance (tel: 232329/232394; www.seychellesbookings.com). Arrive 15 minutes before departure for all ferries.

Schooners run throughout the day with seven daily return journeys departing Praslin Mon–Thu 7am–5.15pm and La Digue 7.30am–5.45pm. On Fri and Sun the last sailing in each direction is 30 minutes later. On Sat the last sailing from Praslin is 6.15pm.

By yacht or motorboat

Day trips or trips of several days on a yacht or motorboat can be arranged through a resort. Or contact a local tour operator for a tailor-made excursion.

By bus

Buses are the prime means of public transport on Mahé and Praslin. In general they are very cheap and reasonably good but times and routes are geared to local requirements, not tourists. On Mahé, if travelling at peak periods you may have to stand and at other times, particularly weekends and public holidays, you may have a long wait at bus stops. Buses are less frequent on Praslin. On La Digue buses take the form of open-sided covered lorries (*camions*) that roam the island with no fixed timetable. Elsewhere there are no buses. Buses on Mahé operate mainly between 5.30am and 8pm and on Praslin between 6am and 6.30pm.

By taxi

There are plenty of metered taxis available on Mahé but not so many on Praslin. It is often necessary to ask the driver to turn on the meter to avoid any argument over the fare at your destination. If the meter is broken (often the case) a fare should be agreed in advance. On Mahé taxis can be found at the airport, Victoria taxi rank in Albert Street (next to

Camion Hall) and by the clock tower in Independence Avenue. Your hotel will also organise one for you.

Taxi drivers can often make very good, amusing and informative guides to the islands and can be hired by the hour or day for negotiable rates, which you must agree on before setting off. On La Digue most people get around on bicycles (available at La Passe); there are only a few unmetered motorised taxis, and several more ox carts, which pass for taxis. They may be encountered driving up and down at La Passe or at the jetty when a ferry arrives from Praslin. None of the other islands has taxis.

Driving

Cars are driven on the left in Seychelles. Standards of driving are not high. Drivers tend to roam onto the wrong side of the road with alarming frequency, veering to the left only when absolutely essential. Tourists unfamiliar with driving on the left sometimes forget which country they are in and create added confusion. There is a drink-drive limit, so the best advice is simply to not drink and drive.

The absence of pavements and the narrowness of roads mean that pedestrians are often added obstacles, particularly at weekends and public holidays when the drink has flowed a little too freely. The rush hour around Victoria should be avoided if possible (either side of 8am and 4pm). None of this should deter you from taking to the road, however – certainly the best way to explore both Mahé and Praslin. Roads on Mahé are very good. Praslin roads are good between Grand Anse, Baie Ste Anne and Anse

Volbert, but deteriorate en route to Anse La Blague and Anse Lazio. Speed limits are 40kmh (25mph) in towns and villages and 65kmh (40 mph) elsewhere, except for Mahé's east coast road, where the limit is 80kmh (50 mph).

Car hire

Cars may be hired only on Mahé and Praslin; several car hire companies are represented at Seychelles International Airport and at the larger hotels. You can arrange to hire a car before you leave home through your tour operator. A national or international licence is required. Vehicle standards are variable and it is useful to inspect prior to making a commitment. Vehicles can be delivered or re-delivered to any point, mutually agreed with the hire company. Jeeps and saloon cars are widely available from most car hire firms.

Service stations

Victoria Service Station, Mahé: daily 7am–11pm
Airport Service Station, Mahé: daily 8am–9pm
Anse Royale Filling Station, Mahé: daily 8am–7pm
Baie Lazare Petrol Station, Mahé: Mon–Sat 7am–7pm
Beau Vallon Service Station, Mahé: daily 6am–9pm
Baie Ste Anne Filling Station, Praslin: daily 7am–8pm
Grand Anse Service Station, Praslin: Mon–Sat 7.30am–6pm, Sun and public holidays 7.30am–noon

Parking

Parking is free in Seychelles except in the centre of Victoria. Even here, there is a free car park on Francis Rachel Street next to the sports stadium, convenient for most requirements. To park on other Victoria streets and car parks requires advance purchase of parking coupons, available through many retail outlets. Traffic police have little to do in Victoria and failure to observe the rules where payment is required will almost invariably lead to a fine. The tourist board's excellent tips for tourist drivers are never leave valuables, such as passports, unattended in the car and never park directly beneath a coconut palm (you'll be paying for the damage if a coconut falls and makes a dent!).

Passenger airplane at Mahé's airport.

SEYCHELLES – A – Z

SEYCHELLES – A – Z

A

Accommodation

Seychelles is an exclusive destination, so prices are usually high and you get a better deal with a package. Private island resorts, such as Frégate, Desroches, Denis and North islands, are very luxurious and tend to attract the rich and famous along with a regular flow of honeymooners. In recent years up-market hotel chains have been attracted to the archipelago, such as Raffles, which has opened on Praslin, and the Four Seasons and Maia resorts on Mahé. However, there are still plenty of independent guesthouses, small hotels and self-catering apartments for those who want to experience local culture on a budget – for a full list go to the Seychelles Tourism Board website, www.seychelles. travel. No camping is permitted in the Seychelles and you'll need proof of accommodation before flying to any of the smaller islands.

Admission charges

Admission charges are in place for practically every tourist attraction here, including islands, nature reserves, botanical gardens and museums. Fees are higher than in many other destinations. Currently there is a discount system for visitors to multiple sites.

B

Budgeting for your trip

Seychelles is an expensive destination and apart from a few items of local produce, prices are higher than for similar products in most countries. Hotels generally charge high mark-ups on everything and offer exchange rates inferior to those of banks.

While travelling around the main islands, you can get a snack or drink at a fraction of hotel or restaurant prices by using local shops. Away from hotels and tourist areas there are some very good restaurants that cater for the local market and charge reasonable prices.

C

Children

Seychellois love children and Seychelles is a very safe place for a family holiday. There is no problem taking well behaved children into any restaurant in Seychelles. However, parents should note that there are few amusements for children away from the beach. The larger hotels offer a babysitting service, though it is usually necessary to give a little notice.

Climate

There are no seasons equivalent to winter, spring or autumn. The climate is tropical: hot and humid year round with temperatures in the region of 24°–30°C (75°–86°F), fluctuating very little from one month to the next or during the day. Rainfall is high, with heavy showers possible at any time of year, particularly during the northwest monsoon from November to April, reaching a peak from mid-December to the end of January. Humidity is at its highest from March to April.

Rainfall and humidity are lowest during the southeast monsoon from May to October. This season brings stronger, more consistent winds producing heavy swells at sea particularly at its peak from July to September. Unpleasant for those without a strong stomach at sea, but the cooling breeze and lower rainfall make this the best time for walking.

Rainfall on coral islands is much lower than on the granitic islands due to the influence of relief. In the southern islands, there is a marked seasonal drought (September to October rainfall on Aldabra averages just 17mm/0.75 ins, compared to 300 mm/12 ins on Mahé).

The islands lie outside the cyclone belt that brings turbulent conditions to the south from January to March. However, strong winds and heavy rain around this time often indicate a cyclone further south and, very occasionally, one may reach the southernmost islands of Seychelles.

When to visit

For birdwatching: April – start of the breeding season; May to September – sooty terns nest on Bird Island; October – migration begins.

For diving: March to May, September to November – best sea conditions, clear and calm, although diving is good all year.

For fishing: October to April, when the gentle northwest trades blow. But for those with good sea legs, fish are plentiful all year round.

CLIMATE CHART

Victoria

□ Maximum temperature
□ Minimum temperature
— Rainfall

For hiking: May to September – drier and less humid.
For sailing: all year round.
For surfing/windsurfing: June to September – when the strong southeast trade winds blow.

Crime and safety

Seychelles is very safe, though crime is not unknown. Some visitors are lulled into a false sense of security by the friendliness of the locals. They make the mistake of leaving their valuables unguarded on the beach while taking a swim, with inevitable consequences. Take the same precautions that you would at home to prevent your holiday being spoiled.

Customs regulations

The duty free allowance is 200 cigarettes (or 250g of tobacco), 2 litres of spirits and wine and 200ml of perfume. In addition, every visitor can import tax-free a video camera, camera, musical instrument, electronic equipment and sports and leisure equipment. If you import goods that are in excess of the above, import tax has to be paid in cash. Spearfishing guns and weapons are prohibited and plants, medicines and chemicals are forbidden without the necessary import permits.

D

Disabled travellers

Most of the larger hotels are geared to accommodate wheelchairs but away from these there are few special facilities. It is very difficult to get around Victoria by wheelchair due to the narrowness of the busy pavements.

E

Eating out

Where to eat

Seychelles is famous for its nature and scenery rather than its cuisine. Common complaints are that restaurants are too expensive and service slow, but if you know where to look it's possible to try delicious Creole cuisine, such as octopus curry or blackened fish, for a reasonable price. There are no beach stalls as in so many other countries, fewer restaurants and if fast food is what you are looking for then you've picked the wrong place. There is no McDonald's – indeed nothing whatsoever very fast in Seychelles, though there are a few takeaways.

Hotels offer a wide choice of meals to keep their clients from straying, often including a barbecue or a Seychellois buffet on certain evenings. However, to sample the finest local cuisine, a new twist on international flavours, and to enjoy informal local surroundings, a trip to a restaurant outside your hotel is an excellent alternative.

Dress is very casual and the atmosphere generally very relaxed. Booking is unnecessary for lunch (which tends to run from noon to 2 or 3pm) but advisable for evenings, indeed essential at some restaurants. Most will open around 6.30pm and by 10.30pm the shutters are beginning to come down. Seychelles isn't a late-night dining spot, although in Victoria you'll find that some of the bars, pizzerias and cafés stay open a little later. It can be a struggle to find places open on a Sunday (outside hotels and resorts), though Sam's Pizzeria in Victoria is a notable exception.

Fish dishes dominate, though meat dishes, mainly chicken and beef, are almost always available. Authentic Seychelles curries are hot, but restaurants will offer chilli sauce on a separate dish to allow the customer to control the temperature.

Embassies and consulates

British High Commission, Oliaji Trade Centre, Victoria; tel: 283666; www.gov.uk/government/world/seychelles
French Embassy, La Ciotat, Mont Fleuri; tel: 4382500
US Consulate, Oliaji Trade Centre, Victoria; tel: 225256; http://seychelles.usvpp.gov

Entry requirements

No visas are necessary for visitors from any country, only a valid passport,

☯ Emergency numbers

Police, fire, ambulance: tel: 999
Central police station in Victoria: tel: 288 000

☯ Electricity

240 volts using three square-pin sockets, the same as in the UK.

proof of accommodation and a return air ticket. A (free) Visitors' Permit is issued on arrival. This is the tear-off portion of the arrivals card distributed on international flights prior to landing. It should be retained and presented along with your passport upon departure. Valid for one month, the Visitors' Permit may be extended for up to three months at no charge by completing an application form available from **Immigration Division**, First Floor, Independence House, Victoria; tel: 293636; www.ics.gov.sc. Processing takes about one week. A fee is payable for extensions beyond three months. Always check the latest entry requirements before you travel.

Etiquette

Seychellois do not like to see scantily clad visitors walking around their towns and villages. Dress respectfully in churches and other holy places. Be sensitive about photographing the local people: it's always polite to ask first. Sunbathing topless is acceptable on the beaches.

H

Health and medical care

Seychelles has a healthy climate. No vaccinations are essential, though some doctors, erring on the side of caution, will recommend typhoid and polio injections. Check the latest health advice before you travel. There is no yellow fever or malaria in Seychelles. The cabins of all flights to Seychelles are sprayed prior to landing to keep such diseases out. If arriving from a country where yellow fever occurs, such as Kenya, you will be required to produce a certificate of vaccination on arrival.

Medical treatment

Essential healthcare services are free of charge to Seychelles residents, while for visitors a small charge is made. There are a large number of local clinics, particularly on Mahé, that visitors may attend, though the waiting time can be frustratingly lengthy.

⊙ Public holidays

1–2 January New Year's Day
March/April Good Friday, Easter Monday
1 May Labour Day
June (Thursday after Trinity Sunday) Corpus Christi
5 June Liberation Day

18 June National Day
29 June Independence Day
15 August Assumption/La Digue Festival
1 November All Saints' Day
8 December Immaculate Conception
25 December Christmas Day

This is particularly true on a Monday morning when the start of the working week coincides with a remarkable peak in illnesses. Treatment at clinics is usually basic.

For those who prefer to spend much of the day somewhere other than sitting on a wooden bench in a waiting room, private doctors are very good and not expensive. It is possible to call in to see a private doctor without an appointment, but a phone call may save waiting time.

Be sure to arrange appropriate medical insurance before you travel.

Hospitals

Anse Royale Hospital: Anse Royale, Mahé; tel: 371222
Logan Hospital: La Passe, La Digue; tel: 234255
Praslin Hospital: Baie Ste Anne; tel: 232333
Silhouette Hospital: Silhouette; tel: 224110
Seychelles Hospital: Mont Fleuri, Mahé; tel: 388000
Private treatment
Euromedical Family Clinic: Providence, Mahé; tel 324999; www.euromedical.info
Psm Dental Clinic: Revolution Avenue, Victoria, Mahé; tel; 324344; www.psmdental.com

Pharmacies

Absolue Pharmacie: Bois de Rose Avenue, Victoria; tel: 511203.
Central Point Pharmacy: Le Chantier Building, Francis Rachel Street, Victoria; tel: 225574; www.centralpointpharmacy.org.

I

Internet

There are many small internet shops on Mahé (mainly in Victoria), Praslin (at Grand Anse and Côte d'Or) and La Digue (at La Passe). All the large hotels and even some smaller premises in the granitic islands will offer Wi-fi for guests (though not always free). In the coral islands, the service may be erratic at best, non-existent at worst, but the situation changes constantly. If you cannot bear to be parted from your email then it is best to check the latest situation with your hotel before arrival.

L

Language

As a rule, English is widely understood in Seychelles. To learn more about Kreol, see the feature Lingua Franca, page 23, and Mauritius Travel Tips, Understanding Language.

LGBTQ travellers

There are no gay bars or other designated gay meeting points in Seychelles, but most Seychellois are open-minded and LGBTQ travellers are unlikely to encounter prejudices.

M

Media

TV and Radio

Radio Seychelles, owned by the government, and 24-hour music and chat Paradise FM, are the only exclusively local radio stations.

The only English-language terrestrial TV station is Seychelles Broadcasting Corporation (SBC), which shows CNN and BBC news programmes in the mornings. Many hotels offer satellite and cable television and a variety of channels, as well as in-house films.

In the Outer Islands, no local radio or TV broadcasts can be received, but some satellite TV channels are received at hotels.

Publications

The government-owned *Seychelles Nation* (www.nation.sc) is published daily except Sunday with articles in English, French and Kreol. It has the latest cinema, TV and radio listings. *TODAY in Seychelles* (www.todayinseychelles.com) launched in 2011 and is a daily, independent, colour newspaper; a digital version is available if you want to read before you fly. *Regar* is a political newsletter run by the Seychelles National Party and *Seychelles Weekly*, published on Thursdays, offers an alternative view of life in Seychelles and is mainly in English.

Antigone Trading in Passage des Palmes, Victoria, and at Mahé international airport, usually holds the latest issues of *Time* and *Newsweek*.

Silhouette, the in-flight magazine of Air Seychelles published three times a year, carries excellent features on the islands.

Money

The **Seychelles rupee** comes in notes of SR500, SR100, SR50, SR25 and SR10. Be careful with SR50 and SR10 notes and SR500 and SR100, which are similar in colour and sometimes muddled. Coins come in denominations of SR5, SR1, 25 cents, 10 cents and 5 cents. Prices in shops may be in amounts that do not end in units of 5 cents and unless paying by credit card will be rounded up or down in your change (usually up!).

Credit cards are accepted at hotels, many guesthouses and the larger restaurants. Visa and Mastercard are most commonly accepted. Diners Club and American Express are also accepted at some locations.

For many years, the Seychelles rupee was pegged at an unrealistically high value. This resulted in a flourishing black market for foreign exchange and gave Seychelles a reputation as a very expensive destination. In November 2008, the Seychelles rupee was floated and promptly sank to more realistic levels.

Tax

A General Sales Tax (GST) of 15 percent is applied to all hotel and restaurant bills. Trades Tax is also levied on almost all goods and this is non-refundable. Only at the **duty-free shop** in Victoria and at **Seychelles International Airport** are goods exempt of Trades Tax.

O

Opening hours

Offices: Mon–Fri 8am–4pm.
Shops: Victoria: Mon–Fri 8.30 or 9am–5 or 5.30pm, Sat 8.30am–12.30pm. Some shops close for lunch 12.30–1.30pm. Elsewhere, small shops are likely to remain open much longer hours. Shops generally close on Sundays.
Banks: Victoria: Mon–Fri 8.30am–2.30pm, Sat 8.30–11am, closed Sun. Praslin: Mon–Fri 8.30am–2pm, Sat 8.30–11.30am, closed Sun. La Digue: Mon–Fri 8.30am–2.30pm, closed Sat–Sun.

P

Postal services

The main post office in Victoria is on Independence Avenue next to the clock tower (Mon–Fri 8.30am–4pm, Sat 8.30am–noon). There are sub-post offices at Grand Anse on Praslin and La Passe on La Digue. Public post boxes are situated outside most police stations. Hotels will sell stamps and post your mail. Airmail collections are made at 3pm Mon–Fri and at noon on Sat.

S

Shopping

The craft industry of Seychelles has shallow roots, having grown up to meet the demands of the tourist industry. This is not to say there are no items unique to Seychelles, for innovation has flourished. However, there are few traditional products on sale.

What to buy

Art There are many art studios well worth visiting, most of which are mentioned in the Mahé, Praslin and La Digue chapters, including Michael Adams, Tom Bowers, George Camille, Gerard Devoud. The Craft Village (Le Village Artisanal), at Anse aux Pins on the east coast of Mahé, is also a good place to see the work of local artists.
Batik Ron Gerlach uses an old Indonesian technique to produce

beach robes, shirts and pareos in a range of attractive colours to his own, unique designs. His work reflects his love of nature (he is also chairman of the Nature Protection Trust of Seychelles).
Coco de mer The world's largest seed, which could weigh as much as your baggage allowance when taken fresh from the tree, makes a novel souvenir when hollowed out. You can buy them at the Rangers Station, Fond B'Offay, Praslin (Mon–Fri 8am–4pm). They are also available from souvenir shops but be sure the vendor gives you an export certificate or you risk confiscation by customs officers at the airport.
Coconut crafts The coconut palm is the artisan's most versatile resource: its leaves are woven into bags and baskets; the nut itself is made into napkin rings, candle holders and trinket pots; coconut oil is used to perfume soaps and bath oils; and the unusual spotted timber is used to make boxes, buttons and beads for necklaces. In the Craft Village, by the entrance to the old St Roch plantation house, is Maison Coco, a shop dedicated to the products of the coconut palm, housed in a building made out of palm tree products itself.
Jewellery Beautiful jewellery, combining gold with mother-of-pearl, sea shells and other local items, is made by Kreolor (tel: 344551; www.kreolorseychelles.com), which has shops at Seychelles International Airport departures lounge, Camion Hall and Kenwyn House, Victoria; Grande Anse in Praslin; and La Passe, La Digue. The sea shells used in the jewellery were acquired following the bankruptcy of a local button factory so there is no impact on the reefs, and there are enough to last another hundred years. The company also manufactures some highly original items combining granite, raffia seeds, coconut wood and espadon – the bill of sailfish discarded by fishermen, which can be made to look like ivory. These include placemats, trays, boxes, bracelets, mirrors and picture frames.
Pearls Praslin Ocean Farm Ltd (tel: 233150; www.blackpearlseychelles.com) culture pearls from the local black-tipped pearl oyster. They produce silvery blue, green, gold and black coloured pearls which are set in jewellery and also baby clams plated with silver and gold. Their shop, Black Pearls of Seychelles, is

opposite Praslin airstrip and is worth visiting not only to see the jewellery, but also their aquarium. You can have a guided tour for a small fee.
Perfume More than 100 local plants are used to produce three perfumes for Kreol Fleurage Parfums of North East Point, Mahé (tel: 241329; www.kreolfleurage.com). On sale at many hotel and souvenir shops – and Harrods in London.
Souvenirs and gifts One of the best places for souvenir shopping is the small mall at Camion Hall in Albert Street, Victoria. Also in Victoria, artist George Camille's Sunstroke Gallery on Market Street sells a range of beachwear, jewellery, printed tablecloths and cushions, while upstairs there is an art gallery featuring several excellent local artists. Outside the capital, the Craft Village is the other main centre on Mahé for gifts and souvenirs. If you happen to be visiting Michael Adams' Studio at Anse aux Poules Bleues, Pineapple Studio (361230; www.pineapplestudio.sc) next door sell their own range of souvenirs, including beautifully hand-dyed pareos in individually woven hessian bags, painted sculptures and wall plaques of fish, beachwear, key rings, letter racks and painted coconuts. (The shop is open weekdays until 5pm, but the owners live next door and will open up any time within reason.)
Stained glass Les and Sharon Masterson produce beautiful jewel-like hangings, lamps, panels and windows at their studio Thoughts, on the Sans Souci Road near Victoria (tel: 321254). Some of their work is also on display at Fisherman's Cove Hotel, Mahé. Sharon's stained-glass windows decorate St Paul's Cathedral, Victoria, the Apostolic Church, Victoria, and a wall at the Benedetti Gallery, Soho, New York.
Tea and spices Packets of spices may be purchased at many places, including Victoria's market and Jardin du Roi, Mahé. Pickled hot chillies and dried vanilla pods, also available at the

---

⏱ Time zone

Seychelles is four hours ahead of Greenwich Mean Time and three hours ahead of British Summer Time. The sun shines for approximately 12 hours a day – sunrise is between 6 and 6.30am and sunset between 6 and 6.30pm.

market, make novel, genuinely local souvenirs to take home. Seychelles Tea Company sells packs of tea with cinnamon, lemon, orange and vanilla flavours, on sale in most supermarkets.

T

Technology

iShop Seychelles: Huteau Lane, Victoria; tel: 224674; www.ishop.sc. A useful place to know about in case you have any Apple equipment problems, from iPad and laptop repairs through to iPhone charger replacements.

Telecommunications

International dialling code: To call Seychelles from abroad dial the international access code followed by 248 then the number you want (there are no area codes in Seychelles). To call overseas from Seychelles the international access code is 00.

Tipping

Tipping is not essential, but is always appreciated at 5–10 percent of the bill. Often, a service charge is included in restaurant bills.

Toilets

Other than at the main taxi stand in Victoria, it's hard to find public toilets in Seychelles. However, if travelling around the main islands it is always possible to call in at a hotel and quietly make use of the facilities – except at the most up-market hotels where security guards only allow paying guests through the main gates.

Tourist information offices

For information before you travel visit www.seychelles.travel, the Seychelles Tourism Board's official site. You'll find everything on here from accommodation listings to information about events, operators, climate and how to plan your trip, plus full contact details of Seychelles' 18 tourist offices around the world.

⊙ Weights and measures

The metric system is used in Seychelles.

Local tourist offices

The Seychelles Tourism Board has its head office at Espace Building, PO Box 1262, Victoria, Mahé; tel: 671300; www.seychelles.travel; Mon–Fri 8am–4pm, closed Sat–Sun and public holidays). There are also information offices on Mahé, Praslin and La Digue, from which many brochures and leaflets are available.
Mahé: Independence House, Victoria; tel: 610800; email: info@seychelles.travelnet; Mon–Fri 8am–4.30pm, Sat 9am–noon
Praslin: Praslin Airport, Amitié and Baie Ste Anne jetty; tel: 233571; email: praslin@seychelles.sc; Mon–Fri 8am–4pm, Sat and public holidays 8am–noon
La Digue: La Passe; tel: 234393; email: stbladigue@seychelles.sc; Mon–Fri 8am–5pm, Sat 9am–noon

Tour operators

Many tour operators offer package and specialist holidays to Seychelles, such as diving, birdwatching or weddings. The following UK-based operators specialise in Seychelles:
Aardvark Safaris Ltd: island hopping combined with an African Safari; tel: 01980 849160; www.aardvarksafaris.co.uk
Abercrombie & Kent Ltd: tailor-made luxury travel; tel: 01242 854468; www.abercrombiekent.co.uk
Aquatours Ltd: diving holidays; tel: 020 8398 0505; www.aquatours.com
Black Tomato: tailor-made trips, multi-destinations; tel: 020 7426 9888; www.blacktomato.com
Cox & Kings Ltd: up-market travel; tel: 020 7873 5000; www.coxandkings.co.uk
Frontiers International Ltd: fly-fishing; tel: 0845 2996212; www.frontierstravel.com
Hayes & Jarvis Ltd: tel: 01293 737640; www.hayesandjarvis.co.uk
Just Seychelles Ltd: tel: 01707 371000; www.justseychelles.com
Kuoni Travel: tel: 0800 0924444; www.kuoni.co.uk
Naturetrek: wildlife; tel: 01962 733051; www.naturetrek.co.uk
Ornitholidays: birdwatching; tel: 01794 519445; www.ornitholidays.co.uk
Seychelles Travel: tel: 01202 877330; www.seychelles-travel.co.uk
Sunset Faraway Holidays: tel: 020 8774 7100; www.sunset.co.uk
Turquoise Holidays: luxury; honeymoons; tel: 0207 1477087; www.turquoiseholidays.co.uk

Virgin Holidays: 0844 557 3865; www.virginholidays.co.uk
The following operators are Seychelles-based:
7°South: Kingsgate House, Victoria; tel: 292800; www.7south.net
Creole Travel Services: Mahé Trading Building, Victoria, Mahé; tel: 297000; www.creoletravelservices.com
Masons Travel: Michel Building, Victoria; tel: 288888; http://masonstravel.com
Seashell Travel: Trinity House, Victoria; tel: 324361
Vision Voyages: Sound and Vision House, Francis Rachel Street, Victoria, Mahé; tel: 323767; www.visionvoyages.com

W

Websites

www.airseychelles.com (airline website))
www.seychellesnewsagency.com (online news)
www.nation.sc (online edition of the Seychelles Nation)
www.seychelles.travel (the official Seychelles Tourism Board website)
www.virtualseychelles.sc (official website of the Seychelles government)

Weddings

For general advice on getting married abroad, see Mauritius Travel Tips, A–Z. Note that regulations on how long before your wedding day you have to be in Seychelles differ from Mauritius – check the current situation before booking your wedding. Note that you need to be 18 years or older to marry in Seychelles.
The Registrar: Civil Status Office, PO Box 430, Victoria, Mahé; tel: (248) 4293 600.

What to bring

Lightweight cotton clothes are standard. You'll also need swimwear; waterproof kagoul or umbrella; plastic sandals or wetsuit boots to protect against spiny sea urchins and broken coral washed up on the water's edge; walking shoes for forests and nature trails; insect repellent; sunglasses, sunhat, high factor sun protection lotion.

Some hotels require men to wear long trousers in their restaurants

GENERAL

Aldabra, World Heritage Site by Mohamed Amin, Duncan Willets and Adrian Skerrett. The best guide to this little-known corner of Seychelles, where giant tortoises still rule supreme.

Beautiful Plants of Seychelles by Adrian and Judith Skerrett.

⊙ Send us your thoughts

We do our best to ensure the information in our books is as accurate and up-to-date as possible. The books are updated on a regular basis using local contacts, who painstakingly add, amend and correct as required. However, some details (such as telephone numbers and opening times) are liable to change, and we are ultimately reliant on our readers to put us in the picture.

We welcome your feedback, especially your experience of using the book "on the road". Maybe you came across a great bar or new attraction we missed. We will acknowledge all contributions, and we'll offer an Insight Guide to the best letters received.

Please write to us at:
**Insight Guides
PO Box 7910
London SE1 1WE**

Or email us at:
hello@insightguides.com

A photographically illustrated guide to some of the commoner plants to be found in Seychelles and, indeed, in many tropical countries.

Beyond the Reefs by William Travis. Tales by an adventurer who abandoned his flying career to explore the Outer Islands of Seychelles.

Birds of Seychelles by Adrian Skerrett, Ian Bullock and Tony Disley. The only guide to all the birds recorded in Seychelles.

Death Row In Paradise by Aubrey Brooks. The fascinating story of an attempted coup d'état which took place more than 20 years ago in Seychelles. A behind-the-scenes account of a mercenary invasion.

Journey through Seychelles photographs by Mohamed Amin and Duncan Willets, text by Adrian and Judith Skerrett. A colourful coffee-table book, with text rich in tales of history and natural history.

Rivals in Eden by William McAteer. Traces the early settlement of Seychelles and the intense struggle that took place between Britain and France to control the sea route

to India, the results of which were to mould the future of the islands.

There's a Centipede In My Pyjamas: An English Family In Seychelles by Martin Varley. Fun account of unemployed conservationist Martin Varley leaving the sodden shores of the UK for a dream job in Seychelles. His wife and their four children join him for the adventure in paradise.

Trouble in Paradise by William McAteer. The sequel to Rivals in Eden, following the story of Seychelles from the British takeover, through the 19th century and up to 1919.

To be a Nation by William McAteer. Third and last volume in the history of Seychelles, taking the story up to Independence in 1976.

OTHER INSIGHT GUIDES

Other Insight Guides to African destinations include: *South Africa*, *Kenya*, *Namibia* and *Tanzania & Zanzibar*, while Insight Guides to Indian Ocean destinations include: *Sri Lanka* and *Oman & the UAE*.

CREDITS

PHOTO CREDITS

Alamy 75ML, 135ML, 255, 327
AWL Images 32, 74/75T, 166, 248
Beachcomber Hotels 6MR, 24, 27, 35, 67B, 107, 109, 110/111, 136, 144
Cerf Island Resort 296, 297
Coco de Mer Hotel 277B
Corbis 74BL, 75TR, 302
Denis Island Resort 33, 335
Dreamstime 79, 82, 115, 117, 124, 260, 261
FLPA 18, 21, 80
Getty Images 6BL, 7ML, 7BR, 7TL, 8T, 10/11, 12/13, 14/15, 19, 23, 30, 31, 34, 42BL, 44/45, 46, 49T, 52, 54, 55, 58, 59, 62/63, 64/65, 66, 68, 69, 72, 76, 78, 81, 83, 85, 89, 91, 92/93, 94, 106, 112, 116, 119, 122, 123, 125, 127, 145, 146, 147, 150, 151, 152, 153, 155, 156, 157, 158, 159, 160/161, 162/163, 164, 174, 186/187, 188, 190, 194, 196, 197, 200, 201, 212, 215, 220, 221, 223, 227, 228/229, 230/231, 232, 234, 237T, 242, 243, 247, 249, 250, 251, 252, 253, 256, 263, 264, 265, 266, 267, 269, 270, 271, 272, 273, 274/275, 280, 281, 284, 285, 286, 287, 292, 294, 295, 298, 301, 307, 308, 309, 312, 314, 316, 317, 318,

319, 321, 322, 323, 324, 325, 328, 329, 332, 333, 336, 340, 341, 345, 346
Hilton Hotels & Resorts 303, 305
IRT/Anakaopress 181
IRT/Cédric Etienne 169, 182
IRT/Emmanuel Virin 7MR, 29, 43BR, 43TR, 43BL, 165B, 172, 178, 193, 195, 204, 205, 206, 211, 366, 370, 373
IRT/Eric Lamblin 9
IRT/frog974 1
IRT/Jérome Martino 170, 173
IRT/Lionel Ghighi 6MR, 22, 74BR, 167, 177, 183, 185ML, 189T, 202, 207
IRT/Luc Perrot 6ML, 184/185T
IRT/Pierre Choukroun 189B
IRT/Sebastien Conjero 365
IRT/Serge Gelabert 42/43T, 179, 185BR, 363T
IRT/Studio Lumière 185TR
IRT/Stéphane Fournet 180
IRT/Stéphane Godin 184BR, 209
IRT/Sébastien Conejero 41, 165T, 210
IRT/Vouschka 208
IRT/Yabalex 176, 184BL
iStock 4, 8B, 16, 36, 37, 38, 39, 40, 42BR, 43ML, 77, 86, 97, 99, 100/101, 134/135T, 134BR, 134BL, 135BL, 135TR, 171, 175, 185BL, 191, 213, 216,

218, 225, 226, 254, 257, 258, 259, 339, 362, 363B, 368, 376, 377, 378, 383
Leonardo 25, 28, 289
Michael Friedel/Rex Features 304
MTPA 7TR, 7BL, 17T, 17B, 47T, 47B, 67T, 70, 71, 73, 84, 87, 90, 95B, 96, 102, 103, 104, 105, 113, 114, 126, 137, 139, 141, 142, 143, 149, 348, 351, 360
MTPA/Saint Aubin 132
National Maritime Museum 240
Oetker Collection 299, 300
Paul Turcotte/Apa Publications 337, 342, 343
Photoshot 20, 49B, 60
Public domain 48, 50, 51, 53, 56, 57, 61, 236, 239, 241, 244, 245, 246
Robert Harding 75BR, 75BL, 168, 219, 262
Shangri-La Hotels & Resorts 26, 95T, 118, 121
Shutterstock 88, 130/131, 133, 135BR, 203, 217, 224, 233T, 233B, 235, 237B, 268, 277T, 282, 283, 288, 290, 291, 293, 306, 311, 315, 330, 331, 334
The Art Archive 238
The Coco de Mer Hotel 313

COVER CREDITS

Front cover: Anse Source d'Argent, Seychelles *Shutterstock*
Back cover: Château de Labourdonnais, Mauritius *Dreamstime*
Front flap: (from top) Le Prince Maurice's pool, Mauritius *Leonardo*;

Chillis *IRT/Sébastien Conejero*; Victoria carnival *iStock*; Giant tortoise on Corieuse Island *iStock*
Back flap: Helicopter over lava flow, Réunion *IRT/Studio Lumière*

INSIGHT GUIDE CREDITS

Distribution
UK, Ireland and Europe
Apa Publications (UK) Ltd;
sales@insightguides.com
United States and Canada
Ingram Publisher Services;
ips@ingramcontent.com
Australia and New Zealand
Woodslane; info@woodslane.com.au
Southeast Asia
Apa Publications (SN) Pte;
singaporeoffice@insightguides.com
Worldwide
Apa Publications (UK) Ltd;
sales@insightguides.com
Special Sales, Content Licensing and CoPublishing
Insight Guides can be purchased in
bulk quantities at discounted prices.
We can create special editions,
personalised jackets and corporate
imprints tailored to your needs.
sales@insightguides.com
www.insightguides.biz

Printed in China by CTPS

All Rights Reserved
© 2019 Apa Digital (CH) AG and
Apa Publications (UK) Ltd

First Edition 2000
Third Edition 2019

Every effort has been made to provide
accurate information in this
publication, but changes are
inevitable. The publisher cannot be
responsible for any resulting loss,
inconvenience or injury. We would
appreciate it if readers would call our
attention to any errors or outdated
information. We also welcome your
suggestions; please contact us at:
hello@insightguides.com

www.insightguides.com

Editors: Carine Tracanelli and Zara
Sekhavati
Authors: Nicki Grihault, Catharine
Cellier-Smart and Amanda Statham
Head of DTP and Pre-Press:
Rebeka Davies
Managing Editor: Carine Tracanelli
Picture Editor: Tom Smyth
Cartography: original cartography
Colin Earl, updated by Carte

CONTRIBUTORS

This new edition of *Insight Guide
Mauritius, Réunion & Seychelles*
was commissioned and edited by
Carine Tracanelli and has been
comprehensively updated by three
local expert writers. **Nicki Grihault**
is an award-winning travel writer
specialising in Mauritius; she
brought her expertise to bear on the
coverage here of all Mascarenes
islands as well as the general Indian
Ocean features. Réunion updater
Catharine Cellier-Smart is a British
expat writer and translator based on
the island, while Seychelles updater
Amanda Statham is the travel editor
for *Cosmopolitan* and a honeymoon
specialist.

ABOUT INSIGHT GUIDES

Insight Guides have more than 45
years' experience of publishing high-
quality, visual travel guides. We
produce 400 full-colour titles, in both
print and digital form, covering more
than 200 destinations across the
globe, in a variety of formats to meet
your different needs.
   Insight Guides are written by local
authors, whose expertise is evident in
the extensive historical and cultural
background features. Each destination
is carefully researched by regional
experts to ensure our guides provide
the very latest information. All the
reviews in **Insight Guides** are
independent; we strive to maintain an
impartial view. Our reviews are
carefully selected to guide you to the
best places to eat, go out and shop, so
you can be confident that when we say
a place is special, we really mean it.

Legend

City maps

Freeway/Highway/Motorway
Divided Highway
Main Roads
Minor Roads
Pedestrian Roads
Steps
Footpath
Railway
Funicular Railway
Cable Car
Tunnel
City Wall
Important Building
Built Up Area
Other Land
Transport Hub
Park
Pedestrian Area
Bus Station
Tourist Information
Main Post Office
Cathedral/Church
Mosque
Synagogue
Statue/Monument
Beach
Airport

Regional maps

Freeway/Highway/Motorway (with junction)
Freeway/Highway/Motorway (under construction)
Divided Highway
Main Road
Secondary Road
Minor Road
Track
Footpath
International Boundary
State/Province Boundary
National Park/Reserve
Marine Park
Ferry Route
Marshland/Swamp
Glacier   Salt Lake
Airport/Airfield
Ancient Site
Border Control
Cable Car
Castle/Castle Ruins
Cave
Chateau/Stately Home
Church/Church Ruins
Crater
Lighthouse
Mountain Peak
Place of Interest
Viewpoint

INDEX

MAIN REFERENCES ARE IN BOLD TYPE

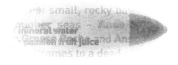

INSIGHT ● GUIDES

OFF THE SHELF

Since 1970, INSIGHT GUIDES has provided a unique perspective on the world's best travel destinations by using specially commissioned photography and illuminating text written by local authors.

Whether you're planning a city break, a walking tour or the journey of a lifetime, our superb range of guidebooks and phrasebooks will inspire you to discover more about your chosen destination.

INSIGHT GUIDES

offer a unique combination of stunning photos, absorbing narrative and detailed maps, providing all the inspiration and information you need.

PHRASEBOOKS & DICTIONARIES

help users to feel at home, when away. Pocket-sized with a free app to download, they go where you do.

CITY GUIDES

pack hundreds of great photos into a smaller format with detailed practical information, so you can navigate the world's top cities with confidence.

EXPLORE GUIDES

feature easy-to-follow walks and itineraries in the world's most exciting destinations, with our choice of the best places to eat and drink along the way.

POCKET GUIDES

combine concise information on where to go and what to do in a handy compact format, ideal on the ground. Includes a full-colour, fold-out map.

EXPERIENCE GUIDES

feature offbeat perspectives and secret gems for experienced travellers, with a collection of over 100 ideas for a memorable stay in a city.

www.insightguides.com